Gender in the Twenty-First Century

Gender in the Twenty-First Century

The Stalled Revolution and the Road to Equality

Edited by

SHANNON N. DAVIS, SARAH WINSLOW,
AND DAVID J. MAUME

University of California Press

University of California Press, one of the most distinguished university presses in the United States, enriches lives around the world by advancing scholarship in the humanities, social sciences, and natural sciences. Its activities are supported by the UC Press Foundation and by philanthropic contributions from individuals and institutions. For more information, visit www.ucpress.edu.

University of California Press
Oakland, California

Library of Congress Cataloging-in-Publication Data

Names: Davis, Shannon N., editor. | Winslow, Sarah, 1978- editor. | Maume, David J., editor.
Title: Gender in the twenty-first century : the stalled revolution and the road to equality / Edited by Shannon N. Davis, Sarah Winslow, and David J. Maume.
Description: Oakland, California : University of California Press, [2017] | Includes bibliographical references and index.
Identifiers: LCCN 2016056689 (print) | LCCN 2016059763 (ebook) | ISBN 9780520291386 (cloth : alk. paper) | ISBN 9780520291393 (pbk. : alk. paper) | ISBN 9780520965188 (ebook)
Subjects: LCSH: Sex role—United States—21st century. | Sex role in the work environment—United States—21st century. | Equality before the law—United States—21st century. | Work and family—United States—21st century. | Sex discrimination in employment—United States—21st century.
Classification: LCC HQ1075.5.U6 G464 2017 (print) | LCC HQ1075.5.U6 (ebook) | DDC 305.30973—dc23
LC record available at https://lccn.loc.gov/2016056689

Manufactured in the United States of America

26   25   24   23   22   21   20   19   18   17
10   9   8   7   6   5   4   3   2   1

Contents

Figures

Tables

Acknowledgments

This volume was borne out of the collaboration that supported the 2015 Southern Sociological Society Annual Meeting, "Stalled Revolutions? Gender Inequality in the 21st Century," with David Maume as president. Shannon Davis and Sarah Winslow cochaired the Program Committee tasked with shaping the intellectual contributions of the annual meeting. Many of the chapters in this volume are revised versions of papers presented at that conference. Shannon Davis was supported by a George Mason University Faculty Study Leave to facilitate the completion of the volume.

We are indebted to our colleagues in the Southern Sociological Society, especially the 2015 Program Committee, as well as those at George Mason University, Clemson University, and the University of Cincinnati for their support in the completion of this volume. Reviewers and editors of University of California Press provided valuable direction and feedback. In addition to our authors, we are grateful for the editorial contributions of M. C. Elias and Sarah Wagner (George Mason University) and the indexing work of PJ Heim of QMFindexing, made possible by financial support from the Charles Phelps Taft Research Center at the University of Cincinnati. We are also deeply appreciative of the support of our families throughout the organization and implementation of the 2015 Southern Sociological Society meeting and our subsequent work on this volume: Frank, Alexandra, and Miles (Shannon), Stephanie, Reeve, and Laken (Sarah), and Debbie (David).

1. Gender as an Institution

Shannon N. Davis, Sarah Winslow,
and David J. Maume

Marcia, age 18, is a senior in high school, while her brother Mark, age 16, is a junior. They live with their biological parents. Both are planning to attend college; Marcia has been accepted at the best liberal arts college in her state. She does well in school, but is so overscheduled that she is tired frequently, leading her parents to make comments about how she needs to worry more about how she looks each day. Mark does well in school, too, but his parents have been pushing him to be more involved in sports so he can look more well-rounded in his college applications. Being president of the Chess Club is important, they say, but he needs to show that he has athletic skills as well. Both Marcia and Mark have many friends, though neither has a steady dating partner. One of the key points of contention in their household is that they have the same curfew, even though Marcia is only a few months away from living on her own.

DEFINING GENDER

If we were writing a script for a twenty-first-century situation comedy about a middle-class white American family, the vignette above would be the ideal backstory for our main characters. The family dynamics that underlie Marcia and Mark's life likely sound familiar. The daughter and son live in the same household but have different expectations placed upon them by their parents. However, their parents are simply trying to encourage them to be the best young woman and man they can be given their presumed natural talents. What is interesting about this vignette is that we find it so normal. Of course young women are going to be interested in the liberal arts. Those disciplines focus on communication and consensus, ideas and collaboration. And shouldn't young men be active in sports? Don't they

1

channel men's natural tendencies to be aggressive and competitive? Young women need to be protected more than young men do, so having the same curfew is simply their parents' way of making sure that Marcia is safe.

These underlying assumptions are gendered assumptions. They presume that because Marcia is female and Mark is male that there are normal, biologically based ways in which they should behave that need to be encouraged through socialization by their parents. However, decades of scholarship in sociology and other disciplines have documented the difference between biological sex (or what we're referring to when we say people are female or male) and gender. Indeed, one of the key contributions of the late twentieth century to the study of gender is that we no longer say that there are sex or gender roles (that is, specific, biologically based roles in society that women and men are supposed to play). Instead, scholars have made the case that gender is socially constructed, with specific meanings for relationships between and among women and men that are temporally and contextually specific and that have implications for individuals, interactions, and societies and social institutions. Importantly, scholars have also highlighted the ways in which differences between males and females and men and women are linked to inequality. It is not just that we ascribe different meanings to being a man or a woman but that these differences are associated with unequal opportunities, constraints, and, ultimately, outcomes. Let's return to Marcia and Mark. Marcia's relatively earlier curfew given her age may limit the employment and extracurricular activities in which she is able to engage, both of which may have negative implications for her future academic and professional achievements. Mark, on the other hand, is encouraged to increase his involvements, including participation in sports, all with an eye toward enhancing his academic and professional prospects. In these seemingly small and taken-for-granted ways, gendered assumptions contribute to unequal outcomes for this brother-sister duo.

In this volume, the chapter authors build on much sociological scholarship to make the case that gender is a social institution,[1] what some have called a social structure,[2] that has implications for individuals, interactions, and institutions themselves. When we say that gender has implications for individuals, we mean that individuals' sense of self, their identity, their personalities, and their actual physical bodies are gendered. In the Western world, we tend to think of gender along a continuum, with women/femininity on one end and men/masculinity on the other. There is the presumption that individuals live their lives at the poles of this continuum, a concept known as gender polarization,[3] as evidenced, for example, by the term "opposite sexes." Further, there is the presumption that biological sex, gender, and gender identity are aligned with one another.

While there is a growing understanding of how each of these possible continua does not match people's experiences, researchers cannot ignore that many individuals think of themselves as existing along each continua. So when we talk about gender as a social structure or social institution having implications for individuals, we mean that individuals think of themselves as more or less feminine or masculine, identify as female/male (and that may or may not match their sex category), and craft a sense of self that is an extension of what they see their sex category and gender identity as being, and that these may or may not align with one another neatly. Marcia, therefore, thinks of herself as a young woman, sees herself that way, and has crafted a sense of self that is (in her mind) consistent with femininity. Mark has done the same for himself, focusing instead on constructing his sense of self around being a young man and masculine. However, while cultural beliefs may allow us to presume that this process of constructing a sense of self reflects the simultaneity of biological sex, gender, and gender identity, some of the chapters in this volume document the more complicated nature of how these continua intersect in our lives.

Gender also has implications for interactions that are based in part on our understanding of individuals. How would we know that Marcia thinks of herself as a young woman? We could ask her but if we were around her we may see that she presents herself as a young woman. She may wear her hair in ways that are consistent with what young women in the United States do, she may dress in a particular way, she may also act in ways that are consistent with how women are expected to act in the contemporary United States. The concept of "doing gender" was coined to explain (in part) this performative component of gender.[4] Individuals expect to be held morally accountable for presenting themselves as a gendered individual. So people who are thought to be women are expected to present themselves as women, and the same for men. Not only present themselves physically (manner of dress and other physical aspects) but also in their mannerisms, interaction style, and general behavior. And when individuals do not conform to what others think a woman or man should be, they are penalized. An example of this comes from recent research on teaching evaluations in college classrooms. Women are held to higher standards for being expected to care for their students than are men, and when they are perceived to be cool or standoffish (or focused more on their research than their students), women are penalized by receiving lower teaching evaluations.[5] Another example is that women who are perceived to be both mothers and employees are penalized with lower salaries in part because they are not living up to their cultural expectations of being focused more on their families than on their work.[6] Indicative of the extent to which gendered expectations are both embedded in interactions and seen as diametrically opposed, men who do not live up to expectations for appropriate masculinity—by, for example, engaging in typically feminine behaviors like dancing or being concerned with their appearance—are chastised and ostracized.[7]

The cultural expectations that we hold individuals to are one of the ways gender has implications for the institutional level. Through our collective attitudes and interactions, we as a culture have general ideas about how women and men are supposed to behave. Individuals internalize those beliefs and they are used to guide our actions and reactions in interactions with others (reflecting how gender at the individual, interactional, and institutional levels is interconnected). Other ways in which gender has implications at the institutional/structural level are through laws that regulate what individuals can do and opportunities of which they are allowed to avail themselves. The United States regulates gender by emphasizing that men are expected to be available to be soldiers, being violent and willing to kill, by requiring that only men register for the Selective Service. In addition, organizations are structured in ways that highlight how there are culturally different expectations for women and men. The ideal worker norm that is a key organizing principle of many organizations is a norm that presumes that workers are devoted only to their work and have no competing interests vying for their time.[8] Historically, this has meant that men could live up to the ideal worker norm but women were penalized (and still are) for focusing on work and not on any family obligations.

INTERSECTIONALITY

This volume highlights how gender is implicated in our social interactions and our social institutions, thus making it one of the key ways in which our everyday lives are organized. However, we do not just experience the world as women or men, nor are interactions and institutions stratified by gender alone. Gender is connected to other forms of inequality, including race and ethnicity, social class, sexuality, nativity, religion, age, and ability.

One important theoretical perspective that highlights the ways that gender and power are intertwined and implicated differently in people's lives is the perspective called intersectionality. Rather than trying to explain experiences as connected to only gender, intersectionality recognizes that gender operates differently when it is intersected with other forms of inequality.[9] Therefore, there are differing expectations and experiences for women and men based upon race and ethnicity, social class, sexuality, nativity, religion, etc.

In the vignette, if Marcia and Mark had been Julia and Julio or Tomeka and Taquan, would their experiences as young women and men have been the same? From your own experience you probably suspect that it is very unlikely that their experiences would have been identical. Indeed, research has shown that not only do parental expectations of young women and men differ by race and ethnicity;[10] parents of Black and Latino youth talk to their children about the intersections of race/ethnicity and gender in ways that parents of white youth do not.[11] Recent controversies around differing expectations among police officers regarding Black and Latino youth versus white youth highlight how race and gender intersect at the interactional level. For example, the Black Lives Matter movement and scholars alike have documented, among other things, the punitive response of law enforcement toward Black youth that is not demonstrated when white youth are accused of similar offenses.[12] One outcome of these differential experiences with law enforcement is the significantly higher rate at which young men of color are incarcerated, which subsequently has deleterious consequences for their access to educational and employment opportunities.[13] Access to education and employment are key examples of the institutional intersection of race/ethnicity and gender.

Similarly, although you may not have thought consciously about it, most readers of this volume likely assumed that Mark and Marcia are heterosexual. This presumption of heterosexuality is referred to as heterocentrism or heteronormativity.[14] Moreover, just as sex and gender are presumed to be compatible, there is also a presumed connection between sex, gender, and sexuality. In other words, appropriately feminine women are expected to be attracted to men, while appropriately masculine men are assumed to be attracted to women. This cultural conception of a series of neat continua (sex, gender, sexuality) that are separate yet aligned does not, however, match the realities of many individuals' lived experiences. Nonetheless, these expectations are institutionalized in cultural norms and formal policies. Although the landmark 2015 Supreme Court ruling in *Obergefell v. Hodges* made same-sex marriage legal throughout the United States, if Marcia is gay she will face a legal climate that does not prohibit discrimination on the basis of sexual orientation in housing, employment, and a host of other matters. Moreover, the typical assumption that sex and gender are compatible denies the lived realities of transgender individuals. Let's assume that Mark is transgender; that is, that his biological sex does not match his gender identity or presentation. North Carolina HB 2, a 2016 bill that required individuals to use restrooms that corresponded to the sex on their birth certificate rather than their gender identity, institutionalizes the link between sex and gender in a legal mandate. Both of these examples emphasize the institutional intersection of sex, gender, and sexuality.

The authors of this volume's chapters present original research investigating the implications of gender at the individual, interactional, and institutional level as it intersects with other forms of inequality. When we examine women's and men's lives, they are never *only* women and men. They are parents or nonparents, immigrants or native-born, heterosexual or LGBTQ, white, Black, Asian, Hispanic, or another racial/ethnic group, may or may not hold formal educational credentials, and may or may not be a professional worker, among other social characteristics. It is our goal to explore the varying ways in which gender has implications in the lives of individuals in the United States through the many ways it intersects with other forms of inequality while emphasizing the key role that gender plays overall in each of our lives.

STALLED REVOLUTIONS

Critics may say that in the United States, women and men are considered equal, that women and men have the same kinds of opportunities and experiences. If there are gender differences, those differences must be based on choices that individuals make. However, sociologists conceptualize these gender differences and the resulting unequal life chances and opportunities as functions not simply of individual choices and preferences. As noted above, interactional pressures lead to patterns of behavior among women and men that generally reinforce what is culturally expected for each gender (based on their race, social class, nativity status, sexual orientation, etc.). And sociologists also routinely document the institutional processes that lead to gender differences in experiences and outcomes, as well as how these gender *differences* are fundamentally linked to gender *inequality*. Sociologists acknowledge that some of the gender differences in educational attainment, labor force participation, pay, and political participation and power, among other experiences, may be in part the result of individual preferences. However, we also see those preferences as only part of the explanation for why gender gaps remain. Cultural norms shape interactions between individuals, leading to discriminatory practices based on stereotypes rather than actual experiences, even when the preferences between individuals are identical (like employers potentially paying mothers less because of the stereotype that they will not be as committed to their jobs and should not be because of the expected primacy of motherhood in women's lives). And institutional policies and practices provide women and men different opportunity structures for success, even when their experiences are the same (like the historic [but now changed] policy of preventing women in the military from being in combat roles, which had the consequence of limiting women's promotion opportunities within the military ranks). Moreover, there is evidence that even preferences themselves are shaped by larger social forces; for example, female faculty members prefer to spend more time on teaching relative to their male counterparts, although this can be largely attributed to educational gaps between the two groups, which are themselves partly shaped by historical barriers that made the pursuit of a doctoral degree more difficult for women.[15]

Certainly much has changed in men's and women's lives—and in gender relations more generally—in the past several decades. Many institutional barriers prohibiting women's full inclusion in important social institutions—such as education, the workplace, and the military—have eroded and landmark pieces of legislation, such as Title IV of the Civil Rights Act of 1964, have made discrimination on the basis of sex (and other protected classes, such as race and religion) illegal. We sometimes call these sweeping changes in women's status since the 1960s a "revolution" and, in fact, many second-wave feminists aspired to a gender-neutral world. Yet, as the vignette with Marcia and Mark reminds us, any such revolution is incomplete at best. College majors and jobs remain gender-typed;[16] the sex gap in pay persists;[17] women are underrepresented in authority positions in the economy, politics, the church, the military, etc.;[18] women still do most of the housework and child care;[19] and traditional beliefs about gender abound.[20] We suspect that if you asked your family and friends whether gender inequality is in the past or if it persists today, you would receive as many different answers as people you queried. Some people may argue that men and women are more equal than ever in all parts of American life, although that does not necessarily mean that gender inequality has been eradicated. Indeed, many scholars recognize both progress and inequality in assessing women's status in society. For example, one prominent gender scholar, Paula England,[21] pronounced the gender revolution uneven and stalled, as recent decades have witnessed progress toward gender equality more in some societal institutions (e.g., education) than in others (e.g., the workplace or the family). Cultural and political conversations about gender-based equality have begun to focus on both women's and men's opportunities to enact their goals and ideals (e.g., men's desire for parental leave) and marriage equality has spread across the United States, but these conversations and policy shifts are uneven at best. This volume focuses on the stalled gender revolution by examining how the progress toward gender equality in the United States has been uneven across many dimensions of public and private life. But instead of focusing only on how gender inequality is produced at the individual, interactional, and institutional levels and how it intersects with other dimensions of inequality, the chapters in this volume offer policy solutions for moving toward gender parity in both the public and the private spheres.

ABOUT THIS VOLUME

The contributors to this volume take on this concept of the stalled gender revolution from two perspectives. First, the authors investigate the gender revolution inside of social institutions, focusing on institutions within the United States (although several chapters explicitly draw comparisons with other nations). Second, the authors highlight the gendered implications of policies, both those that currently exist and those implied by their empirical work.

The remainder of this book is structured in two parts that correspond to these two approaches to examining the stalled gender revolution. In the first part of the book we have included original chapters that assess the gender revolution in society's core institutions: the family, higher education, the workplace, religion, the military, and sport. These chapters will assess progress toward gender equality and what policies are needed to promote equality. The second part of the book focuses on gender politics and policies, and examines more specific examples of gender inequality in political and economic leadership, work-family integration, health, immigration, globalization, and sexuality. Each part concludes with a set of reflection questions to inspire your own imagination as to how you can build on the research presented in order to investigate the social world.

Three additional features of this volume warrant noting here. First, although each piece focuses on one of the broad areas mentioned above, the authors of each chapter investigate specific phenomena or themes within those broad areas. We have listed the pieces under broad headings in the table of contents to direct the readers' attention to the larger area of investigation and to assist readers in matching the pieces in this volume to other published work. Our overall goal is to illustrate a perspective—assessing progress toward gender equality and suggesting policies needed in achieving that end—and we encourage the reader to see the included chapters as illustrating one way (among many) of addressing the associated questions in any given institutional or policy realm. It is our hope that these examples, rather than being the definitive or comprehensive investigation of the topic, serve to generate additional ideas and questions in our readers.

Second, the pieces in this volume represent a range of methodological approaches, from sophisticated yet accessible quantitative analyses to qualitative interviewing to first-person ethnographic narrative. Moreover, some pieces represent an investigation of a specific empirical research question, while others present more of a retrospective and prospective overview of a larger issue. In this way, we present Sociology as a living scientific discipline involving research informed by a number of methodological, empirical, and theoretical traditions. Thus a further feature of the volume is to illustrate how these various approaches can all be employed to study how gender is created, re-created, and institutionalized—and, in fact, how our understanding of the stalled gender revolution is enhanced as a result. Third and finally, and in part as a direct result of the two previous features, each piece in this volume takes on the "voice" of its author(s) and the style related to its methodological approach. While we have attempted to maintain consistency in the structure of the chapters, if read in succession, they will and do sound as if they stem from slightly different styles of writing—styles that are inherently tied to the approach taken in the chapter.

Our goal in this volume is to assess progress toward gender equality in institutions in the United States, coupled with discussions of public policies needed to further the goal of achieving gender equality. We conclude the volume with our own reflection on the contemporary state of the relationship between scholarship on gender inequality and policies working to unstall the gender revolution, situating the policies presented throughout the chapters by level of policy (e.g., local, organizational, governmental) as a way to think through the connections between the polity as a social institution and gender as a social institution.

NOTES

1. Martin, Patricia Yancey. 2004. "Gender as Social Institution." *Social Forces* 82:1249–1273.

2. Giddens, Anthony. 1984. *The Constitution of Society: Outline of the Theory of Structuration.* Berkeley: University of California Press; Risman, Barbara J. 1998. *Gender Vertigo: American Families in Transition.* New Haven: Yale University Press.

3. Bem, Sandra L. 1993. *The Lenses of Gender: Transforming the Debate on Sexual Inequality.* New Haven: Yale University Press.

4. West, Candace, and Don H. Zimmerman. 1987. "Doing Gender." *Gender & Society* 1:125–151.

5. Sprague, Joey, and Kelley Massoni. 2005. "Student Evaluations and Gendered Expectations: What We Can't Count Can Hurt Us." *Sex Roles* 53:779–793.

6. Benard, Stephen, and Shelley Correll. 2010. "Normative Discrimination and the Motherhood Penalty." *Gender & Society* 24:616–646.

7. Pascoe, C.J. 2007. *Dude, You're a Fag: Masculinity and Sexuality in High School.* Berkeley: University of California Press.

8. Acker, Joan. 1990. "Hierarchies, Jobs, Bodies: A Theory of Gendered Organizations." *Gender & Society* 4:139–158; Acker, Joan. 2006. "Inequality Regimes: Gender, Class, and Race in Organizations." *Gender & Society* 20:441–464.

9. Crenshaw, Kimberle. 1991. "Mapping the Margins: Intersectionality, Identity Politics, and Violence against Women of Color." *Stanford Law Review* 43:1241–1299; Collins, Patricia Hill. 1990. *Black Feminist Thought: Knowledge Consciousness, and the Politics of Empowerment.* New York: Routledge; West, Candace, and Sarah Fenstermaker. 1995. "Doing Difference." *Gender & Society* 9:8–37.

10. Hill, Shirley, and Joey Sprague. 1999. "Parenting in Black and White Families: The Interaction of Gender with Race and Class." *Gender & Society* 13:480–502.

11. Dow, Dawn Marie. 2016. "The Deadly Challenges of Raising African American Boys Navigating the Controlling Image of the 'Thug.'" *Gender & Society* 30 (2): 161–188; Johnson, Waldo E., Lauren M. Rich, and Lance C. Keene. 2016. "Father–Son Communication." *Journal of Men's Studies* 24 (2): 151–165; Whitaker, Tracy R., and Cudore L. Snell. 2016. "Parenting while Powerless: Consequences of 'the Talk.'" *Journal of Human Behavior in the Social Environment* 26:303–309; Lareau, Annette. 2011. *Unequal Childhoods: Class, Race, and Family Life.* 2nd ed. Berkeley: University of California Press.

12. Alexander, Bryant Keith. 2014. "Call for Papers—Special Issue 'Hands Up! Don't Shoot!': Policing Race in America." *Cultural Studies ↔ Critical Methodologies* 14 (6): 626–626.

13. Kirk, David S., and Robert J. Sampson. 2013. "Juvenile Arrest and Collateral Educational Damage in the Transition to Adulthood." *Sociology of Education* 86:36–62; Pager, Devah. 2007. *Marked: Race, Crime, and Finding Work in an Era of Mass Incarceration.* Chicago: University of Chicago Press.

14. Rich, Adrienne. 1980. "Compulsory Heterosexuality and Lesbian Existence." *Signs* 5:631–660.

15. Winslow, Sarah. 2010. "Gender Inequality and Time Allocations among Academic Faculty." *Gender & Society* 24 (6): 769–793.

16. England, Paula, and Su Li. 2006. "Desegregation Stalled: The Changing Gender Composition of College Majors, 1971–2002." *Gender & Society* 20:657–677; Padavic, Irene, and Barbara F. Reskin. 2002. *Women and Men at Work.* 2nd ed. Thousand Oaks, CA: Sage.

17. Maume, David J., and Leah Ruppanner. 2015. "State Liberalism, Female Supervisors, and the Gender Wage Gap." *Social Science Research* 50:126–138.

18. del Río, Coral, and Olga Alonso-Villar. 2015. "The Evolution of Occupational Segregation in the United States, 1940–2010: Gains and Losses of Gender–Race/Ethnicity Groups." *Demography* 52:967–988; Paxton, Pamela, and Melanie M. Hughes. 2017. *Women, Politics, and Power: A Global Perspective.* 3rd ed. Thousand Oaks, CA: Sage.

19. Bianchi, Suzanne M., Melissa A. Milkie, Liana C. Sayer, and John P. Robinson. 2000. "Is Anyone Doing the Housework? Trends in the Gender Division of Household Labor." *Social Forces* 79:191–228.

20. Davis, Shannon N., and Theodore N. Greenstein. 2009. "Gender Ideology: Components, Predictors, and Consequences." *Annual Review of Sociology* 35:87–105.

21. England, Paula. 2010. "The Gender Revolution: Uneven and Stalled." *Gender & Society* 24:149–166.

PART I

Changing and Unchanging Institutions

2. There's No Such Thing as Having It All

Gender, Work, and Care in an Age of Insecurity

Kathleen Gerson

Danny and his wife are committed to their jobs—his as a financial advisor and hers as a real estate broker. They are also committed to sharing as equally as possible in the care of their young son. Danny believes children are best reared by their parents and does not want to surrender the chance to create a strong bond during his son's early years. He also believes motherhood should not imperil his wife's career, which is as important as his in securing the family's financial security. For all of these reasons, he is splitting his working time between home and office, trading off with his wife so that one of them is always home. This arrangement has made it possible to spend time with his son, but it has also left him feeling torn between the needs of his child and the expectations of his boss. Danny is proud of his efforts to share work and caregiving, but he is also beginning to wonder how much longer he can maintain this pace.

Dolores met her husband when they were both students working their way through college. After graduation, he encouraged her to continue her studies in biology and followed her to a new city, where they decided to start a family. As the years passed, Dolores completed her training and found a series of better jobs in new places, while her husband followed her. As Dolores thrived in her career, he took the jobs he could find and became the family's main caregiver for their three children. Yet despite her work success and husband's support, Dolores finds it burdensome to support the family on her paycheck alone, worries about her husband's growing frustration, and wonders how much longer her marriage can survive the financial and emotional strains.

After years of seeking a good job and satisfying relationship, Michelle seemed to achieve both as she reached her midthirties. She was appointed the director of a nonprofit agency helping the poor, and she was happy in a two-year relationship. Then, unexpectedly, she found herself pregnant. Though unplanned, she greeted the news with hope that it would mark the beginning of starting a family. She soon discovered, however, that her partner did not share her vision of the future. He told her that he would not take responsibility for supporting or caring for a child. Aware this might be her last chance to have a child, Michelle decided to go forward with her pregnancy on her own. Today, Michelle is a devoted single mother, who relies on the help of good friends and paid caretakers to help care for her young daughter. Faced with the need to support a child and have a less demanding schedule, she has had to give up the nonprofit directorship for a less exciting but more secure and less demanding job at a for-profit firm.

Now in his late thirties, Jason lives alone and holds no paid job. Over the years, he has held a series of jobs, but these never offered a comfortable income or prospects for a better financial future. His experiences in intimate relationships have proved equally unstable, with live-in girlfriends who moved out or were asked to leave. Instead, Jason gets up every morning and goes to a local coffee house where he works on developing an app he hopes will jumpstart a career in tech. Jason is not sure whether he prefers his "freedom" to a stable job and family life, but he is convinced that he isn't "entitled" to have a family as long as his finances remain so precarious.

The clear boundary between earning and caretaking, which once provided the core rationale for gender arrangements in American families, no longer comes close to describing the lives of today's women and men. While many households continue to depend on a primary breadwinning father and homemaking mother, this arrangement no longer describes the circumstances of most women and men today. Consider the lives of the four people described above, all members of the generation that came of age during the gender revolution that offered them new options but no clear resolutions to the conflicts between working and caring. While Danny is endeavoring, often against the odds, to integrate work and parenting and sustain an egalitarian partnership, Dolores has unwittingly found herself in a different situation. Unlike both Danny and Dolores, Michelle is shouldering the responsibilities of both work and parenthood without the help of a partner for either breadwinning or caretaking. Finally, in contrast to all of these parents, Jason faces no obligations to a family or a job. Yet his situation poses its own dilemmas.

These four stories illustrate the variety of new patterns that are emerging in response to the financial and interpersonal uncertainties of today's "new economy." The once-predominant "traditional" arrangement of homemaking mothers and breadwinning fathers can still be found, but it exists alongside a patchwork of alternative patterns like those of Danny, Dolores, Michelle, and Jason. Why has such a diverse set of approaches to work and care emerged? How do young women and men choose among them? And what challenges do they pose? To understand the options facing today's families and their prospects for the future, we first need to answer these questions.

INTRODUCTION

Today's "Great Transformation" in Economic and Personal Life[1]

Like the shift to an industrial system, the rise of a "new economy" is reshaping the organization of American work and family life in fundamental ways. Service, information, and technology jobs are on the rise, while manufacturing jobs continue their steep decline. The location of paid work is also changing, with employees logging on to their jobs from distant locales as work sites move out of the traditional office into the home and the coffee house. Finally, the composition of the labor force continues to transform, with the gender gap in work participation shrinking to the point of disappearing. The implications of these economic shifts for gender and family life are enormous. They mark the end of an era that demarcated clear boundaries between homes and workplaces, paid workers and unpaid caretakers, and mothers and fathers. Today, women and men alike face blurring—and typically conflicting—boundaries between work and family life.

One of the most important consequences of these changing economic arrangements is the emergence of new uncertainties in both jobs and intimate bonds. The erosion of job security is an integral aspect of the new economy, and it is reshaping work trajectories among workers in all levels of education and income. As unionization has declined, low-wage service work has grown, the pool of workers has expanded beyond national borders, the unskilled and semiskilled can no longer count on unions or local labor markets to protect their jobs or provide a predictable work path. Education offers an expanded set of opportunities, to be sure, but the white-collar jobs that accompany higher levels of education also no longer guarantee a secure financial future. Like their working-class peers, middle-class workers face a job market in which workers are increasingly "disposable" and career paths increasingly haphazard.[2]

On the private side of the work-family divide, a similar shift has occurred. People have far more options in their personal lives—not just about whether, when, and how to form an intimate relationship, but also whether to stay or leave a relationship. The option to end a relationship may be welcomed by those who wish to leave or rued by those who wish a partner to stay, but the expansion of the choice to leave has eroded everyone's sense that they can count on a relationship to endure. For this reason, getting married (like finding a job) no longer offers a predictable point along a steady path toward family and career building.

The rise of insecurity in work and personal life has profound implications for the gender bargain between breadwinning husbands and caretaking wives that rose to prominence in the mid-twentieth century. Since this "separate spheres" bargain depends on the assurance that men can and will provide a steady income large enough to support a wife and children, the rising unpredictability in men's and women's work and marital commitments erodes the foundation upon which it rests. Today, for example, breadwinner mothers account for around 40 percent of US households with children under 18, with one-third of this group consisting of married mothers who earn more than their husbands and the remaining two-thirds consisting of single mothers.[3]

Now that so many families depend on a mother's earnings, it would be reasonable to expect that work and caretaking pressures would lighten so that everyone could more easily blend and share the two. Yet the opposite has occurred. Workers increasingly sense they need to work longer and harder just to keep a job or find a better one. An ideal worker was once expected to put in 40 hours a week, but today he—or she—often needs to devote 50, 60, or more hours a week with far less assurance that these efforts will lead to financial security or a stable career.[4] What's more, changes in caretaking norms add another layer to the pressures on workers and parents. Today's parents, and especially mothers, are expected to practice a level of "intensive parenting" that would have seemed extreme even to the full-time mothers of America in the 1950s.[5] In fact, even though the proportion of mothers who work outside the home has grown exponentially since that time, mothers and fathers now spend more time with their children than did previous generations of parents.[6]

Taken together, the rising insecurity and increasing demands in public and private life have intensified the conflicts between work and caretaking. These conflicts reflect a deep disconnect between the realities facing ordinary people and the institutions of work and family, which have yet to recognize or adapt to these new realities. This clash between changing lives and resistant institutions has created cross-pressures on three levels. At the institutional level, the "greedy institutions" of work and family are on a collision course.[7] At the individual level, women and men face growing dilemmas about how to balance and choose between financial self-reliance through paid work and commitments to care for others. And at the interpersonal level, the conflicts between work and care create tensions about how to divide and share earning and caretaking.

BACKGROUND

Making Sense of Change

How are Americans responding to these growing cross-pressures? Others have offered conflicting answers to this question. One view argues that we have reached a standstill, with change not only at an end but possibly undergoing a reversal.[8] This view points to evidence showing a stall in women's progress at work. Not only have rates of labor force participation leveled off, but glass ceilings and walls at the workplace continue to leave most women segregated in lower-paying jobs. Surveys also show that women still do more than men at home, even though the gender gap has narrowed, and that many continue to feel ambivalent about mothers who work when their children are young.[9] Given these statistics, it is not surprising that anecdotal stories abound about women opting out of jobs and careers to stay home and rear children.[10]

In contrast to the view that gender and family change has stalled and even reversed, another scenario posits an opposite picture. This view focuses on a different set of findings that appear to point to women's growing independence and men's declining advantages. Younger generations of women are outpacing men in college attendance, educational attainment, personal earnings, and career aspirations.[11] At the same time, men's labor force participation is declining.[12] One pundit has even argued that the confusion and sense of threat this loss of status evokes signal "the end of men."[13] Yet whether the focus is on women's gains or men's losses, this scenario depicts a future populated by single adults who build solitary lives rather than lives with a lifelong partner.[14] The most alarmist vision of this future sees rampant individualism replacing lasting commitments to marriage, family, and community.[15]

Revolutionary times are always confusing, and this period is no exception. It is thus not surprising that people will come to different conclusions about the direction and nature of change. Yet both of these views, despite their starkly different depictions of the future, implicitly assume a linear trajectory going forward. Neither is wrong, but each is incomplete. Placing these apparently contradictory trends in a larger context reveals change that is uneven, creating cross-pressures that require new integrations of work and care without offering the necessary social supports to do so. These cross-pressures undermine earlier practices, but they do not provide new resolutions that are clear, viable, or socially accepted.

In this climate, American women and men are left to devise their own strategies to reconcile the conflicting pressures to be *both* a committed worker and a devoted caretaker.[16]

How are they navigating these conflicts, and what strategies are they crafting? Since uneven change has created unavoidable dilemmas that require innovative responses, we need to know the full range of strategies people are pursuing as well as the obstacles that prevent them from achieving a more satisfying and secure blending of work and care.

CASE STUDIES

Findings from Research on the Children of the Gender Revolution

To understand how people are navigating these revolutionary changes, I conducted two studies. The first consists of interviews with young adults between the ages of 18 and 32 who grew up during the last several decades of rapid family shifts.[17] In wide-ranging conversations, these "children of the gender revolution" reflected on their experiences in families that underwent transitions and discussed their own hopes, expectations, and plans for the future. The second study seeks to discover the strategies people are pursuing as they attempt to build families and careers by interviewing women and men between the ages of 34 and 46.[18] By drawing on findings from both studies, it is possible to construct a picture of how today's women and men are responding to growing uncertainties in work and personal life as they attempt to cope with the conflicts between work and care.

Children of the Gender Revolution Consider Their Options   What options do new generations perceive as they consider their future plans? My interviews with young women and men in early adulthood saw three alternatives.[19] One, which I call "neo-traditional," represents an updated version of what we conceive to be the traditional pattern of breadwinning husbands and homemaking wives. The neo-traditional option also stresses permanent, heterosexual marriage in which one partner specializes in breadwinning and the other in caregiving, but it also includes the possibility that a

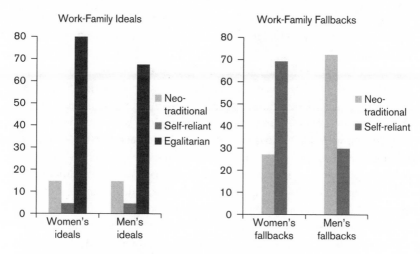

FIGURE 2.1.   Ideals and Fallback Positions of Young Adults.

mother may hold a paid job as long as she also takes responsibility for the "second shift" of domestic work.[20]

At the other end of the spectrum, a second option stresses "self-reliance." In this model, marriage remains an option, but it does not provide economic security or relieve a person's need to be able to survive on one's own. Self-reliance thus means retaining a sense of independence rather than depending on a partner for economic support.

These contrasting models echo the scenarios posited by analysts and pundits, with neo-traditionalism depicting a stall in the move toward gender equality and self-reliance depicting a move toward individualism for women and men alike. A third alternative, "egalitarianism," contains elements of each model but diverges from each. To reconcile the seemingly incompatible goals of personal autonomy and commitment to an intimate partner, the egalitarian option emphasizes fairness, equity, and flexibility in apportioning responsibility for work and care. In this scenario, intimate partners share earning and caretaking and balance these pursuits in their own lives.

Which options do young adult Americans prefer, and which do they expect to achieve? As figure 2.1 shows, the overwhelming majority of those I interviewed wish to have an egalitarian balance of work and care. Indeed, four-fifths of women and two-thirds of men said they hope to create an egalitarian relationship where both paid work and family caretaking are shared. Yet most of these young adults also concluded that their options going forward are likely to fall substantially short of these ideals. Anticipating great barriers to achieving the egalitarian option, they formulated fallback strategies. Unlike their ideals, however, these fallback positions are quite different for women and men.

Most young women—regardless of class, race, or ethnic background—said they were reluctant to surrender their autonomy in a traditional marriage and thus were determined to remain financially self-reliant. Almost three-fourths of women said they plan to build a base and independent identity through paid work in order to avoid becoming trapped in an unhappy marriage or abandoned by an unreliable partner. Young men, however, said they were more inclined to fall back on neo-traditionalism. While acknowledging a woman's right to work outside the home, men nevertheless felt a need to be a breadwinner and rely on their partner to be the primary caretaker.

These findings reveal two different divides in American life. While popular attention remains focused on gender differences, there is also a rising conflict between the ideals younger generations espouse and the options available to accomplish these ideals. Women and men appear to be converging in their aspirations, but they face large obstacles to achieving them.

Emerging Strategies of Work and Care

How are today's adults coping with the conflict between rising egalitarian ideals and the lack of egalitarian options? My interviews with women and men in their prime career- and family-building years show the emergence of four general strategies.[21] The two most evident patterns reflect the fallback positions of neo-traditionalism and self-reliance. About a third were in a relationship where men had become the primary breadwinners and women the primary caretakers, while another third were living on their own or as a single parent.

Among those living in gender traditional families, most were "reluctant traditionals" who had originally hoped to create more equal relationships. Yet economic pressures left fathers coping with time-demanding jobs and excessive workweeks that allowed little time for domestic involvement. Mothers thus had to step up and into this void, becoming the default family caregiver even when that meant pulling back from jobs they enjoyed or dropping out of the workforce altogether. These couples conform to the image of a stalled revolution, in which the arrival of children prompts parents to divide paid work and caretaking in gender-specific ways, even when the original hope had been to avoid this outcome.

In contrast to these reluctant traditionals, another third embody the concerns of those who see a trend away from marital commitment. These singles found themselves on their own rather than in a committed relationship because they faced setbacks in their intimate relationships and often setbacks at work as well. Yet single women and men took a variety of paths to reach this destination. Many women, like Michelle (described in the introduction), became single mothers when boyfriends or husbands left them to rear children on the own. Most men, along with some women, opted to remain single and childless in the wake of unsatisfying relationships and work experiences that left them ill-prepared to take on the emotional or financial obligations of marriage and parenthood. Yet, like their traditional peers, these singles had also hoped for an egalitarian partnership at an earlier stage of their lives. They may have ultimately concluded that the costs of commitment were too great, but they did not anticipate this outcome.

If these two patterns exemplify the dual, if divergent, concerns of those who argue that the gender revolution has stalled and those who see the triumph of uncommitted individualism, they do not tell the whole story. Another third of my interviewees developed a different set of strategies. About 15 percent became "reversers," who developed relationships in which mothers and fathers reversed responsibility for earning and caretaking, while the remaining 15 percent became "egalitarians," who were taking extraordinary steps to resist gender divisions so they might share work and care as equally as possible.

Like reluctant traditionals and singles, the mothers and fathers who reversed responsibility for paid work and caretaking did not start out seeking this arrangement. Yet, over the years of their partnerships, the men hit roadblocks at work while the women were able to find stable—if not always inspiring—jobs and careers. What began as an agreement to share crystallized into a reversed division of work and care. Able to bring in a steady if not necessarily abundant income, women became the primary breadwinners, leaving men to take on the greater share of caretaking, as Dolores's story exemplifies. The reversed arrangement represents a practical adjustment to the changing mix of options found in an economy dominated by service and high-tech jobs, and it is not as unusual as might be expected. In 2012, for example, 15 percent of American households with children younger than 18 depended on a married mother who outearned her husband (up from 4 percent in 1960).[22]

Another pattern among my interviews also represents a new, less rigid approach to enacting gender arrangements. Unlike the reversers, however, this group comes closest to achieving the egalitarian ideal that most of the interviewees claim to prefer. Like Danny, these "egalitarians" forged relationships built on the principle of equal sharing, even when doing so meant personal sacrifices of time, money, and sleep. It also involved significant trade-offs. For example, Danny and his wife chose to reconfigure their work schedules, knowing that these choices might endanger their future work prospects. Other egalitarian couples opted for a different choice, deciding instead to postpone or reject childbearing. In the absence of employer support or affordable child care, the commitment to equality prompted couples to devise creative strategies, but it could not provide a solution to the conflicts between work and care. Egalitarian women and men thus wondered how long they could defy the odds and sustain their ideals.

All of these patterns contain diversity, and the distinctions among traditionals, singles, reversers, and egalitarians can blur as individuals move from one category to another as their lives change in unexpected ways. Indeed, the decline of financial and interpersonal predictability suggests that most will undergo some kind of change going forward. It is also clear that none of these strategies is straightforward or easy. Each contains drawbacks, and most developed a pattern they had once hoped to avoid. Even those who were able to achieve their earlier aspirations encountered unforeseen challenges and difficulties. It is thus not surprising that most reported feeling vaguely dissatisfied and some reported feeling intensely conflicted. Taken together, these groups nevertheless provide a roadmap for charting the options people face and the paths they are blazing as they respond to the conflicts between work and care in today's uncertain landscape.

THE CONTEMPORARY SITUATION

Implications for the Popular Debate

Considering the full array of strategies among my interviewees, it is important to see their commonalities as well as their differences. Each strategy represents a different compromise to shared dilemmas. Yet neither gender identity nor personal preferences can explain why individuals developed such different strategies. Women and men from all social backgrounds articulated aspirations to integrate and share work and care with a life partner. Yet people traveled different paths and developed divergent commitments despite the similarities in their expressed personal preferences.

Stepping back to look at the whole landscape reveals the ways that disparate social contexts prompted people to respond in different ways to the new conflicts and insecurities of work and care. While some were able to find secure, flexible work and to build a stable, egalitarian relationship, only a small minority enjoyed these propitious circumstances. Most coped with work and family circumstances that fell far short of their ideals. In the case of traditional and reversed couples, the partner with the more stable but also more demanding job became the main breadwinner, leaving the partner with less promising work options to take on primary caretaking duties. In most instances, men enjoyed the best prospects at work and also confronted the most intense work pressures; but when a woman's job offered more security, income, and/or advancement opportunities, she became the primary financial provider despite the cultural norm of male breadwinning. Whether the job of breadwinning fell to a man or a woman, the need for one person to hold on to a job by working long hours placed limits on the options of the other. The person with fewer opportunities at work thus became the default caretaker.

In contrast, others were unable to establish a stable relationship, although this situation had different implications for men and women. When men were unable to find secure work, they tended to avoid marriage as well.[23] Single women were more likely to face a different dilemma, either opting to remain childless or to rear children without the help of an intimate partner. While single men faced a dearth of commitments to work or care, single mothers sought ways to combine work and care on their own. Finally, egalitarians confronted a different set of options than their traditional, reversed, or single peers. Although they were able to find satisfying jobs and to create relationships with partners who were also committed to work, most found that "doing it all" did not mean "having it all." Lacking flexible career options and high-quality child care, they faced a trade-off between childlessness and exhaustion.

All of these patterns reflect different ways of organizing work and care, but each entails difficulties and sacrifices. Egalitarian strategies offer an alternative to neo-traditional, self-reliant, and gender-reversed models, but the egalitarian ideal remains vague and difficult to attain. Indeed, the variety of patterns is itself an indication that an adequate set of institutionalized supports for the preferred egalitarian pattern—including secure jobs, flexible, workplaces, and child-care resources—has yet to emerge.

FUTURE DIRECTIONS AND POLICIES
Where Do We Go From Here?

Today's women and men say they want to "have it all," but they also believe such a goal is an impossible and even self-centered dream.[24] Yet the desire to blend satisfying work with a rich family life is not selfish and should not be out of reach. To the contrary, the ability "to work and love" is the mark of a healthy person, and providing the means to blend work and love is the mark of a healthy society.[25] Framing these desires as selfish and unrealistic is thus not just inaccurate but counterproductive. It obscures the institutional roots of the shared dilemmas facing new generations and prevents us from discovering and developing the solutions. The first step toward creating a society that supports women, men, and children from all social classes and backgrounds is thus to jettison the idea that integrating work and care is a selfish pursuit confined to middle-class women.

The new economy has transformed our ideals but left people facing a gap between their aspirations and their options. The erosion of job security for men means that women and men must share in the work of supporting their households. Similarly, the erosion of marital security means the women cannot afford to confine their lives to caretaking alone. Amid this irreversible gender transformation, restructuring our work and caretaking institutions holds the key to lessening the work-care conflicts and pressures for everyone. Creating supports for integrating work and care means changing our work and caretaking norms as well as reorganizing our workplace and caretaking structures. Here are some immodest proposals.

First, we need to replace the "ideal worker" norm, which rewards workers who put work first regardless of life stage or the needs of their dependents, with a new set of norms that value carework and reward the "flexible worker." A commitment to the norm of work flexibility has two implications. In the short term, it values workers' *contributions* rather than the amount of time they put in at the workplace. In the longer run, it allows women and men alike to build work careers that allow them to take time for their families without absorbing long-term penalties.

Next, just as we need to create more flexible workplaces that value the unpaid work of caretaking, we also need to jettison an "intensive parenting" norm that defines time-intensive, exclusive devotion by mothers and (to a lesser extent) fathers as the only responsible parenting style. A "flexible parenting" norm, in contrast, would place mothers and fathers at the center of a wide network of caretakers that stretches out into the community and beyond. This more expansive vision of childrearing not only recognizes the realities facing today's parents. It also recognizes the benefits for children when they are exposed to diverse environments and can count on the support of many caretakers as they grow up.

Changes in norms are necessary but not sufficient. Indeed, American values appear to be far ahead of the country's institutional structures when it comes to acknowledging and supporting more flexible, egalitarian forms of work and parenting.[26] The challenge is to reorganize our work and caregiving structures to fit with the more nuanced views now emerging among American women and men. Employers need to restructure jobs and careers to provide their employees with the flexibility to accomplish their breadwinning and caregiving tasks how (and when) they deem best. Flexible work and career structures would empower workers to shape their daily schedules and career trajectories to better fit the ebb and flow of their caregiving responsibilities.

We also need to reorganize the structure of care in our neighborhoods, communities, and cities. In today's economy, it takes a very large village to raise a child and any dependent—whether young, old, or disabled—who needs the care of others. Now that women are no longer able to provide this support free of charge, it is time to recognize the inherent value, economic worth, and social necessity of providing universal, high-quality, and well-compensated care for all the life stages and situations, from infancy through childhood and adolescence and into old age, that require it.

Three principles should guide the construction and implementation of these new norms and structures—gender equality in work and caregiving; integration between the workplace and the home; and support for all workers to balance earning an income with caring for others. The principles of equality, integration, and balance are as necessary as they are just. These proposals may seem unrealistic, but it is even more unrealistic to imagine we can continue to build a thriving society without them. Indeed, in lieu of institutional realignments that offer a range of egalitarian resolutions to intensifying work-care conflicts, our nation and its economy will struggle amid a patchwork of inadequate, individual strategies that leave rising numbers of our citizens facing insecurity and overload.

The good news is that popular support for these institutional supports is widespread. Recent research shows, for example, that Americans want egalitarian work and family policies and support employed mothers and caretaking fathers when their circumstances allow.[27] The political challenge may appear daunting, but new efforts to enact policies such as paid family leave and workplace protections are signs that Americans can overcome the stalemate, stop blaming ordinary women and men for the problems they did not create, and create new supports for blending work and care in the ways that each family deems best. The future is not preordained, and there has never been a better opportunity to overcome the stall and finish the gender revolution that can no longer be denied.

NOTES

1. Polanyi, Karl. 1944 (reissued in 1957). *The Great Transformation: The Political and Economic Origins of Our Time.* Boston: Beacon.

2. Hacker, Jacob S. 2008. *The Great Risk Shift: The New Economic Insecurity and the Decline of the American Dream.* New York: Oxford University Press. See

also Kalleberg, Arne L. 2011. *Good Jobs, Bad Jobs: The Rise of Polarized and Precarious Employment Systems in the United States, 1970s to 2000s.* New York: Russell Sage Foundation; Cooper, Marianne. 2014. *Cut Adrift: Families in Insecure Times.* Berkeley and Los Angeles: University of California Press; Pugh, Allison J. 2014. *The Tumbleweed Society: Working and Caring in an Age of Insecurity.* Oxford: Oxford University Press; Silva, Jennifer. 2103. *Coming Up Short: Working Class Adulthood in an Age of Uncertainty.* New York: Oxford University Press.

3. Wang, Wendy, Kim Parker, and Paul Taylor. 2013. *Breadwinner Moms.* May 29. Washington, DC: Pew Research Center. See also Glynn, Sarah Jane. 2014. *Breadwinning Mothers, Then and Now.* June. Washington, DC: Center for American Progress.

4. Williams, Joan. 2000. *Unbending Gender: Why Family and Work Conflict and What to Do about It.* New York: Oxford University Press. See also Moen, Phyllis, and Patricia Roehling. 2004. *The Career Mystique: Cracks in the American Dream.* Lanham, MD: Rowman & Littlefield; and Jacobs, Jerry A., and Kathleen Gerson. 2004. *The Time Divide: Work, Family, and Gender Inequality.* Cambridge, MA: Harvard University Press.

5. Hays, Sharon. 1996. *The Cultural Contradictions of Motherhood.* New Haven: Yale University Press.

6. Bianchi, Suzanne M., John P. Robinson, and Melissa A. Milkie. 2007. *Changing Rhythms of American Family Life.* New York: Russell Sage Foundation.

7. Coser, Lewis A. 1974. *Greedy Institutions: Patterns of Undivided Commitment.* New York: Free.

8. Belkin, Lisa. 2003. "The Opt-Out Revolution." *New York Times Magazine,* October 26.

9. England, Paula. 2010. "The Gender Revolution: Uneven and Stalled." *Gender & Society* 24:149–166.

10. Cotter, David A., Joan M. Hermsen, and Reeve Vanneman. 2011. "End of the Gender Revolution? Gender Role Attitudes from 1977 to 2008." *American Journal of Sociology* 117:259–289.

11. DiPrete, Thomas A., and Claudia Buchmann. 2013. *The Rise of Women: The Growing Gender Gap in Education and What It Means for American Schools.* New York: Russell Sage Foundation. See also Wang, Wendy. 2014. *Record Share of Wives Are More Educated Than Their Husbands.* Washington, DC: Pew Research Center (February); Lang, Molly Monacan, and Barbara J. Risman. 2010. "A 'Stalled' Revolution or a Still Unfolding One?" In *Families as They Really Are,* edited by Barbara J. Risman, 408–412. New York: Norton; Cotter, David A., Joan M. Hermsen, and Reeve Vanneman. 2014. "Back on Track? The Stall and Rebound in Support for Women's New Roles in Work and Politics." Council on Contemporary Families Gender Rebound Symposium. https://contemporaryfamilies.org/gender-revolution-rebound-brief-back-on-track/.

12. Patten, Eileen, and Kim Parker. 2012. *A Gender Reversal on Career Aspirations: Young Women Now Top Young Men in Valuing a High-Paying Career.* April 25. Washington, DC: Pew Research Center.

13. Rosin, Hanna. 2012. *The End of Men and the Rise of Women.* New York: Riverbed.

14. Klinenberg, Eric. 2012. *Going Solo: The Extraordinary Rise and Surprising Appeal of Living Alone.* New York: Penguin. See also DePaulo, Bella. 2006. *Singled Out: How Singles Are Stereotyped, Stigmatized, and Ignored, and Still Live Happily Ever After.* New York: St. Martin's.

15. Wilcox, W. Bradford. 2010. *When Marriage Disappears: The Retreat from Marriage in Middle America.* Charlottesville, VA: National Marriage Project. See

also Putnam, Robert D. 2000. *Bowling Alone: The Collapse and Revival of American Community.* New York: Simon & Schuster.

16. Beck, Ulrich. 1992. *Risk Society: Toward a New Modernity.* Thousand Oaks, CA: Sage.

17. Gerson, Kathleen. 2011. *The Unfinished Revolution: Coming of Age in a New Era of Gender, Work, and Family.* New York: Oxford University Press.

18. Gerson, Kathleen. 2016. "Different Ways of Not Having It All: Work, Care, and Shifting Gender Arrangements in the New Economy." In *Beyond the Cubicle: Insecurity Culture and the Flexible Self,* edited by Allison Pugh. New York: Oxford University Press.

19. Gerson (2011).

20. Hochschild, Arlie R., with Anne Machung. 1989. *The Second Shift: Working Parents and the Revolution at Home.* New York: Metropolitan.

21. Gerson (2016).

22. Wang et al. (2013).

23. Wilson, William Julius. 1975. *The Truly Disadvantaged.* Chicago: University of Chicago Press.

24. Slaughter, Anne-Marie. 2012. "Why Women Still Can't Have It All." *Atlantic,* July.

25. Erikson, Erik. 1963. *Childhood and Society.* New York: Norton.

26. Jacobs, Jerry A., and Kathleen Gerson. 2016. "Unpacking Americans' Views on the Employment of Mothers and Fathers: Lessons from a National Vignette Survey." *Gender & Society* 30 (3): 413–441. http://gas.sagepub.com/content/early/2015/08/05/0891243215597445.full.pdf?ijkey = HyVJlcqtcMnTnWg&keytype = finite.

27. Pedulla, David, and Sarah Thebaud. 2015. "Can We Finish the Revolution? Gender, Work-Family Ideals, and Institutional Constraint." *American Sociological Review* 80 (1): 116–139.

3. Community Colleges as a Pathway for Low-Income Women to Enter the Engineering Technology Workforce

Chrystal A. S. Smith

Recently divorced, Honoria is a 44-year-old Hispanic woman with three children. A housewife for many years, she had to find a job to support her children financially. Honoria considered entering the fast food industry, but decided that while a college education would take a year or two and be costly initially, it was a worthwhile long-term investment that would help her to obtain a higher paying job. When Honoria attempted to enroll in a health degree program at the nearby Florida community college, she was informed that there was a wait list of two years. Determined to start her college degree immediately, she explored the other programs offered by the community college and in the process discovered the engineering technology program. Her children encouraged her to pursue the engineering technology degree because as a teaching assistant at her son's robotics camp, she displayed the skills to build computers. Honoria is now enrolled full-time in the engineering technology program (the only woman in her cohort) and works part-time at the community college. Spanish is her first language so she often struggles to understand the coursework. She has worked assiduously to overcome this language barrier and has become the top student in her cohort. Honoria would like to get a full-time job in the engineering technology workforce, working in quality control rather than with machines. Ultimately, she is interested in pursuing an online four-year engineering degree, which will allow her the flexibility to work and support her children.

INTRODUCTION

Honoria's story highlights the diverse pathways taken by women who enroll in engineering technology (ET) programs at community colleges.

28

Driven by the need to support her children, Honoria initially sought to enroll in one of the health-related degree programs offered by the community college before deciding to enter into a two-year ET degree program. Graduates from two-year community college ET programs are technicians who have the knowledge and applied skills to work in support of engineering activities in high-tech manufacturing and other industries.[1] The health-related occupations that women traditionally pursue typically have lower wages and fewer opportunities for career advancement than the male-dominated technology-related occupations requiring similar levels of education. Thus, Honoria has potentially increased her future earnings by pursuing an ET degree with the goal of obtaining a technology-related job.

In this chapter, I first review the recent literature and data on women pursuing ET degrees/certificates and their subsequent employment in the science, technology, engineering, and mathematics (STEM) workforce, specifically in the ET workforce. Next, I present a discussion of interviews conducted with Honoria and five other women who participated in our research study funded by the National Science Foundation (NSF) that examined community college ET degrees as pathways into the ET workforce. We conducted follow-up interviews with five of the six women. These interviews provide insight into the challenges that women encounter as they pursue ET degrees and the strategies that they use to overcome obstacles and achieve their academic and career goals.

BACKGROUND

Women, Unemployment, and Community Colleges

In the economic recovery that followed the Great Recession (2007 to 2009), women are less likely to regain employment and more likely to be unemployed in low-wage jobs than men.[2] African American women, in particular, are more likely to be unemployed than are white men and women with the same educational background. In part, this disparity in employment is due to the lack of recovery of public sector jobs where women and ethnic minorities have been overrepresented because of government policies committed to equal opportunity and affirmative actions.[3]

To gain employment in the private sector, it is critical that women, ethnic minorities, and low-income individuals obtain a college degree or certificate. Well-paying jobs that do not require a college degree are becoming increasingly scarce. Analysts predict that by 2020 postsecondary education and/or some form of training post–high school will be required for two out of every three jobs.[4] In addition, college-educated workers earn higher wages and have lower levels of unemployment.[5] A review of unemployment data found that enrollment rates in community colleges spike during periods of high unemployment,[6] an indication that the general public is aware of the importance of attaining a college degree to retrain and acquire new skills to obtain employment in growing sectors of the economy.

Community colleges provide women, ethnic minorities, and low-income individuals with the opportunity to obtain an affordable, accredited, convenient, and flexible degree or certificate as well as the opportunity to transfer to four-year colleges. In 2010, women were 57 percent of community college students, three out of 10 were women of color, and one out of four were mothers with work, family, and caregiving responsibilities.[7] Women are more likely to attend community colleges part-time than women who attend four-year colleges and men who pursue postsecondary education. Unfortunately, a review of national community college data found that over a six-year period (initial enrollment fall 2009) only 38.2 percent of students earned a degree or certificate at their starting community college or a different community college or a four-year college.[8] Overall, women were 54 percent of this cohort of community college students, yet only 41.5 percent of these women earned a degree or certificate.[9] The low completion rates of community college students have been attributed to a lack of academic preparation, limited financial resources (including financial aid), work-and-life-balance issues, and insufficient academic advising.[10]

Barriers to Women Enrolling in Community College ET Programs

One of the fastest growing areas of employment, STEM occupations are predicted to increase 26 percent by 2020.[11] Yet women continue to be underrepresented in the STEM workforce.[12] Of the women employed in the STEM workforce, approximately 28 percent are Asian/Pacific Islander, 4.9 percent are white, 2.8 percent of black/African American, and 2.3 percent are Native American and Hispanic.[13] A review of the National Science Board: Science and Engineering Indicators[14] shows an overall decline in the number of women earning ET degrees from 2000 to 2013 (see figure 3.1).

Although there is a gender disparity in salaries in the STEM workforce as in the non-STEM workforce, women in STEM occupations have higher average earnings and opportunities for advancement compared to women in the non-STEM workforce.[15] For example, individuals with associate's degrees in STEM fields such as mechanics and electricians have higher lifetime earnings than individuals with four-year degrees such as teachers,

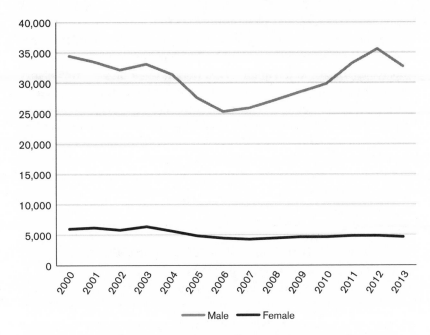

FIGURE 3.1. Earned ET Associate's Degrees by Sex, 2000 to 2013. *Source:* Author's Review of the National Science Board: Science and Engineering Indicators 2014.

school administrators, and writers/editors.[16] In addition, women with bachelor's and master's degrees are more likely to have attended a community college STEM program.[17]

The primary barrier to women enrolling in ET programs at community colleges is culturally dictated gender roles. Despite having the similar aptitude and interest in STEM as men, culturally determined gender roles and stereotypes influence women's decisions not to pursue occupations in STEM fields.[18] Women like Honoria who enroll in community colleges most frequently choose to pursue degrees or certificates in areas considered "appropriate" occupations for women, e.g., health sciences, teaching, child care, and administration.[19] Unfortunately, these occupations, traditionally dominated by women, have lower wages and few opportunities for career advancement compared to other fields that are typically dominated by men, such as STEM.[20] These culturally determined gender roles and stereotypes along with implicit bias lead women to believe that (1) they have a lower aptitude in math and science compared to their male counterparts and (2) only men should pursue occupations in STEM.[21] Also, high school and community college advisors/counselors/teachers, influenced by culturally determined gender roles and stereotypes, often neglect to inform female students about employment opportunities in the STEM workforce.[22] Consequently, women make decisions about their postsecondary education and enter the workforce lacking crucial information regarding the variety of available technology-related occupations as well as the affordable flexible training offered by community colleges.

CASE STUDIES

Research Design

This National Science Foundation–funded study was designed to examine the pathways into community college ET programs. Our University of South Florida research team led by Dr. William Tyson, PI, conducted 57 semistructured interviews with students who were enrolled in ET programs at five southwest Florida community colleges. In collaboration with the community colleges, research team members visited core ET classes to explain the purpose of the study. Students interested in participating in the study were asked to write their contact information on provided forms. Research team members contacted students within a week to schedule the interviews. Most of the interviews were conducted in person at the community colleges or at locations convenient for students; a minority were conducted over the telephone.

Six of the total interviews were conducted with women enrolled in ET programs at these community colleges. After analyzing the women's initial interviews, I sought to learn more about their pathway into community college ET programs by conducting follow-up interviews. Approximately one year after the initial interviews, I conducted these follow-up interviews with five of the six women so we could learn about their academic and career progress. I was unable to contact the sixth woman. To develop the follow-up interview protocols, I reviewed the literature about the experiences of women at community colleges in STEM and non-STEM programs and in collaboration with the Co-PI and qualitative lead, Dr. Lakshmi Jayaram, identified the following research questions:

- What are the experiences of women enrolled in ET degree programs at community colleges?
- To what extent are the experiences of these women similar and/or different?

- Why do/did these women decide to enroll in community college?
- Why do/did these women decide to pursue ET degree/certification?
- What are the career ambitions of these women?

These research questions sought to gain additional insight into the women's pathways into ET along with the cultural and financial barriers and work-life balance issues that they encounter and overcome.

The follow-up interview protocols asked the women for specific examples about their experiences related to their ET programs at community colleges and included "tell-me-more" probes.[23] I conducted the interviews in person as well as over the phone to accommodate the women's busy schedules. The interviews ranged from 35 minutes to one hour. The interviews were audio-recorded with the women's informed consent and then transcribed for analysis. After the interview transcripts were entered and coded in ATLAS.ti 6, I merged the initial and follow-up interview transcripts for five of the six women and systemically reviewed each transcript to identify emerging themes and patterns. Next, I present the analysis of both the initial and the follow-up interviews conducted with the six women who participated in this study.

Women's Characteristics

Before conducting the initial interviews, we administered a sociodemographic questionnaire to each woman (see table 3.1). The average age of the women in our study was 42 years with an age range from 30 to 56 years. Four of the six women were married and five of the six women had childcaring responsibilities. Five of the six women funded their ET degree using a combination of personal savings, federal student loans, and federal grants and scholarships. The sixth woman was a veteran whose ET degree was primarily funded through the Veterans Retraining Assistance Program (VRAP) GI Bill.

Analysis of Women's Interviews and Case Studies

To analyze the interviews, I reviewed the transcripts meticulously and identified themes that focused on the women's (1) pathways into community college ET programs, (2) experiences in the ET program, (3) financial support, (4) work-life balance issues, (5) experience with cultural and social stereotypes about entering ET fields, and (6) career goals and aspirations. I wrote extensive case studies for each woman. Using pseudonyms, the abbreviated case studies for each woman presented below focuses on the following:

TABLE 3.1 Sociodemographic Characteristics of Women Enrolled in ET Programs at Community Colleges

Characteristics	Number
Ethnicity	
White American	4
Latino/Hispanic	2
Marital Status	
Married	4
Single	2
Caregiving—Children	
Yes	6
No	0
Education	
High school diploma	3
Associate's degree	1
Bachelor's degree	2
Current Employment	
Yes	4
No	2
Full-time Employment	
Yes	4
No	2

Adriana, a 30-year-old married Hispanic American woman, works at a temporary full-time job at the nearby community college, where she is pursuing her ET degree full-time. She has an associate's degree in elementary education and recently obtained a bachelor's degree in business administration from her current community college. Adriana decided to pursue the ET degree when one of her professors mentioned the need for a qualified workforce in advance manufacturing. She obtained a production technician certificate, but did not get any interest from potential employers because she lacked experience, so she then decided to take the extra credits necessary to obtain an ET degree. Adriana's work schedule made attending classes challenging because her classes started just as her job ended for the day. She found it difficult to get to class on time and it caused her to miss several classes. However, she was able to focus and study with her classmates so she passed the course. Adrian also found it difficult being the only woman in her courses and not having hands-on experience in technology. However, her classmates have been helpful and the director of the program, who is also an instructor, became her mentor. Adriana thinks that the Open Entry-Open Exit[24] method that her program is implementing will give her the flexibility to continue working and complete her degree sooner.

Adriana is the sole income earner in her family. Her husband is unemployed and stays at home caring for their three children. Financial constraints hampered her ability to pursue her education, but she was able to obtain funding from various sources including the Workforce Investment Act and scholarships from her community college along with her personal savings. Overall her family is supportive of her pursuit of an ET degree. However, her husband is somewhat opposed to the idea of her working in the industry that is highly dominated by men because he fears that she could be harassed and one of her sisters thinks that she should be working, not pursuing a new degree. Adriana is always debating whether she should enter the workforce now or finish the program. She has been seeking job opportunities in manufacturing and engineering through Employ Florida, Job Monster, local companies, and Google. She is also researching programs that assist women in finding opportunities. Adriana is seeking an internship, preferably paid, so she will gain experience in the manufacturing field. The community college's internship coordinator is confident that Adriana will get an internship shortly. She would like to wear a "space suit" and "work in [an] anti-static room." She aspires to find an employer who would support her efforts to continue her education.

Candace, a 40-year-old, married, white American woman, works full-time in international sales for a midsize electronic company that was recently bought by a Fortune 100 company. She has a bachelor's degree teaching foreign languages (French and Spanish). She has a background in the fundamentals of electricity. But when she started producing more technical presentations for clients, she felt that she would make more progress in her job if she had a technical degree that would earn her higher visibility, allowing her to pursue international sales or become a sales engineer. She enrolled in the ET program at the nearby community college part-time with the intention of eventually transferring to a four-year state university and majoring in electrical engineering. She takes both online and in-person classes. She wishes that she could take more than two classes at a time. She has classes with one other woman and they get along with their male colleagues. So far Candace has not found the information challenging in the ET program. In fact, she had discovered that she is more knowledge about ET than she realized when she entered the program. Yet she has gained additional knowledge that she has applied directly to her job. For example, she now has an improved understanding about electrical circuits so she can better meet the specific demands of her global customers.

Candace pays for her part-time ET program with partial tuition reimbursement from her employer and her personal savings. Her husband, who is employed full-time, is supportive and helps care for their children so she can attend class and study. Although her father, an engineer, is very proud of her, it was difficult for Candace tell him that she was pursuing her engineering degree because she was uncertain of his reaction. However, he reacted positively and has been supportive of her pursuit of an engineering degree. Candace hopes that once she gets her electrical engineering degree that she will earn more money, but does not see her job changing substantially. She does believe that she will be "a lot smarter" and will not have to rely on engineers at her company to give her advice, which will earn the respect of her colleagues.

Helena, a 56-year-old, married, white American woman, recently started a full-time position as an operations and manufacturing manager. When first interviewed, Helena was a purchasing manager for a medium manufacturing company, which paid for her to obtain a manufacturing certificate. She decided to enroll in the community college ET program part-time because she wanted to transfer to the engineering department in a supervisory position with an increased salary at that company. In the supervisory position, she would have worked more with her hands, drawing parts, which she considered more interesting and challenging. Helena took 90 percent of her ET courses online because they were more convenient for her busy lifestyle. She believes that pursuing her ET degree not only helped her get her new job, but has increased her understanding of the maintenance of the machinery, the manufacturing flow processes, and the quality processes in the factory she supervises.

Helena used her personal savings and grants/scholarships to pay for the community college ET program. She has two in-person classes remaining to graduate, but she has not spoken to her new employers about obtaining the time needed to complete her degree. Helena had two women in her classes and they got along well with their male classmates. She had the support of her family and friends as she pursued her ET degree. She thinks that woman have more employment opportunities and higher rates of pay in ET than in the typical office jobs that more women pursue.

Honoria, a recently divorced, 44-year-old Hispanic woman, works full-time at the nearby community college, where she is enrolled part-time in an ET program. She enrolled in the ET program because there was a wait list for the health degree program she was originally going to pursue. Honoria feels that at the beginning her male cohorts in the ET program were uncomfortable with her as the only woman in the class because they had to control their language, but over time they became comfortable with each other. They are very respectful and help her understand some of the course material. She has found everything about the program challenging because Spanish is her first language. To overcome this obstacle, she used dictionaries, additional books, and online videos; studied with a classmate; and asked the teacher to explain term meanings after class. She would help the other students and they helped her. They would tease her because she was a woman with no experience and a Spanish speaker and yet she was the top student in the class. She did not think the teasing was serious and thought that they were just kidding.

Honoria is using federal grants and scholarships to pay for her ET program. She has not as much time to spend with her three children because she has to go to school and study. Outside of her children, her family does not understand ET and she has to keep explaining it to them. She has recommended her women friends pursue an ET degree, but she says until she gets a job, they will not take her seriously. Currently, she is taking sociology, her final course to graduate with her associate's degree. She has already applied to a four-year online ET degree program. She is looking for a full-time job in quality control.

Megan, a single, 47-year-old, white American woman, is unemployed after being laid off as an electronics assembler after 20 years at the same company. As a veteran, she is able to get one year of education benefits through the Veteran Retraining Assistance Program (VRAP) so she decided to go back to school full-time and get a technical degree. She considered attending ITT Technical Institute, a for-profit technical postsecondary school, but its tuition was double the price of the conveniently located nearby community college. A former coworker suggested that she enroll in an ET program. In her ET program, Megan is taking new courses that she finds challenging and her math skills have improved. One of her friends who is an engineer helps her with her mathematics and electronics assignments. Megan wishes that there was more hands-on teaching and more labs instead of teachers using PowerPoint slides for instruction.

Megan is paying for her ET program with federal student loans and the GI Bill/military assistance. She is the part-time caregiver of her four-year-old granddaughter. Megan is not sure what jobs are available with an ET program degree, but is confident that she will get a job as a technician in manufacturing when she has completed the program. She prefers to work at a small company, possibly in research and development. She found out about these jobs through the Internet, Craig's List, and General Electric's listserv. Being an assembler did not pay that well and it was difficult to get promoted in the company without advancing your education, so she is confident that her ET program degree will help her make more money and get better job opportunities.

Sarah, a 35-year-old, married, white American woman, works as the director of marketing and operations for a small- to midsize company in the Florida energy technology sector. She has a four-year degree in energy technology management. In her initial interview, she was enrolled full-time in the last year of her program after losing her job in the insurance field. She became interested in the energy technology program at the nearby community college after seeing an ad in the newspaper. Several years prior, Sarah had majored in computer science at a four-year state university for one year. These credits were accepted by the community colleges so she was able to complete her energy technology degree in approximately three years. She believes that the energy technology program would be improved with more in-person classes so that there is more hands-on training and face-to-face interaction. She had minimal hands-on training because approximately 90 percent of the courses are online. She also feels that the program should teach more of the technical aspects of energy technology. Sarah got along with her male classmates and worked closely with the two other women in the program. They studied and worked on assignments together.

Sarah paid for her full-time bachelor's degree in energy technology management with a combination of her personal savings and federal loans/grants/scholarships. Her husband's job is flexible and he has been supportive, assisting in the care of their two children. After Sarah lost her job, she felt that the community college officials were uncommunicative and unhelpful when she attempted to get financial aid. Also, she did not have an assigned advisor; rather, the department chair advised her about her coursework and career goals. In her final year in the program, Sarah found an uncompensated internship at this company without the assistance or support of her program. She used the knowledge from her energy technology program to help organize the company and to assist in the installation of products. Her male colleagues were surprised that she was knowledgeable about energy technology and willing to do the manual labor such as going up on roofs. The company owner and manager considered her contribution invaluable. After she completed her internship and graduated, he hired her full-time.

Overview of Women's Case Studies

I found that the women interviewed in this study were uniformly talented, hardworking, ambitious, committed to pursuing their postsecondary education, and determined to improve their socioeconomic status. They shared the belief that pursuing a degree in ET at a community college was a viable means to obtaining employment in the STEM workforce, advancing their careers, increasing their salaries, and gaining the respect of their male colleagues. With the exception of Candace and Sarah, the women were working-/lower-class and first-generation college students. They chose to enroll in ET programs that were offered at community colleges because they were conveniently located, offered flexible courses (e.g., online courses), and were affordable compared to for-profit technology institutes. The women attended both in-person and online classes, worked on lab assignments, studied alone and with classmates, and overcame challenges to their academic success. For example, Honoria worked long hours outside of classes to overcome a language barrier (Spanish as a first language) to become the top student in her cohort. They also experienced periodic financial difficulties that made it difficult for them to continue their ET courses, causing them to occasionally rely on their personal savings. These women stressed the importance of having supportive spouses and families to assist them with their child care obligations and the financial challenges as they pursued their ET degrees.

UPDATING THE CONTEMPORARY SITUATION

This research contributes to the nascent literature on women enrolled in ET programs at community colleges, much of which focuses on women transferring from community colleges to four-year universities to pursue STEM degrees. However, with the increase in the number of technology jobs in the STEM workforce, researchers have began to explore community college ET programs as a pathway into these jobs for women, minorities, and low-income individuals because of the higher wages and opportunities for advancement. For example, many companies offer in-house training or will pay for employees to take technology courses at community colleges or technical institutes over a three- to six-month period, leading to promotions and salary raises.

My analysis of the interviews with the women participating in this study captures some of the barriers that many women face pursuing ET degrees and certificates as well as obtaining employment in the STEM workforce. The following primary themes related to STEM emerged from the interviews: (1) women were not advised about ET as a possible pathway to employment opportunities in the STEM workforce by their high school and community colleges, (2) women were apprehensive about taking technology courses and lacking hands-on experience, and (3) women frequently encountered negative cultural stereotypes about entering male-dominated occupations.

Insufficient Advising about ET

Most of the women in this study did not receive sufficient advising about pursuing an ET degree or certificate. Research has found that advising at community colleges is crucial to the success of women, minorities, first-generation college students, and other marginalized individuals.[25] Advising, academic and career, is even more crucial for women who enter community college lacking awareness about the benefits of pursuing ET degrees and certificates and often have misconceptions that all manufacturing jobs require manual labor and are dirty. None of the women in this study had been informed about ET programs at community colleges or about the employment opportunities in ET by their high school or community college advisors. They learned about the employment opportunities available with ET degrees and/or certificates from instructors in other programs, from work colleagues, and in one case through a newspaper advertisement. Describing how she found out about the ET program, Honoria stated:

> I visited every department here [at the community college], I went because when I was registered for dental hygiene I realized I have to be on a waiting list for two years and I can't, I cannot wait, I have to graduate to get a job and then when I find out that, I just begin to visit all the departments and I say, but I don't like this, I don't like this, well this is kind of but then I find out this one [ET] and I say, okay. That sounds interesting.

This finding suggests that both community colleges and high schools need to put mechanisms in place to ensure that advisors/counselors are aware of ET programs and the potential earnings and opportunities for career advancement that are available in ET fields. This information must be conveyed to women as well as male students to broaden the participation of women in STEM occupations.

Inadequate Experience in ET

Most women do not have experience working a technology job prior to entering ET programs, which can make them apprehensive about the technical coursework. Yet, if they are to gain employment in the STEM workforce on completing their degrees and certification, it is vital that they gain experience working in technology fields through their programs.[26] In this study, women expressed confidence about their ability to complete the mathematics and science coursework required for their ET program, but most of them were apprehensive about the technology courses, especially the hands-on lab activities. Their lack of experience in technology fields contributed to their apprehension about the unfamiliar technology courses such as hydraulics. They reported having to study more hours and reaching out to the instructor and their male classmates for assistance. Describing the challenge of her technology courses, Adriana stated:

The hydraulics course was really hard for me because the way that the ET program accepted me . . . I had articulated credits from a previous certification. The certification in itself was a huge milestone for me because it was really, really challenging. I didn't have the background in manufacturing or mechanics or electronics. However I'm a pretty good student so I would study and I would just study, study, study and so I passed all those exams for the certification . . . but again I didn't have any confidence since I had never really done hands-on work in mechanics or manufacturing so hydraulics and pneumatics class truly was overwhelming because I didn't have the applicable experience, not just that but our laboratories were quite limited, we worked in group settings and the labs were not available throughout the week, they were only available during scheduled courses so I felt that was kind of a disadvantage for me because I would've benefited from additional lab time.

The women proudly shared their stories of persisting in the technology courses, which built their confidence in their ability to be successful in the STEM workforce. In contrast to Helena, who got a high-paying position prior to completing her degree because of her years of experience, Adriana was unable to find a job with her ET certificate so she chose to pursue a degree to gain the experience through the required internship. Sarah discovered that finding a paid internship was difficult, so she chose to work for free for several months. Her effectiveness in this internship resulted in her supervisor offering her a permanent position. For most women, finding an internship without contacts in the ET industry, especially an internship that is paid, is difficult and an unpaid internship is not financially viable.

Community colleges must be sure that they have programs in place to assist women in gaining experience in ET fields as well as assisting them in finding paid internships in their field of interest. All five Florida community college ET programs in this study had partnerships with manufacturing companies in their regions. From the interviews, we learned that while the directors and instructors would email ET students with employment opportunities at these companies, there was no established job placement or assistance program in place to match students with these employment opportunities.

Negative Cultural Stereotypes about Women in ET Occupations

Gender stereotypes about what is "women's work" vs. "men's work" are embedded in our society. Despite the decline of heavy manufacturing in the United States, STEM fields continue to be considered male occupations that are dirty and grimy and require strength to lift machinery. These gender stereotypes or biases can contribute to advisors at both the high school and the community college levels dissuading women from pursuing ET, especially when assessment tests biased toward men are involved.[27] The women in this study often encountered negative cultural stereotypes about women entering male-dominated occupations from family, friends, and male colleagues in their cohort and at work. While supportive, their families and friends were unfamiliar with ET and equated it with heavy manufacturing, which is considered "men's work." Reflecting on the challenges that women in her program face as they pursue employment in the STEM workforce, Sarah stated:

> I think probably one of the challenges is acceptance into the workforce. I mean, I even experience it because I'm a woman. When I started my internship like they didn't expect me to be able to do the same things that the guys were doing and you know they were really surprised that I was willing to get up on the rooftop and do all the same things that they were doing and that I could do just as well if not better than them. So I think that there's a little bit of a stigma that it's not really a place for women still.

While the women were enthusiastic about pursuing careers in the STEM workforce and confident in their abilities, they acknowledged that they must overcome these gender stereotypes about STEM occupations that have been traditionally held by men.

FUTURE DIRECTIONS AND POLICIES

Traditionally policies and research addressing gender inequality in STEM have focused on students at four-year universities and their experiences in the workforce. As the debate about income inequality has come to the forefront of our society, there has been a growing conversation about the role that community colleges can play in diversifying the STEM workforce. Community college are not merely a means of educating students who transfer to four-year universities; rather, there should be a focus on the affordable and flexible STEM two-year degrees and other certificates that they offer, which can lead to higher average earnings and career advancement for women, ethnic minorities, and low-income individuals. I propose that improving community college advising and job placement assistance and increasing the funding for the research into the barriers that women encounter pursuing ET programs at community colleges will broaden their participation in STEM and contribute to efforts to reduce income inequality in our society.

Community Colleges Advising and Job Placement Assistance

Our research indicates that community colleges need to improve the advising about ET programs and careers for women. Most women enter community colleges intending to obtain degrees in fields that women traditionally occupy such as health sciences and education.[28] Community colleges should require that their advisors inform women about the opportunities for higher earnings and career advancement in the STEM workforce. They should also use other forms of marketing such as featuring the ET program on the front page of their websites, sending emails to students about ET, and giving out brochures featuring women during registration.

Community college advising should also focus on providing students with information about the federal financial aid for which they are eligible rather than relying on their financial aid office. As in our study, community college students are older first-generation students who work full-time and attend community college part-time, and thus have limited time to make multiple visits to campus. Research shows that community college students are approximately a third of Pell Grant recipients, but almost two-thirds of all eligible students attended community colleges.[29] These community college students did not complete the Free Application for Student Aid (FAFSA) required to apply for Pell Grants because they were unaware that they were eligible for financial aid or underestimated their need for assistance and found the FAFSA too difficult to complete.[30] Yet community college students who completed the FAFSA were more likely to persist in their programs, particularly the ones who attended part-time.[31] Community colleges need to develop mechanisms that streamline their advising to incorporate information about financial aid into their academic advising and provide students with assistance in completing the FAFSA.

Community colleges should also support women enrolled in their ET degree programs by developing and implementing programs to assist them in finding jobs/internships. These programs should have commitments from their partner corporations to provide students with compensated internships and opportunities to interview for open positions. This program would be an invaluable resource for women, who usually lack experience in ET. They lack the "insider" knowledge and contacts to access the internships necessary to gain experience or to enter the STEM workforce.

Increase Research

Our research suggests the need for further exploration of the barriers to women pursuing ET degrees and certificates at community colleges. The development of policies to broaden the participation of women in the ET workforce through community college programs has been stymied by a dearth of targeted research. If our goal as a society is to broaden the participation of women (and minorities) in STEM education and occupations, researchers must design studies and write proposals that examine the challenges that women encounter pursuing ET degrees and certificates and employment in ET fields as well as develop interventions to increase their success.

The NSF Advanced Technological Education (ATE) division funds regional centers that partner with local community colleges to offer technical education programs. ATE also funds targeted research that investigates the experiences of women and minorities in ET, develops interventions to increase their numbers, and examines the barriers that they face in the STEM workforce. The resulting research data can be used to shape policies to increase the numbers of women and minorities pursuing ET degrees and certificates and to address the gender and ethnic disparity in earnings that currently exists.

CONCLUSION

In response to the growing debate about gender inequality in the STEM fields negatively impacting women's incomes and career advancement, I decided to further explore the pathways of the women in our sample of community college ET programs as well as the barriers that they encountered academically as well as related to work-life balance issues. The findings of this study indicate that (1) community colleges must be more proactive in advising women about opportunities and earning potential in ET as well as incorporate guidance about financial aid, (2) women need more hands-on experience in technology to build their confidence and give them experience that increases their likelihood of obtaining a job in ET, and (3) negative cultural stereotypes about women entering male-dominated occupations such as ET continue to be prevalent in our society.

These findings are limited by the small number of women in the sample. I propose that larger mixed-method research studies should be conducted to examine the factors that impact the experiences of women pursuing ET degrees and certificates at community colleges. These studies should be longitudinal so as to follow women's progress in their ET programs, their job search experiences, and their employment. It is important to track their employment and salaries so they can be compared to their male counterparts. Ultimately, this research will inform the development and implementation of public policy that addresses (1) broadening the participation of women in ET through the community college pathway and (2) the gender disparity in salaries in the technology workforce.

ACKNOWLEDGMENTS

This research was funded by the National Science Foundation Grant no. 1104214, "Successful Academic and Employment Pathways in Advanced Technology" (PathTech), through the Advanced Technological Education (ATE) division. My thanks to our research team: Dr. William Tyson, Principal Investigator, Dr. Lakshmi Jayaram, Co-Principal Investigator and Qualitative Lead, Dr. Rebecca Heppner, Dr. Margaret Cooper, Pangri Mehta, and David Zeller. My thanks also to Dr. Michelle Hughes Miller for her editorial contribution to this chapter.

NOTES

1. Accreditation Board for Engineering and Technology. 2015. "Engineering vs. Engineering Technology." Baltimore: Accreditation Board for Engineering and Technology. www.abet.org/accreditation/new-to-accreditation/engineering-vs-engineering-technology/.

2. National Women's Law Center. 2014. *Underpaid and Overloaded: Women in Low-Wage Jobs*. Washington, DC: National Women's Law Center. https://nwlc.org/wp-content/uploads/2015/08/executivesummary_nwlc_lowwagereport2014.pdf.

3. Cooper, David, Mary Gable, and Algernon Austin. 2012. *The Public-Sector Jobs Crisis: Women and African Americans Hit Hardest by Job Losses in State and Local Governments*. Washington, DC: Economic Policy Institute. www.epi.org/publication/bp339-public-sector-jobs-crisis/.

4. Carnevale, Anthony P., Nicole Smith, and Jeff Strohl. 2013. "Recovery: Job Growth and Education Requirements through 2020." Georgetown Public Policy Institute, Center on Education and the Workforce. http://cew.georgetown.edu/recovery2020.

5. Carnevale et al. (2013).

6. Betts, Julian R., and Laurel L. McFarland. 1995. "Safe Port in a Storm: The Impact of Labor Market Conditions on Community College Enrollments." *Journal of Human Resources* 30:741–765; Johnson, Nate. 2015. *The Unemployment-Enrollment Link*. Washington, DC: Inside Higher Education. www.insidehighered.com/views/2015/08/27/unemployment-rate-community-college enrollments-and-tough-choices-essay.

7. Goldrick-Rab, Sara, and Kia Sorensen. 2011. "Unmarried Parents in College: Pathways to Success." *Fast Focus*. Institute for Research on Poverty University of Wisconsin-Madison. www.irp.wisc.edu/publications/fastfocus/pdfs/FF9–2011.pdf; St. Rose, Andresse, and Catherine Hill. 2013. *Women in Community Colleges: Access to Success*. Washington, DC: Women in Community Colleges, Access to Success. www.aauw.org/files/2013/05/women-in-community-colleges.pdf.

8. Shapiro, Doug, Afet Dundar, Phoebe Khasiala, Xin Yuan Wakhungu, Angel Nathan, and Youngsik Hwang. 2015. *Completing College: A National View of*

Student Attainment Rates—Fall 2009 Cohort (Signature Report No. 10). Herndon, VA: National Student Clearinghouse Research Center. https://nscresearchcenter.org/wp-content/uploads/SignatureReport10.pdf.

9. Shapiro et al. (2015).

10. St. Rose and Hill (2013); Attwell, Paul, Scott Heil, and Laurel L. Reisel. 2011. "Competing Explanations of Undergraduate Noncompletion." *American Educational Research Journal* 48 (3): 536–559; Hillard, Tom. 2011. *Mobility Makers.* New York: Center for an Urban Future. https://nycfuture.org/pdf/Mobility_Makers.pdf; Miller, Kevin, Barbara Gault, and Abby Thorman. 2011. *Improving Child Care Access to Promote Postsecondary Success among Low-Income Parents.* Washington, DC: Institute for Women's Policy Research. www.iwpr.org/publications/pubs/improving-child-care-access-to-promote-postsecondary-success-among-low-income-parents.

11. Carnevale et al. (2013).

12. St. Rose and Hill (2013); Institute of Women's Policy Research. 2015. "The Status of Women in the States: 2015 Employment and Earnings." Washington, DC: Institute of Women's Policy Research. http://statusofwomendata.org/app/uploads/2015/02/EE-CHAPTER-FINAL.pdf.

13. Institute of Women's Policy Research (2015).

14. National Science Board. 2016. "Science and Engineering Indicators 2016." Arlington, VA: National Science Foundation. www.nsf.gov/statistics/2016/nsb20161/#/report.

15. Attwell et al. (2011); Institute of Women's Policy Research (2015); Carnevale, Anthony, Nicole Smith, and Michelle Melton. 2011. "STEM: Science, Technology, Engineering, Mathematics." Washington, DC: Georgetown University Center on Education and the Workforce; Costello, Cindy. 2012. *Increasing Opportunities for Low-Income Women and Student Parents in Science, Technology, Engineering and Math at Community College.* Washington, DC: Institute for Women's Policy Research. www.iwpr.org/publications/pubs/increasing-opportunities-for-low-income-women-and-student-parents-in-science-technology-engineering-and-math-at-community-colleges.

16. Carnevale et al. (2011).

17. Costello (2012).

18. Hill, Catherine, Christianne Corbett, and Andresse St. Rose. 2010. *Why So Few? Women in Science, Technology, Engineering, and Mathematics.* Washington, DC: American Association of University Women. www.aauw.org/files/2013/02/Why-So-Few-Women-in-Science-Technology-Engineering-and-Mathematics.pdf.

19. Costello (2012).

20. Institute of Women's Policy Research (2015); Costello (2012).

21. Hill et al. (2010).

22. St. Rose and Hill (2013).

23. Bernard, H. Russell. (2011). *Research Methods in Anthropology: Qualitative and Quantitative Approaches.* 5th ed. Walnut Creek, CA: Altamira.

24. The Open Entry-Open Exit method allows students enroll in courses at their convenience and progress through the material as their schedules permit. They participate in lab sessions independently with a lab manager to guide them through the assigned modules. They must pass competency-based assessments to pass the course and receive a grade. Choitz, Vickie, and Heath Prince. 2008. *Flexible Learning Options for Adult Students.* Washington, DC: US Department of Labor. www.jff.org/sites/default/files/publications/FlexibleLearning.pdf.

25. St. Rose and Hill (2013); Costello (2012); Starobin, Soko S., and Frankie Santos Laanan. 2010. "Broadening Female Participation in Science, Technology,

Engineering, and Mathematics: Experiences at Community Colleges." *New Directions for Community Colleges* 16 (1): 67–84.

26. Costello (2012).

27. Lester, Jamie 2010. "Women in Male-Dominated Career and Technical Education Programs at Community Colleges: Barriers to Participation and Success." *Journal of Women and Minorities in Science and Engineering* 16 (1): 51–66.

28. St. Rose and Hill (2013).

29. Kantrowitz, Mark 2011. "Reasons Why Students Do Not File the FAFSA." *Student Aid Policy Analysis.* http://finaid.org/educators/20110118nofafsareasons.pdf.

30. Kantrowitz (2011).

31. McKinney, Lyle, and Heather Novak. 2012. "The Relationship between FAFSA Filing and Persistence among First-Year Community College Students." *Community College Review* 41 (1): 63–85.

4. "Separating the Women from the Girls"

Black Professional Men's Perceptions of Women Colleagues

Adia Harvey Wingfield

Karina is an attorney in California. She is in her late thirties and works in a small firm practicing marriage and family law. Karina enjoys what she does for a living, though it can sometimes be dispiriting to navigate couples through contentious divorces and handling custody cases. One of her bigger issues, though, is that like many other women in the legal field, she also copes with the challenges of being a woman in a male-dominated industry.

In a conversation one afternoon, Karina described one of the key male attorneys who was an exception to this norm. "Leon always had my back," she said. "He was hard on me—on all the women in the firm—because he knew what we were up against. He knew how men are in this field. They don't take women seriously. They don't think we're cut out to practice law. He heard all the things guys said, but he didn't buy into any of it. He just pushed us all to be better so that we would be prepared to counter that mindset." When I expressed some surprise, given the descriptions she'd given of men expressing the opposite behavior, she said, "Well, it's different with black men in the legal field."

INTRODUCTION

In my discussion with Karina, I wanted to know what sort of challenges she encountered as a female lawyer. I was curious about whether they were consistent with the things I'd read about how women, particularly women of color, often confront sexist behaviors from male colleagues. Karina confirmed that the legal field was definitely an "old boys club." But when our discussion turned to Leon, I was struck by the way she described how he'd always supported and encouraged her.

Karina's comments made me realize that there is an understudied dynamic to the general, gendered assumptions we have about men and the ways they treat women in male-dominated occupations. The common narrative—backed by a great deal of sociological literature—is that in jobs where women are in the minority, men are often hostile, unwelcoming, and isolating, and that these processes keep women underrepresented in the high-status jobs where men are in the majority. But what if there are racial- and class-based components to this gendered story as well?

This chapter investigates this question in more detail. Generally speaking, we know that men's perceptions of and interactions with women can be a critical factor in curtailing their assimilation and inclusion in these types of jobs. In occupations that have traditionally been the province of men, women often face a rocky entrée as men engage in various practices (closing social networks, harassment, and so forth) that intentionally or unintentionally create an unwelcoming environment. These are all examples of the types of interactions Karina typically encountered from men in the legal profession. And studies that document these sorts of processes have great utility and importance. By identifying and addressing these social behaviors, sociologists and policymakers can illuminate the problematic actions that keep women underrepresented in certain fields. Perhaps more importantly, however, these studies can also help expose alternative ways to structure the workplace that enhance all employees' productivity and minimize the ways underrepresented groups are especially disadvantaged in settings where they are in the minority.

In this chapter, I take a different approach to understanding how workplaces are gendered. Rather than revisit the narrative that men, as a group, perceive women as unsuited for male-dominated occupations and thus behave in ways that contribute to their difficulties in these fields, I focus on the ways this process may be complicated by other factors. Specifically, I consider how this gendered dynamic is influenced by race and class in ways that influence how racial-minority men perceive and describe their interactions with women coworkers. Research has documented that men in male-dominated occupations can be instrumental in creating and maintaining obstacles to women's success. In this chapter, I investigate how this process is not only gendered, but shaped by race and class. By looking at the ways black professional men working in white male-dominated occupations understand their relationships with their women colleagues, I am able to suggest strategies organizations can adopt that could potentially facilitate more gender-equitable work environments.

BACKGROUND

The research on women in male-dominated occupations typically finds evidence of numerous obstacles and blocked paths to upward mobility. Early on, Kanter studied women executives working in a male-dominated corporation and coined the term "tokenism" to describe the social and cultural processes they encountered. Kanter argued that women faced perceptual tendencies, including heightened visibility, contrasting, and role encapsulation. These perceptual tendencies led to performance pressures, exaggerated boundary drawing, and difficulties assimilating, respectively, and ultimately made women's incorporation into the predominantly male organization difficult or even impossible. Specifically, men viewed women as representatives of their gender rather than individuals (especially when they made mistakes), went out of their way to isolate them, and treated women as secretaries and assistants even when they were there in executive capacities.[1]

Kanter's conclusions have been echoed in other studies. For instance, in her study of the construction industry, sociologist Kris Paap argues that this field is structured by race, gender, and class in such a way as to facilitate risk taking and dangerous behavior among white working-class men. Specifically, Paap contends that as skilled jobs are disappearing, white working-class men act to preserve construction as a safe space that privileges the whiteness and masculinity that they believe is declining in other settings. They do this by devaluing femininity, taking extreme physical risks in their work, and marginalizing men of color who work on their construction sites. Based on her ethnographic research in this field, Paap concludes that the pressures which push women out of male-dominated fields persist in this industry, and that broader social trends increasing the precariousness of skilled wage labor help make it inhospitable and unwelcoming for women working construction.[2]

Jennifer Pierce observes similar trends among women in the legal field. In her classic ethnography of a law firm, Pierce studies the way gender is embedded in multiple occupations in that field. Comparing occupational expectations, emotional labor (the ways that emotions are subject to organizational control in the workplace), and social networks among attorneys (a male-dominated occupation) and paralegals (predominantly female), Pierce concludes that gendered norms, roles, and beliefs remain remarkably consistent regardless of the gender composition of occupations in the legal field. In the case of women attorneys, men often penalized them for appearing aggressive, belligerent, combative, or otherwise insufficiently feminine, despite the fact that culturally feminized emotions such as being nurturing, caretaking, and being deferential were considered inappropriate for attorneys. In this context, men constrained women's access to and success in this field by policing their emotional displays and holding them to gendered standards that were inconsistent with the job expectations.[3]

As these studies indicate, the research on women in male-dominated occupations is largely consistent with Kanter's original findings. However, many of these early studies neglect to consider how race and class inform the ways men reproduce these gendered patterns and processes in their work environments. Theorists like Patricia Hill Collins have argued persuasively that gender, race, and class are intersecting factors that must be understood in conjunction with one another rather than as discrete categories. This is supported by research that shows that women of color in white male-dominated jobs encounter gatekeeping mechanisms that reflect both gender *and* race—difficulties accessing same-race mentors, stereotypes about their sexuality, racialized stereotypes of their inferiority and lack of intelligence, and presumptions that they received their positions due to racial preferences rather than merit, skill, or hard work.[4]

This theoretical approach emphasizing intersections of race, gender, and class has been used in a few studies to assess how women of color (most frequently black women) face uniquely racialized, gendered challenges as *black* women in predominantly white male occupational settings. However, it has rarely been used to assess how these same intersecting factors inform the ways men perceive and relate to their female coworkers of all races. Though intersectionality calls us to consider how these overlapping categories inform power relations, there are few applications of the ways that it influences occupational interactions that are shaped simultaneously by privilege and disadvantage. Attention to the ways men's responses to women in male-dominated occupations are not just gendered but also raced and classed can help illustrate potential strategies for making the professional workplace a more equitable and inclusive environment.[5]

In the remainder of this chapter, I focus on black professional men to explore the ways men's perceptions of and responses to women workers in white male-dominated occupations are raced, classed, and gendered social phenomena. We know that men's responses to women in these professions are gendered. Further, research shows us that it is important to consider how gender is simultaneously constructed by race and class. What does this mean for black men in these occupations? How does the combination of gender and class privilege coupled with racial disadvantage inform the ways these men perceive and interact with their female coworkers? How do these intersections reproduce and/or challenge inequalities? And what policies can be implemented as a result?

CASE STUDY

To answer these research questions, I conducted intensive interviews with 42 black men working as doctors, lawyers, bankers, and engineers. Interviews allowed respondents to offer detailed assessments of various aspects of their work, including but not limited to their pathways into these occupations; relationships with mentors, colleagues, and supervisors; the challenges and opportunities they observed; and parallels and dissimilarities between their work experiences and those of other colleagues. Respondents ranged in age from 33 to 60. All held at least a college degree, with all lawyers and doctors holding terminal degrees in their fields (JDs and MDs, respectively). Four of the 10 engineers interviewed held doctorates, two more were working on postgraduate degrees, and two bankers had earned their MBAs by the time of the interview. Thirteen respondents were lawyers, 12 were doctors, 10 were engineers, and 7 were bankers. As such, they were employed in occupations where black men constitute a very small minority of workers. All respondents identified themselves as the only black male worker or one of two or three black male workers in their particular offices, sometimes in the entire company at their level. The majority of their colleagues were white males, though three engineers described working with a handful of Asian American men, and all of the lawyers identified one to three women who were associates at their firm, while support staff (e.g., nurses, legal assistants, administrative assistants) were mostly white women.

All interviews were transcribed and analyzed, and all names and identifying details used here have been changed. Data were coded by themes that emerged deductively, such as perceptions of advantages vs. disadvantages relative to women colleagues; feeling assimilated vs. feeling isolated at work; or being perceived as a threat vs. being perceived neutrally. Based on this analysis, I was able to develop a narrative of the ways that race, gender, and class intersect to shape aspects of work for black professional men. In the next section, I elaborate on these themes to discuss how these overlapping categories influenced social interactions and everyday dynamics of work for black men in white male-dominated occupations.

UPDATING THE CONTEMPORARY SITUATION

For black men working in white male-dominated jobs, there were several key ways that their interactions with women reflected gendered processes that were simultaneously raced and classed. Respondents observed that the occupational culture in their work environments served to exclude their women counterparts. Often they noted that as men, they were cushioned from some of these gendered disadvantages. More importantly, they asserted that their own experiences with racial discrimination rendered them more sensitive than their white male counterparts to the challenges facing women. Finally, these men described ways they were able to leverage their gendered privileges to help create more equitable work environments for their female peers. These observations highlight how race, gender, and class are operative in constructing men's perceptions of women colleagues, but they also give rise to ways that policies might be constructed to build on black professional men's work experiences to help increase gender equity in male-dominated jobs.

Position Relative to Women

Black professional men are in a unique position in professional environments due to their race, gender, and class status. Gender and class generally function as advantages, allowing them to assimilate into the broader mainstream in their work environments. Yet race intersects with gender and class to impact the degree to which these categories privilege black men and enable them to fit into these predominantly white male spaces. Many black men discussed the ways these intersecting factors positioned them relative to women of all races, and spoke of how gender allowed them to avoid some of the challenges women encountered working in a male-dominated environment, but their experiences in the racial minority allowed them to empathize with and in some cases address the challenges they observed women facing.

Frederick, a banker, described his observations of the ways that the financial industry presented specific challenges for women workers:

> It's tough from a woman's perspective because it's a male-dominated business. Very few women are necessarily looked at as peers, and then the family piece kicks in. You know: Are you going to have a career? Are you going to have a family? And those women that chose to take the family route first—there are all kind of negative connotations that are given to them in terms of whether they're going to be career-oriented. Just the whole dynamic is different.

In his assessment of the occupational culture in finance, Frederick notes that both the demographics and the gendered assumptions create difficulties for women. His observation that women are not only in the minority but perceived to be less diligent workers who prioritize family is supported by a wealth of research.[6]

Dennis, a cardiologist, also discussed observations of bias against women in medicine:

> There is absolutely more gender bias than racial. This is an environment where it's mostly male, and people say things. There are so many issues of bias. It's considered part of the club, and men enter because of different credentials. I'm a man, I'm in the gentleman's club.

Like Frederick, Dennis notes the ways that cultural dynamics of the medical field—specifically, the "gentleman's club" mentality—create gender dynamics that are unfavorable to women doctors.

Still other respondents noted the ways that intersections of race and gender uniquely disadvantaged women of color. Jared, an attorney, described a number of ways that he felt the legal field was unwelcoming to racial-minority lawyers—higher scrutiny, presumptions of incompetence, and so forth. Yet, he remarked:

> I would think that an African American woman is facing far more of a challenge than an African American male. Not only does she deal with the burden of being black and being perceived as not as qualified as these other people. In this profession, let's say, for example, in court, unless the judge is a woman—and you'll probably see my own stereotypes that are coming up—the comments that are associated with women are that they're not strong, that you could probably trust a man with legal issues and not a woman, especially when it comes to weaving together these complex legal issues. I just think [women] have to fight beyond that.

Though Jared is familiar with the challenges facing black men in the legal profession, he astutely observes that these are compounded for black women, who must also contend with gendered perceptions that they do not belong in the legal field. He even notes the pervasiveness of these images, as he acknowledges that even while he describes the barriers women face, he instinctively envisions judges as men.

Empathy with Women

Respondents not only identified ways that women faced issues that they did not; they asserted that their position as black men made them uniquely empathetic to the challenges women encountered. Richard, an engineering professor, stated:

> I think being a black man, I'm very [cognizant] of the challenges women face. Especially in a place like this where they are in the minority. In some ways, I'm less of a minority than they are . . . I really understand the things they are going through and am much more

sensitive than probably the majority of my colleagues are. [Being black] does make me more sympathetic to what women go through. And very much more sensitive, and I try to be understanding.

Richard parallels his experiences as a black male in a predominantly white male-dominated profession with the challenges that women face. From his description, they share a common experience of being in the minority—his due to race, women's due to gender. Note that he also indicates that due to his gender, the racial challenges he encounters are less daunting than those facing women—"in some ways, I'm less of a minority than they are." This is an important indication of the ways that race and gender intersect to shape his work experience in a way that offers him particular advantages relative to his female counterparts.

Randall, an engineer, drew a similar link between the ways race constructed his own experiences and the ways he related to the issues women faced:

In this country, women have traditionally had unnecessary and unfair bias placed upon them just because they are women. And then you add a minority card on top of it, and it's a little bit worse. And they tend to get underestimated more so. If you have a professional black man and a black woman, then they'll assume that because he's a man that he is more qualified than she is, which may not be the case. Once you have been subjected to that sort of behavior, you tend to not exert any expectations on other people . . . Because I've been the subject of unfair treatment at times, and I tend not to do it to others because I know how it feels.

Richard draws a clear parallel between his personal experience of unfair treatment and what he sees for women in engineering. Encountering these low expectations helps make him more aware of the ways these processes occur for women.

Finally, Michael, a doctor, explicitly made these connections between the ways race and gender operated in parallel ways to construct his experiences and those of his women colleagues:

I think being a black male, I understand a lot about what they are going through. A lot of women [doctors] will complain that when they walk into the room, patients will say, "I have to hang up the phone because my nurse is in the room." [Women colleagues] used to say that to me all the time. But I would tell them that I would much rather be a nurse than an orderly or an X-ray technician.

Michael offers here an insightful analysis of the ways patients' perceptions of jobs are not only gendered but simultaneously raced and classed. He identifies that his position as a black male enables him to relate to women doctors' frustration at being assumed to be nurses, because these sorts of mistaken assumptions characterize his interactions with patients as well. Yet he also suggests that these presumptions reflect racial and class stereotypes that suggest black men working in health care are more suited for technical or janitorial work than specialized, professional medical care. In doing so, Michael highlights the ways intersections of race, gender, and class structure (white) women's and black male doctors' occupational lives in parallel but distinct ways. Neither is immediately assumed to be the doctor, but white women are cast in white-collar, professional roles as nurses, while black men are cast in still lower-skilled, less prestigious roles as orderlies or technicians.

Leveraging Gendered Advantages for Equality

In addition to recognizing women's challenges, some respondents took the important step of taking action to address the issues they saw women facing. These men saw commonalities between women's experiences and their own; yet they also perceived that the masculine occupational culture in their jobs offered them some advantages relative to their female counterparts. Consequently, these men made efforts to leverage these privileges to help offset what they saw as the gender bias women faced in male-dominated occupations.

Consider this statement from Gerald, an attorney, who describes the importance of engaging in services that will help erase the gender bias in the legal field:

> Certainly, in the private practice women have it tougher. Women of color have it tougher than that. I'm active, you found me through the State Association for Black Female Lawyers. I'm on the foundation board . . . I recognize that we are all in the same boat.

Gerald is describing extracurricular projects—what legal scholars Mitu Gulati and Devon Carbado call "lumpy citizenship tasks," which are not explicitly mandated by an organization but are informally expected of workers.[7] Many workers, particularly in law firms, avoid these responsibilities because they can be time-consuming with little reward. Significantly, Gerald voluntarily takes on a citizenship task that explicitly works on behalf of black women. While Gulati and Carbado rightfully note that diversity-related obligations like these can backfire by making people of color appear too militant, Gerald's sense that "women of color have it tougher" and his perception that "we are all in the same boat" prompt him to use his position on behalf of his women counterparts.

Another attorney, Anderson, was a partner in his firm at the time of our interview. He described the importance of working with and mentoring women associates:

> I sympathize [with them] because I understand the issue. And I can look at the numbers and tell that women aren't being as successful as white men. So there's a solidarity in the sense that if there were two people similarly situated with the same credentials, and both could offer me the same things in a project, I would pick the woman. Just because inherently, in my mind, I'm thinking, if I don't do it, things aren't going to change.

Because of his awareness of the ways gender dynamics in the legal field operate to women's disadvantage, Anderson intentionally seeks opportunities to work with women associates who might otherwise fall through the cracks. Once again, his position as a black male—someone who also imperfectly fits the normatively white, male cultural image of an attorney—helps him empathize with the ways women are similarly marginalized. However, as a partner and someone with relative power within the firm, Anderson takes steps to try to help offset this cultural bias against women associates.

A final quote from Jared, an engineering professor, provides an additional example of this process:

> One of the things that I've tried to do is sometimes do little things that would tend to make women feel more included. Like when I write a scenario that involves somebody, I will often make that somebody female. So I say, "Suppose a bike rider wants to stop her bike in the quickest time possible or whatever, what should she do?" So it's a little thing, but it does sort of change the expectations. Or one of the things I know I've said is, "This exam will really separate—" instead of saying "the men from the boys" I'll say "the women from the girls." So even though there's eight or 10 women and 40 males, why not say it? There's no great campaign that I have, but there's certain things I do because I just can appreciate that part of the game is to feel like you're part of the equation. And if you feel like you're part of the equation, and you feel like you belong, then that tends to bring out your best performance.

Jared offers both a subtle critique of the ways that innocuous processes can reinforce women's marginalization in engineering and an insightful discussion of simple strategies that can be used to address them. As he notes, those in the minority often encounter subtle (or overt) cues that they do not belong and are not suited for particular areas. When it comes to engineering, this can be true for women of all races and for racial-minority men. Based on his firsthand experience with this process, he intentionally takes steps to make his classrooms more inclusive and welcoming for his female students.

The ways respondents interact with women colleagues reveal notable patterns about the ways race, gender, and class construct aspects of black men's work in professional occupations. For black men in predominantly white male-dominated jobs, the intersections of gendered and class advantages coupled with racial disadvantage place them in a unique space. They still encounter racial biases and prejudices from colleagues, but recognize that their gender—being men in male-dominated occupations—can often put them in a more favorable location than their women counterparts. Yet at the same time, the racial prejudgments they encounter lead them to empathize with women and the challenges they face. These intersecting factors put black professional men in a position where they leverage their gendered advantages to advocate for and support women in subtle but critical ways.

FUTURE DIRECTIONS AND POLICIES

Given this finding that black men recognize and in some cases take steps to help alleviate the challenges women encounter in male-dominated occupations, it makes sense to consider drafting suggestions for changing workplaces in ways that take them into account and build on this outcome. Researchers who study race and antiracism have noted that white allies are a critical component of establishing procedures and building support for initiatives designed to address racial stratification. In particular, working-class white women are often identified as those who may be most sympathetic to the challenges facing people of color, due to their encounters with sexism and class inequality.[8]

I suggest here several strategies that those working in professional white male-dominated occupations like law, medicine, engineering, and finance can adopt that build on the expressions of support black men report in this chapter. These take into consideration both the ways race, gender, and class intersect for these workers and how these overlapping factors can potentially have utility for helping to create more gender-equitable workplaces. This is particularly critical in fields where women of all races and racial-minority men are underrepresented.

Rewarding Citizenship Tasks

One strategy for helping to create more gender-equitable work environments might be to recognize and place greater weight on service tasks designed to support underrepresented groups. Note that Gerald, the attorney quoted above, references his volunteer work with the State Association for Black Female Lawyers. This is work that he takes on because of his personal commitments to greater equality and his recognition of the challenges that women, particularly black women, face in the legal field. Yet this is the type of "citizenship task" that often goes overlooked, undervalued, and ignored. As such, many professional workers avoid this type of service work because it does not offer rewards that facilitate advancement.

Gulati and Carbado note that while they are typically devalued, these tasks are particularly complicated for workers of color. Often, they are in the numerical minority in their work environments. They also are likely to feel a sense of social pressure to support and mentor other workers of color. However, because there are so few of them, they are frequently stretched so that the act of mentoring becomes both rewarding and burdensome— rewarding because of the opportunity to help nurture younger workers of color, but burdensome due to the fact that they become responsible for a great deal of additional work that is not expected of other colleagues and that often gets ignored.[9]

If institutions gave greater credit to mentoring efforts, particularly those that work with underrepresented populations, then black men's efforts in this regard could possibly gain greater traction. Were organizations to take mentoring and support initiatives into consideration when making decisions and evaluations about hiring, firing, and promotions, this might incentivize black men who are empathetic to the challenges women encounter in these jobs, but feel similarly overwhelmed with other extensive mentoring. Given that black men express awareness of the challenges women face in these occupations and are also attuned to the ways they escape these potential pitfalls by virtue of being men in male-dominated occupations, they may be especially helpful mentors for women workers in these professions.

Of course, challenges accompany this as well. Many black men also reported treading very carefully when it came to interactions with white women colleagues. This caution has its roots in the long and ugly history of black men's representation as sexual predators who were especially dangerous to white women. Interactions between black men and white women can raise this caricature, and black professional men were very cognizant of avoiding behavior that might evoke this image in colleagues' minds. As such, initiatives to give more weight to mentorship of underrepresented groups must take into consideration the ways these particular racial/gender dynamics are present for black professional men.

Moving from Diversity (Back) to Affirmative Action

Another potential tactic involves placing more emphasis on affirmative action rather than on diversity. In public discourse, these terms are often used interchangeably. However, sociologists have shown that as the political economy has changed and support for overt policies of racial redress has waned, managers face declining support for policies explicitly designed to reduce racial and/or gender inequities.[10] In response, they switched their emphasis from a focus on these systemic processes, and began to recenter their work to address issues of "diversity," very broadly defined. Consequently, managers in charge of diversity are more likely to use loose definitions of this term, and consider more individualized factors like geographical region, personal interests, and even "diversity of thought" as criteria for building more "diverse" workplaces. While these strategies enable these workers to tailor their jobs to a new political-economic reality, they also leave more systemic processes that reproduce racial and gender inequities in place in professional workplaces.

However, a return to a more intentional focus on affirmative action could be beneficial in minimizing these structural inequalities. In a study of the strategies that are most effective in increasing diversity, Kalev, Dobbin, and Kelly found that oft-used tactics such as networking programs and employee groups were much less effective than simply tasking a manager with the responsibility of shaping a more diverse work environment. Should organizations require managers to increase racial and gender diversity in male-dominated occupations, this may have more efficacy than current colorblind policies and initiatives.[11]

There is some indication that diversity officers are moving in this direction. In a study of how diversity officers described their work, I found that using a "business case" provided language that justified their focus on erasing racial and gender differences.[12] Thus, while these workers at large certainly face pressures to focus on diversity that is decoupled from historical and ongoing processes of inequality, they also are able to use a discourse that supports efforts to bring more women of all races and minority men into upper level roles in their organizations. Should organizations evince support for managers who are explicitly tasked with minimizing racial and gender inequalities, they may find that black professional men are particularly adept partners in these initiatives.

An added benefit to this strategy is that more support for affirmative action may lead to more black men themselves in high-ranking positions in these organizations. It is important to remember that while the results of this research indicate that black men can be important allies for women in male-dominated occupations, this will not uniformly be the case among all black men, and that they also encounter racially specific challenges that stem from being in the minority. In order for black professional men to foster effective cooperation and support with women colleagues, it is important to address the processes that keep them underrepresented as well.[13]

It is also important to emphasize that these strategies for capitalizing on black men's support for women are organizational ones that must be enacted at that level. It is not enough, nor is it fair, to suggest that black men should simply be responsible for ensuring that their women colleagues encounter a welcoming environment. Despite their perception that gender helps mitigate some of the racial challenges they encounter in these workplaces, it is important to keep in mind that these men face their own stereotypes, misperceptions, and processes of exclusion in white male-dominated workplaces. Thus, initiatives to build on their support for women colleagues must be implemented at the organizational level in order to avoid taxing them further. I suggest here that black professional men be identified as potential *partners* in organizational efforts to make workplaces more racially and gender diverse, not that organizations absolve themselves of this responsibility by situating it with their black male employees. Hopefully, with more initiatives like these, black men's willingness to be allies to their women counterparts will help more women like Karina encounter fewer occupational obstacles.

NOTES

1. Britton, Dana. 2003. *At Work in the Iron Cage.* New York: New York University Press; Kanter, Rosabeth Moss. 1977. *Men and Women of the Corporation.* New York: Basic; Pierce, Jennifer. 1995. *Gender Trials.* Berkeley: University of California Press; Yoder, Janice, and Patricia Aniakudo. "Outsider within the Firehouse: Subordination and Difference in the Social Interactions of African American Women Firefighters." *Gender & Society* 11 (3): 324–341.

2. Kanter (1977); Paap, Kris. 2006. *Working Construction.* Ithaca, NY: ILR.

3. Pierce (1995).

4. Bell, Ella, and Stella Nkomo. 2001. *Our Separate Ways.* Cambridge, MA: Harvard Business Review; Chou, Rosalind. 2013. *Asian American Sexual Politics.* New York: Routledge; Collins, Patricia Hill. 2000. *Black Feminist Thought: Knowledge, Consciousness, and the Politics of Empowerment.* 2nd ed. New York: Routledge; Higginbotham, Elizabeth, and Lynne Weber. 1997. "Perceptions of Workplace Discrimination among Black and White Professional-Managerial Women." In *Latinas and African American Women at Work,* edited by Irene Browne. New York: Russell Sage; Kanter (1977).

5. Higginbotham and Weber (1997).

6. Budig, Michelle, and Paula England 2001. "The Wage Penalty for Motherhood." *American Sociological Review* 66 (2): 204–225; Kmec, Julie. 2011.

"Are Motherhood Wage Penalties and Fatherhood Bonuses Warranted?" *Social Science Research* 40:444–459.

7. Gulati, Mitu, and Devon Carbado. 2013. *Acting White*. New York: Oxford University Press.

8. Frankenberg, Ruth. 1993. *White Women, Race Matters.* Minneapolis: University of Minnesota Press.

9. Gulati and Carbado (2013).

10. Bell and Nkomo (2001); Berrey, Ellen. 2015. *The Enigma of Diversity.* Chicago: University of Chicago Press; Collins, Sharon. 2011. "Diversity in the Post Affirmative Action Labor Market: A Proxy for Racial Progress?" *Critical Sociology* 37 (5): 521–540.

11. Kalev, Alexandra, Frank Dobbin, and Erin Kelly. 2006. "Best Practices or Best Guesses? Assessing the Efficacy of Corporate Affirmative Action and Diversity Policies." *American Sociological Review* 71 (4): 589–617.

12. Wingfield, Adia Harvey. 2016. "Advocating Affirmative Action in the Days of Diversity: How the Business Case Enables Attention to Race and Gender." In *Underneath the Thin Veneer: Critical Diversity, Multiculturalism, and Inclusion in the Workplace,* edited by David G. Embrick, Sharon Collins, and Michelle Dodson. Netherlands: Brill.

13. See Wingfield, Adia Harvey. 2013. *No More Invisible Man: Race and Gender in Men's Work.* Philadelphia: Temple University Press, for a more detailed discussion of the challenges black men face in these occupations.

5. True Love Had Better Wait, or Else!

Anxious Masculinity and the Gendered Politics of the Evangelical Purity Movement

Sierra A. Schnable

Dear Clayton, I know you are a busy guy, traveling and preaching all the time. But I really need your help because I feel like I am always trying so hard to get victory in the area of sexual purity, but I just keep failing over and over again ... You said I had victory in Jesus, but if I really do, how does that work when I am being tempted to mess around with my boyfriend? I am not a virgin. I really love my boyfriend, and we're both Christians. We know it's wrong to sleep together, but we just can't stop. We pray, and we've even read the Bible together, but nothing works ... I am doubting my own salvation. I am so confused. If I were really saved, I feel like this wouldn't be so hard. HELP![1]

INTRODUCTION

The struggles with sexual purity experienced by the young woman above prompted her to reach out to Clayton King, the leader of the modern True Love Waits revival. That these struggles are common among evangelical young women points to a larger culture of shame around female sexuality—a culture that Clayton King and other evangelical leaders draw upon when preaching to large audiences around the United States and authoring devotional readers on sexual purity. For more mainstream Americans, it is tempting to dismiss the purity movement, with its promise rings, abstinence pledges, and purity balls, as obsolete and irrelevant to the lives of most girls and women. However, evangelical religious traditions continue to thrive and maintain considerable influence in contemporary institutions in the United States; even a cursory glance at the popular and controversial conversations that occurred on the Twitter hashtag #PurityCultureTaughtMe in 2015 reveals the profound impact that the teaching of abstinence-only sex education, which is currently required in over half of the states in the United States,[2] has had on countless individuals. The purity movement has undoubtedly achieved national success over the last several decades and is currently being revitalized and refocused by a group of fresh, young evangelical Christian leaders. Uncovering the layers of this movement reveals that it is engaged in the ongoing construction of femininity, masculinity, sexuality, and the family in ways that position young women's bodies as the battleground upon which patriarchy and progress war for control of sexual agency.

This chapter points to the importance of taking conservative religious movements seriously by interrogating how the largest evangelical organization of the purity movement, True Love Waits, creates discourse around female sexuality that permeates other institutions. After tracing the emergence of the purity movement, I discuss how biblical expectations for gender roles become naturalized and lay the framework for the purity movement's guiding ideologies. This necessarily incorporates the concept of "soft patriarchy," or the new evangelical vision for men that positions them as emotionally connected but unquestionably authoritative figureheads to the family.[3] I then use materials from the True Love Waits campaign to argue that young women find their sexuality policed by a three-headed male figure comprising their fathers and male church leaders, Jesus Christ, and their future husbands. Finally, I return to the construction of masculinity to assess how this control of the subversive potential of female sexuality signals a form of "anxious masculinity," perhaps best described by Mark Breitenberg as "the anxiety and violence engendered in men by a patriarchal economy that constructs masculine identity as dependent on the coercive and symbolic regulation of women's sexuality."[4] I contend that anxious masculinity is thus the driving force behind the culture that demands young women surrender their sexual decisions to male control. The vast reach of the movement further prompts a discussion of how our current sex education system is implicated in the same ideologies that True Love Waits promotes and thus fails to adequately prepare girls and young women for safe, healthy, and unconstrained sexual experiences and relationships.[5] Although the purity movement has attracted the recent attention of several feminist scholars,[6] this chapter contributes new dimensions to the study of the purity movement by analyzing the role of anxious masculinity and creating a model for the three-headed male figure to which girls and young women owe their purity.

The Emergence of the Purity Movement

The purity movement—also known as the abstinence movement—is a modern phenomenon created by the evangelical church and the Religious Right in the United States. It is commonly associated with its largest social movement organization, True Love Waits (abbreviated as TLW), a project launched in 1993 under the umbrella of the Southern Baptist Convention and managed by LifeWay Christian Resources. Initially the goal of TLW was to teach young people about biblically mandated sexual purity and persuade them to sign abstinence pledge cards explicitly promising that they would refrain from sexual activities outside of the confines of heterosexual marriage. Just a year after the launch of this endeavor, TLW brought together over 200,000 signed abstinence pledge cards and displayed them on the National Mall in Washington, DC, during a rally; within six months of this event, 400 news outlets had covered the purity movement and the True Love Waits campaign.[7] Since this impressive genesis, TLW has continued to steadily attract more individual and institutional followers.

Over the last two decades, TLW has engaged a global audience through ambassadors that take purity-based programs to various countries as well as through philanthropic and issue-oriented aid to underdeveloped nations. The organization has permeated not only churches but also the education system, the government, and health organizations.[8] Its reach is further than is perhaps expected—an estimated four to five million young people have participated in the purity movement through various organizations and churches to date. Currently, TLW is refocusing its goals toward a 20-year resurgence. Its mission, according to evangelical leader Clayton King, is to help students understand their sexuality in light of the gospel and to promote holistic biblical living that is held accountable to parents, church authorities, and peers.[9]

The purity movement emerged during a historical moment characterized by sympathetic political allies, state facilitation, and an opening in the political system that was consistent with its underlying ideology.[10] The political opportunity structure that gave rise to the purity movement was also distinctly gendered in that fluctuating cultural notions of gender and sexuality allowed for a model of submissive female abstinence to gain a good deal of support.[11] This occurred, in part, because the Religious Right rose to prominence in the wake of the sexual revolution with the large-scale political shift under the Reagan and Bush administrations during the 1980s. A power structure that was supportive of sexual conservatism allowed fundamentalist leaders to set an antifeminist—and, arguably, anti-woman—agenda by lobbying for increased funding for abstinence-only sex education in schools and spreading a "profamily" ideology that emphasized traditional, 1950s-era gender roles.[12] The evangelical church also successfully lumped premarital sex in with other "social ills" like abortion, divorce, and homosexuality that, for evangelicals, signaled a shift away from traditional biblical morality.[13] It is in this cultural climate that the purity movement gained momentum.

BACKGROUND

The Foundation of Purity: Naturalized Gender Differences

The purity movement is built on a foundation of evangelical thought that produces and necessitates ideologies of biblical femininity, godly masculinity, and conservative heterosexuality. These constructs rest, first and foremost, on a strong "separate spheres" doctrine that requires women to exert their "natural abilities" in caretaking work while men assume their rightful role in securing economic stability.[14] The strength of the church rests on the stability of the family, which, in turn, relies on an enactment of these naturalized sex differences. Although the evangelical church has moved slightly toward more flexibility in terms of gender roles,[15] it is still largely characterized by what Katherine Jones calls a "moderate essentialism" that is just orthodox enough to maintain its religious roots yet just malleable enough to appeal to a broader base outside of the church.[16]

The goal of wifely purity that girls and women are taught to aspire to is decidedly unattainable, largely due to the fact that the female body is distinguished from the male body by being sexually problematic. The concept of "original sin" articulated in the creation narrative of Genesis lays the groundwork for the pervasive inferiority of women expressed throughout the Bible. The association of Eve with the first human act of evil is deeply embedded in the Christian tradition and has influenced the conception of female bodies as evil, closer to nature, and sexually sinful.[17] This association, however, must be maintained in institutional and cultural ways in order to protect biblical patriarchy. Rosemary Radford Ruether, noted feminist theologian, writes: "It must be reiterated generation after generation, by repeating the myths of woman's original sin to the young, both male and female, and by reinforcing laws and structures that marginalize women from power roles in society."[18] That the assumption of natural differences between the sexes must be continually agreed upon by both women and men is a testament to the fragility of its construction; that it *is* continually and uncritically agreed upon reveals the pervasive roots of sexism and male dominance in the church.

Essentialized female and male bodies become the achieved genders of woman and man, which are reified through their repeated performance over time.[19] This relies on a conventional Western gender binary that constructs woman and man as mutually exclusive, dichotomous categories that are maintained through cultural sanctions. Indeed, "publicly practicing masculinity and femininity is necessary for boundary maintenance and for authenticating allegedly natural sex differences."[20] Thus, over time and through repetition, socially constructed genders begin to appear as inherent and natural manifestations of bodies that are labeled either female or male. One particularly pervasive version of this biological determinism is the biblical ideal of the "Proverbs 31 woman," so named for the biblical passage where it can be found. A Proverbs 31 woman is one who exemplifies beauty and strength through grace, virtue, steadfastness, wisdom, and deference to her husband. She is, according to Proverbs, worth more than rubies.[21] Both women and men are engaged in the maintenance of this ideal—women by aspiring to it, and men by demanding it. The primacy of the Proverbs 31 woman model prevents women from developing aspects of their identity that are "undesirable" in the evangelical church, driven by a fear of female power that curtails the potential of women for the husband's benefit.[22]

The naturalized gender differences of evangelical Christianity, then, create a system where the inferiority of women is a biological given and their protection by men is a biological necessity. Men are best positioned to offer this protection in the context of the heterosexual family structure, which is a biblical mandate for evangelical Christians.[23] (Hetero)sexuality is appropriately expressed in ways that resemble traditional sexual morality.[24] Feminine and masculine gender roles are *assumed* to be complementary and are enacted by bodies that are *constructed* as biologically matched opposites, which should then make for a naturally balanced marriage. The extension of this traditional morality is the strong belief that sexual activity is designed for the marriage covenant between one woman and one man.[25] In this family structure, men are the protectors of women and are responsible for being connected to their families, since depriving children of the "vital" male role means failing at their masculine duties.[26] Like the strict yet gentle God they worship, modern evangelical fathers are not detached and distant but rather are warm, affectionate, and expressive.[27] This affirmative style, however, is combined with strong disciplinary practices and unquestioned male authority. This is the essence of a "soft patriarch": powerful but compassionate, ruling with a velvet glove.[28] Such a caretaking mentality is motivated by assumptions of female inferiority and thus relies on benevolent sexism to recast patriarchal authority as "traditional values."[29]

CASE STUDY: TRUE LOVE WAITS

Methodology

This study draws on both primary data from the purity movement's largest social movement organization, True Love Waits, and secondary resources documenting movement activities and ideologies. Primary materials include the documentary *True Love Waits: The Complicated Struggle for Sexual Purity,* released in 2014, and two devotional guides written by married evangelical figures Clayton and Sharie King in their revival of the True Love Waits program: *True Love Project: How the Gospel Defines Your Purity* and *True Love Project: 40 Days of Purity for Girls.* Other promotional resources produced by TLW were also consulted in an effort to triangulate the analysis that emerged from the main primary source materials and verify that specific ideologies function cohesively across purity movement materials. TLW and the purity movement that it represents are both engaged in the process of framing, or creating "packages" that help individuals relate events to one another. However, perhaps more importantly, the movement is continually constructing gender discourses and ideologies that convey specific values and normative claims.[30] It is these ideologies that this study is concerned with interrogating through thematic qualitative coding and analysis.

A distinctly feminist approach guides this research. It takes the experiences of girls and women as central, seeking to understand both how social structures constrain experiences and how individuals make meaning within those structures. It also examines the construction of femininity and masculinity through this particular movement, revealing what it means to be a woman or a man within evangelical Christianity. Finally, it exposes structures of inequality and harmful ideologies that directly impact women's lives.

As a researcher, I am in a unique position to study this movement due to my extensive experience in Christian traditions. My upbringing included education in the Christian school system and participation in multiple evangelical churches in various ways, and my current relationship to religion includes regular participation in mainline Protestant churches. This involvement in the church is inseparable from my position as a woman, as I have felt the full force of the church's control of female sexuality and have experienced the purity movement firsthand. Having an insider status is consistently an advantage in my academic work, as it helps me to understand what questions to ask, where to find the answers, how to speak in the language of the church, and where to look for meaning-making processes.

Performing Purity

Like complementary feminine and masculine gender roles, purity is a ritualized, repetitive, and performed process rather than an inherent or bodily trait that exists independent of the social world. Girls and young women must not simply abstain from sexual acts; they must also convey to their peers, elders, and community that they are committed to a *lifestyle* of fleeing from sexual impurity in its myriad forms. The words of Sharie and Clayton King appropriately capture this element of purity accountability that is enforced upon girls and young women: "Nothing feels worse than disappointing God, yourself, your parents, your future husband, your friends, or pretty much anyone who expected you to be the Christian you portrayed yourself to be . . . And somehow messing up in our sexual lives feels so much more disappointing than other sins."[31] The thread binding the message of TLW together, then, is that female worth lies only in the ability to adequately perform sexual purity for the evaluation of others.

Two important studies on the performance and social organization of sexuality are useful to understanding how TLW creates expectations of purity accountability. Gul Ozyegin, in her research on upwardly mobile, educated young Turkish women, created the concept of "virginal facades" to encompass the practices that young women engage in to signal their purity to others, regardless of their actual sexual behaviors and ideologies.[32] Virginal facades emphasize the *audience* and the *evaluation* of purity, allowing women to receive the benefits of being read as virginal while negotiating a sex-obsessed society and shifting sexual norms. Ozyegin's work decentralizes the intact hymen as the site of purity and repositions the "moral expressions" of virginity as the site of judgment and guilt surrounding women's sexual experiences. Much like girls engaged in TLW through the evangelical church, the upwardly mobile Turkish women in Ozyegin's study must negotiate an audience of God, parents, and future husbands when performing and constructing their sexual identities. Although the larger cultural context differs, Ozyegin's virginal facades are enacted in comparable ways by girls and women in the United States.

Breanne Fahs similarly analyzes the performance element of purity in her work on ritualized abstinence.[33] Of particular importance in Fahs's research is her interrogation of chastity balls, ornate and marriage-like ceremonies in which young girls publicly promise to their fathers that they will live a life of purity for God and their future husbands. In this phenomenon, which is an extreme extension of purity pledges, girls become property to be traded between men and are entered into a system of sexual commerce at ages as young as 10, often without full understanding and agency. These group pledging ceremonies are grand events often accompanied by elaborate hair, makeup, and clothing, dinner, dancing to sentimental music, and prominent evangelical speakers, obliging girls to solidify a promise that they may not yet fully comprehend in front of their entire religious community. This community, then, becomes each girl's accountability partner and gains the right and responsibility of continually evaluating her claim to purity as she matures into adolescence and adulthood.

In looking across the literature on ritualized purity and sexuality, it is clear that girls' sexual expressions are intended to be on display for others to police. These others are, conspicuously, fathers, future husbands, God or Jesus, pastors, and the church community at large; at their core, these are all supported by anxious masculinity as it functions to regulate and constrain sexuality through various individuals with authority over the feminine. A girl or young woman does not immediately become tainted when she engages in a sexual activity with a man, but rather when these others *perceive* her to be inadequately performing purity and infer that she must have engaged in some such impure act. Thus virginity is not defined by the state of the hymen, but instead in the social enactment of a virginal facade consisting of promises, behaviors, attitudes, and values that fulfill expectations of purity and appropriate femininity.

The Three-Headed Male Figure

Clayton and Sharie King assert, "The foundation for the *True Love Project* is an issue of ownership. It's about who's in charge of your life. Either Jesus is Lord or you are Lord. You're not big enough or strong enough or smart enough to be Lord, but Jesus is."[34] The gender ideologies operating within TLW and the purity movement at large can be theorized as a framework of "ownership" that positions fathers and male church leaders as the keepers of female sexuality, Jesus Christ as the ultimate owner and ruler of female sexuality, and future husbands as the receivers of female sexuality. The purity of girls is owed to each member of this figure individually as well as collectively, merging them into a three-headed machine with interlocking gears that systematically governs female purity in its support of anxious masculinity. Breitenberg's[35] formulation of anxious masculinity as the impetus for the regulation of female sexuality across historical periods is thus useful for understanding that the three-headed male figure is not isolated or unique. Instead, it is but one iteration of anxious masculinity that draws on existing cultural ideologies and institutions to control women's pleasure, desire, and performance of purity.

The Paternal Figure: Fathers and Church Leaders   Evangelical fathers are responsible for protecting the sexual honor of the women in their families, especially as women's bodies are the bearers of familial and community honor. In addition to being personally shameful, sexual activity outside of the bounds of marriage also reflects poorly on the family; indeed, "since women often carry the honour of their family, their behaviors are often regulated and policed. Their virginity can be crucial to the honour of the family within the community, so that fathers and brothers feel responsible for their protection."[36] For fathers, this means, in large part, maintaining control of their daughter's sexual behavior until she can be passed off to her future husband. To that end, fathers and church leaders often facilitate the courtship of young women, drawing on reputable young men in the evangelical community and acting as the gatekeepers that control men's access to women.

Like their courtship, the Godly submission of young girls is often channeled through a church leader—nearly always male, since women are prohibited from pastoral leadership in evangelical communities beyond their typical duties of overseeing music and children. The abstract concept of "spiritual maturity" positions them as advisors to girls and young women on how to be properly moral individuals. Clayton King, in his leadership of the TLW resurgence, exemplifies the paternal figure that controls female sexuality as he writes books and guides, oversees his extensive ministry, and travels widely to speak on the subject. He frequently uses his own marriage as a testimony to the virtues of abstinence until marriage, inspiring girls to follow in the footsteps of his (appropriately feminine) wife, Sharie. He communicates, "Sex is a good gift given to us by a good God who intentionally created sex as a means of pleasure and procreation . . . The bedroom in a marriage can become a playground for adults when there is mutual trust, patience, and understanding. Sharie and I make love without guilt or shame because we know and trust each other. It's often playful and silly."[37] TLW materials push girls to save their sexuality for marriage in the hopes that young men are doing the same, and that the eventual union of two pure people in front of their church leaders will lead to a satisfying sex life inside of marriage as exemplified by Clayton and Sharie King.

This particular dimension of male control of female sexuality is deeply invested in performance rituals for enacting purity. A girl's commitment to purity, as mediated through father figures, is communicated in very public ways with the signing of abstinence pledge cards and the adorning of purity rings. When girls engage in these enactments of purity, they are signaling to their fathers and, to a lesser extent, their church leaders and brothers that they will preserve the honor of the family by refraining from sexual activity. Sharie and Clayton King directly instruct young women: "decide now that you will not experiment sexually with a guy. Put it in writing and sign it. Give it to your parents, your pastor, or youth leader for accountability."[38] They further compare purity to a "team effort," noting that "you're going to need people around you to help you win. People who will create a safe place for you to learn how to resist temptation, to confess your sin when you blow it, and to watch how older men and women love each other and treat each other. You need people in the church to teach and preach God's Word, to instruct and correct you so you don't walk into a bad situation."[39] Positioning church-wide accountability as key to purity reinforces that the *ritual* is what determines a girl's worth, and that her audience is not only her father but also male church leaders.

Abstinence pledge cards and purity rings are symbols of performance on their own; however, in many cases they are institutionalized as performed purity through purity balls, described above in Fahs's work on ritualized abstinence. In this startlingly popular component of evangelical purity culture, daughters pledge ownership of their bodies and purity to their fathers, surrendering control of their sexual choices to the male head of household who will eventually give them to their husbands.[40] In these cases, "purity balls enter women into a system of commerce in which their sexuality becomes an object to be traded by and between men,"[41] tying them to a commitment that they may not entirely understand and wooing them to promise their abstinence at a very young age. The language utilized in these balls further undermines female agency by infantilizing young women while simultaneously constructing their fathers as battle-tested warriors. Fathers are called upon to go to war for the purity of their daughters against an enemy that is twofold: the sex-crazed boys who will try anything to "violate" innocent young women, and the supernatural forces that conspire to tempt and tease girls away from their commitments to purity.

The Spiritual Figure: Jesus Christ   The purity mandate is frequently cloaked in an ideology of submission to and worship of God, where the emphasis is not only on sexual purity but also on developing a holistic personal relationship with Jesus Christ through which He becomes the ultimate authority. In the words of Sharie and Clayton King, "When He is our focus, we will inevitably develop a spiritual intimacy that will undeniably produce the fruit of sexual purity in our lives . . . Virginity is a by-product of our love and passion for Christ."[42] According to TLW, the ultimate goal is submitting to the "lordship" of Christ, which will naturally manifest itself through sexual purity. The goal of the purity movement, then, is not only to control female sexuality but to persuade young women to surrender all of their choices to the commands of Jesus and to make pleasing Him the central aim of their lives.

The language of primary TLW texts heavily features authoritative signifiers for Jesus, referring to Christ as a master, boss, ruler, and king. The fallibility of humanity is further emphasized in these materials with statements that point to our need for a higher power: "The job of ruler, boss, and master needs to be filled by someone who is smart and experienced enough to see things that you don't see and to know things that you couldn't possibly know. You need a boss that can handle the job."[43] This language may seem bold to outsiders, but young women are likely familiar with this language if they are a part of the evangelical church as this ideology is a foundational tenet of conservative Christianity. The espoused motivation for this submission is simple and direct: God created you and Jesus Christ paid for you with His life, so your obedience, especially in matters of sexual purity, is owed to Him. For evangelical Christians, the doctrine further asserts that individual bodies, once devoted to God's service, become houses for God Himself in the form of the Holy Spirit.[44] King and King are drawing on this rhetoric when they note, "You practice sexual purity because you belong to Jesus, because your body is now His dwelling place and He is using your life as a witness to the world that His gospel is true and His kingdom is coming."[45] Positioning women's bodies as "the Temple of the Holy Spirit" easily lends credibility to the purity movement's assertion that individual choices about the body do not belong to individuals but instead to Jesus.

A further metaphor that reinforces male ownership of women is the comparison of an earthly marriage relationship to a biblical marriage relationship, which features prominently in evangelical movement ideology as it argues that the church is the bride of Christ. According to the book of Ephesians, Christian women are to be "married" to Jesus just as they are to be wedded to their earthly husbands; indeed, "the husband is the head of the wife, as also Christ is the head of the Church."[46] This transforms girls and young women into property to be owned by men through marital ties—even before they can be married to a *physical* man, they are married to a *metaphysical* one.

The Marital Figure: Future Husbands   Finally, when it comes to abstinence, the emphasis for girls is on making the choice to be pure for their
future husbands. Purity is something that can be *given* to future husbands
on the wedding night when they have sex for the first time—virginity is
framed as a *gift* that girls should save, wrapped and sealed, in order to please
their future husbands.[47] According to King and King, practicing purity for
a satisfying marriage should be a central concern for girls: "I talk to a lot of
girls who want an amazing marriage and a loving husband, but they are
making relationship choices now that contradict what they hope to have in
the future. If you want to honor God with your body, with your relationships, and eventually with your marriage, you need to start practicing right
now."[48] Even before they meet, girls are encouraged to pray for their future
husbands and to invest in the relationship by preserving all sexual thoughts,
feelings, and activities for them.

Donning a purity ring is an outward symbol of this inward commitment to
abstinence *until marriage.* In her study of the rhetorical strategies employed
by the abstinence movement, communication scholar Christine Gardner discusses the importance of the purity ring:

> it functions as a reminder to the wearer of her commitment to
> abstinence, but it also functions as the material manifestation of the
> symbolic gift of her virginity for her future spouse. Purity rings play a
> significant role in the evangelical abstinence campaigns' promotion of
> the goal of the good marriage. The ring and corresponding pledge
> ceremony foreshadow the wedding ring and wedding ceremony. In this
> way, the use of the purity ring trains people for a traditional wedding
> and marriage.[49]

That the purity ring is intended to be worn on the third finger of the left
hand and that it is often bestowed in an elaborate and public abstinence
pledge ceremony are both features relating participation in the movement
to a future marriage covenant that follows traditional (heterosexual) biblical morality.

TLW is clear and direct in enforcing the evangelical ideology that heterosexual, biblical marriage is the proper place for expressing sexuality.[50] This
is based on the naturalization of gender differences that extends from anatomy to gender roles and is exemplified when, for instance, Adam and Eve
are used to demonstrate the complementarity of men and women: "God
engineered those first two human bodies to go together. They were vastly
different in anatomy yet undeniably attractive to each other. Even the physical body parts themselves fit perfectly with each other, as they still do,
allowing the woman and the man to experience the full measure of joy dur-

ing sex."[51] In invoking Adam and Eve, TLW leaves no room for "alternative" expressions of sexuality that engage in loving, fulfilling, committed relationships. The purity mandate does not—indeed, according to evangelical thought, *cannot*—extend to nonheterosexual relationships.[52] TLW's discourse is entirely unambiguous on this front; King asserts of the sexual marriage bond that husband and wife "actually become one flesh. This kind of strong language isn't used in the Bible to describe parents and their kids or the relationship between friends. And it isn't used to describe a sexual relationship between two men or between two women."[53] It is clear that girls who pledge their purity are doing so to and for their future husbands.

UPDATING THE CONTEMPORARY SITUATION

Protecting Anxious Masculinity

The data presented above provide a compelling case for understanding the regulation of female sexuality through the purity movement as a function of anxious masculinity, which relies upon being understood by others as able to govern women's bodies and performances in order to remain hegemonic. Several prominent scholars of gender have established that masculinity is a fragile social construct that is dependent upon evaluation by peers through interaction.[54] Masculinity does not naturally proceed from the male body, but rather is an accumulation of bodily and discursive practices that conform to collective social expectations of how men should behave in the world. To be successful, it depends upon being recognized and accepted by others as appropriate masculinity; the pressure of evaluation and potential failure makes it a deeply anxious and unstable construct. In other words, men enact the conventions of masculinity *with* other men and *for* them to assess; thus a man's status can easily be challenged if he is deemed to be failing at appropriate masculinity.[55] For instance, lacking in sexual prowess and virility by not partnering with women is a decisive affront to masculinity and must be avoided by demonstrating relationships with women.[56] Gender scholars have argued that heterosexuality is a governing social structure that both women and men are forced into in order to become acceptable members of society and have their humanity validated.[57] Perhaps the most pertinent argument concerning compulsory heterosexuality as a violent institution is that it is not inherent in human nature or organization but is produced and reproduced as a social construction. Of course, subscribing to and displaying traditional sexual morality are biblical mandates and position men as fully complying with this structure of obligatory heterosexuality.[58]

The intense panic that socially progressive causes are weakening the traditional family leads men of the Religious Right to engage in activist causes that will ultimately reaffirm patriarchy and protect their anxious masculinity.[59] This masculine reassertion is accomplished by arguing that the downfall of society is directly tied to feminism, homosexuality, multiculturalism, and communism, which all signal the feminization of men in some way.[60] In their study of ex-gay therapies, Robinson and Spivey illuminate a fundamental piece of conservative ideology: "Social changes brought about by gay liberation and feminism have contributed to gender confusion and the demasculinization of men. This is considered to be the source of most social problems today, including family breakdown, poverty, welfare dependency, and crime."[61] The purity movement is a startlingly clear example of this belief, as its leaders have spent decades connecting teen premarital sex with every social ill imaginable, from abortion to divorce to sexually transmitted disease.[62] The solution that we are presented with by organizations like True Love Waits is apparent—control female sexuality and reinstate the traditional family.

Acceptable masculinity in the evangelical church is closely tied to authoritative leadership, particularly requiring men to prove that they have control over their homes and the sexuality of the women inside them.[63] Sharie and Clayton King reinforce this idea when they tell young women, for instance, that "sometimes an appetite must be controlled because an appetite without limits is destructive."[64] Uncontrolled female sexuality is perhaps the greatest threat to the gender order that evangelical movements strive to maintain.[65] Women making educated, healthy choices to engage in sexual activity according to their own rules is incredibly subversive in the context of a structure that systematically denies them that ability. Indeed, Breitenberg writes, "the preoccupation among men with female chastity maintains such a universal hold on the imaginations and social practices of Western culture that we can hardly envision patriarchy without it."[66] The purity movement is merely one such evangelical endeavor that aims to control female sexuality through the three-headed male figure in order to preserve its fragile, anxious masculinity.

FUTURE DIRECTIONS AND POLICIES
Policy Implications: Structure, Agency, and Gender

The reach of the evangelical purity movement is deep and wide, and any analysis of sexuality that fails to consider the continued impact of religion is neglecting a core institution that shapes sexual attitudes, behaviors, and meanings. TLW and the purity movement draw on existing ideologies concerning naturalized gender roles, the performance of female purity for an audience, and the demonstration of male control of female sexuality as a function of anxious masculinity. Beyond the three-headed male figure, the major, longstanding impacts of the purity movement are both tangible and ideological in nature. Despite purporting to reduce teen pregnancy, prevent premarital sex, stymie sexually transmitted infection, and prevent psychological and emotional hardship for young women and men, the purity movement and its educational companion, abstinence-only sex education, have not achieved these very practical outcomes. Ultimately, girls and young women who participate in evangelical purity culture are no less likely than their secular counterparts to engage in premarital sexual activity, and have actually been found to be *more* susceptible to human papillomavirus (HPV) and nonmarital pregnancies than their counterparts who do not take abstinence pledges.[67] Indeed, statistical research consistently reports that approximately 80 percent of young adults who make purity pledges have vaginal or oral sex before marriage[68] and do not significantly delay the timing of first sexual activity,[69] yet feel high levels of shame, regret, and stigma around sexual activity.[70] When young adults who take purity pledges do engage in sexual activity, they are less likely to use condoms, birth control, and other forms of protection.[71] Enforcing abstinence on girls and limiting their access to knowledge do not solve the social problems that purity culture aims to solve; abstinence-only sex education may be most in line with the evangelical church's ideologies and goals, but it is not appropriately preparing girls and young women to navigate sexuality and intimacy.

Abstinence-only sex education is so deeply rooted in purity movement ideologies that even secularized versions taught across the United States, such as "Sex Respect," utilize the gendered frameworks described above.[72] If abstinence-only sex education does not equip young adults with the necessary knowledge and skills to make informed and healthy sexual decisions, yet purity culture is meaningful for many individuals and cannot be overlooked, then what does it mean to effectively prepare teens to navigate a sex-saturated society? The insular nature of the evangelical purity movement coupled with federal support for abstinence-only sex education[73] means that girls and young women are often singularly exposed to purity movement ideologies and lack medically accurate knowledge about their bodies and developing sexuality. Research shows that many young adults who participate in purity culture desire and support comprehensive sex education,[74] yet even this solution does not address the gendered roots of purity movement ideology that have been so pervasive in education. Rather than neglect the religious influence that many students bring to sex education in schools *or* promote abstinence as the only acceptable sexual pathway, a holistic focus on the overall emotional, sexual, and intimate wellness of young adults that considers abstinence to be one choice among many is a more satisfying balance of structure and agency. To only consider outcomes such as sexually transmitted infections, premarital sex, and use of protection is to overlook the deep-seated gender ideologies that many young adults bring to their understanding of sexuality and relationships. When these gender ideologies imitate those of the purity movement, women simultaneously become sexual property to be traded among men and sexual gatekeepers that must "slow down the young man" in order to safeguard the integrity of both individuals.[75] Modeling relationships between women and men in this way has potentially dangerous implications for teens as they navigate sexual choices, yet both abstinence-only and comprehensive sex education programs fail to interrogate these underlying gender ideologies.

In communicating information about sexuality to teens and young adults, schools make value judgments about what information is necessary for them to negotiate this complex aspect of themselves and society. In his global history of sex education, Jonathan Zimmerman notes that sex education is "a mirror, not a spearhead," since it reflects society's ideological constructs around sex and sexuality; he further argues that these ideological constructs must shift *first* in order to support a change in how we communicate sexuality to children and teens.[76] To present abstinence as one choice among many would undoubtedly require a paradigm shift in the evangelical church. However, the church and sexual openness are not incompatible and the beginnings of this evolution are already in place, as the modern iteration of TLW draws on biblical descriptions of sex as beautiful and life-affirming rather than shameful and dirty, positioning intimacy and sexuality as key features of humanity.

Choosing abstinence until marriage is not, in itself, inherently disempowering to women. Rather, it is the constraints placed on the choices of girls and women through the purity mandate, driven by anxious masculinity, that oppress women by stifling and subduing female sexuality. The overarching message of the purity movement is that the burden of performing ritualized purity, the burden of controlling the "natural" sexual urges of men by remaining pure, and the burden of enacting adequate virtue and submission in their relationships with men all fall on girls and women. When these constraints are replicated in other institutions, such as education, women become trapped in a system of sexual commerce that positions their bodies as objects over which they have little control. Breaking down this system requires the reenvisioning of ideological constructs and their practical implications in such a way that girls and women are appropriately educated about a diverse array of sexual and bodily choices *and* are free of the pressures and constraints of institutions on those choices, without being forced to abandon participation in institutions and movements that may provide them with meaning and fulfillment.

NOTES

1. King, Clayton, and Sharie King. 2014a. *True Love Project: How the Gospel Defines Your Purity.* Nashville: B & H, 162–163.

2. Guttmacher Institute. 2015. "State Policies in Brief: Sex and HIV Education." www.guttmacher.org/statecenter/spibs/spib_SE.pdf.

3. Kim, Nami. 2011. "'Lord, I Am a Father!': The Transnational Evangelical Men's Movement and the Advent of 'Benevolent' Patriarchy." *Asian Journal of Women's Studies* 17 (1): 100–131; Wilcox, William Bradford. 2004. *Soft Patriarchs, New Men: How Christianity Shapes Fathers and Husbands.* Chicago: University of Chicago Press.

4. Breitenberg, Mark. 1993. "Anxious Masculinity: Sexual Jealousy in Early Modern England." *Feminist Studies* 19 (2): 377–398, 377.

5. Paik, Anthony, Kenneth J. Sanchagrin, and Karen Heimer. 2016. "Broken Promises: Abstinence Pledging and Sexual and Reproductive Health." *Journal of Marriage and Family* 78 (2): 546–561.

6. Baumgardner, Jennifer. 2011. *F'em!: Goo Goo, Gaga, and Some Thoughts on Balls.* Berkeley: Seal; Gardner, Christine J. 2011. *Making Chastity Sexy: The Rhetoric of Evangelical Abstinence Campaigns.* Berkeley: University of California Press; Valenti, Jessica. 2010. *The Purity Myth: How America's Obsession with Virginity Is Hurting Young Women.* Berkeley: Seal.

7. Mills, Scott. 2014. *True Love Waits: The Complicated Struggle for Sexual Purity.* DVD. LifeWay Films.

8. Valenti (2010).

9. King and King (2014a).

10. For a useful discussion of political opportunity structure that is beyond the scope of this chapter, see: Staggenborg, Suzanne. 2011. *Social Movements.* New York: Oxford University Press.

11. Taylor, Verta. 1999. "Gender and Social Movements: Gender Processes in Women's Self-Help Movements." *Gender & Society* 13 (1): 8–33.

12. Faludi, Susan. 1991. *Backlash: The Undeclared War against American Women.* New York: Anchor.

13. Wilcox (2004).

14. Fahs, Breanne. 2010. "Daddy's Little Girls: On the Perils of Chastity Clubs, Purity Balls, and Ritualized Abstinence." *Frontiers: A Journal of Women's Studies* 31 (3): 116–142; Robinson, Christine M., and Sue E. Spivey. 2007. "The Politics of Masculinity and the Ex-Gay Movement." *Gender & Society* 21 (5): 650–675.

15. Bloch, Jon P. 2000. "The New and Improved Clint Eastwood: Change and Persistence in Promise Keepers Self-Help Literature." *Sociology of Religion* 61 (1): 11–31.

16. Jones, Katherine. 2013. "Children of Christ and Sexual Beings: Sexuality and Gender in an Evangelical Abstinence Organization." *International Journal of Religion and Spirituality in Society* 3 (2): 1–14, 9.

17. Ruether, Rosemary Radford. 1993. *Sexism and God-Talk: Toward a Feminist Theology*. Boston: Beacon.

18. Ruether (1993): 169.

19. Butler, Judith. 1988. "Performative Acts and Gender Constitution: An Essay in Phenomenology and Feminist Theory." *Theatre Journal* 40 (4): 519–538; West, Candace, and Don H. Zimmerman. 1987. "Doing Gender." *Gender & Society* 1 (2): 125–151.

20. Robinson and Spivey (2007): 659.

21. Proverbs 31:10–31, New King James Version.

22. Breazeale, Kathlyn A. 2010. "There Goes the Bride: A Snapshot of the Ideal Christian Wife." In *Women and Christianity*, edited by Cheryl A. Kirk-Duggan and Karen Jo Torjesen, 3–25. Santa Barbara: ABC-CLIO, 3.

23. Gardner (2011).

24. Wilcox (2004).

25. Gardner (2011); Pruss, Alexander. 2013. *One Body: An Essay in Christian Sexual Ethics*. Notre Dame: University of Notre Dame Press.

26. Kimmel, Michael. 2010. *Misframing Men: The Politics of Contemporary Masculinities*. New Brunswick, NJ: Rutgers University Press.

27. Bartkowski, John P., and Xiaohe Xu. 2000. "Distant Patriarchs or Expressive Dads? The Discourse and Practice of Fathering in Conservative Protestant Families." *Sociological Quarterly* 41 (3): 465–485.

28. Bartkowski, John P. 2001. *Remaking the Godly Marriage: Gender Negotiation in Evangelical Families*. New Brunswick, NJ: Rutgers University Press; Lienesch, Michael P. 1990. "Anxious Patriarchs: Authority and the Meaning of Masculinity in Christian Conservative Social Thought." *Journal of American Culture* 13 (4): 37–55; Kim (2011); Stein, Arlene. 2005. "Make Room for Daddy: Anxious Masculinity and Emergent Homophobias in Neopatriarchal Politics." *Gender & Society* 19 (5): 601–620; Wilcox (2004).

29. Becker, Julia C., and Janet K. Swim. 2011. "Seeing the Unseen: Attention to Daily Encounters with Sexism as Way to Reduce Sexist Beliefs." *Psychology of Women Quarterly* 35 (2): 227–242; Ferree, Myra Marx, and David A. Merrill. 2000. "Hot Movements, Cold Cognition: Thinking about Social Movements in Gendered Frames." *Contemporary Sociology* 29 (3): 454–462.

30. Ferree and Merrill (2000).

31. King, Sharie, and Clayton King. 2014b. *True Love Project: 40 Days of Purity for Girls*. Nashville: B & H, 70.

32. Ozyegin, Gul. 2009. "Virginal Facades: Sexual Freedom and Guilt among Young Turkish Women." *European Journal of Women's Studies* 16 (2): 103–123.

33. Fahs (2010).

34. King and King (2014a): 47.

35. Breitenberg (1993).

36. Seidler, Victor J. 2006. *Transforming Masculinities: Men, Cultures, Bodies, Power, Sex and Love*. London: Routledge, 74–75.

37. King and King (2014a): 62 and 68.

38. King and King (2014b): 36.

39. King and King (2014b): 39.

40. Baumgardner (2011); Fahs (2010); Valenti (2010).

41. Fahs (2010): 133.

42. King and King (2014b): 28 and 99.

43. King, Clayton. 2014c. *The True Love Project: How the Gospel Defines Your Purity, Student Book*. Nashville: B & H, 16.

44. King (2014c).

45. King and King (2014a): 72–73.

46. Ephesians 5: 22–33, New King James Version.

47. Carpenter, Laura M. 2005. *Virginity Lost: An Intimate Portrait of First Sexual Experiences*. New York: New York University Press; Fahs (2010).

48. King and King (2014b): 34–35.

49. Gardner (2011): 52.

50. Gardner (2011); Jones (2013).

51. King and King (2014a): 65.

52. Although, according to evangelical thought, nonheterosexual individuals cannot use the language of purity and marriage, there is research suggesting that they may rework, amend, and even embrace biblical directives in their own relationships according to their needs and desires. See, for instance, Yip, Andrew K.T. 1997. "Gay Male Christian Couples and Sexual Exclusivity." *Sociology* 31 (2): 289–306.

53. King and King (2014a): 64.

54. Connell, R.W. 2005. *Masculinities*. 2nd ed. Berkeley: University of California Press; Kimmel, Michael. 1996. *Manhood in America: A Cultural History*. New York: Free Press; Messner, Michael A. 1997. *Politics of Masculinities: Men in Movements*. Lanham, MD: Altamira Press.

55. Heath, Melanie. 2003. "Soft-Boiled Masculinity: Renegotiating Gender and Racial Ideologies in the Promise Keepers Movement." *Gender & Society* 17 (3): 423–444; Kimmel, Michael. 1994. "Masculinity as Homophobia: Fear, Shame, and Silence in the Construction of Gender Identity." In *Theorizing Masculinities*, edited by Harry Brod and Michael Kaufman, 119–141. Thousand Oaks, CA: Sage.

56. Ducat, Stephen J. 2004. *The Wimp Factor: Gender Gaps, Holy Wars, and the Politics of Anxious Masculinity*. Boston: Beacon.

57. Connell (2005); Katz, Jonathan Ned. 1995. *The Invention of Heterosexuality*. New York: Penguin; Rubin, Gayle. 1975. "The Traffic in Women: Notes on the 'Political Economy' of Sex." In *Toward an Anthropology of Women*, edited by Rayna Reiter, 157–210. New York: Monthly Review Press.

58. Stein (2005).

59. Brubaker, Pamela K. 2010. "Gender and Society: Competing Visions of Women's Agency, Equality, and Well-Being." In *Women and Christianity*, edited by Cheryl A. Kirk-Duggan and Karen Jo Torjesen, 93–114. Santa Barbara: ABC-CLIO; Stein (2005).

60. Connell (2005); Ducat (2004); Kimmell (2010).

61. Robinson and Spivey (2007): 665.

62. Williams, Jean Calterone. 2011. "Battling a 'Sex-Saturated' Society: The Abstinence Movement and the Politics of Sex Education." *Sexualities* 14 (4): 416–443.

63. Breitenberg (1993); D'Angelo, Mary Rose. 2003. "'Knowing How to Preside over His Own Household': Imperial Masculinity and Christian Asceticism in the Pastorals, *Hermas*, and Luke-Acts." In *New Testament Masculinities*, edited by Stephen D. Moore and Janice Capel Anderson, 265–295. Atlanta: Society of Biblical Literature.

64. King and King (2014b): 51.

65. Fahs (2010); Valenti (2010).

66. Breitenberg (1993): 377.

67. Paik et al. (2016).

68. For an insightful assessment of premarital sexual activity in Southern Baptist settings, see Rosenbaum, Janet E., and Byron Weathersbee. 2013. "True Love

Waits: Do Southern Baptists? Premarital Sexual Behavior among Newly Married Southern Baptist Sunday School Students." *Journal of Religion and Health* 52 (1): 263–275.

69. Bersamin, Melina M., Samantha Walker, Elizabeth D. Waiters, Deborah A. Fisher, and Joel W. Grube. 2005. "Promising to Wait: Virginity Pledges and Adolescent Sexual Behavior." *Journal of Adolescent Health* 36 (5): 428–436; Rosenbaum, Janet Elise. 2009. "Patient Teenagers? A Comparison of the Sexual Behavior of Virginity Pledgers and Matched Nonpledgers." *Pediatrics* 123 (1): e110–e120.

70. Carpenter (2005); Rosenbaum and Weathersbee (2013).

71. Brückner, Hannah, and Peter Bearman. 2005. "After the Promise: The STD Consequences of Adolescent Virginity Pledges." *Journal of Adolescent Health* 36 (4): 271–278; Rosenbaum (2009).

72. Carpenter (2005).

73. Even with the Obama administration's efforts to reduce funding for abstinence-only sex education, it still proliferates in many school systems; perhaps more importantly, the culture of purity and abstinence taught in these forms of sex education is pervasive in the culture at large.

74. Rosenbaum and Weathersbee (2013).

75. Carpenter (2005).

76. Zimmerman, Jonathan. 2015. *Too Hot to Handle: A Global History of Sex Education.* Princeton: Princeton University Press.

6. Gender, Residential Segregation, and Military Enlistment Patterns

Allison Suppan Helmuth and Amy Kate Bailey

Rob and Keisha share a triplex with their mother, Jeanette, in the neighborhood where they grew up. Nearly all of their neighbors are black, like them. Keisha is divorced, and her children go to the neighborhood high school. Keisha's car hasn't worked in months, and her commute takes more than an hour each way on public transit, although the national chain hardware store where she works as a cashier is only six miles from the house. Rob is an Army veteran who completed an apprenticeship program in construction and is currently looking for work. Keisha's oldest daughter isn't sure how she will pay for college and doesn't see many good jobs in the neighborhood, so she is thinking about following her Uncle Rob into the Army.

Benny and Rhonda are white and they live across town, each about two blocks away from their mother, Veronica. Like Rob and Keisha, they also live in the neighborhood where they grew up, but this neighborhood is nearly all white. Rhonda works as a file clerk in a medical office about half a mile from her apartment. Rhonda's ex-husband agreed that she should keep the minivan when they divorced, so she is able to get to the grocery store and her children's afterschool activities pretty easily. Benny is a plumber who found his most recent job through his upstairs neighbor. Rhonda's daughter has started doing some clerical work after school for Benny's boss and plans to continue working there when she starts community college in another year.

Veronica, Benny, and Rhonda have similar levels of education as Jeanette, Rob, and Keisha. Each family's neighborhood environment, however, has a major impact on their lives and level of economic security. Their neighborhoods shape their social networks and their access to transportation, both of which are critical in finding and keeping jobs that are close to home. Neighborhoods can also affect young men and women differently, by shaping the different opportunities they face as they finish high school and move into adult roles and responsibilities.

In this chapter, we review current research and incorporate original data analysis to examine how gendered military enlistment patterns might be linked to a phenomenon that has typically been understood to be racial: residential segregation. We hope that this will help scholars consider how residential segregation supports not only race and class inequality, but gender inequality, too.[1] Women—especially women of color—have been significantly marginalized within both contemporary and historical urbanization processes. The mainstream retelling of the history of residential segregation focuses primarily on race and class.[2] In contrast, a feminist, intersectional approach to studying racial segregation helps us to identify and uncover how women's experiences in particular are shaped by these processes. An intersectional approach can help us examine how race, class, and gender operate together as social structures that constrain or expand our resources and opportunities.[3] Given the way that racial segregation differently structures the opportunities that are available to men and to women, we can imagine that people from various kinds of neighborhoods might evaluate the risks and benefits associated with specific economic decisions differently.

One example might be the decision whether or not to join the military. Enlistment seems to be most attractive to people from communities with fewer economic opportunities, suggesting that it is often a decision at least partly motivated by economic concerns. People of color—particularly black Americans—are also overrepresented in the armed forces, meaning that people of color comprise a higher percentage of those on active duty than of the American population overall. There is also a tremendous gender difference in military participation, with women much less likely to join the armed forces than men.[4] Many people are probably aware that higher rates of enlistment mean that men shoulder a larger burden of death and disability, but military employment also provides real economic advantages. Compared to other entry-level jobs, people in the armed forces earn higher average pay, universally gain health insurance for themselves as well as their spouse and children, and receive financial subsidies to pursue a college education. Many *veterans* also receive funding for college, as well as low-cost loans to purchase a home and lifetime hiring preference in governmental jobs. Joining the armed forces, then, provides an array of economic benefits that are currently claimed overwhelmingly by men. Because the distinct economic consequences of living in a racially segregated neighborhood are gendered, in this chapter, we examine how enlistment patterns might differ for men and women who live in neighborhoods where their local opportunities are impacted by varying levels of racial diversity.

In our analysis of men's and women's military enlistment, we tried to understand how gendered employment patterns in one major sector of the labor market—the military—might be linked to racially segregated neighborhoods. We focus on their employment in the US military because of its importance as a major employer in the US labor market, as well as the role it plays as an "invisible welfare state"[5] that is primarily available to working-class men.

BACKGROUND

Racial Residential Segregation and Gender

Racial residential segregation is the process by which people come to live in neighborhoods that are largely populated by members of a single racial or ethnic group. It is a pattern of urban life that has persisted throughout the twentieth century to the present. This form of segregation is associated with a host of negative outcomes. People who live in racially segregated neighborhoods of concentrated poverty have limited access to job opportunities, healthcare, and education.[6] Although we understand these racial effects, we do not often think of segregation as a process that *also* reproduces gender inequality. Many sociological accounts of residential segregation emphasize how race and class inequality have contributed to the creation and reproduction of racially segregated neighborhoods with concentrated urban poverty.[7] Feminist scholars have sought to make interventions into these mainstream narratives, emphasizing how the policies and legal frameworks that supported and upheld racial inequality and segregation simultaneously upheld and reproduced gender inequality.[8]

The earliest examples of this come from the federal policy that provided subsidies for public housing and home ownership in the mid-1930s. In 1936, "Greenbelt Towns" were established in Ohio, Milwaukee, and Maryland to encourage city dwellers to move to the rural outskirts of the urban area. Leases for homes in these new suburban neighborhoods often prohibited married women from engaging in any economic activity within the home, and the preferred tenants were heterosexual married couples who had a commuting husband and stay-at-home wife.[9] In this sense, in addition to being racially segregated for white families only, the federally subsidized suburbs also regulated which kinds of families were permitted to move there, and they hastened a spatial pattern in cities in which single people, people in poverty, people of color, and LGBT people were prohibited from settling in the suburbs, and instead clustered in urban neighborhoods.[10] In this sense, neighborhoods were not only segregated by race and class, but also by family type, gender, and sexuality.

Federal housing policies also stipulated which kinds of urban neighborhoods were eligible for home ownership loans. Racial segregation in neighborhoods and metropolitan areas was strengthened by discriminatory federal policies that denied the mortgage and housing subsidies that benefited residents of all-white neighborhoods to (primarily black) people living in more racially diverse areas. Some of these mortgage and housing subsidies were tied to military service: beginning in 1944, veterans were the recipients of massive public spending on home loans as part of the GI Bill,[11] and the dispersal of these benefits disproportionately went to white veterans.[12]

Other public policies, including "urban renewal" and exclusionary zoning, combined with private practices, such as real estate discrimination and "white flight" from integrated neighborhoods, to entrench segregation in US cities and create all-white suburbs.[13] Black women were doubly disadvantaged by policies like these, as the federal government routinely discriminated against women in determining home buyers' mortgage eligibility.[14] Because black men were disproportionately excluded from military service and therefore unlikely to qualify for subsidized VA loans, or to receive benefits for which they were eligible,[15] black families—including women who became widowed or divorced—were denied the ability to build home equity or inherit wealth in the form of real estate.

The contemporary consequences of these policies are reflected in what is known as the "racial wealth gap." In 2011, the median black family held less than 10 percent of the wealth held by the median white family, and much of that disparity was driven by differences in home ownership.[16] Employment-linked ramifications of living in racially segregated areas emerged during the late-twentieth-century transition away from an economy based on manufacturing to a "postindustrial" reliance on technology, the service sector, and finance.[17] These economic changes, while race-neutral on the surface, reorganized economic activity within metropolitan areas and isolated black people in high-poverty neighborhoods.

As the number of manufacturing jobs in US cities declined and economic activity shifted to the suburbs, joblessness among black men skyrocketed. The number of service sector jobs in central city areas increased, but these jobs paid lower wages, tended to be nonunionized, and were more likely to employ women.[18] This gendered division of labor and the devaluation of women's work worsened poverty in segregated black neighborhoods, especially for households headed by single women. The spatial separation of black residents of segregated urban neighborhoods from family wage jobs is called "spatial mismatch,"[19] and results in higher joblessness in these neighborhoods. This problem is exacerbated for black men living in segregated communities due to high rates of incarceration. People who are formerly incarcerated are likely to struggle with unemployment and homelessness, and employers routinely discriminate against younger black men based on the presumption that they have been or may become involved with the criminal justice system.[20]

The structure of local labor markets—particularly the limited number of secure jobs—has strong effects on wage inequality for all workers, but also distinct effects by gender.[21] Residential segregation is linked to a higher racial earnings gap, and greater income inequality between social classes, for men. Simply put, higher-status blacks, and black men in particular, suffer greater wage penalties when they live in more highly segregated metropolitan areas.[22] Niki Dickerson[23] theorizes that residential segregation combines with labor market segregation to produce inequalities that cleave along lines of both race *and* gender. In order to test this relationship, she proposes that research should specify the mechanisms through which residential segregation leads to labor market stratification and how these mechanisms may operate differently for men and women, sorting men and women into different jobs depending on their residential origin. Our analysis of men's and women's military participation enables us to identify how enlistment patterns differ by gender, depending on the diversity of one's neighborhood of origin, and to speculate on the mechanisms that lead to these differences.

Women in the Military

Women have traditionally been limited in their access to military employment, with consequences for their claims on the full rights of citizenship.[24] The public discussion about women's inclusion in the armed forces, and implications for gender roles and women's rights and responsibilities as citizens, dates back to at least World War II.[25] The onset of the Cold War and its expansive needs for military staffing created the first conditions under which women were allowed into the armed forces without need to rely on the pretext of active war.[26] As the role of the US military changed, however, and personnel became more professionalized, the concept of military as a form of citizen service grew in importance.[27] Women's exclusion from many opportunities in the armed forces also diminishes women's inclusion in the civic polity,[28] and through it, claims on citizenship rights. Currently, fewer than one in seven active duty members of the American armed forces are women,[29] a proportion that has remained relatively stable for 25 years.

The armed forces are not merely an arbiter of political inclusion, however. They also serve a massive role in redistributing public resources to a select group of people—people who are disproportionately male. Joining the military provides stable employment for moderately skilled young adults, the overwhelming majority of whom have not completed college.[30] These jobs provide opportunities for paid education and training, earnings that are higher than those of three-fourths of comparable civilian jobs, and an array of employer-provided benefits such as access to family health care unavailable to many young workers. Indeed, the US Department of Defense spends $500 million annually on tuition assistance for active duty personnel,[31] with more than $30 billion additionally on college assistance between 2009 and 2013 via the Post-9/11 GI Bill,[32] and roughly $1.4 billion just in 2013 on loan guarantee programs.[33] Because of the gender imbalance in military enlistment, the lion's share of those public resources are redistributed to men. While enlistment is frequently framed in public discourse as a patriotic decision based on self-sacrifice—and many people with military experience identify patriotism and a sense of service with their time in uniform—there are also tangible economic benefits that come with armed forces employment.

Different processes seem to govern military enlistment for men and women. Women, for example, are likely to abandon delinquent behaviors following enlistment, while men are not,[34] and the curvilinear relationship between delinquent behavior and enlistment is more pronounced for girls than it is for boys.[35] Women also tend to have a more careerist approach to the military than is true for men, with higher levels of participation in training and educational programs, both while on active duty and as veterans.[36] Women who are drawn to the military seem to value the highly regulated nature of the armed forces, which allows for less discrimination than in civilian jobs. In fact, military women report higher levels of job satisfaction and perceptions of fairness than is true for white military men.[37]

US veterans have access to an array of social and economic benefits not provided to people without a history of military employment, including education and training, subsidized home loans, and a specialized health care system.[38] Veterans also receive preferential treatment in government hiring. The erosion of employment protections and increased privatization and "new governance" approaches, however, have reduced the benefits to veteran status.[39] Black women veterans have similar earnings to other black women, while white female veterans suffer an earnings penalty compared to other white women, even controlling for education and work experience.[40] The economic consequences associated with military employment, then, stretch across the life course, and vary somewhat by race and gender. Our research takes a first step toward understanding how the constraints imposed by one type of structural inequality—residential segregation— might help drive gender disparity in access to these economic resources.

CASE STUDY

We are interested in whether a community's level of racial diversity or homogeneity is linked to women's enlistment patterns. We suspect men's and women's economic motivations for enlistment might be related to the gendered opportunity structures they face. These opportunity structures are shaped at least in part by segregation. Our research combines two sources of information. First, we use data from the US Census Bureau on the social, economic, and demographic characteristics of people who live in each US ZIP Code. This includes information that might be linked to local economic conditions, like the percentage of children who live below the federally defined poverty level, the percentage of all workers who are employed in a variety of industries, and the share of adults who hold different levels of education—like high school dropouts, high school graduates, and so on. For each ZIP Code, we also use information from the Department of Defense on how many people joined the military from that ZIP Code in four specific years (1990, 1995, 2000, and 2005), along with each person's gender.

To assess the general racial composition of a ZIP Code, we measure the number of racial or ethnic groups who live in that ZIP Code, as well as how large each group is, relative to the others. Based on that information, we calculate what is called an "entropy score." ZIP Codes that have a smaller number of racial or ethnic groups living within them, or where one of the groups is much larger than the other groups, have smaller entropy scores. More diverse local neighborhoods, with a larger number of racial and ethnic groups, and the groups being more equal to one another in size, have larger scores.

We calculate enlistment rates, the total number of enlistments, and the probability of *any* enlistment in each ZIP Code separately for men and women, although our discussion focuses on women's enlistment. When we calculate an enlistment rate, the number of new male or female enlistees is the numerator and the number of men or women age 18–24 recorded as having lived in that ZIP Code is the denominator. We select the range 18–24 because more than 90 percent of people who join the armed forces for the first time are between these ages. We don't examine the relationship between diversity and enlistment for ZIP Codes with a total population less than 100, including at least five young adults aged 18–24. In our statistical analyses, we take into account the number of people between the ages of 18 and 24 living in each ZIP Code, since it is reasonable to expect that the number of *most likely enlistees* will be linked to the number of *enlistments*.

We try to identify which economic and demographic factors, especially residential segregation, can help predict enlistment for men and women. For example, if veterans are more likely to have a positive view of the military, and to encourage young adults they know to join the armed forces, we would expect to find higher levels of enlistment in places where a larger share of the adults are veterans. Similarly, if young people living in communities where adults have to commute long distances in order to find full-time work are disheartened at their own job prospects, they find the military a more attractive employment option than young people who live where well-paying jobs are plentiful and close by. All of the factors we account for in our statistical analyses, grouped by category, are presented in table 6.1.

In each of the years we analyze, there were no enlistments reported for between 25 percent and 35 percent of all ZIP Codes, and no female enlistments in roughly two-thirds of all ZIP Codes. We used a statistical technique (called logistic regression) that predicts the odds of something happening, as compared to its not happening. In this case, we were predicting the odds of a ZIP Code having at least one female enlistment relative to the odds of it not having any women enlist. Our analyses suggest that more diverse ZIP Codes have a higher probability of experiencing female enlistments when compared to more segregated ZIP Codes. Note that there are many other factors that may be associated with racial composition *and with military enlistment*. In our assessment, we accounted for each variable listed in table 6.1 and still arrived at this conclusion.

Figure 6.1 depicts how the probability that at least one woman enlists from a specific ZIP Code increases as its level of racial diversity increases in each of the four years we are analyzing—1990, 1995, 2000, and 2005. The axis along the bottom of the figure identifies the level of racial and ethnic diversity, as measured by its percentile among all ZIP Codes on the entropy score. ZIP Codes at the 10th percentile are relatively homogenous, having higher entropy scores than only one in 10 ZIP Codes. ZIP Codes at the median are more diverse than half of all ZIP Codes, and so represent the average. Those with entropy scores in the 90th percentile are more diverse than nine out of 10 ZIP Codes. The left-hand axis identifies the probability that a ZIP Code at each level of racial diversity would have at least one woman living there join the armed forces in a given year. In all four years,

TABLE 6.1 Social and Economic Factors Used to Predict Gender Enlistment Patterns

Spatial Mismatch	Labor Market Conditions	Military Culture	Social Conditions	Young Adult Prospects
Percent workers whose jobs are in the county	Percent workers in each of the following industries: manufacturing; transportation and trade; finance, insurance, and real estate; professional services; public administration; education; and health and social services	Percent working-age adults who are veterans	Child poverty rate	Percent of people age 16–19 who are in the military, in school full time, working and not in school, unemployed and not in school, and not working or in school
Percent workers who commute 45 minutes+		Percent working-age adults on active military duty	Percent of adults who did not attend high school, dropped out of high school, (only) graduated from high school, completed some college, and completed a four-year college degree.	Total number of men or women in the ZIP Code age 18–24
Percent men who work full time, year-round			Percent living in urban areas	
Percent women who work full time, year-round			Percent who recently moved within the county and who moved in from another county or state	
			Percent age 65 and older	
			Total population	

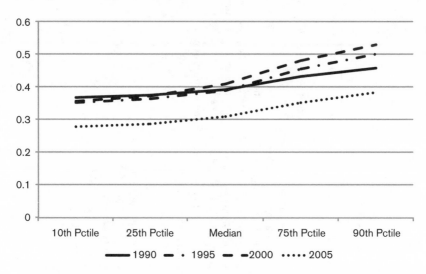

FIGURE 6.1. Probability a ZIP Code Has at Least One Female Enlistment, by Racial Diversity.

the more diverse a ZIP Code is, the more likely it is that at least one woman living there decided to join the armed forces.

We should note that the trend line for 2005 is far below the lines for the other years. Fewer ZIP Codes experienced any female enlistments in 2005 than was true in 1990, 1995, or 2000. This reflects the general decline in women's enlistment once the United States invaded Iraq. Simply put, as the risks of deployment and combat increased, fewer Americans, including women, were willing to accept the potential negative consequences of being employed by one of the armed forces. We believe it is important that even in that time of relative uncertainty and declining overall military participation, we observe the same basic relationship between the probability of female enlistment and racial segregation or integration as we do in periods when there were fewer risks associated with being in uniform.

We also wanted to understand whether a ZIP Code's entropy score was linked not just to the probability of *any* enlistment among women, but also to the *number* of women living there who decided to join the armed forces. We asked whether, taking into account all of the factors listed in table 6.1 that might be related to a community's level of either diversity or homogeneity *and its level of military enlistment*, diversity might help explain *how many* female enlistments it launched in a given year. In all four years that we examined, ZIP Codes with higher entropy scores were likely to send larger numbers of women into the military. Again, we took all of the other

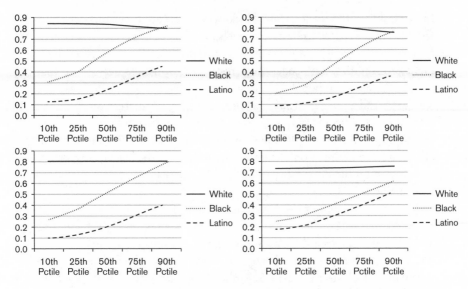

FIGURE 6.2. Probabilities of Race/Ethnic Enlistment from ZIP Codes by Racial Diversity. Top: 1990, 1995; bottom: 2000; 2005.

community-level characteristics listed in table 6.1 into consideration—including the number of people living there who were in the age range that is most likely to enlist.

In general, we find that diverse ZIP Codes are more likely to witness women joining the armed forces and that more women enlist from ZIP Codes with higher levels of racial diversity. ZIP Codes with higher entropy scores are also more likely to experience male enlistments, and to send a larger number of their young men into uniform, but these relationships appear to be stronger for women—in both the size and the strength of the relationship. We believe that these gender patterns are driven at least in part by the different racial composition of men and women in the military. Roughly half of all women in uniform are black, which means that low levels of enlistment from segregated communities in large part reflect the disadvantages faced by black women living in highly segregated contexts. Similarly, although the percentage of non-Hispanic white men in the military is smaller than their percentage in the civilian population, they still make up the majority of male enlisted personnel. The somewhat weaker relationship between rates of male enlistment and residential diversity reflects the fact that both white men and women tend to live in communities that are mostly white.

The relationship between enlistment by racial and ethnic group and residential neighborhood diversity is displayed in figure 6.2, which presents the probability that at least one black, white, or Latino person will enlist from an observed ZIP Code across levels of residential segregation, in each of our four observational years. Note that in assessing race-specific enlistment probabilities, ZIP Codes were restricted to include only those that reported at least 100 population, as well as at least five people between the ages of 18 and 24 *in the racial and ethnic category of interest,* and took the total number of people in this age range into account. Similarly, the effects of all other variables in the model are held constant at their mean levels, allowing us to examine only the effects of changing the level of residential segregation on the probability of a black, white, or Latino person enlisting from a given ZIP Code.

We see that in all four years, a large majority of ZIP Codes were predicted to experience at least one non-Hispanic white person enlist. In both 1990 and 1995, more diverse ZIP Codes were slightly *less* likely to generate white enlistments, while in 2000 and 2005, there was virtually no difference in the probability of white enlistments regardless of the level of diversity. For both blacks and Latinos, however, the story looks quite different. It was very unlikely, in all four observational years, that either blacks or Latinos enlisted from segregated ZIP Codes, and the probability that a person of color enlisted increased rapidly as the ZIP Codes became more diverse.

Additional evidence lends support to the idea that women's enlistment is linked to local economic circumstances. For example, a ZIP Code is more likely to have women enlist, and to have a larger number of female enlistments, when lower percentages of its workers have to cross county lines, or endure long commutes, to get to their jobs.[41] Female enlistment is also more likely from ZIP Codes where fewer adults have completed a four-year college degree, and in places where a larger share of the population has recently moved. We also observe higher numbers of women enlisting from ZIP Codes where a larger share of workers are employed in economic sectors with heavy concentrations of public employment, where veterans enjoy a hiring advantage—public administration, education, and health and social services. We see smaller numbers of women enlist from ZIP Codes with higher shares of workers employed in professional services and finance, insurance, and real estate, where being a veteran brings no specific, guaranteed advantage.

UPDATING THE CONTEMPORARY SITUATION

Our findings demonstrate that diverse neighborhoods are more likely to generate female enlistment than are black or white segregated neighborhoods, and that larger numbers of women enlist from more diverse neighborhoods. These differences hold when taking into account a number of economic and social factors that might be linked to enlistment or to segregation. But what does that mean? Why should we care? And what are the real consequences?

Surely Americans hold a diversity of ideological opinions about whether joining the armed forces is a desirable choice. Our argument is not to encourage or discourage enlistment, but merely to point out how the military serves as a key institution of redistribution, both to active duty personnel and to veterans. To the extent that gender-based differences persist in military participation, men and women will have unequal ability to make claims on the economic benefits available through this institution.

Our findings contribute to the body of literature that links segregation with unequal access to key social institutions. Prior research has shown that racial and economic integration across cities is associated with increased access to education, healthcare, and other supports that have been systematically disinvested from many segregated urban neighborhoods.[42] We suggest that reducing gender inequalities in segregated neighborhoods could lead to more gender egalitarian enlistment patterns. One in four American teens do not meet the armed forces' minimum standards for educational credentialing, cognitive capacity, and/or physical fitness, and would be rejected if they attempted to enlist.[43] Many of the factors that block women's eligibility for serving in the armed forces are conditions that are prevalent in segregated neighborhoods of concentrated poverty: health disparities, such as asthma and obesity, and educational disparities, such as lower rates of attaining a high school diploma.

While disparities in racial inequality and the benefits of military service have been examined,[44] these issues have been largely ignored as a continuing source of gender inequality. We also know very little about how residential segregation operates in combination with gendered rates of enlistment, and the corresponding gender disparity in men's and women's use of and eligibility for VA benefits. It is possible, for example, that greater gender parity in enlistment could allow more women to access the economic resources needed to help them move into neighborhoods with more desirable opportunity structures and environments.

Our research seeks to move the literature in this direction, but we agree with Dickerson,[45] who proposes that future scholarship should strive to identify the mechanisms through which residential segregation leads to gendered inequalities in employment outcomes. For example, we think that future research should employ an intersectional analysis to identify how gendered patterns in enlistment may differ for men and women of different racial groups, and to test the influence of a host of local economic character-istics that may be associated with differential labor market outcomes for men and women. These characteristics may serve as a link between the two systems of residential segregation and labor force segregation that result in gender disparities. We expect that differential access to education, health-care, and employment for men and women in segregated neighborhoods would influence one's interest in enlisting in the armed forces. Future research should continue to investigate this relationship.

FUTURE DIRECTIONS AND POLICIES

So where does this leave us? On December 3, 2015, Ashton B. Carter, the United States' secretary of defense, announced that all military occupations, including those acknowledged to involve combat, would be open to all quali-fied applicants, regardless of gender.[46] This move toward more complete gen-der integration could have wide-reaching effects for women's advancement within the armed forces, as well as their career opportunities and mobility into higher-paying jobs outside of the military. This is a critical step in the right direction, particularly in advancing women's claims to full citizenship rights. In light of such wide gender disparity in enlistment, and the links we have uncovered between women's enlistment patterns and their residential contexts, it seems, however, that more affirmative steps could be taken.

Given women's significant underrepresentation within this institution, the employment benefits and other opportunities for advancement that are associated with military service reflect a tremendous transfer of public resources to men. Increasing women's access to these benefits will lead to a more gender-egalitarian institution within the military, and may also help to reduce gender inequality as women move from military occupations into the civilian labor force over the course of their careers. Additionally, service in the military is associated with numerous gendered economic outcomes and veterans' benefits, including subsidies for homeownership or small business ownership, preferential hiring in government employment, fund-ing for education, and access to healthcare, additional social services, and pensions.

In the interest of making data-driven policy, the gendered consequences of this relatively generous (by US standards) social safety net should be empirically investigated. To date, we have a (still too limited) body of work that identifies how these policies have affected inequality between races and across cohorts, but much less work that interrogates consequences by gender. In addition to comparisons between male and female veterans, or between women who are and are not veterans, scholars and policymakers also need to know how the severe underrepresentation of women in the military perpetuates gender inequality, and transfers economic resources from women (as taxpayers) to men. Only with access to complete information can we competently suggest policy remedies.

Similarly, in light of our findings about the link between segregation and lack of participation in this institution, there is a need for residents, policymakers, city planners, and legislators to distinguish between policies that produce segregation and those that produce integration. Policies that promote integration help to enforce antidiscrimination laws, while also protecting and expanding affordable housing for residents at the lowest income levels to attain housing in their preferred neighborhoods. Among others, these policies may include rental vouchers for low-income households, inclusionary zoning that requires a percentage of units in any new development to be reserved for low-income households, or incentives for real estate developers to include in their plans affordable, 3+ bedroom units that are suitable for family housing.

One promising development at the federal level is the Department of Housing and Urban Development's adoption of a new rule for Affirmatively Furthering Fair Housing (AFFH), which was announced in 2015.[47] AFFH aims to provide cities and communities with the tools, resources, and guidance necessary to plan, implement, and adopt policies that support economic and racial residential integration. In an effort to better enforce one of the provisions of the Fair Housing Act of 1968, the new rule requires that communities complete a Fair Housing Assessment, using data made available through HUD, to identify barriers to integration and the factors within the community that contribute to these patterns. This effort complements other provisions of the Fair Housing Act that prohibit discrimination. Such a step, we hope, will hasten the decline of racial residential segregation, and in turn reduce men and women's disparate experiences in segregated neighborhoods.

NOTES

1. Dickerson, Niki T. 2002. "Is Racial Exclusion Gendered? The Role of Residential Segregation in the Employment Status of Black Women and Men in the US." *Feminist Economics* 8 (2): 199–208.

2. Spain, Daphne. 2005. "What Happened to Gender Relations on the Way from Chicago to Los Angeles?" In *Gender and Planning: A Reader,* edited by Susan S. Fainstein and Lisa J. Servon, 15–30. New Brunswick, NJ: Rutgers University Press.

3. Glenn, Evelyn Nakano. 2004. *Unequal Freedom: How Race and Gender Shaped American Citizenship and Labor.* Cambridge, MA: Harvard University

Press; Ken, Ivy. 2008. "Beyond the Intersection: A New Culinary Metaphor for Race-Class-Gender Studies." *Sociological Theory* 26 (2): 152–172; Ken, Ivy. 2010. *Digesting Race, Class, and Gender: Sugar as a Metaphor.* New York: Palgrave McMillan.

4. Office of the Deputy Assistant Secretary of Defense (Military Community and Family Policy). 2013. *2012 Demographics. Profile of the Military Community.* Washington, DC: Department of Defense.

5. Campbell, Alec. 2004. "The Invisible Welfare State: Establishing the Phenomena of Twentieth Century Veteran's Benefits." *Journal of Political and Military Sociology* 32 (2): 249–267.

6. Wilson, William Julius. 2009. *More Than Just Race: Being Black and Poor in the Inner City.* New York: Norton.

7. Massey, Douglass S., and Nancy A. Denton. 1993. *American Apartheid: Segregation and the Making of the Underclass.* Cambridge, MA: Harvard University Press; Wilson (2009).

8. Reid, Megan. 2010. "Gender and Race in the History of Housing Policy and Research: From Industrialization to Hurricane Katrina." *Sociology Compass* 4:180–192; Howard, Clayton. 2013. "Building a Family-Friendly Metropolis: Sexuality, the State, and Postwar Housing Policy." *Journal of Urban History* 39 (5): 933–955; Howard, Madeline. 2013. "Subsidized Housing Policy: Defining the Family." *Berkeley Journal of Gender, Law, and Justice* 22 (1); Hayden, Dolores. 2005. "What Would a Nonsexist City Be Like? Speculations on Housing, Urban Design, and Human Work." In *Gender and Planning: A Reader,* edited by Susan S. Fainstein and Lisa J. Servon, 47–66. New Brunswick, NJ: Rutgers University Press.

9. England, Kim V. L. 1991. "Gender Relations and the Spatial Structure of the City." *Geoforum* 22 (2); C. Howard (2013).

10. M. Howard (2013).

11. Friedman, Lawrence M. 1966. "Public Housing and the Poor: An Overview." *California Law Review* 54 (2): 642–669; McFadden, Joan R. 1993. "Housing Policy in the United States: A Contemporary Analysis." *Housing and Society* 19 (2).

12. Katznelson, Ira. 2006. *When Affirmative Action Was White: The Untold History of Racial Inequality in Twentieth Century America.* New York: Norton.

13. Jackson, Kenneth T. 1985. "Federal Subsidy and the Suburban Dream: How Washington Changed the American Housing Market." In *Crabgrass Frontier: The Suburbanization of the United States,* 190–218. New York: Oxford University Press; US Riot Commission. 1968. *Report of the National Advisory Commission on Civil Disorders.* New York: Bantam; Wilson (2009); Massey and Denton (1993).

14. Reid (2010).

15. Katznelson (2006).

16. Sullivan, Laura, Tatjana Meschede, Lars Dietrich, Thomas Shapiro, Amy Traub, Catherine Ruetschlin, and Tamara Draut. 2015. *The Racial Wealth Gap: Why Policy Matters.* New York: Demos and the Institute for Assets and Social Policy, Brandeis University.

17. Wilson (2009).

18. Collins, Jane L., and Victoria Mayer. 2010. *Both Hands Tied: Welfare Reform and the Race to the Bottom in the Low-Wage Labor Market.* Chicago: University of Chicago Press; Collins, Patricia Hill. 2000. *Black Feminist Thought: Knowledge, Consciousness, and the Politics of Empowerment.* 2nd ed. New York: Routledge; Wilson (2009).

19. Kain, John F. "Housing Segregation, Negro Employment and Metropolitan Decentralization." *Quarterly Journal of Economics* 82:175–197.

20. Pager, Devah. 2007. *Marked: Race, Crime, and Finding Work in an Era of Mass Incarceration.* Chicago: University of Chicago Press; Roman, Caterina Gouvis, and Jeremy Travis. 2006. "Where Will I Sleep Tomorrow? Housing, Homelessness, and the Returning Prisoner." *Housing Policy Debate* 17 (2): 389–418; Western, Bruce, Anthony A. Braga, Jaclyn Davis, and Catherine Sirois. 2015. "Stress and Hardship after Prison." *American Journal of Sociology* 120 (5): 1512–1547.

21. McCall, Leslie. 2000a. "Gender and the New Inequality: Explaining the College/Non-College Wage Gap." *American Sociological Review* 65 (2): 234–255; McCall, Leslie. 2000b. "Explaining Levels of Within-Group Wage Inequality in US Labor Markets." *Demography* 37 (4): 415–430.

22. Thomas, Melvin, and Richard Moye. 2015. "Race, Class, and Gender and the Impact of Racial Segregation on Black-White Income Inequality." *Sociology of Race and Ethnicity* 1 (4): 490–502.

23. Dickerson (2002).

24. Segal, David R. 1989. *Recruiting for Uncle Sam: Citizenship and Military Manpower Policy.* Lawrence: University Press of Kansas.

25. Fenner, Lorry M. 1998. "Either You Need These Women or You Do Not: Informing the Debate on Military Service and Citizenship." *Gender Issues* 16 (3): 5–32.

26. Bellafaire, Judith Lawrence. 2006. "Public Service Role Models: The First Women of the Defense Advisory Committee on Women in the Service." *Armed Forces and Society* 32 (3): 424–436.

27. Janowitz, Morris. 1960. *The Professional Soldier: A Social and Political Portrait.* Glencoe, IL: Free Press.

28. Office of the Deputy Assistant Secretary of Defense (2013).

29. Snyder, R. Clare. 2003. "The Citizen-Soldier Tradition and Gender Integration in the U.S. Military." *Armed Forces & Society* 29 (2): 185–204.

30. Asch, Beth J., M. Rebecca Kilburn, and Jacob Alex Klerman. 1999. *Attracting College-Bound Youth into the Military: Toward the Development of New Recruiting Policy Options.* Santa Monica, CA: RAND Corporation.

31. United States Government Accountability Office. 2011. *DOD Education Benefits: Increased Oversight of Tuition Assistance Program Is Needed.* Washington, DC: United States Government Accountability Office.

32. Office of Public and Intergovernmental Affairs. 2013a. "VA and the Post 9/11 GI Bill." US Department of Veterans Affairs. www.va.gov/opa/issues /post_911_gibill.asp; Office of Public and Intergovernmental Affairs. 2013b. "One Million Now Benefit from Post-9/11 GI Bill." November 8, 2013. http://va.gov /opa/pressrel/pressrelease.cfm?id = 2490.

33. Department of Veterans Affairs. 2014. "FY13 Summary of Expenditures by State, Expenditures in $000s." www.va.gov/vetdata/expenditures.asp.

34. Craig, Jessica, and Holly Foster. 2013. "Desistance in the Transition to Adulthood: The Roles of Marriage, Military, and Gender." *Deviant Behavior* 34 (3): 208–223.

35. Teachman, Jay, and Lucky Tedrow. 2014. "Delinquent Behavior, the Transition to Adulthood, and the Likelihood of Military Enlistment." *Social Science Research* 45:46–55.

36. Teachman and Tedrow (2014).

37. Lundquist, Jennifer Hickes. 2008. "Ethnic and Gender Satisfaction in the Military: The Effect of a Meritocratic Institution." *American Sociological Review* 73:477–496.

38. Campbell (2004).

39. Wilson, George, Vincent J. Roscigno, and Matt Huffman. 2015. "Racial Income Inequality and Public Sector Privatization." *Social Problems* 62:163–185.

40. Cooney, Richard T., Mady Wechsler Segal, David R. Segal, and William W. Falk. 2003. "Racial Differences in the Impact of Military Service on the Socioeconomic Status of Women Veterans." *Armed Forces and Society* 30 (1): 53–86.

41. These effects are less consistent in predicting the number of enlistments, and the relationship between spatial mismatch and the probability of any female enlistments emerges in 1995.

42. Hartmann, Chester, and Gregory Squires. 2010. *The Integration Debate: Competing Futures for American Cities.* New York: Routledge; Cashin, Sheryll. 2005. *Failures of Integration: How Race and Class Are Undermining the American Dream.* New York: Public Affairs.

43. Asch, Beth J., Christopher Buck, Jacob Alex Klerman, Meredith Kleykamp, and David S. Loughran. 2009. *Military Enlistment of Hispanic Youth: Obstacles and Opportunities.* Santa Monica, CA: RAND Corporation.

44. Katznelson (2006).

45. Dickerson (2002).

46. Rosenberg, Matthew, and Dave Phillips. 2015. "All Combat Roles Now Open to Women, Defense Secretary Says." *New York Times,* December 3.

47. Greene, Solomon, and Erika C. Poethig. 2015. "Creating Place of Opportunity: HUD's New Data and Community Driven Approach." Washington, DC: Urban Institute.

7. Conference Realignment and Its Impact on Women Student-Athletes

Earl Smith and Angela J. Hattery

Maya Moore plays forward for the WNBA Minnesota Lynx. Her story is similar to all women who play intercollegiate and professional sports: (In) Visibility. Moore played college basketball for the University of Connecticut, winning two NCAA national championships (2009 & 2010), earning All-Star recognition across four years, and helping to put UConn on the national basketball map. Once she entered the women's professional basketball league, the WNBA, she saw a considerable drop in attention to women playing basketball. Empty seats. No national TV coverage and as she put it: (In)Visibility:[1]

> *Wait, what happened here? That's a question we as WNBA players ask ourselves. We go from amazing AAU experiences to high school All-American games to the excitement and significant platform of the collegiate level to . . . [a]ll of that visibility to . . . this. Less coverage. Empty seats. Fewer eyeballs. In college, your coaches tell you to stay focused on your team and the game—not the media attention. But you know you're on national television. You know people are following you. You can feel the excitement. And then as a professional, all of that momentum, all of that passion, all of that support—the ball of momentum is deflating before my eyes. I went No. 1 in the 2011 WNBA Draft. That's when I felt the drop. Gone.*

Moore's story is similar to that of most women who play intercollegiate sport and enter one of the few opportunities to play professional sports, whether in basketball, Mixed Martial Arts (MMA) fighting, ski sports, or track and field. As we have observed in other research on women in sports, we argue in this chapter that conference realignment pushes women athletes further from the center of the conversation.

The Maya Moore story *is* the story of women who play sports. That story just got worse, especially at the intercollegiate level of sports participation as we analyze in this chapter. Why? Conference realignment. Conference realignment is one of the most important issues facing intercollegiate sports today.[2] This is especially true with the establishment of the "Power 5" conferences. The use of the term "power" is deliberate. This is precisely what conference realignment is about, the concentration of power, power over resource allocation, power over scheduling, power over establishing national championships, in a relatively small number of athletic programs. The Power 5 conferences are the 65 universities and colleges organized into 5 conferences, the ACC, SEC, Big 10, Big 12, and Pac 12. Prior to the birth of the "Power 5" the most elite athletic programs were organized into 6 conferences—the SEC, the ACC, the Big 10, the Big 12, the Pac 10, and the Big East, which were then referred to as Division 1, with all of the other Division 1 programs belonging to Division 1A conferences. During the conference realignment explosion of 2012 and 2013 the Big East was dismantled, and each of the surviving conferences that became the Power 5 reorganized, with some losing teams (the Big 12 now only has eight teams) and some adding teams (the Big 10 now has 14 teams). After the dust settled, the total number of teams in the NCAA's most elite set of conferences grew by only 1, from 64 to 65. And thus the total number of athletes, playing on both men's and women's teams, competing in the most elite set of conferences did not change appreciably.

The Power 5 conferences have "won" several of the battles with the NCAA over power that have allowed them to have more control over their programs than colleges and universities in the other athletic conferences. For example, the teams in the Power 5 have much greater autonomy from the NCAA, including the vested authority to run championship events in the sport of football. Add to this the "cost of attendance" plans, wherein the Power 5 conferences, whose member schools have more financial capital, allow programs like Michigan, Alabama, and other "powerhouse" athletic programs to have the ability to set in place "cost of attendance" funds to be paid directly to their football and basketball players at $5,000 to $6,000 per player per year. Institutions outside of the Power 5 have fewer resources; hence, athletes in those conferences will receive less money, if any at all.

Because power is at stake, athletic programs have been scrambling to gain entry into one of the Power 5 conferences. The commissioners of the Power 5 conferences have made admission not only difficult but also costly. The University of Maryland, for example, paid $50 million dollars to exit the ACC and enter the Big 10. And any athletic program that seeks entrance into a Power 5 conference must demonstrate not only their ability to compete on the national stage, but also their ability to fill stadiums beyond 25,000 seats and provide a higher number of scholarships to all sports, including 85 scholarships to the football team. These requirements ensure that the Power 5 conferences are comprised only of the most elite athletic programs and those with the financial resources to afford the standards imposed by the conference. For example, the University of Connecticut, despite its storied reputation in both men's and women's basketball, was left out of the Power 5 conferences during the dismantling of the Big East, largely because of its football program, which was underperforming and unable to garner all of the resources necessary. The goal, then, of the Power 5 conferences is to grow, yes, but only to grow by consolidating the most elite and wealthy programs while shedding those that do not meet these strict requirements.

Though the focus of this chapter is on the Power 5 conferences, it is important to note that there has been a trickle-down effect. As programs like the University of Connecticut get shifted to midmajor conferences, programs in the midmajor conferences shuffled to improve their status by moving to a midmajor with a better athletic reputation and more resources. The university where we are currently employed, George Mason, got into the game and paid $1 million dollars to move out of the Colonial Athletic Conference and into the American Athletic Conference, all in an attempt to better its position.

Both the establishment of the Power 5 conferences and the cost of attendance will have a significant impact on maintaining any progress that was made since the implementation of Title IX in 1972.

In this chapter the goal is to analyze the question posed long ago by sociologist Harry Edwards as well as others over the mechanisms that allowed for the exploitation of the student-athlete, especially at the level of intercollegiate competitive sports.[3] Consistent with a feminist approach to research, we interrogate not only those disadvantaged by the distribution of resources and opportunities in SportsWorld but also those who benefit from a structure that preferences some athletes and sports over others and herein this reference is to women athletes.

Definitionally speaking, "SportsWorld" is a term coined by one of the authors, Earl Smith, and is defined as the constellation of major institutions in not only American society but also abroad that interconnects the economic, political, societal, and commercial interests that revolve around the making of money for athletic programs. Going further, SportsWorld refers to local, regional, and international webs of interest that coalesce around institutional sports teams and their events (e.g., March Madness) and the hosting of American football and men's basketball games in foreign lands. These events may also include booster club fundraising activities, special financial deals to booster club members at local automobile dealers, the awarding of construction company contracts, the setting up of bank accounts at local banking institutions, the rental of hotel beds and conference rooms for *home games,* and/or educational institutions, including high schools, that overall have become dependent on each other in the promotion of athletics from Little League play to professional games.[4]

This chapter will examine the recent and dramatic conference realignment movement. At times this refers to institutions moving to a new conference or teams within institutions being in different conferences. Notre Dame is the best example of this latter change. Notre Dame moved to the Atlantic Coast Conference (ACC) in all sports except football, which remains independent. Though colleges and universities have engaged in shuffling for many decades, between 2012 and 2013, 20 percent of Division 1 colleges and universities "switched" athletic conferences. Therefore, our analysis is focused on this time frame. We should note that the term "conference realignment" only comes into widespread use during this time period reflecting the enormity of the shift.

We examine this realignment movement that has taken place in intercollegiate sport and analyze the ways in which this movement further exacerbates the disadvantaging of women student-athletes while pandering to the male student-athletes playing the sports of football and basketball.

Throughout the chapter, we use Gaul's language of "poor sports" rather than the often-used "Olympic Sports"; they are called "poor sports"

> because they had no money of their own and no visible way of making any, short of lucking into a rich benefactor. These were the sports living from paycheck to paycheck—track and field, field hockey, women's rowing, the programs that athletic directors often refer to as the "Olympic sports" because you only see them on television once every four years.[5]

This conceptualization of "poor sports" is useful in examining both the impetus for and the impact of conference realignment on athletic programs, teams, coaches, and student-athletes. Though there are always individual differences, there are several distinct patterns to the ways in which resources are allocated in athletic programs, across conferences, and even across divisions. As noted, conference realignment is about the consolidation of power and resources. Clearly, then all athletic programs that have membership in the Power 5 will generally have larger athletic budgets than those in the other conferences. For example, an athletic program in a midmajor conference will have an annual budget ranging from $75 to $100 million, whereas athletic programs in the Power 5 have budgets that often exceed $150 million dollars. In contrast, the average Division 2 athletic program will have an annual budget that is only about 10 percent of that associated with a midmajor program, or approximately $10 million. It goes without saying, then, that there are significantly more resources available to teams, including access to travel, equipment, coaches, salary and benefits (cars, country club memberships), and, of course, scholarships for athletes. In fact, this is crystal clear in the fact that the scholarship requirements for athletic programs to qualify for membership in Division 2 are significantly lower than Division 1, with most athletes in all sports receiving only partial scholarships, if they receive scholarships at all, which many student-athletes playing "poor sports" do not.

Across conferences and divisions, sport and gender also shape resource allocation. Almost without exception, football programs receive the bulk of the resources, even when we consider per capita spending. The only exceptions to this are the resources allocated for a very small number of head basketball coaches, including Mike Krzyzewski, the head basketball coach at Duke University, who demand extraordinary salaries and travel budgets. With regard to gender, again, consistent across conferences and divisions, *there are no women's teams with greater resource allocation than comparable men's teams.* As our previous research demonstrated, the gender gap in resource allocation is highest in the most resourced sports, especially basketball, and lowest in what Gaul terms "poor sports" like track and field. The logic follows such that gender disparities in resources are narrower in the midmajor conferences and in Division 2, but in all cases, gender continues to shape resource allocation.

LITERATURE REVIEW

The arrangement of playing intercollegiate sports in conferences has existed since before the setup of the National Collegiate Athletic Association (NCAA) in 1906. The modern era of NCAA governance over intercollegiate athletics begins in 1951 with the reign of the late Walter Byers,[6] lasting until 1988. It is under Byers's rule that the exchange for playing a sport was rewarded with an athletic scholarship, a practice that has not only persisted but grown in the decades since its inception. It is critical to note that athletic scholarships did not come to women student-athletes until 1974,[7] and they continue to provide less financial support than scholarships for men's teams, even today, just one example of the gender inequality among student-athletes.

Byers is also the architect of the concept "student-athlete," which was created to do two things:

1. Establish that college athletes are students first and athletes second;

2. Clearly establish that the scholarship is an academic, not athletic, award, so as to protect the NCAA in legal battles that may arise over worker compensation benefits.

Consistent with the classic rules of the scientific research model wherein the researchers read critically the existing literature in order to situate their research, we conducted a thorough review of the existing literature and came up with only a few scholarly works on conference realignment. This is not surprising given that the massive conference realignment we describe in this chapter really only began in 2011, and thus there has not been an adequate amount of time for scholarly research to be conducted, vetted, and published.[8] The few publications we did find were by legal scholars and most focused primarily on debating the rules of disengagement from one conference and moving to another.[9] None took on questions of gender inequalities. This is not surprising for several reasons, including the fact that overall there is little attention to discussion of gender inequality in the research on SportsWorld; this is exacerbated in discussions about conference realignment by the fact that the entire conference realignment movement is all about football,[10] a sport women are not allowed to play.

Thus, most of the literature that frames our argument comes from documents and journalistic accounts from noted sports writers who cover college sports. They, too, have focused their discussions on football and, to a lesser degree, basketball. One of the major basketball coaches in college sports said as much; we quote from legendary Syracuse basketball coach Jim Boehiem responding to a reporter about leaving the Big East conference and moving to the Atlantic Coast Conference (ACC):

> Where would you want to go to a tournament for five days? Let's see: Greensboro, North Carolina or New York City? Jeez. Let me think about that and get back to you.

Coach Boehiem goes even further illustrating his disappointment with moving out of the then most powerful basketball conference in the country, the Big East:

"If conference commissioners were the founding fathers of this country, we would have Guatemala, Uruguay and Argentina in the United States," Boeheim said. "This audience knows why we are doing this. There's two reasons: Money and football . . . We're going to end up with mega conferences and 10 years from now either I'm going to be dead wrong or everybody is going to be like, why did we do this again? Why is Alabama playing Texas A & M this week and going to Texas Tech next weekend? And why is Syracuse going to Miami in basketball this week and next week they're going to play Florida State?"[11]

In short, it is clear to sports writers, coaches, and legal scholars that conference realignment is all about football. Though a few commentators and coaches have raised issues related to men's basketball, virtually no one until now has focused on the impact of conference realignment on women's teams and women athletes.

Theoretical Framework

We use two theoretical lenses to frame our analysis, Merton's theory of accumulation of advantage and disadvantage[12] and feminist theory.

Merton's theory of accumulation of advantages and disadvantages can be applied to intercollegiate sports,[13] providing the framework for understanding the uneven distribution of resources and talent in a relatively small pool (just 120 colleges and universities field Division 1 football and just more than 300 round out Division 1 men's basketball) that is at the root of conference realignment. The theory demonstrates that even small initial imbalances accumulate and are compounded by conference realignment. Specifically, conference realignment was more than a random movement of teams, but rather a deliberate concentration of power located in what were determined to be the most powerful conferences—now dubbed "the Power 5." The advantages that accrue to even the least successful athletic departments who are members of one of the Power 5 conferences dwarf the most successful programs that are unfortunate enough to be excluded and housed in an inferior conference.

Much of the "power" associated with the Power 5 conferences results from a series of financial decisions that include TV rights, seat taxes and other money, and prestige-generating strategies.[14] One illustration is the consummation of the 24-hour—around the clock—radio and TV deal that the University of Texas made public on January 19, 2011. This arrangement is with ESPN and the University of Texas IMG College, a company that handles marketing and licensing contracts for the university, for 20 years and is worth at least $300 million dollars.[15] Once Texas opened the door to

establishing television contracts that are independent, immune to conference administration oversight, and very lucrative, other institutions and
entire conferences followed suit. Schools began jockeying for membership
in the conferences with the most lucrative television contracts. At the
same time as the television contracts were being negotiated, the Bowl
Championship Series (BCS) was establishing the first playoff system in
college football. This playoff was negotiated outside of the auspices of the
NCAA and contributed significantly to conference jumping, as every major
athletic program understood the importance of being in a conference
that would be included, or not included, by the BCS commissioners in the
playoff system. And once conference realignment got started it would not
end. Schools were jumping all over the map, many in a geographically
illogical way.[16]

Feminist theory provides the framework for understanding more deeply
and in more nuanced ways the process by which the accumulation of
advantage to men's teams and male athletes in the Power 5 conferences
results in a net disadvantage for women's teams and female athletes. The
riches accumulated in the Power 5 conferences are not distributed equitably
to all of its members, with the most glaring inequality remaining that associated with gender.

Lorber[17] elucidates gender as a social structure: gender is

> an institution that establishes patterns of expectations for individuals,
> orders the social processes of everyday life, is built into the everyday
> social organization of society, such as the economy, ideology, the family,
> and politics, and is also an entity in and of itself.

Feminist theory is a framework that focuses on the ways in which gender
as a social structure shapes the outcomes for individuals who identify as or
are perceived to be female. Feminist theorists, including Cynthia Fuchs
Epstein, in her Presidential Address to the American Sociological Society,
have argued persuasively that, though gender inequality is intimately connected with and mutually supportive of other systems of oppression including racism and classism, gender oppression is the most primary and fundamental structure organizing inequality.[18] In short, though there are
variations by race, class, sexuality, age, ability, religion, and so forth, there is
no place or time in the world in which it is better to be a woman than a man.

We analyze the impact of conference realignment through a feminist
lens because SportsWorld, like every other institution, is gendered, and
women are disadvantaged in every case. Title IX is based on the feminist
presumption, which was and continues to be demonstrated empirically, that

gender inequality and gender discrimination exist in all areas of the social world and in all social institutions, including in higher education and in particular in SportsWorld.[19] The women who compete in SportsWorld have fewer opportunities, earn less money, and have very few routes for professional careers as coaches, as analysts, and in leadership positions such as athletic directors or conference commissioners. The persistence of gender inequality 45 years after the passage of Title IX is a clear testament to the power of gender as a social structure, and therefore, *not* attending to gender in a discussion of SportsWorld, and in this case conference realignment, is to render invisible the gendered distribution of power and privilege and access that pervades the world of sports, from the playing fields of Little League to the professional ranks of modern day sports.

THE CASE STUDY: CONFERENCE REALIGNMENT AND THE IMPACT ON WOMEN'S TEAMS AND WOMEN ATHLETES

For this chapter "conference realignment" is to mean the systematic movement of institutions from one athletic conference to another in order to concentrate power and resources as well as create a multitiered system of haves and have-nots. As stated above, the movement from one conference to another is primarily about football, yet it has implications for all NCAA sports and all student-athletes who play them.

Conference Realignment: An Overview

Though colleges and universities have moved between conferences in the past, most of this previous movement has been about conference expansion. What is unique about the movement since 2012 is both the cause and the volume of movement. Since 2012 approximately 13 teams, or 20 percent of the programs in Division 1, moved to a new conference. Only one team— Utah—moved *into* the newly configured Power 5 conferences, whereas all of the other movement involved institutions shifting from one powerful conference to another. Notably, five (West Virginia, Notre Dame, Pittsburg, Syracuse, and Louisville) of the 13 teams moved out of the previously powerful Big East and into the newly configured Power 5 conferences. A double winner in all of this movement is Notre Dame; they maintain the independence of their football program (and their NBC TV contract worth $38 million dollars) while moving to the ACC in basketball and all other sports.

Not only did teams move but the realignment involved the dismantling of a major conference—the Big East, which no longer includes institutions with football programs and focuses instead on retaining its title as the premier league for men's college basketball. We note that the biggest "loser" in this reconfiguration is arguably the University of Connecticut (UConn), which was forced out of the old Big East because they do field a football team. It is now in the American Athletic Conference. We use the term "loser" to mean UConn wanted to move to a Power 5 conference and did not receive any invitations. Another "loser" has to be Boise State. Boise jumped to the Big East and after they moved there the Big East dissolved. Hence, Boise had to move back to the Mountain West Conference. Using Merton's typology here, UConn moved from a major conference playing on a major stage to the American Athletic Conference, putting them in a position where, as Merton would say, they are now competing in a nonaccumulating conference.

The Gender Implications of Conference Realignment

We now turn to the unintended consequences of conference realignment as it impacts female student-athletes and Title IX. Title IX can be applied to any aspect of the educational experience, although its most common application has been to the world of sports. And, as a result, there have been many significant gains. For example, in 1972, roughly 300,000 females competed in high school athletics. That figure skyrocketed to 3.2 million girls participating by 2010–2011. Yet, this increase of girls and women in sports has a downside as well. According to Acosta and Carpenter and Hattery, the equality promised via the Title IX legislation has not yet been fully achieved. As we argue herein, though most colleges and universities are technically in compliance with Title IX—they meet the letter of the law—few offer truly equal or even equitable experiences for female and male athletes, leaving the spirit of the law unmet. For example, Hattery[20] notes that, despite the explosion in athletic participation for girls and women, the opportunities for women to coach have declined precipitously, from 95 percent of women's basketball teams being coached by women in 1972 to less than 50 percent in 2015. In 2015 sociologist Michael Messner and his colleague Cheryl Cooky wrote[21] that women's sports continue to receive little coverage in the media. Sociologist Mary Jo Kane from the University of Minnesota underscored the substance of the research,[22] and several years later, when the Minnesota Lynx won the Women's National Basketball title, not one major TV network, including ESPN, covered the achievement, even though the Lynx have won this championship title three times in the last five years, a feat few NBA teams have accomplished. Ironically, the star player on the Lynx, Maya Moore, made her comments about the lack of media attention on the WNBA *before* she led her team to their third WNBA championship.

A common experience that takes place on college and university campuses occurs when there are highly successful women's teams and mediocre men's teams. For example, we were privileged to teach at a small liberal arts university in the southeast in the early 2000s when the women's field hockey team "three-peated" winning the NCAA Division 1 title, a record. In the fall of 2004 they won their third national championship, and that same fall the football team won the ACC conference title. In response, the football players were featured at a ceremony that the entire campus attended. And it was indeed wonderful to celebrate with them. Sadly, there was not even a mention of the incredible feat the women field hockey players had accomplished, many of them contributing to all three of the national championship wins. In response, the team wrote an open letter to the university expressing their hurt in not even being acknowledged. In their case, they were denied a compensatory celebration. The letter of the law may have been met, but definitely not the spirit of the law. The story told to us is amazing and it goes like this:

> We were winners on the field. We won three straight national NCAA titles and not a word of congratulation came from the administration even though they would routinely send out a note telling us how great the football team was even though they could barely win five or six games of a 12-game schedule. To make matters worse we traveled as second-class citizens. The basketball and football teams flew chartered flights. One team even had their own airplane. And for road games we doubled up (triple) in hotel rooms. When we played our home games we did not get to stay in luxury hotels the night before the games nor did we get to have our meals at the pricey steak house in town where the basketball team had all of their home game meals. This duplicitous treatment sucked!

There are many consequences of conference realignment. Not surprisingly, absent in the public and academic discourse on conference realignment is any consideration of the impact of conference realignment on the student-athletes who do not play football or basketball. Digging deeper, in the limited discussions of the costs of conference realignment to student-athletes there is virtually no discussion of the ways in which the impact is *shaped by gender*. In fact gender matters so much in intercollegiate sports, yet no one has stepped back from the euphoria many university presidents, NCAA officials, athletic directors, and coaches feel from the possibilities of money to seriously consider the unintended and unanticipated consequences of the gender implications of conference realignment and specifically the threat to Title IX.

1. The complete and final disruption of the academic mission of colleges and universities as these apply to student-athletes: We simply can no longer say that student-athletes, at least those playing Football Bowl Subdivision (FBS) football and men's basketball, can realistically earn an education, and this is especially detrimental to women student-athletes; for many of these women student-athletes, their only route to an education is via an athletic scholarship;

2. The expectation that conference realignment will turn back some of the gains achieved under Title IX, specifically vis-à-vis the new cost of attendance policy.

Because this movement is so recent, as noted (49 teams were "realigned" on July 1, 2013, alone), there is not yet a scholarly literature on this issue. Thus, our discussion here is very theoretical and is based on examination of news accounts as well as scholarly literature that focuses on discrimination and the second-class citizenship of women student-athletes.

The Dismantling of the "Student" in "Student-Athlete"

One of the hallmarks of conference realignment is disruption of the geographic organization of conferences, and with it, the increased travel that is required to compete in conference games and matches. Extensive travel inevitably means more time away from campus and thus more classes missed and more difficulty completing class assignments. This will likely be exacerbated for female athletes, whose teams rarely fly to competitions and instead are already relegated to long bus trips. We have reviewed decades' worth of graduation rate data,[23] which shows disturbingly low graduation rates for African American men who play football and basketball. Based on data obtained in 2014, among student-athletes in the Power 5 conferences, Black football players graduated at a record high rate of 68 percent. The overall rate for black athletes, which has typically lagged behind that of white athletes, was 70 percent, a 3-percentage-point increase from 2013. Women continue to outpace their male counterparts, with white female athletes graduating at a rate of 93 percent and black female athletes graduating at a rate of 81 percent, a disturbing racialized trend. We anticipate that this trend in lower graduation rates for Black women will be exacerbated under conference realignment.[24] Why? Because, like football and men's basketball players, conference realignment will keep women's basketball players away from campus for longer periods of time, they will miss more classes and tutoring sessions, and they will have less time to complete work.

Why do we care if women student-athletes graduate or not? First of all, we should care. As the NCAA is fond of advertising, there are more than 400,000 student-athletes and most will "go pro" in something other than sports. And whether they want to believe it or not, this applies to the vast majority of women who play college sports as well. Thus, getting a college education is still their primary route to accessing the American Dream. Why? Because so few of these athletes will ever make it to the professional leagues, a fact exacerbated for women because of the overall dearth of professional opportunities available for women as athletes or coaches.[25] Take, for example, professional women's basketball, as Maya Moore laments. With only 12 teams in the league, there are typically no more than 25 players drafted in any given year, which does not provide much opportunity for the thousands of women playing college basketball at the Division 1 level.

Turning Back Title IX

As we have demonstrated elsewhere,[26] college and university athletic departments are nearly always in compliance with Title IX, but they rarely deliver an equal or even equitable experience for women's teams and female athletes. Our second concern is that conference realignment may further exacerbate this inequality, what we refer to as the "spirit" of Title IX. For example, resource differences almost always produce experiential differences. That is to suggest that male athletes playing "revenue generating sports" (football and basketball) are far more likely to travel by air, travel on chartered flights, and stay in more upscale hotels than their female counterparts and those men playing "poor sports," who are far more likely to travel by van, even long distances, and often report staying in substandard motels. Men's basketball players report pregame meals for home games being eaten in upscale steak houses whereas women's basketball players report having pregame meals catered by the on-campus food provider (e.g., Aramark, Sodhexho). Even farther down the rung, cross country runners, both men and women, report being given $5 each and stopping at a convenience store to pick up pregame food; granola bars for athletes who routinely run 100 miles per week!

In 2008 we used the Equity in Athletics Data (EADA) to analyze the financial records of men's and women's basketball and soccer teams at 50 Division 1 colleges and universities. We quote directly from that paper here:[27]

> We chose to analyze soccer and basketball for several reasons. First, the majority of schools in our sample had basketball and soccer teams for both men and women. Second, scholars have identified soccer as a sport in which gender equity has been achieved. Third, because basketball is a

high profile, revenue generating sport—increasingly for women as well as men—and soccer is not—for either gender—we were able to explore the presence (or absence) of gender equity in resources in high profile sports as compared to non-revenue sports.

The data in table 7.1 indicate several important measures of continued gender inequity in resource allocation. We summarize:

- Male student-athletes receive, on average, $598 more in aid per year than female student-athletes
- Coaches of male teams earn, on average, $190,310 more than coaches of female teams
- Men's teams have, on average, $271,490 dollars more to spend on recruiting than women's teams

Given the ways in which differences in experience already exist, we can predict that not only will these kinds of differences persist under conference realignment, but because of the pressure to maintain football and men's basketball players and teams at continued luxury levels, without additional sources of revenue generated by college and university athletic programs, these inequalities will likely worsen. Conference realignment has disrupted the natural geographical boundaries that shaped most conferences before 2012. These changes increase the costs of travel to compete in conference contests. The additional resources that football teams, men's basketball teams, and to a lesser extent women's basketball teams will require for increased air travel and perhaps additional hotel nights, depending upon the game schedule, will have to come from somewhere. And that "somewhere" will be further gutting the support of the already under resourced "poor sports."

Many college and university athletic departments are "resolving" these challenges by restricting contests for "poor sports" to local competition that is almost always outside of the conference. In other words, some teams will travel more and some will travel less. For example, field hockey and lacrosse are primarily east coast sports. So, when the University of Maryland moved from the ACC to the Big 10 they moved from a lacrosse and field hockey powerhouse conference to a conference that has few teams fielding either sport. The Maryland lacrosse and field hockey teams may now find themselves playing mostly out-of-conference matches, against their former ACC rivals as well as teams like Johns Hopkins, most of which are within a five-hour drive, significantly closer than other teams in the Big 10. This is not inherently problematic, as teams may continue to play the best compe-

TABLE 7.1 Gender Differences (Men-Women) in Selected College Sports Expenditures

	Soccer operating expenses	Soccer per-capita spending	Basketball operating expenses	Basketball per capita spending	Aid-scholarships-per capita women	Aid-scholarships-per capita men	Head coach salary TEAMS	Recruiting spending
Mean	−22,708	−901	275,050	12,303	9,633	10,231	190,310	271,490
Median	−4,100	−165	211,559	8,786	9,491	9,921	154,779	225,818
Standard Deviation	89149	2737	280371	21271	3900	3614	195104	210586

tition in out-of-conference contests, but it does produce a different experience. It may engender less allegiance to the conference for these athletes and in some cases it may result in competing on a significantly smaller stage and with less media attention for sports that already receive only a fraction of the media coverage afforded to football. This is yet another example of failing to meet the "spirit" of Title IX. Gender continues to shape the experiences of student-athletes; women's basketball players will bear the burden, as will men's basketball and football players, of longer travel, and women playing "poor sports" will travel less but be less engaged in their conferences and potentially have fewer opportunities to perform on a bigger stage. Additionally, in many ways, travel will pit women against each other: basketball players will have an experience that is closer to that of male athletes than to that of their female counterparts.

Cost of Attendance

Making matters worse is a new policy referred to as "cost of attendance." Cost of attendance (COA) was approved by the NCAA in 2015 and allows college and university athletic departments to provide cash payouts to student-athletes as a measure to close the gap between what the scholarship and housing allowance pay for and the actual cost to attend college. For example, anyone who has been to college or who has paid tuition knows that the estimates produced by financial aid offices do not account for things like travel to and from campus each semester, the cost of necessities like haircuts and clothes and automobile oil changes, and many of the other items that college students truly need. The argument that student-athletes don't have enough money for incidentals was fueled by several high-profile male athletes stating publicly that sometimes they were hungry.

The cost of attendance policy soon followed, thus allowing athletic departments to provide student-athletes with a stipend, based on a series of calculations, that is intended to close that gap between an athletic scholarship and the actual overall cost for attending a college or university. There is no question that there is a gap between the cost estimated by the financial aid office and the actual cost to attend college. That said, we argue that the cost of attendance policy will exacerbate inequalities of all kinds, and particularly the inequalities faced by women student-athletes who play on teams without the plentiful resources that are available for the men who play football and basketball.

The cost of attendance has become a pathway for the "Power 5" conferences to add upward of $160 million a year in additional benefits to student-athletes, thus improving the "haves" ability to recruit.[28] For example, Auburn is already paying all football players a $5000 per year stipend, whereas schools with tighter athletic budgets, like Boston College, are paying just a quarter of that figure. It's not hard to imagine the role that the stipend will play in recruiting! A sport column by *Chronicle of Higher Education* writer Brad Wolverton says that a fear looming is that coaches will take the extra money (COA) and use it in ways not originally intended. He put it thusly:[29]

> But some programs are using the money as a kind of blank check to coaches, allowing them to disperse it largely at their discretion. That could lead coaches to allocate the money based on athletic performance—play better one year, get more money the next—the way they often allocate their scholarship budgets. In other cases, coaches are planning to hand out the extra dollars to players who have the least aid. Coaches have also discussed using the money to add roster spots, putting more players on scholarship rather than helping the players who are already on their teams. Mr. Stricklin says he has discouraged his coaches from taking that approach. "Adding more players or spreading scholarships out among additional athletes defeats the purpose of what we're trying to accomplish here," he says.

Another essential, and often overlooked, way that SportsWorld and conference realignment are gendered is in the way women who are not athletes are used as recruiting tools for the biggest programs in the country, including Oklahoma State, Penn State, Vanderbilt, and the University of Louisville. In the powerhouse programs of football and basketball the athletes are flown in for their recruiting visits. The process includes meeting with coaches and visiting the fields, courts, and other facilities (mainly locker rooms and lounges).

Included in the visit are the social hours set up by the coaches and players to entertain the highly valued recruits. They are sometimes shown the town; in other visits, like those to Oklahoma, Vanderbilt, and Louisville, they are given access to "Hostess Squads" of women who "work" for the athletic department. These women greet the athletes at the airport, take the athletes to dinner, take them around campus to meet other students, and often "escort" them to parties. In the cases of Oklahoma State, Vanderbilt, and most notably Louisville they also have sex with the recruits. The 2015 case at Louisville has garnered significant national attention because of the direct link to the athletic department: the assistant basketball coaches paid female escorts to come to campus, specifically to the basketball dorm, to dance, drink alcohol, and have sex. Based on the testimony of the madam, Louisville coaches paid across a four-year period (2010–2014) over $10,000.[30] All of this, coaches argue, in the name of recruitment.

Although all of this is widely know, ESPN analyst Jalen Rose (a member of the Michigan Fab Five basketball team, 1992–1993) confirmed the importance of using sex to recruit:[31]

> First off, if I'm not getting laid, I'm not coming. I'm not signing. I'm not coming.

The fact that the allegations at Louisville run directly to officials of the university reveals the deliberate and coordinated nature of these recruiting visits and allows for them to be analyzed as not simply individual acts of one coach or one player, like Jalen Rose, but more so institutionally.

CONCLUSION

Conference realignment is perhaps the most significant shaper of the future of intercollegiate sports and also the most unpredictable. Even four years ago there were just whispers about the possibility of massive conference realignment and the probability of individual conferences negotiating lucrative television contracts separate from the NCAA's gaze and control. And, though there have long been discussions and debates about a playoff system in college football, we could not have predicted even just a few years ago the ways in which this playoff system and the television contracts, and the millions and millions of dollars associated with each, would drive conference realignment to the point that on July 1, 2013, 49 teams were involved in moving from one conference to another.

As important as the magnitude of these shifts is, as we argue above, we are quite certain that conference realignment will have consequences that are gendered. Quite simply, we predict that conference realignment and the cost of attendance policy will turn back the clock on Title IX.

Conference realignment coupled with the cost of attendance policy will require many athletic departments to identify and funnel greater resources (e.g., money) to football programs in order to provide cost of attendance funds, which will be critical in recruiting, and to accommodate the increased travel costs that are inevitably associated with conference realignment; the University of Maryland football team must now fly to Lincoln, Nebraska, and the University of Colorado football team must now fly to Seattle. And, though conference commissioners and athletic directors may suggest that joining a power conference will increase revenue, there is no clear indication of exactly how this will happen or that it will. Though the athletic directors will argue that membership in a power conference will give them access to television revenue based on the agreements between a given conference and the broadcaster, how these funds will be distributed remains to be seen. The distribution of television revenue and the payouts when teams compete in the NCAA tournament apply only to men's teams. For example, under the current NCAA structure, each conference is given a percentage of the revenue of the men's basketball tournament based on their representation in the tournament. If eight ACC teams are selected in the field of 64, then the ACC will receive one-eighth of all revenue from that round. And the same applies in subsequent rounds. In fantasies of ACC Commissioner John Swofford, the final game in the men's national championship would find Duke playing Carolina, and the ACC would receive 100 percent of the revenues from that game. There is no similar pay out structure for women's basketball. And, though their revenues are certainly smaller, the fact that women's basketball teams are not rewarded through this structure exacerbates the gendered inequalities of college sports.

Early indications are that the big, powerful football programs will consume most of the conference share of TV and radio and advertising money returned to the conferences. This is where the money will come from.[32] As one of the authors has demonstrated elsewhere,[33] the vast majority of FBS football programs are not profitable; they lose money and thus require subsidies from the general operating budget of the university that houses them in order to bring them into the "black." This practice will not only continue but in fact will most likely *increase* in response to the increased costs of travel and the cost of attendance stipends, and all of this will ultimately impact all students at the university, as these subsidies will likely be generated by increasing tuition and student fees.[34]

In short, we argue that conference realignment has the potential to have devastating consequences for all of the "poor" sports and for women's teams and women athletes in particular. It is highly likely that the women's sports will see their budgets trimmed as a result of the increased costs of travel and the cost of attendance policy, which will benefit only the football and men's basketball teams. Women's athletic budgets will be trimmed by reducing the opportunities for travel, by competing in geographic contests rather than conference contests, and by trimming perks such as the quality of the pregame meal. Other strategies to funnel more and more money to pay for the increased cost of (especially) football may lead to other types of budget cuts to women's sports as well, which could impact coaches' salaries, the number of assistant coaches, equipment budgets, and food budgets. All of these restrictions will create a different—and inarguably *inferior*—experience for women athletes. It will turn back the clock on Title IX and squash any opportunity for women athletes to have any resemblance of an equitable student-athlete experience.

Finally, though the focus of this chapter has been on the "on the field" experiences of student-athletes, we are deeply concerned that an unintended consequence of greater equality for women's basketball will be a decline in the likelihood of women's basketball players graduating. That is not a form of Title IX equality that has drawn interest.

Policy Recommendations

Our policy recommendations are actually quite simple and straightforward. If the Department of Education were to enforce the "spirit" of Title IX rather than just the "letter" of the law, then nearly every collegiate athletic department would immediately be out of compliance and budgets would have to be given serious scrutiny in order to create equality and equity for women's teams and their athletes. Our model is simple: funding should be driven by need, not want. All athletes should travel in reasonable accommodations that limit their time away from campus (and thus, it is hoped, improve graduation rates), they should have adequate food to meet their nutritional needs, they should have equipment that allows them to compete safely, and they should have support to close the gap between the scholarship and the actual costs incurred to attend college.

As research demonstrates,[35] football and men's basketball are funded based on wants—a new pair of shoes every week, chartered flights to games that are just a few hours' drive away, coaches' salaries that exceed college presidents by 10-fold,[36] dinners at expensive steak houses where most Americans cannot afford to eat, and, worst of all, the use of strippers, prostitutes, and hostess squads, which are funded by athletic departments. The pathway to gender equity in SportsWorld is achievable; we just have to decide, as a society with a huge sports culture, that we value women's contributions as much as we value men's.

NOTES

1. Moore, Maya. 2014. "(In)visibility." http://bit.ly/1EUxXto

2. Smith, Earl. 2014. *Race, Sport and the American Dream*, 3rd ed. Durham: Carolina Academic Press.

3. Edwards, Harry. 1979. "The Olympic Project for Human Rights: An Assessment Ten Years Later." *Black Scholar* 10:2–8; Greene, Linda. 2012. "Head Football Coaches: Ending the Discourse of Privilege." *Wake Forest Journal of Law & Policy* 2 (1): 115–142; Olson, Jack.1968. "The Black Athlete—A Shameful Story." *Sports Illustrated*, July 1. http://sportsillustrated.cnn.com/vault/article/magazine/MAG1081325/.

4. Smith (2014).

5. Gaul, Gilbert. 2015. *Billion Dollar Ball: A Journey through the Big-Money Culture of College Football*. New York: Viking, 180.

6. Byers, Walter. 1995. *Unsportsmanlike Conduct: Exploiting College Athletes.* Ann Arbor: University of Michigan Press.

7. Acosta, Vivian, and Linda Carpenter. 2015. "Women in Intercollegiate Sport: A Longitudinal National Study, Thirty-Seven Year Update, 1977–2014." www.acostacarpenter.org/.

8. Zimbalist, Andrew. 2013. "Inequality in Intercollegiate Athletics: Origins, Trends and Policies." *Journal of Intercollegiate Sport* 6:5–24.

9. Dennie, Christian. 2011. "Conference Realignment: From Backyard Brawls to Cash Cows." *Mississippi Sports Law Review* 1:249–279.

10. Robinson, Andrew. 2011. "Conference Expansion Affects More Than Football." http://bit.ly/1VUTnZS.

11. Smith, Erick. 2011. "Syracuse Coach Jim Boeheim Not Happy about Move to ACC." *USA Today.* http://usat.ly/pfvTid.

12. Merton, Robert. 1988. "The Matthew Effect in Science, II." *ISIS* 79:606–623.

13. Gaul (2015).

14. Haurwitz, Ralph, and John Maher. 2011. "UT Sets New Standard with $300 Million ESPN Deal: Few If Any Other Schools Could Match Such a TV Network Arrangement, Officials Say." *American-Statesman.* http://atxne.ws/1PmhyS7.

15. Smith (2014).

16. Hoffer, Adam, and Jared Pincin. 2014. "The Effects of Conference Realignment on NCAA Athletic Departments." http://ssrn.com/abstract = 2578333.

17. Lorber, Judith. 1995. *Paradoxes of Gender.* New Haven: Yale University Press, 1.

18. Epstein, Cynthia Fuchs. 2007. "Great Divides: The Cultural, Cognitive, and Social Bases of the Global Subordination of Women." *American Sociological Review* 72:1–22.

19. Hattery, Angela J. 2012. "They Play Like Girls: Gender and Race (In)Equity in NCAA Sports." *Wake Forest Journal of Law & Policy* 2:247–265. http://bit.ly/1IODKNc.

20. Hattery (2012).

21. Cooky, Cheryl, Michael A. Messner, and Michela Musto. 2015. "'It's Dude Time!': A Quarter Century of Excluding Women's Sports in Televised News and Highlight Shows." *Communication and Sport* 3:1–27.

22. Kane, Mary Jo. 2013. "The Better Sportswomen Get, the More the Media Ignore Them." *Communication & Sport* 1 (3): 231–236.

23. Smith (2014).

24. Hosick, Michael. 2014. "Student-Athletes Earn Diplomas at Record Rate." *NCAA.* http://on.ncaa.com/1PF38YA.

25. Beamon, Karen, and Patricia Bell. 2002. "Going Pro: The Differential Effects of High Aspirations for a Professional Sports Career on African-American Student-Athletes and White Student-Athletes." *Race and Society* 5:179–192.

26. Hattery, Angela J., Earl Smith, and Ellen Staurowsky. 2008. "They Play Like Girls: Gender Equity in NCAA Sports." *Journal for the Study of Sports and Athletes in Education* 1:249–272.

27. Smith et al. (2008): 260–263.

28. Berkowitz, Steve, and Andrew Kreighbaum 2015. "College Athletes Cashing in with Millions in New Benefits." *USA Today.* http://usat.ly/1hmqsBj.

29. Wolverton. Brad. 2015. "Disparities in New Aid for Athletes Could Alter Recruiting Dynamics." *Chronicle of Higher Education.* http://bit.ly/1LhOFCM.

30. Forde, Pat. 2015. "NCAA Interviewed Ohio State's JaQuan Lyle about Louisville Recruitment." *Yahoo Sports,* October 7 http://yhoo.it/1LDmr8V.

31. Schrader, Steve. 2015. "Former Pacer Jalen Rose on College Recruiting: It's Like a Bachelor Party." *Detroit Free Press,* October 21. http://indy.st/1PX5C8O.

32. Mandel, Stewart. 2015. "Biggest Winners, Losers Five Years after Realignment Hell Broke Loose." http://foxs.pt/20bBEEZ.

33. Smith (2014).

34. Ridpath, David. 2015. "Who Actually Funds Intercollegiate Athletic Programs?" *Forbes.* http://onforb.es/1VvIDSp.

35. Gaul (2015); Smith, Earl, and Angela J. Hattery. 2015. "Conference Realignment and the Demise of the Academic Mission." In *Introduction to Intercollegiate Athletics,* edited by Eddie Comeaux, 219–230. Baltimore: Johns Hopkins University Press. http://bit.ly/144Noza.

36. Branch, Taylor. 2011. "Shame of College Sports." *Atlantic.* http://theatln.tc /1MD1D1H.

Review Questions

Part I: Changing and Unchanging Institutions

1. Gerson cites rising economic insecurity as a key explanation for young women's and men's changing ideas about their expected roles in family life. Explain how economic insecurity also underlies Smith's findings about the changing role of higher education in women's lives, Wingfield's results regarding Black women's and men's experiences in the workplace, and Helmuth and Bailey's findings regarding military enlistment. Would you expect the results of these four studies to be different if economic insecurity were not a concern in the United States? Why or why not?

2. Schnable's work on the purity movement documents how religion is an important component of the cultural fabric of the United States that reinforces gender as a social institution and yields different and unequal outcomes for women and men. Provide one other example of how religious organizations and/or practices structure women's and men's lives at the individual, interactional, and institutional levels in the United States. That is, like Schnable, provide evidence (using appropriate scholarly sources and available data) for how religion as an institution reinforces different and unequal outcomes for women and men. Then provide evidence of one example of how religion as an institution may be changing in the United States to challenge the different and unequal outcomes of gender as an institution.

3. How do the experiences of male and female athletes at your college or university differ (e.g., in terms of opportunities, resources, recognition, etc.)? How have their experiences changed as a result of the conference realignment discussed by Hattery and Smith? Using archival data from your institution (visit the DOE/OPE website http://ope.ed.gov/athletics/ and search for your institution) and interviews with key individuals

(coaches for women's and men's sports, male and female athletes), describe (1) the experiences of and support for male and female sports and athletes generally and (2) whether and how sports have changed at your institution in response to conference realignment. In your investigation, be sure to examine how women's and men's sports were treated both before and after conference realignment, including funding mechanisms, travel arrangements and schedules, and facilities, as were discussed by Hattery and Smith in their chapter.

4. Find a popular blog that discusses scholarly research on gender (e.g., http://speak4sociology.org/, https://thesocietypages.org/socimages/blog/, https://gendersociety.wordpress.com/, https://familyinequality.wordpress.com/) in one of the social institutions studied in this part of the volume (family, higher education, work, religion, the military, sport). Using what you have learned about gender as a social institution that has implications at the individual, interactional, and institutional levels, describe how the blog presents the research findings about gender. Read the original research that is being discussed. Does the blog post highlight certain findings (e.g., implications for gender at the individual level) and underemphasize others? For further challenge, find a different blog that discusses research on gender in a different social institution and compare the presentation of the findings on gender. Does it seem that blogs about different institutions focus on gender differently? Why would that be the case?

PART II

Gender Politics and Policies

8. Gender Parity on Corporate Boards

A Path to Women's Equality?

Martha Burk and Heidi Hartmann

The cosmetics company Max Factor, founded in 1909, was the premier Hollywood movie makeup studio and the first to makeup actresses for color movies. With just one woman ever serving on its board, however, Max Factor failed to anticipate changing product demands, and in 1973 the company was bought by Norton Simon and eventually consolidated into Procter & Gamble. Today the company lives on only in nostalgic memories of Hollywood glamour. Let's imagine how this story might have ended differently. Winning Factor, an early 1900s beauty product company, recognized early on the crucial role women board members played in its success. By actively recruiting women to its board, the company made better decisions and successfully predicted market changes. With global growth, its profits soared. It developed and included women-owned business in its supply chain, diversified its global staff and management, and became a major philanthropic donor to women's rights organizations around the world. Today, Winning Factor is enormously profitable, its personnel are diverse and creative, women's businesses thrive in many unexpected parts of the world, and many women's organizations are well funded by Winning Factor and its network of suppliers. Winning Factor is a household name and held up as a shining example of the broader benefits of gender equality in the corporate world.

INTRODUCTION

Today, gender inequality infiltrates all spheres of the labor market, including the corporate boardroom. This chapter investigates the issue of gender equity in the realm of corporate boards, assessing the economic and social benefits of and strategies to increase women's representation on boards. Because corporate boards are at the apex of the corporate world, controlling—along with the top management they hire—all aspects of corporate behavior, getting more women on corporate boards is seen as an important way to advance all women. Does having more women on corporate boards help women generally? This chapter examines and compares "supply-side" and "demand-side" approaches to understanding and remedying the scarcity of women on corporate boards, reviewing numerous recent government and private efforts to increase women's share of seats. The chapter then reviews evidence on the impact on broader gender equality of having more women on corporate boards.

When we ask the question of whether gender parity on corporate boards is a path to women's equality, we must separate the question into two parts: (1) Is it a path to equality in the corporate world, in terms of equal representation in decision making, gender equitable pay at all levels of corporate employment, and equal opportunity in hiring and promotions? (2) Can equality on corporate boards (even if only partially realized) contribute to equality of women in general, particularly in the economic realm? To the degree that we can answer these questions, we will know the extent to which achieving gender parity on corporate boards is a path to equality more broadly. We conclude that demand-side tactics, particularly mandatory quota systems, are most effective at achieving gender parity in the corporate realm. Whether equal representation on corporate boards will lead to broader gains for women remains to be seen, given the limited evidence of its effects; however, research suggests it would help achieve both business and moral goals.

BACKGROUND

Women on Corporate Boards—by the Numbers

Women's representation on corporate boards varies widely around the world, depending on several factors, including but not limited to country culture, laws, and advocacy efforts by women's groups and investors. The United States is not a leader when it comes to gender parity. Female membership on boards in the Fortune 1000 companies increased by less than 1 percent a year from 2011 to 2014 (14.6 percent to 17.7 percent).[1] The rates are even lower in Silicon Valley, where women make up just 9.1 percent of board members.[2] In 2014 in the S & P 500, women held 19.2 percent of board seats in the United States.[3] At this rate it will take another 30-plus years to reach parity, assuming companies maintain the same (low) level of effort.

As can be seen in figures 8.1 and 8.2, a number of other countries, most prominently in Europe, have outstripped the United States in gender parity

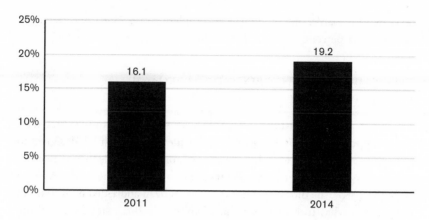

FIGURE 8.1.   Percent of Board Seats Held by Women in the United States, 2011 vs. 2014. *Source:* 2011 analysis based on 497 companies listed in Fortune 500; 2014 analysis is based on 500 companies from the S & P Index. Data provided by Catalyst, *2011 Catalyst Census:* Fortune 500 Women Board Directors: www .catalyst.org/system/files/2011_Fo.

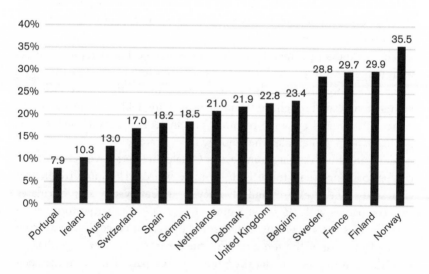

FIGURE 8.2.   Percent of Board Seats Held by Women at European Stock Index Companies, 2014. Data from October 2014. Europe is represented across the following indices, providing the percentage of board seats held by women across a specific number of companies: Austria (20 companies), Belgium (20), Denmark (19), Finland (22), France (40), Germany (30), Netherlands (27), Norway (24), Portugal (19), Spain (35), Sweden (29), Switzerland (20), and the United Kingdom (101). Data provided by Catalyst, *2014 Catalyst Census: Women Board Directors:* www .catalyst.org/system/files/2014_catalyst_census_women_board_directors_0.pdf.

on corporate boards, though none is at complete parity. Norway is the highest with 35.5 percent.

CASE STUDY I: THE SUPPLY-SIDE APPROACH TO GENDER PARITY

The justification for parity on corporate boards has historically centered on two arguments: the moral case and the business case. Both are designed to persuade companies to act voluntarily. The moral case holds that companies should strive for gender parity because it's the right thing to do. At least since the 1980s, the moral case has most often been addressed by initiatives to influence what authors Kramer and Wolfman call the *supply side* of the issue—trying to increase the number of qualified women and make them more easily available.[4] This has often been accomplished by constructing databases with names of qualified women and publicizing them (or what Mitt Romney infamously described as "binders full of women").[5] This might also be called the "shaming strategy," a tactic used by many actors, including social movement organizers, nongovernmental organizations, and state governments for many issues (e.g., to enforce international human rights norms and laws).[6]

The business case maintains that more female board representation leads to higher profits. The business case is often accompanied by the argument that more diversity also leads to more innovation, since different points of view are brought to the problem-solving table. The business case has been bolstered by some research, and in recent years a good deal of publicity. It might be called the "money talks strategy."

Companies with higher numbers of female directors have better financial performance than those with all-male boards. The most frequently cited study, by the research and advocacy group Catalyst in 2007, calculates that companies with the most women board directors outperform those with the least by 53 percent, as measured by return on equity, comparing the performance of the top quartile firms in terms of women on boards with those in the bottom quartile.[7] Table 8.1 compares data from the 2007 Catalyst study with that from their 2011 report, showing data from 2002–2004 compared with data from 2004–2008, when the advantage of women on boards of directors is shown to be somewhat lower. Returns are shown for three different measures of performance. It is perhaps understandable that returns on equity in a time period ending in 2008 in the depth of the Great Recession might be out of step with other measures of performance.

TABLE 8.1 Correlation between Rates of Return and Women on Boards, 2002–2004 and 2004–2008

	Female Representation			*Female Advantage: Financial Performance Gain for Top Quartile Compared with Bottom Quartile (B–A)/A*
	Bottom Quartile (A)	*Top Quartile (B)*	*Three or More Women on Board (C)*	
Return on Equity				
2002–2004	9.1%	13.9%	16.7%	53.0%
2004–2008	13.7%	12.9%	15.3%	Not Significant (−0.8%)
Return on Sales				
2002–2004	9.7%	13.7%	16.8%	42.0%
2004–2008	11.6%	13.4%	14.0%	16.0%
Return on Invested Capital				
2002–2004	4.7%	7.7%	10.0%	66.0%
2004–2008	7.2%	9.1%	10.4%	26.0%

[i] Correlation does not imply causation.

SOURCES: Carter, Nancy M., and Harvey M. Wagner. 2011. *The Bottom Line: Corporate Performance and Women's Representation on Boards (2004–2008).* American Express Company, BMO Financial Group, Chevron Corporation, Deloitte LLP, Desjardins Group, Deutsche Bank AG, Ernst & Young LLP, Hewlett-Packard Company, IBM Corporation, McDonald's Corporation, and UPS. New York: Catalyst. www.catalyst.org/system/files /the_bottom_line_corporate_performance_and_women's_representation_on_boards_ %282004–2008%29.pdf; Joy, Lois, and Nancy M. Carter. 2007. *The Bottom Line: Corporate Performance and Women's Representation on Boards.* Chubb Corporation. New York: Catalyst. www.catalyst.org/system/files/The_Bottom_Line_Corporate_Performance_and_ Womens_Representation_on_Boards.pdf. Note that data shown in this report are for 2002–2004.

The US Securities and Exchange Commission also reports that companies with a high rate of diverse board seats exceed the average returns of the Dow Jones and NASDAQ indices over a five-year period.[8] And a 2012 study found that a firm generates on average "one percent (or over $40 million) more economic value with at least one woman on its top management team than without any women on its top management team and also enjoys superior accounting performance."[9] Further, a 2015 report found that companies with strong female leadership (i.e., if three or more women sat on its board, if the percentage of women on the board was above the country average, or if the company had a female CEO and at least one woman on the board) performed better than companies without strong female leadership on two key indicators: average annual ROE (10.1 percent versus 1.56 percent) and average valuation (price-to-book ratio of 1.76 versus 1.56). Due to limited historical data, the report could not posit a causal link between women in leadership and corporate performance, but does conclude that "enhanced decision making capacity of more diverse boards is likely an important benefit of having more women on boards."[10]

Both moral case and business case strategies have relied on tracking and reporting of female board membership by organizations such as Catalyst, ION, Corporate Women Directors International, Government Metrics International, and others that issue periodic reports on progress or lack thereof. Both strategies also rely on good intentions and voluntary efforts by corporations to bolster their female board membership.

Regardless of which argument is made, in the United States the needle has barely moved in the past few years. A Government Accountability Office report from December 2015 finds that even if half of all new board members were women beginning in 2015, it would still take more than 40 years for women to reach parity with men.[11] In short, neither the moral case nor the business case has been sufficient to bring about robust change in the United States. The subtitle on a Catalyst press release announcing their annual census says it all: "Incremental Progress Not Sufficient to Disrupt Status Quo," followed by the statement "Companies that are not making diversity on boards a priority should be embarrassed."[12]

The reasons why progress is slow to nonexistent have not been formally researched over a broad range of companies. But one in-depth company-wide assessment of the corporate culture at Goldman Sachs, led by Jackie Zehner, a former partner, is perhaps indicative. The study revealed that while the white male majority strongly believe the company is a meritocracy and the best people (usually like themselves) get promoted, females and nonmajority males view the corporate culture differently. Nonmajority members are more likely to say that there are hidden rules for success, and that it is harder to get the right opportunities and more difficult to be sponsored. Zehner's conclusion: "It is my belief that the main reason why there has been so little progress in terms of the numbers is because the dominant belief at most companies is that they are a meritocracy. In other words, nothing is really broken. There is no deep examination of corporate culture, but rather a long list of programs aimed at 'fixing' less qualified and able people."[13] In other words many firms take a supply-side approach in developing their leadership; they do not recognize that there may be inadequate demand.

A September 2011 conference in Washington, DC, sponsored by Johns Hopkins University School of Advanced International Studies (SAIS), underscored Zehner's point, concluding that the problem is not on the supply side. While it is important to continue to prepare women (and men) for board service and to promote women into the leadership positions that qualify them for such service, there currently is a considerable untapped pool of women candidates. The challenge is getting boards to look beyond their usual pool of candidates for board positions.[14]

We are compelled by the numbers to accept the fact that current efforts to reach gender parity on corporate boards in the United States are not working as hoped and intended, and other avenues must be explored.

CASE STUDY II: THE DEMAND-SIDE APPROACH TO GENDER PARITY

Tactics other than those depending on corporate good will or persuasion have been called *demand-side* efforts. Initiatives on the demand side are exactly what they sound like—recommendations or imperatives from governments, regulators, shareholders, and stock exchanges that firms change how they recruit and select board members.

Continental Europe: Government Mandates

Norway, with the highest percentage of female corporate board members in the world at 35.5 percent, serves as one example of how demand-side tactics can make change, and also what the limits of that change might be. The Norway experience is instructive in a variety of ways, as reported in a study by Marianne Bertrand and several coauthors that was published by the National Bureau of Economic Research in its Working Paper Series.[15]

In 2003, Norway passed a law mandating that public limited-liability corporations (for which none of the shareholders is personally liable for the company's debts) create boards with no less than 40 percent of each gender represented. Even so, most companies did not do much to increase female participation. By 2005, only 17 percent of board positions were held by women. So the government added sanctions, which took effect in 2008. That's when the average share of women on the boards of those companies approached 40 percent.

The results, however, look better than they actually are. A majority of the 563 public limited-liability companies subject to the law in 2003 went private or otherwise changed their corporate status (delisted), leaving only 179 firms subject to the legislation by 2008. Although not all of this decline can be attributed to the mandate, the shift in status of firms limits the number of firms affected by the law and thus the law's potential impact.

Despite the smaller number of companies, some results are instructive. Before reform was enacted, corporate leaders argued there were not enough qualified women to fill the board positions. Female board members post-reform were actually better-educated than the prereform cohort. The study found they had an extra half-year of education and the representation of MBA degrees was on a par with the male board members. The pay gap of female board members compared with male board members shrank. But 10 years into this experiment, which now is being copied in other countries, the research found little evidence of a trickle-down effect for other women in the workforce, nor did it find evidence of changing work environments in affected firms. The authors conclude that the small sample size and relatively short time frame since reforms were enacted may have contributed to the lack of more positive results on these dimensions.

Without doubt Norway's quota system has served as a model and/or incentive in other countries. In the three European countries immediately below Norway in the ranking on share of corporate board membership that is female (Finland, France, and Sweden—see figure 8.2), all have a demand-side component.

Unlike Norway, there are no statutory quotas for the private sector in Finland (second in Europe), though in stock-exchange-listed companies there is mandated self-regulation by the Finnish Securities Market Association (FSMA) based on the FSMA's Corporate Governance Code (CG Code).

The CG Code states that "both genders shall be represented on the board," and listed companies must follow the CG Code on a "comply or explain" basis, meaning that they must specify and explain the basis for each deviation on their website and in their annual corporate governance statement. The application guidelines for the CG Code state that it is not sufficient to explain that a suitable female director could not be found or that the annual meeting decided on a different board composition. Despite this, the FSMA has found that exceptions concerning the gender composition of boards are among the most common deviations made by listed companies, and that the explanations given by companies are too general in nature and not sufficiently informative. That said, the policy is working to the extent that female board membership in Finland at (29.9 percent) is second among European countries, and since the updated CG Code was issued in 2008, the percentage of listed companies with an all-male board of directors has fallen from close to 50 percent to only 13 percent in 2013.[16]

In July 2014, the French Parliament adopted a bill referred to as "real equality between women and men." It touches on the issue of women on boards, as well as many aspects of French life, and reaffirms the application of the Zimmermann Copé law of 2011, which requires French public companies employing more than 500 workers to have 40 percent female board representation by 2017. It also requires that lists of candidates for a board must be divided between men and women, with a maximum difference of one. If the board has eight members or less, the difference between the genders cannot exceed two. When the composition of the governing board changes and no longer fulfills the quota, temporary nominations must be made. If these thresholds are not reached, the directors will not be paid. The real equality bill extends the Zimmermann Copé requirements to smaller companies (with more than 250 employees), with a goal of achieving the 40 percent threshold by 2020.[17]

Sweden's current policies require publicly traded companies to disclose the gender breakdown of their board members and management, and a 2010 policy also urges companies to strive for equal gender distribution when determining their boards, both voluntary measures. Swedish finance minister Anders Borg, who held office from 2006 to 2014, considered legislation to impose quotas, since women hold only 24 percent of the board seats at private Swedish companies, according to Statistics Sweden. They also make up just 22 percent of senior managers at the country's 25 largest firms. At companies that are owned by the government, on the other hand, women make up nearly half of all board members.[18]

Though Germany is ninth among EU countries at 18.2 percent female board membership, it bears discussion because of its place in the economic pantheon and recent legal changes. In late 2014, Angela Merkel's coalition government announced that as of 2016, a 30 percent female quota would be instituted for board seats in all exchange-listed companies that are subject to "codetermination" (firms that are subject to codetermination are those that are required by law to have representatives of their workers on their supervisory boards). The law contains an "empty chair" requirement, which stipulates that an election violating the quota will be considered null and void, and the seat left empty until a woman is elected to fill it.[19] Several companies, including BMW, have threatened to leave the country, and many more have claimed "there are not enough qualified women," but it is too early to tell whether either of these types of statements will come true.

In any case it might not matter, unless all corporations want to relocate outside Europe, assuming the European Parliament adopts a proposed law by the European Commission to improve gender balance on the boards of EU companies. The legislation would require that nonexecutive board directors of large listed companies be 40 percent female by 2020 (up from 16.6 percent in 2013). Small and medium-sized enterprises (companies with fewer than 250 employees and an annual worldwide turnover not exceeding 50 million EUR) are excluded, but member states are invited to support and incentivize those companies to improve the gender balance at all levels of management and on boards significantly.[20] Sanctions for failure to respect provisions for board selection procedures would include exclusion from public procurement and partial exclusion from European structural funds awards. To become law, the commission's proposal needs to be adopted jointly by the European Parliament and by the EU member states in the council (which votes by qualified majority).[21]

United Kingdom and United States: Limited Government Pressure

In the United Kingdom and the United States, government action is limited to recommendations and disclosure requirements to leverage action by corporations. An exhaustive review and criticism of UK companies and women on the Financial Times Stock Exchange (FTSE) 100 boards—the 100 companies listed on the London Stock Exchange with the highest market capitalizations—was released by the UK Government in 2011, authored by Mervyn Davies, then UK minister of state (Department for Business, Innovation, & Skills). In the report, Davies recommended against quotas, but noted, "Government must reserve the right to introduce more prescriptive alternatives if the recommended business-led approach does not achieve significant change." The "recommended business-led approach" included, among other measures, that (1) all chairmen of FTSE 350 companies should set out the percentage of women they aim to have on their boards in 2013 and 2015, (2) FTSE 100 companies should aim for a minimum of 25 percent female representation on their boards by 2015, (3) chairmen should announce their aspirational goals by September 2011, (4) chief executives are expected to review the percentage of women they aim to have on their executive committees in 2013 and 2015, (5) public companies that are on the London Stock Exchange should be required to disclose each year the proportion of women on the board, women in senior executive positions, and female employees in the whole organization.[22]

A progress report released in March 2014 by the UK Department for Business, Innovation, & Skills showed that the representation of women on the boards of FTSE 250 companies rose from 12.5 percent in 2011 to 20.7 percent in 2014. The report highlighted progress made in placing women on boards and in opening new avenues to leadership positions for women, but also addressed the challenges of reaching the targets set by the original 2011 report of 25 percent board representation. The report found that only 25 percent of executive search firms claim a commitment to the code on their websites, and just 12 percent share data on their success rate in placing women. The report goes on to recommend creation of a database of board-ready women to share with search firms and boards.[23]

Clearly concerned with the progress to date, UK secretary of state for business and innovation Vince Cable, an opponent of quotas, expressed concern in the press in February 2015. Cable was blunt in his warning: "Our target of 25 percent women on boards by 2015 is in sight. However, the threat of EU mandatory targets remains a reality if we do not meet it. If we are to avoid action from Brussels, we must continue to demonstrate that our voluntary approach is the right one and is working."[24]

Like the United Kingdom, the United States has no laws regarding gender balance on corporate boards, not even for companies receiving government contracts. In 2009 the Securities and Exchange Commission (SEC) passed a new rule requiring management of publicly held companies to disclose (1) whether diversity is a factor in considering candidates for nomination to the board of directors, (2) how diversity is considered in that process, and (3) how the company assesses the effectiveness of its policy for considering diversity. While "diversity" is not specifically defined, a reading of the rule makes it clear that it refers to women and minority men, though no specific numbers are required, nor is disaggregation by race and gender required. In other words, the rule has no actual requirements that companies strive for diversity, and in fact does not even require a commitment to diversity (a company could merely state that diversity is not a factor in board selection, or that it has no diversity policy at all), rendering it almost completely ineffective. A recent resolution passed in June 2015 by the Illinois House of Representatives does "encourage equitable and diverse gender representation on corporate boards and directors," and includes aspirational target numbers.[25] By 2018, it urges publicly held corporations with nine or more seats to have a minimum of three women on their boards, those with between five and nine seats to have two women, and those with fewer than five seats to fill at least one with a woman.[26] Though it is not legally binding or mandatory, this resolution citing specific numbers of women who should hold seats on corporate boards offers a model for government action encouraging changes in norms.

The ineffectiveness of the 2009 Securities and Exchange Commission (SEC) rule was highlighted by SEC commissioner Luis Aguilar, in a speech a few months after it was instituted. He said that initial examination of the reports submitted showed that while a few companies provided useful information in the spirit of the SEC rule, many others provided only abstract disclosure—oftentimes limited to a brief statement indicating that diversity was something considered as part of an informal policy. Moreover, many companies reported no concrete steps taken to give real meaning to its efforts to create a diverse board.[27]

A 2015 report by the US Government Accountability Office summarizing developments in the United States regarding increasing the representation of women on corporate boards concluded that clarifying the SEC rule would be useful. In response, Representative Carolyn Maloney, who, as the ranking member of the Subcommittee on Capital Markets and Government Sponsored Enterprises of the House of Representatives Committee on Financial Services, requested the report, wrote a letter calling on the Securities and Exchange Commission to update its diversity disclosure requirements, so that corporations have to report each board nominee's gender, race, and ethnicity.[28]

UK and US Nongovernmental Advocacy: Shareholder Influence

In the absence of meaningful legislation or regulatory reform in the United Kingdom and the United States, demand-side initiatives continue to be led by outside groups seeking to put pressure on companies to change. The 30% Club in the United Kingdom was launched in 2010 by fund executive Helena Morrissey, and remains one of the forerunners in pushing for greater female representation on boards. The club members are chairs, CEOs, or equivalent roles at companies and other organizations who support the mission of placing more women on corporate boards without the use of government-mandated quotas. Their primary tactic is one-on-one lobbying of corporate executives by peers. Although the group was founded to push for more female representation in the United Kingdom, by 2014 the group boasted clubs either recently launched or starting in Australia, Canada, Hong Kong, Ireland, and the United States. Since 2003, the 30% Club has helped to double the percentage of women on major British companies' boards, to 23 percent.[29]

Demand-side efforts by US advocacy organizations and institutional investors have so far borne little fruit in the last few years, and the results are still meager. In 2012 and 2013, less than one-fifth of Fortune 500 companies had 25 percent or more women directors, while one-tenth had no women serving on their boards. Less than one-quarter of companies had three or more women directors serving together in 2012 and 2013. Women of color held 3.2 percent of board seats, essentially the same as 2012 (3.3 percent), and two-thirds of the companies had no women of color.[30]

Perhaps the most prominent and most active advocacy organization in the United States is the Thirty Percent Coalition, founded in late 2011 and based in New York. As the name implies, the group is committed to the goal of women holding 30 percent of board seats. The group's membership includes institutional investors, public officials such as state treasurers and others responsible for investing public funds, senior business executives, national women's organizations, and corporate governance experts.[31]

The institutional investor initiative of the Thirty Percent Coalition has already had an impact on the corporate landscape. Cochaired by Janice Hester-Amey of the California State Teacher Retirement System (CalSTRS), one of the largest investors in the country, and Tim Smith of Walden Asset Management, the coalition's institutional investors initiated engagement with corporations in their portfolios following an initial letter-writing campaign reaching over 160 companies with no women on their boards. Subsequently, 17 companies appointed women to their boards of directors, and 25 received shareholder resolutions from their investors pushing the boards to take steps to diversify. The initiative more than doubled the assets under management represented in the current letter-writing campaign, adding an additional 27 new investors as signatories to the letter. Their most recent letter is one component in a series of planned actions by investor members of the coalition, including engaging companies in private dialogue, shareholder resolutions, and its recently launched Champions for Change program.

The Champions of Change initiative was launched in March 2014 to convince US corporations to place more women on their boards. Principles for gender diversity on boards advanced by the group include (1) corporate leaders committing to developing and recruiting talent, (2) boards adopting best practices for improving gender diversity, including changes in governance and nominating committee charters, (3) expanding director searches to include director nominees from corporate positions beyond chief executive officer and from diversified environments such as former government, academia, and nonprofit organizations. Champions for Change has attracted an impressive roster of leaders, including current or former CEOs and board members of AOL, Ernst & Young, Citigroup, Emerson Electric, Walmart, Glaxo Wellcome, and the Pennsylvania Real Estate Investment Trust.

Institutional investors, many at the urging of, and in cooperation with, the Thirty Percent Coalition, are starting to push harder for corporate reform when it comes to board selection. Launched in November 2014, by New York City comptroller Scott M. Stringer on behalf of the $160 billion New York City Pension Funds, the Boardroom Accountability Project[32] is a national campaign to give shareowners a greater voice in how corporate boards are elected at every US public corporation. Stringer will submit a proposal at each of 75 public corporations, asking for adoption of a bylaw allowing shareholders who have owned at least 3 percent of its stock for three years or more to nominate directors for election to the board. One of the three areas of emphasis is board diversity. Twenty-four of the targeted companies have few or no women directors, and little or no apparent racial or ethnic diversity. Institutional supporters of the Boardroom Accountability Project include California Public Employees' Retirement System (CalPERS), the Illinois State Board of Investment, California State Teachers' Retirement System, Philadelphia Board of Pensions and Retirement, and a number of other municipal and public sector union funds. Though there is no mention of divestment if targeted companies don't comply, it would seem to be an unspoken future possibility.

Asset management firms are also stepping up the pressure. In 2013 shareholder resolutions concerning board composition were filed with more than 25 corporations, according to the Thirty Percent Coalition. Filers included Pax World, Calvert, Walden Asset Management, New York City Pension Funds, Mercy Investment Services, United Methodist Foundation, New York State Pension Funds, Trillium Asset Management, United Auto Workers Pension, Episcopal Church, AFL-CIO, CalSTRS, Sustainability Group, North Star Asset Management, Catholic Health Partners, Evangelical Lutheran Church of America, UMC Foundation, and Trinity Health.

During the fourth quarter of 2014, Trillium Asset Management filed shareholder proposals related to board diversity with Chipotle Mexican Grill, Citrix Systems, Discovery Communications, and eBay, asking company boards of directors to report to shareholders on their practices to increase diversity on the board as well as to provide an assessment of the effectiveness of these efforts. The proposals also asked for a description of how the Nominating and Corporate Governance Committee takes steps to include women and minority candidates in the pool of board candidates. Trillium was joined by Mercy Investment Services, Calvert Investments, and Portico Benefits (an affiliate of the Lutheran Church) with support from Boston Common Asset Management, in the Discovery action. The

New York State Common Retirement Fund joined Trillium in a separate filing at eBay with Pax World and the United Methodist Foundation joining as cofilers. Increasing female participation was particularly emphasized in the Trillium announcement, which noted that improved governance practices and financial health have been particularly noticeable when there are three or more women on a board.[33]

Without filing a shareholder proposal, Trillium and the Sustainability Group were also successful using behind-the-scenes pressure to persuade Apple to add language to a board committee charter, vowing to diversify its board and add more female directors and executives. The shareholders had met with Apple representatives several times and promised to bring the issue to a vote at a 2014 shareholder meeting. They withdrew the threat after Apple added language to its charter that promises to consider women and minorities as board candidates. The language, however, stops short of making any specific commitments.[34]

Business advocates are getting into the gender parity act as well, albeit with persuasion instead of demands, for example, the Committee for Economic Development of the Conference Board (CED), a business-led public policy and research organization based in Washington, DC. The organization actively petitions corporations to increase female board membership, seemingly in an attempt to stave off government-mandated quotas. CED has always advocated progressive corporate policies regarding gender parity on boards, including widening the criteria, supporting public pressure and shareholder resolutions, and numerical monitoring. Recently the organization went a step further and announced a personal outreach initiative that will "focus on one-on-one contact with nominating committee members and chairs, most of whom are male . . . and will support supplementary seminars, luncheons, and dinners to highlight this program."[35]

THE CONTEMPORARY SITUATION

Reaching gender parity on corporate boards remains a problem, not only in the United States but around the developed world (gender parity on Asian boards is 10.2 percent or less; Japan is at only 3.1 percent). Advocates have tried for years to convince companies that gender balance on boards is both a moral imperative and a sound business decision, with very limited success. At the same time various groups have assembled "binders full of women" in an attempt to convince companies that qualified females are available for board seats and to refute the decades-old "pipeline" argument that there are not enough qualified women to be found.

Key points that emerged from the SAIS conference (referenced above) serve as an accurate assessment of such efforts to date. First, the problem is not lack of research, though continued research is always important. Second, the issue is not at this point the business case or trying to convince people of the business case. Third, the problem is not on the supply side. While it is important to continue to prepare women (and men) for board service and to promote women into the leadership positions that qualify them for such service, there currently is a considerable untapped pool of women candidates. Finally, the challenge is getting boards to look beyond their usual pool of candidates for board positions.

To put it bluntly, supply-side tactics, such as begging and cajoling, expanding the potential candidate pool, and even embarrassment, have not worked in the past except at the margins, and are not likely to work any better in the future.

Demand-side tactics such as investor and shareholder action and regulatory measures by various governments and stock exchanges are more effective, but still fall short of reaching the gender parity goal in a reasonable length of time. The demand-side tactic that makes the most change is the stronger government policy of mandated quotas, as instituted in Norway. Whether the mere *threat* of quotas such as the proposed EU mandate (see UK discussion) will work as well remains to be seen.

There is no shortage of critics of mandatory quotas. Business groups have consistently opposed them, and some companies have gone to great lengths to avoid them where instituted, most prominently in Norway, where a large number delisted from the stock exchange to avoid the requirement. Nevertheless, quotas are by far the most effective method to date of increasing gender parity on corporate boards, and in fact are gaining acceptance among business executives.

A 2014 Grant Thornton report, *Women in Business: From Classroom to Boardroom*, finds more leaders warming to a quota system, with 45 percent of international business leaders supporting quotas: up from 37 percent just a year previously.[36] A follow-up study finds that in 2015, 56 percent of both male and female senior managers support quotas to increase the ratio of women on the boards of large listed companies, an increase from 30 percent in 2014.[37]

FUTURE DIRECTIONS AND POLICIES

We cannot yet answer whether gender parity on corporate boards is a path to equality in the corporate world in terms of equal representation in decision making, equal pay, and equal opportunity in hiring and promotion, because gender parity has not yet been achieved. Indeed, only one country (Norway) cited in this review has even reached 30 percent, a number generally accepted as a critical mass in decision making enabling minority voices to be heard. Many people believe that parity on boards is a path to corporate equality, and when achieved will open doors for more women in the executive ranks, bringing women greater influence and pay parity with their male peers.

Whether equality on corporate boards (even if only partially realized) will contribute to women's equality throughout corporations or an economy is a much harder question. The only study available indicates there is no evidence of those benefits yet in Norway. The authors found no evidence that the mandate benefited women besides newly elected board members. Specifically, they found no statistically significant change in the gender wage gap or female representation in top positions within companies, in the gender wage gap or likelihood of filling a top business position for highly qualified women who were not appointed to boards, in women's enrollment in business education programs, in early-career women's fertility plans, in the gender wage gap for early-career women, or in work-life balance policies within companies whose boards gained women members. The authors caution, however, that not enough time has passed to make an informed judgment.

The experience of the US Congress is perhaps instructive when it comes to the potential for women making systemic change as their numbers reach critical mass in corporate governing bodies. Once female numbers became high enough for women not to be considered a "special interest group" (approaching critical mass) women in Congress sometimes began to vote as a bloc regardless of party.[38] In other words, on legislation affecting females in general (equal pay, abortion rights, child-care funding), female legislators voted together to make change for all women. It is not unreasonable to assume the same dynamic will apply in corporate decision making when women reach parity on corporate boards.

Even if it were to be reached quickly and become institutionalized, gender parity in corporate boardrooms is neither the shortest nor the most obvious path to economic equality for women in the workplace in general. A much more direct route would be stronger supports for working women, including subsidized child care, paid family leave, and paid sick leave. While these supports could be instituted by corporations without government mandates, they are much more likely to come from government action, as they have in many industrialized countries other than the United States.

Stronger government laws and enforcement could increase collective bargaining rights and encourage more aggressive public and private action to close the gender pay gap. In a small step forward, the US Department of Labor was directed by an executive order by President Obama to gather more data regarding compensation for women and men in companies receiving government contracts. In some states public disclosure of pay statistics by gender and race for contractors is gaining traction. This type of mandate could eventually lead to denial of government contracts to companies that do not pay women fairly, a powerful motivation for corporate leaders to change hiring and pay practices.

In sum, gender parity on corporate boards is a worthwhile goal, and equal representation will break down one more barrier for women in the workplace, particularly at the higher levels. The moral case is clear, the business case is clear, and the benefits may eventually trickle down to rank-and-file working women. What is needed now is a change in corporate culture, and government and regulatory mandates appear to be the fastest way to achieve that goal.

ACKNOWLEDGMENTS

The authors thank members of the staff of the Institute for Women's Policy Research who contributed to this chapter. Elyse Shaw, Research Associate; Emma Williams-Baron, Mariam K. Chamberlain Fellow; Gina Chirillo, Coordinator, Office of the President; and Hero Ashman, former Research Intern, all provided assistance with research and fact-checking. Emma Williams-Baron also researched and drafted the opening paragraph about Max Factor and Winning Factor.

NOTES

1. 2020 Women on Boards. 2014. "Steady Gains Made by Women on Fortune 1000 Company Boards." www.2020wob.com/about/press/release/2020-women-boards-releases-2014-gender-diversity-index.

2. Streitfeld, David. 2012. "Lawsuit against Kleiner Perkins Is Shaking Silicon Valley." *New York Times,* June 2.

3. Catalyst. 2015. *2014 Catalyst Census: Women Board Directors.* New York: Catalyst. February 6. www.catalyst.org/knowledge/2014-catalyst-census-women-board-directors.

4. Kramer, Vicki, and Toni Wolfman. 2011. *Major Approaches to Making Change.* Thirty Percent Coalition. New York: 30 Percent Coalition. www.30percentcoalition.org/files/Major%20Approaches%20to%20Making%20Change.pdf.

5. See the 2012 *Guardian* article "'Binders Full of Women': Romney's Four Words That Alienated Women Voters." www.theguardian.com/world/shortcuts/2012/oct/17/binders-full-of-women-romneys-four-words.

6. Hafner-Burton, Emilie M. 2008. "Sticks and Stones: Naming and Shaming the Human Rights Enforcement Problem." *International Organization* 62 (4): 689–

716; Meernik, James, Rosa Aloisi, Marsha Sowell, and Angela Nichols. 2012. "The Impact of Human Rights Organizations on Naming and Shaming Campaigns." *Journal of Conflict Resolution* 56 (2): 233–256.

7. Joy, Lois, Nancy M. Carter, Harvey M. Wagner, and Sriram Narayanan. 2007. *The Bottom Line: Corporate Performance and Women's Representation on Boards.* Chubb Corporation. New York: Catalyst. www.catalyst.org/system/files/The_Bottom_ Line_Corporate_Performance_and_Womens_Representation_on_Boards.pdf.

8. Korbel, Pam Watson, and Donna Evans. 2012. *Women on Boards = Peak Performance in Organizations: A White Paper on the High Value That Women Directors Bring to Corporations and Non-Profit Organizations.* Denver: Women's Leadership Foundation. http://cloud.chambermaster.com/userfiles/UserFiles /chambers/427/File/womenonboardswhitepaperver4pwkde.pdf.

9. Dezso, Cristian L., and David Gaddis Ross. 2012. "Does Female Representation in Top Management Improve Firm Performance? A Panel Data Investigation." *Strategic Management Journal* 33:1072–1089. http://onlinelibrary.wiley.com .proxygw.wrlc.org/doi/10.1002/smj.1955/pdf>.

10. Lee, Linda-Eling, Ric Marshall, Damion Rallis, and Matt Moscardi. 2015. *Women on Boards: Global Trends in Gender Diversity on Corporate Boards.* MSCI ESG Research. www.msci.com/documents/10199/04b6f646-d638–4878–9c61– 4eb91748a82b.

11. Sherrill, Andrew. 2015. *Corporate Boards: Strategies to Address Representation of Women Include Federal Disclosure Requirements.* Washington, DC: United States Government Accountability Office. www.gao.gov/assets/680/674008.pdf.

12. Catalyst. 2015. *New Global 2014 Catalyst Census: Women Board Directors.* www.catalyst.org/media/new-global-2014-catalyst-census-women-board-directors.

13. Zehner, Jackie. 2014. "The Road Not Taken: What If I Had Never Left Goldman Sachs?" *Linked In Pulse.* November 20. www.linkedin.com/pulse/road- taken-what-i-never-left-jacki-zehner?trk = prof-post.

14. Kramer and Wolfman (2011).

15. Bertrand, Marianne, Sandra E. Black, Sissel Jensen, and Adriana Lleras- Muney. 2014. *Breaking the Glass Ceiling? The Effect of Board Quotas on Female Labor Market Outcomes in Norway.* Cambridge, MA: National Bureau of Economic Research. www.nber.org/papers/w20256.

16. Giunta, Tara, and Michelle Cline. 2014. *Breaking the Glass Ceiling: Women in the Boardroom: A Study of Major Global Exchange.* Washington, DC: Paul Hastings Law Firm. www.paulhastings.com/docs/default-source/PDFs/gender_ parity_report_exchanges.pdf.

17. Orsagh, Matt. 2014. "Women on Corporate Boards: Global Trends for Promoting Diversity." *CFA Institute Market Integrity Insights,* September 24. http://blogs.cfainstitute.org/marketintegrity/2014/09/24/women-on-corporate- boards-global-trends-for-promoting-diversity/.

18. Covert, Bryce. 2014. "Sweden May Establish Quotas If Companies Don't Hire More Female Board Members." *Think Progress,* February 13. http:// thinkprogress.org/economy/2014/02/13/3287791/sweden-boards-quota/.

19. Binder, Ulrike, and Guido Zeppenfeld. 2015. "Germany Introduces Rules on Female Quota for Supervisory Boards." www.mondaq.com/x/381586 /Employee+Benefits+Compensation/Germany+Introduces+Rules+on+Female+Q uota+for+Supervisory+Boards.

20. European Commission. 2012. "Women on Boards: Commission Proposes 40% Objective—European Commission." http://ec.europa.eu/justice/newsroom /gender-equality/news/121114_en.htm#Press.

21. Orsagh (2014).

22. Davies, E. Mervyn. 2011. *Women on Boards*. United Kingdom Government. February. www.gov.uk/government/uploads/system/uploads/attachment_data /file/31480/11-745-women-on-boards.pdf.

23. Davies, E. Mervyn. 2014. *Women on Boards: Davies Review Annual Report 2014*. United Kingdom Government. March. www.gov.uk/government/publications /women-on-boards-2014-third-annual-review.

24. Goodley, Simon. 2015. "Cable Hints at Mandatory EU Quotas for Female Executives." *Guardian*, February 3.

25. House of Representatives of the Ninety-Ninth General Assembly of the State of Illinois. 2015. *Resolution HR 0439*. Illinois. www.ilga.gov/legislation /billstatus.asp?DocNum'0439&GAID'13&GA'99&DocTypeID'HR&LegID'91204& SessionID'88.

26. House of Representatives of the Ninety-Ninth General Assembly of the State of Illinois (2015).

27. Aguilar, Luis A. 2010. "Speech by SEC Commissioner: Board Diversity: Why It Matters and How to Improve It." November 4. www.sec.gov/news /speech/2010/spch110410laa.htm.

28. Wheeler, Lydia, and Tim Devaney. 2016. "Overnight Regulation: GAO Faults Corporate Boards on Diversity." *Hill*, January 4. http://thehill.com /regulation/overnights/264700-overnight-regulation.

29. Smale, Alison, and Claire Cain Miller. 2015. "Germany Sets Gender Quota in Boardrooms." *New York Times*, March 6. www.nytimes.com/2015/03/07/world /europe/german-law-requires-more-women-on-corporate-boards.html.

30. Soares, Rachel, and Liz Mulligan-Ferry. 2013. *2013 Catalyst Census: Fortune 500 Women Board Directors*. Catalyst. New York: Catalyst. www.catalyst.org /knowledge/2013-catalyst-census-fortune-500-women-board-directors.

31. Thirty Percent Coalition. 2014. "CalSTRS and The Thirty Percent Coalition Expand Campaign For More Women on Corporate Boards." California State Teacher's Retirement System. October 22. www.30percentcoalition.org/news.

32. New York City Comptroller. 2014. "Comptroller Stringer, NYC Pension Funds Launch National Campaign to Give Shareowners a True Voice in How Corporate Boards Are Elected." November. http://comptroller.nyc.gov/boardroom-accountability/.

33. Trillium Asset Management. 2014. "Trillium Files Four Board Diversity Shareholder Proposals for 2015." December. www.trilliuminvest.com/14405/.

34. Satariano, Adam. 2014. "Apple Facing Criticism about Diversity Changes Bylaws." *Bloomberg Business*. January 6. www.bloomberg.com/news/articles /2014-01-06/apple-facing-criticism-about-diversity-changes-bylaws.

35. Brooke-Marciniak, Beth A., and Debra Perry. 2014. *Every Other One: More Women on Corporate Boards: An Update of a Policy Statement*. Committee for Economic Development's Policy and Impact Committee. Washington, DC: Committee for Economic Development. www.ced.org/reports/single/every-other-one-more-women-on-corporate-boards.

36. Orsagh (2014).

37. Grant Thornton LLP. 2015. "U.S. Businesses Show Little Progress in Advancing Women during Past Decade." *MarketWatch*. March 5. www.marketwatch .com/story/us-businesses-show-little-progress-in-advancing-women-during-past-decade-2015-03-05.

38. Burk, Martha. 2014. *Your Voice, Your Vote: The Savvy Woman's Guide to Power, Politics, and the Change We Need*. Austin, TX: A.U.; Newton-Smalls, Jay. 2013. "Women Are the Only Adults Left in Washington." *Time*, October 16. http:// swampland.time.com/2013/10/16/women-are-the-only-adults-left-in-washington/.

9. Hispanic Inclusion at the Highest Level of Corporate America

Progress or Not?

Lisette M. Garcia and Eric Lopez

Five years ago my then board chairman suggested that we diversify our board, saying, "we have to do it . . . It's not just the right thing to do . . . but it's the smart thing to do. Our customer base is becoming increasingly diverse and their opinions, values, tastes, and beliefs aren't reflected around this table. What are you waiting for?" What was I waiting for? The reality of the situation was that we were losing market share and we needed to do something different. Diversity would infuse our board with fresh ideas, fresh perspectives, and perhaps be the game changer to get us back to the level of sales we had grown accustomed to before. So we did, one person at a time and here we are five years later with one of the most diverse boards in our sector and with record sales. Did the diversity cause the increase in sales? Well, of that I am not sure, but I can tell you they are related and because of it I am still gainfully employed as the CEO.

Ask any diversity professional in corporate America and they will tell you that over the years the narrative that surrounds diversity in the corporate world has changed from one of legal obligation to one of maintaining a competitive advantage. One might expect that such changes in the framing of diversity might result in increased gains for women and minorities, but the reality of the situation is that, to date, minimal gains for underrepresented populations at the highest levels of corporate America have been made.

This chapter will investigate the extent to which corporate boards have diversified over the last 20 years, focusing on the gains that Hispanics, especially Hispanic women, have made in that time period. The importance of the Hispanic community as a demographic group is highlighted by their rapidly growing representation in the US population. Hispanics have come to represent over 17 percent of the US population,[1] as well as over 15 percent of the US labor force,[2] and, due to their growing purchasing power, are an increasingly dominant presence in the US economy.[3] Yet, despite their growing market share, Hispanics remain underrepresented at the highest levels of corporate America.

Hispanics are now the largest minority group and one of the fastest growing minority groups in the United States.[4] The latest Census figures have the Hispanic population at over 55 million, about half of which are female.[5] Projections have shown that by 2050, the Latina share of the US female population will increase to 25.7 percent.[6] Latinas also represent the fastest growing sector of the entrepreneurial market[7] and for the majority of Hispanic households, they are the primary financial decision makers.[8] Coupled together, these facts show the competitive advantage Hispanic females' knowledge and expertise could bring to corporate America. Unfortunately, without a seat at the table, their underrepresentation continues to manifest itself as a lack of executive leadership and corporate board positions. These figures are clear indicators that, as the US population, workforce, and consumer base continue to diversify, companies wishing to remain competitive will also need to continue diversifying their ranks at all levels—particularly their boards.

BACKGROUND

Why Is Diversity Important?

In the early 1960s the United States was in a state of civil unrest. Years of pervasive and egregious discrimination and segregation experienced by minority groups had created a divided workforce. Employers openly instituted policies that would deny minority groups access to most jobs,[9] resulting in negative immediate and generational effects for minority groups across the country. The strain of these experiences on families and communities of color severely limited their opportunities for social mobility. Citizens, through protests and demonstrations, began expressing their frustrations in cities across the country. Finally, in 1963, President Kennedy called on Congress to act. One year later, on July 2, 1964, President Johnson signed the Civil Rights Act into legislation, laying the foundation for the diversity work that continues today. However, the passage of the Civil Rights Act was just the beginning. In his Howard University commencement address in 1965, President Johnson noted:

> You do not wipe away the scars of centuries by saying: "now, you are
> free to go where you want, do as you desire, and choose the leaders you

please." You do not take a man who for years has been hobbled by chains, liberate him, bring him to the starting line of a race, saying, "you are free to compete with all the others," and still justly believe you have been completely fair . . . This is the next and more profound stage of the battle for civil rights. We seek not just freedom but opportunity—not just legal equity but human ability—not just equality as a right and a theory, but equality as a fact and as a result.

President Johnson's words echo the sentiments of the time—planned, purposeful diversity, since individuals could not be relied on to do it for themselves. His speech to the graduating class of Howard University that day became the frame for the precursor of diversity—affirmative action. While critics continue to argue whether affirmative action is or was a flawed policy, few today disagree that it was a critical first step in diversifying corporate America.[10]

Since the passage of the Civil Rights Act of 1964, there has been growing interest in the origins and advancement of diversity in corporate America. Some experts have noted that early adopters of diversity policies may have been seeking to protect themselves from lawsuits and not diversifying their employee base, and have accused them of not being diverse enough or treating their employees differently based on race, gender, or religion.[11] As evidence, researchers point to the superficial public discourse used by companies to tout interest and support of diversity initiatives while paying little attention to measurable success and the sustainably of these efforts.[12] To date a great deal of academic literature has been dedicated to the understanding of the motivations and conditions under which diversity has been "successful,"[13] the role race and gender still play in determining work outcomes,[14] and, to a lesser extent, the experiences of underrepresented individuals in the workplace.[15] The research thus far has certainly provided helpful data on the work conditions of underrepresented groups in corporate America where there previously was none; however, a great deal more remains to be understood before it can be definitively said that corporate America has moved on from its initial motivations, toward more sustainable models of diversification. Furthermore, today's shifting demographics necessitate a close reexamination of diversity and why it continues to be important more than 50 years after the passage of the Civil Rights Act of 1964.

According to population estimates by the US Census Bureau, Hispanics are the fastest growing minority population. In fact, Census projections indicate that the Hispanic population in the United States will have grown to 119 million people, about 28.6 percent of the population, by the year 2060.[16] Other projections indicate that growth in the Hispanic population

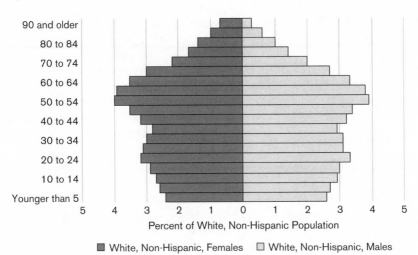

FIGURE 9.1.　Population Distribution of the US White, Non-Hispanic Population. Author calculations from US Census data showing the overall distribution of the US white, non-Hispanic population by age reflecting greater proportions of both males and females at older ages.

is expected to outpace growth of all other groups in the United States.[17] This unprecedented growth is driven in part by the fact that US Hispanics are younger compared to the US white non-Hispanic population, with greater proportions of Hispanic women within childbearing age. Figure 9.1 and figure 9.2 illustrate these population differences.

Figures from the 2010 Census have nearly 50 percent of Hispanic women within childbearing age (defined as ages 15 through 44), compared to only 40 percent of women in the US population more generally. Add to this the fact that nearly 30 percent of the Hispanic population is also under 15 years of age compared to fewer than 20 percent of the rest of the US population and it becomes clear that the potential for future growth in the United States lies with this population.

US Hispanics have become the foundation on which corporate America will come to rely on to build on their past successes and move more confidently into the future. These are outcomes corporate America can ensure for itself by entrusting the Hispanic population to both renew the United States' aging labor force and continue to preserve its market position in the global economy. In addition to representing a growing percentage of the US labor force, Hispanics have come to represent a growing share of the US population's purchasing power.[18] Hispanics account for over 50 million consumers, who collectively possess $1.3 trillion in buying power,[19] with a per

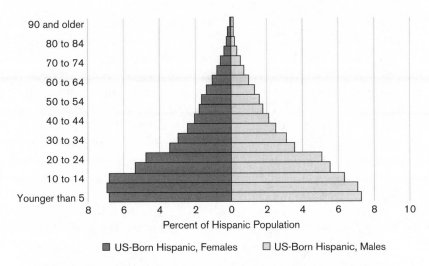

FIGURE 9.2. Population Distribution of the US Hispanic Population. Author calculations from US Census data showing the overall distribution of the US Hispanic population by age reflecting the greater proportion of both Hispanic males and females at younger ages.

capita income higher than those found in Brazil, India, or China.[20] Given these trends, it is no surprise that the shifting demographics have brought the Hispanic population to the forefront of the US political, financial, and business realms. As the population of Hispanics continues to grow, corporate America will undoubtedly need to step up and take notice of this population.

The Business Case for Diversity

Business attitudes about diversity have changed overtime. In the past, it was seen by most as a legal obligation; today it is being accepted as a business imperative with the potential of impacting a company's "bottom line." Echoes of the changing climate can be heard in a set of interviews from 2013 by Groysberg and Connolly. In them, Groysberg and Connolly interview 24 CEOs in order to better understand why diversity had become a strategic initiative at their companies and how they were integrating it into their corporate culture.[21] Among the most cited reasons contributing to the business value of diversity was feeling not only that companies would be better positioned to meet the needs of their customers, but also that it increased their ability to drive creativity and innovation.[22] Diversity of people brings with it diversity of thought and diversity of ideas, outcomes that have compelled companies to integrate diversity into their culture and decision-making process. The results have been innovation as diverse working groups can and do challenge each other to reach breakthroughs, think outside the box, and offer a fresh perspective on problems,[23] without which business operations become stale, doldrum, and perhaps even inefficient.

However, some research has pointed out that the benefits of diversity can have some drawbacks. For instance, it has been cited that a homogenous workforce can work "better" together with less conflict.[24] Conflict can result in higher levels of dissatisfaction, which can ultimately impact productivity and turnover.[25] So it seems that the jury is still out on whether or not the impact of diversity on the corporate culture is sufficient to outweigh the impact of heterogeneity on individuals or groups of similar people.

Nevertheless, there are things that can be done in order to encourage increased diversity and reap its benefits. Much of the research conducted thus far indicates that support from the top levels of an organization has to be present in order for diversity to take root[26] and that a commitment to diversity has to be made real with concrete, actionable items,[27] not something that is simply paid lip service as part of a corporation's narrative. However, even when these conditions are met, the potential to derail diversity efforts may still exist and sometimes these conditions are not seen or felt; they are unconscious. DiTomaso and colleagues highlighted the impact of "homophily," or preferences for individuals with similar backgrounds, tastes, and experiences, on workplace experiences for women and people of color.[28] If the majority of individuals making decisions about promotions are white men, then it stands to reason that because of homophily, we would find other white men being selected for executive positions as well as to serve on corporate boards.

Although arguments can be made for or against diversity, it is the position of these authors that there is certainly value in diversity at the highest levels of corporate America. This is especially true when it comes to Hispanic representation in corporate America. Given the facts thus far (Hispanics are the fastest growing population in the United States, they are now the largest minority group in the United States, with the largest workforce participation among US minority groups, and a buying power larger than some of the largest countries in the world), it is plain to see that the future of corporate America and the American economy is, in large part, tied to the inclusion of Hispanics in the development, evolvement, and prosperity of corporate America. However, there are not many studies that look at the degree of Hispanic inclusion in corporate America. Since 1993, the Hispanic Association on Corporate Responsibility (HACR), a nonprofit organization whose mission it is to advance the inclusion of Hispanics in corporate America, has conducted one of the few analyses looking at corporate governance among America's largest companies. HACR's Corporate Governance Study (CGS) looks at the number of seats held by Hispanics and the number of corporations addressing the need for more diversity in their boardrooms and C-suites. Below is a description of its 2013 findings.

CASE STUDY

Tracking Hispanic representation on corporate boards is, at best, like trying to hit a moving target. Corporate governance is quite dynamic and can be influenced by a number of factors, including the financial position of the company, operating strategies, and other appointments held by prospective board members.[29] Nevertheless, for the past several years HACR has been tracking Hispanic representation on the boards of some of the largest, most profitable companies in the United States, the Fortune 100, in an effort to understand what prevailing trends are saying about the state of diversity and inclusion (D & I) in corporate America and how this information can be used to inform policies and practices aimed at improving the representation of Hispanics at the highest levels of corporate America.

Between 1993 and 2003, there was significant momentum in Hispanic representation in the corporate boardroom.[30] However, more recent data from 2013 suggests that the momentum has been lost. While an increase of more than 2 percent in Hispanic representation on corporate boards between 1993 and 2003 can and should be counted as an improvement in D & I, it is also important to highlight that this gain was, at best, minimal— and not nearly representative of the size and financial strength of the US Hispanic population.

The data collected for this study is unique and time-consuming to collect. The data-collection process for this study started in July of 2012. We began by creating a listing of Hispanic board directors and company officers in Fortune 100 companies using the 2012 filings of SEC Form DEF 14A with US Securities and Exchange Commission (SEC). Form DEF 14A, also known as a definitive proxy statement, "must be filed by or on behalf of a registrant when a shareholder vote is required."[31] Upon collecting available board information from the SEC, it was then compared to what was reported on each company's website in order to confirm that the information is current.

Once the preliminary data was compiled, a letter was sent to the chairman and/or chief executive officer (CEO) and the general counsel of each of the Fortune 100 companies requesting information regarding the status

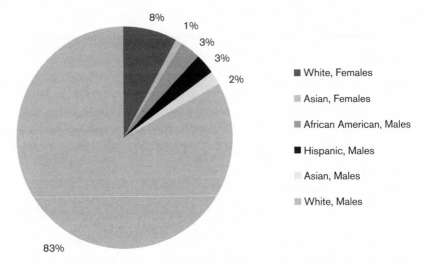

FIGURE 9.3.   Race and Gender Distribution of 2015 Fortune 100 CEOs. Author calculations from author collected original data showing the distribution of race and gender among the CEOs of the Fortune 100 companies.

of Hispanic directors and officers of the company. Extensive research on each individual identified is conducted to identify their race, gender, and citizenship status. Changes in board or executive appointments after June 30, 2013, are not reflected in the CGS.

Of the companies in the Fortune 500, 110 companies responded to requests for information. For companies that did not respond, HACR reported information that was publicly available from SEC filings and/or company websites between January 1 and June 30, 2013. The result of all this effort is a unique, author-collected data set.

Hispanic Inclusion: How Far Have We Come?

Fortune magazine ranks the 100 largest and most profitable companies in the United States annually. While there is some movement in the companies that make this list, the variation in the companies on the list year after year is minimal. Historically, the majority of these companies have been led by white males with very few companies led by women or people of color.[32] In 2015, 83 of the top 100 companies were led by white males, while only 17 of the top 100 companies in the United States are led by women or people of color, as shown in figure 9.3.

Among those companies led by women or people of color, only three are led by Hispanic males and none by Hispanic females. Two of those three

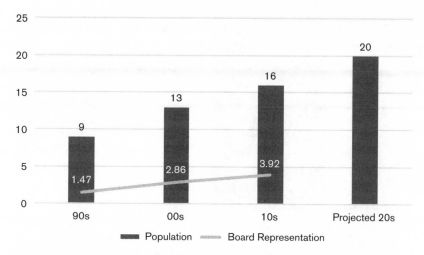

FIGURE 9.4. Hispanic Population vs. Hispanic Board Representation. Author calculations from US Census data and author collected original data showing the differences in the population growth of the US Hispanic population and representation of Fortune 100 company boards.

Hispanic CEOs only recently assumed the helm of the companies they lead. For nearly 10 years George Paz, the CEO of Express Scripts Holdings, was the only Hispanic CEO in the Fortune 100. Research has shown that there has been a steady increase in the number of companies led by white women while the number of CEOs of color has in fact declined over time.[33] The recent appointments of Juan Luciano at Archer Daniels Midland and Oscar Muñoz at United Continental Holdings, however, represent a potentially positive outlook for Hispanic representation at the CEO level of Fortune 100 companies (at least for men).

As for board representation, between 1993 and 2013 Hispanic representation in the corporate boardroom of Fortune 100 companies more than doubled, increasing from just under 1.5 percent to just under 4 percent. However, the reality of the situation is that while this represents a significant increase in representation, it remains a relatively small increase given that it has taken over 20 years to occur. Additionally, despite these gains in representation, Hispanic board members remain vastly underrepresented relative to the share of the US population or their potential for continued growth (see figure 9.4).

Companies often cite their inability to find qualified Hispanics to fill vacant board positions, indicating the pool of potential executives from which to draw on is nonexistent.[34] Figure 9.5 shows that in 1993, the

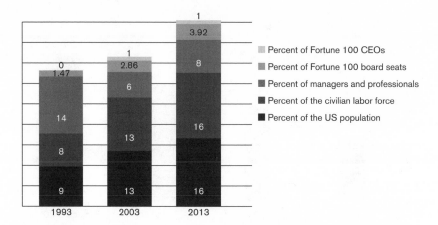

FIGURE 9.5.   Hispanic Population and Labor Market Trends. Author calculations from US Census data and author collected original data showing the differences in the population growth of the US Hispanic population and representation of Hispanics in managerial positions, in Fortune 100 boardrooms, and as CEOs of Fortune 100 companies.

proportion of Hispanics occupying managerial and professional positions was actually larger than the overall proportion of Hispanics in the population. Yet, in spite of this discrepancy, the number of Hispanics selected to serve on boards or in executive positions was rather small in 1993. There is research which supports the notion that it is not a lack of qualified diverse candidates that limits diversity, but rather flawed methods for selection of new directors and executives,[35] a point we will revisit in the discussion.

Figure 9.5 also shows that this pool of potential candidates did decline between 1993 and 2003 before experiencing a slight increase in 2013. Could this increase be a sign that the pool of potential candidates for board appointments or CEO positions has increased perhaps as signaled by the recent appointment of two new Hispanic CEOs? Additional research is still needed to determine whether the pool of qualified candidates has increased over time.

The picture for women, however, continues to be dismal. Latinas currently hold slightly more than 1 percent of board seats in the Fortune 100, which represents a significant increase from 1993, when Latinas only held 0.28 percent of board seats in the Fortune 100. But as mentioned above, currently not one company in the Fortune 100 is run by a Latina. And while we have generally seen improvements in the representation for white women, Latinas assuming the helm of a Fortune 100 company remains an elusive goal.

UPDATING THE CONTEMPORARY SITUATION

In the past 20 years there has been an increase in the representation of Hispanics and Latinas in the corporate boardroom. However, these increases still reflect an extremely small proportion of total board seats. Furthermore, any movement toward including Hispanics at the highest level of corporate America has since essentially flatlined.

There's a general optimism that there will be positive change in the near future. The recent appointments of Oscar Muñoz and Juan Luciano may be signaling a change in the guard and in the mindset regarding the value of having global insiders on your executive team and board. Zweigenhaft and Domhoff cite the importance of being multilingual and multicultural, and being increasingly adept at handling global business and negotiations for future CEOs, a fact not lost on many Asian and Hispanic CEOs.[36] A company's bottom line is inextricably linked to its ability to compete in an increasingly global economy; diversity among directors who serve in the boardrooms of corporate America's largest firms is required to provide the necessary leadership in an ever-changing global marketplace. Hispanics bring different insights, different experiences, and guidance to the table— all essential components for continued success in today's global environment.

Until that time comes, however, increased attention must be paid to the current situation and trends, which, once again, are not overwhelmingly encouraging. The growing Hispanic population is ripe with the talent that can be picked to serve on the boards or other leadership positions within corporate America. But corporate America has yet to make diversity a strategic imperative on whose value they could be capitalizing now. By virtue of the changing demographics of the United States, corporate America will diversify, but why wait? Why not leverage the benefits of diversity now by creating sustainable, socially responsible business practices that will lead to greater diversity at the top?

To do so requires a shift in the traditional methods by which board directors are identified and selected. Historically, director nominations have been limited to the networks of existing directors or the company CEO. By virtue of the way the corporate elite tends to be structured in the United States, this typically meant other elites, usually white men—homophily in action. Historically, women and people of color were excluded from these networks; therefore, relying on the traditional method to fill board positions limited the opportunity to diversify boards.[37] These traditional methods must be replaced by ones that can produce more diverse slates for open positions. Otherwise, we will never truly see diversity in the boardroom at levels commensurate with population representation.

Another factor impacting board diversity, similar to historical reliance on personal networks, is the historical reliance on sitting or former CEOs to fill open board positions.[38] These credentials limit the pool of diverse candidates who could potentially fill board vacancies since very few women and people of color have served as CEOs of Fortune 100, 500, or even 1000 companies in recent times.

It seems easy; simply changing these two historical methods for new director selection could potentially have a huge impact on the level of diversity within a company's board. But pushing boards to go outside their traditional methods for seeking new candidates requires work and effort. It is much easier to pull candidates from those who are already familiar to the current board, rather than vetting a new potential board member. These flawed methods for director selection have led us to the place where we find ourselves now, and until companies reconceptualize how directors are selected, we may continue to see limited gains for diverse populations.

FUTURE DIRECTIONS AND POLICIES

HACR's research has revealed that in the past 20 years there have only been minimal gains in Hispanic representation on corporate boards. Since 1993, the proportion of board seats held by Hispanics has increased from roughly 1.5 percent to nearly 4 percent. The exciting thing about this work is that there are lots of potential directions to go to from here.

Census projections indicate that there will be over 119 million Hispanics in the United States by 2060, nearly 30 percent of the nation's total population.[39] The resulting reality emerging from this shift in the US population is one in which corporations will have to increasingly rely on Hispanics to replace their aging workforce as well as attract customers and investors. Doing so will provide corporations with the foundation on which their governance boards will be able to harness the experienced and diverse talent that will solidify their future. However, the gains in Hispanic representation on corporate boards experienced thus far are not enough, given the trajectory of the population laid out above.

As the size of the Hispanic population increases, so will their political and economic power as well as their share of the labor force—companies should be looking for ways of engaging the voice of this population around their decision-making tables. Hispanics have a higher labor force participation rate than any other group in the United States and the growth in the nation's labor force will be driven by the growth in the Hispanic population.[40] Their voice needs to be represented among those who are making the decisions. As educational attainment continues to increase for the Hispanic population and entrepreneurial opportunities abound, there is no legitimate reason why increased board representation cannot follow.

Lack of Hispanic inclusion is a missed opportunity for corporate America. Companies are missing out on this voice and the innovation, creativity, and insights they can provide. Hispanics can bring with them the required experience of managing successful business operations as well as a significant understanding of the Hispanic community. Failure to capitalize on this knowledge and experience is another missed opportunity for corporate America.

So how can corporate America increase its diversity efforts? They can start by first establishing partnerships with the Hispanic community to help build a pipeline of talented executives that could fill vacancies. Nonprofit organizations, such as the Association of Latino Professionals for America, HACR, and the National Society of Hispanic MBAs, as well as Employee Resource Groups (ERGs), are just a few examples of organizations that can help corporations gain direct access to the Hispanic community—its talent, entrepreneurs, and leadership—in order to increase their representation. Once a critical mass of qualified individuals has been established, the pathway to greater Hispanic inclusion becomes clearer.

Another potential opportunity to increase diversity on corporate boards is to consider instituting term limits for board positions.[41] Term limits are not uncommon in the nonprofit sector, even in the government, but they are essentially nonexistent in the corporate world. Term limits would necessitate that companies refresh their board periodically, which could lead to increased diversity.

Requiring diverse slates for open board positions is also another possibility for picking up the pace to diversity. The SEC requires all publicly traded companies to have a statement regarding diversity as part of their governance protocol, yet it doesn't specify what that means or even that diverse candidates should be considered for vacancies. Perhaps simply creating something similar to the NFL's "Rooney Rule," which requires that minority candidates be interviewed for head coaching and senior positions, in corporate governance would go a long way toward facilitating diversity and Hispanic inclusion.

Finally, we cannot ignore the larger discussion in the corporate world about quotas. Quotas require a fixed number or percentage of seats for underrepresented minorities. The European Union has adopted quotas in the hopes of mandating a greater gender balance on their corporate boards. However, not all companies required to abide by these guidelines have; and those that have are going about it in very different ways, leading to mixed results in terms of (1) the effectiveness of the quotas and (2) the value of women on boards. Research has indicated that some companies were more "carefree" in their appointments and have appointed women for the sake of appointing women without careful consideration of their knowledge, competencies, or what they could bring to the board.[42] The effect of this on the perception of the quotas and the contributions that women make to governance could do irreparable harm for the case of diversity.

Unfortunately, exclusion from corporate boards and executive teams in corporate America is not a problem that is unique to Hispanics. White women and members of other racial and ethnic groups are faced with the same dismal picture, but this is something that can be changed. If left to voluntary diversity, eventually it will happen, but why wait to capitalize on the value diversity brings to the table?

NOTES

1. United States Census Bureau, Population Division. 2015. *Annual Estimates of the Resident Population by Sex, Age, Race, and Hispanic Origin for the United States and States: April 1,2010 to July 1,2014.* http://factfinder.census.gov/faces /tableservices/jsf/pages/productview.xhtml?src = bkmk.

2. United States Department of Labor. 2012. *The Latino Labor Force at a Glance.* www.dol.gov/_sec/media/reports/HispanicLaborForce/HispanicLaborForce.pdf.

3. Nielsen. 2014. *A Fresh View of Hispanic Consumers.* www.nielsen.com/us /en/insights/news/2014/a-fresh-view-of-hispanic-consumers.html.

4. United States Census Bureau. 2014. *Facts-for-Features: Hispanic Heritage Month 2015.* www.census.gov/newsroom/facts-for-features/2015/cb15-ff18.html.

5. Pew Research Center. 2008. *Hispanic Women in the United States, 2007.* www.pewhispanic.org/2008/05/08/hispanic-women-in-the-united-states-2007/.

6. Jackson, Mareshah. 2013. *Fact Sheet: The State of Latinas in the United States.* Center for American Progress. www.americanprogress.org/issues/race/ report/2013/11/07/79167/fact-sheet-the-state-of-latinas-in-the-united-states/.

7. United States Hispanic Chamber of Commerce. 2010. *America's Business Trailblazers—the Impact of Hispanic Business Women.* http://ushcc.com/americas- business-trailblazers-the-impact-of-latina-entrepreneurs/.

8. Nielsen. 2013. *Latinas Are a Driving Force behind Hispanic Purchasing Power in the U.S.* New York: Nielsen. www.nielsen.com/us/en/insights/news/2013 /latinas-are-a-driving-force-behind-hispanic-purchasing-power-in-.html.

9. Amesen, Eric, ed. 2007. *Encyclopedia of U.S. Labor and Working-Class History,* vol. 1. New York: Routledge.

10. Reskin, Barbara. 1998. *The Realities of Affirmative Action in Employment.* Washington, DC: American Sociological Association.

11. Embrick, David. 2011. "The Diversity Ideology in the Business World: A New Oppression for a New Age." *Critical Sociology* 37 (5): 541–556; Kalev,

Alexandra, Frank Dobbin, and Erin Kelly. 2006. "Best Practices or Bests Guesses? Diversity Management and the Remediation of Inequality." *American Sociological Review* 71:589–617.

12. Cook, Alison, and Christy Glass. 2014. "Above the Glass Ceiling: When Are Women and Racial/Ethnic Minorities Promoted to CEO?" *Strategic Management Journal* 35:1080–1089; DiTomaso, Nancy, Corinne Post, and Rochelle Parks-Yancy. 2007. "Workforce Diversity and Inequality: Power, Status, and Numbers." *Annual Review of Sociology* 33:473–501; Embrick (2011); Herring, Cedric. 2009. "Does Diversity Pay? Race, Gender, and the Business Case for Diversity." *American Sociological Review* 74:208–224; Williams, Christine L., Kristine Kilanski, and Chandra Muller. 2014. "Corporate Diversity Programs and Gender Inequality in the Oil and Gas Industry." *Work and Occupations* 41 (4): 440–476.

13. Dobbin, Frank, Alexandra Kalev, and Erin Kelly. 2007. "Diversity Management in Corporate America." *Contexts* 6 (4): 21–27; Giscombe, Katherine, and Mary Mattis. 2002. "Leveling the Playing Field for Women of Color in Corporate Management: Is the Business Case Enough." *Journal of Business Ethics* 37:103–119; Kim, Soohan, Alexandra Kalev, and Frank Dobbin. 2012. "Progressive Corporations at Work: The Case of Diversity Programs." *NYU Review of Law and Social Change* 36:171–213; Williams et al. (2014).

14. Cianni, Mary, and Beverly Romberger. 1997. "Life in the Corporation: A Multi-Method Study of the Experiences of Male and Female Asian, Black, Hispanic and White Employees." *Gender, Work, and Organizations* 4 (2): 116–129; DiTomaso et al. (2007); Stainback, Kevin, and Donald Tomaskovic-Devey. 2009. "Intersections of Power and Privilege: Long-Term Trends in Managerial Representation." *American Sociological Review* 74:800–820; Tomaskovic-Devey, Donald, and Kevin Stainback. 2007. "Discrimination and Desegregation: Equal Opportunity Progress in U.S. Private Sector Workplaces since the Civil Rights Act." *Annals of the American Academy of Political and Social Science* 609:49–84; Williams, Katherine, and Charles O'Reilly. 1998. "Demography and Diversity: A Review of 40 Years of Research." In *Research in Organizational Behavior*, edited by Barry M. Staw and Robert I. Sutton, 77–140. Greenwich, CT: JAI.

15. Cianni and Romberger (1997); DiTomaso et al. (2007); Stainback and Tomaskovic-Devey (2009); Tomaskovic-Devey and Stainback (2007).

16. Colby, Sandra L., and Jennifer M. Ortman. 2015. "Projections of the Size and Composition of the U.S. Population: 2014 to 2060: Population Estimates and Projections." *Current Population Reports*. US Census Bureau. March 2015.

17. Colby and Ortman (2015).

18. Nielsen. 2014. *A Fresh View of Hispanic Consumers*. www.nielsen.com/us/en/insights/news/2014/a-fresh-view-of-hispanic-consumers.html.

19. Nielsen (2013).

20. Goldman Sachs. 2011. *Global Economics, Commodities & Strategy Research: BRICS Monthly Issue 11/06*.

21. Groysberg, Boris, and Katherine Connelly. 2013."Great Leaders Who Make the Mix Work." *Harvard Business Review* September 2013:2–10.

22. Groysberg and Connelly (2013).

23. Di Tomaso et al. (2007); Groysberg and Connelly (2013); Herring (2009); Williams and O'Reilly (1998).

24. Herring (2009).

25. Herring (2009).

26. Groysberg and Connelly (2013).

27. Groysberg and Connelly (2013).

28. DiTomaso et al. (2007).

29. Kamonjoh, Edward. 2015. *Boardroom Refreshment: A Review of Trends at U.S. Firms.* Institutional Shareholder Services.

30. Hispanic Association on Corporate Responsibility. 2013. *Corporate Governance Study.*

31. Investopedia. 2016. www.investopedia.com/terms/s/sec-form-def-14a.asp.

32. Russell Reynolds Associates. 2014. *Diversity in Leadership: Minority and Female Representation on Fortune 250 Boards and Executive Teams.* Washington, DC: Russell Reynolds Associates; Zwigenhaft, Richard L., and G. William Domhoff. 2006. *Diversity in the Power Elite: How It Happened, Why It Matters.* Lanham, MD: Roman & Littlefield; Zwigenhaft, Richard L., and G. William Domhoff. 2011. *The New CEOs: Women, African American, Latino, and Asian American Leaders of Fortune 500 Companies.* Lanham, MD: Roman & Littlefield; Zwigenhaft, Richard L., and G. William Domhoff. 2015. "Diversity in the Corner Office from 2005–2014: Yes but Mostly No." Unpublished manuscript.

33. Zwigenhaft and Domhoff (2015).

34. Brady, Diane. 2014. "The Crumbling Case against Women on U.S. Boards." *Bloomberg Business.* www.bloomberg.com/bw/articles/2014–04–17/the-crumbling-case-against-adding-more-women-to-u-dot-s-dot-corporate-boards; Catalyst. 2015. *Still Too Few Women on Boards.* New York: Catalyst; Russell Reynolds Associates (2014).

35. Catalyst (2015).

36. Zwigenhaft and Domhoff (2015).

37. Catalyst (2015); Russell Reynolds Associates (2014).

38. Catalyst (2015); Russell Reynolds Associates (2014).

39. Colby and Ortman (2015).

40. US Bureau of Labor Statistics. 2015. "Labor Force Characteristics by Race and Ethnicity, 2014." *BLS Reports: Report 1057.* November 2015.

41. Brady (2014).

42. Kamonjoh, Edward. 2014. *Gender Diversity on Boards: A Review of Global Trends.* Institutional Shareholder Services.

10. Work-Life Balance and the Relationship between Women in State Legislatures and Workers' Schedule Control

Beth A. Rubin, Sabrina Speights, Jianhua Ge, Tonya K. Frevert, and Charles J. Brody

Ramona wakes up at 4:00 in the morning so that she has time to get to her new job as a food prep cook in a major health food store. While she's never been a morning person, she quit her previous, better-paying job as a culinary arts teacher at a fee-based culinary institute because she couldn't take the unpredictable work schedules anymore. In that job, she sometimes had split shifts working in the morning and evening with the afternoon "free"; sometimes she had all-day shifts. The final straw was when her schedule suddenly shifted to Saturday morning. This change conflicted with her time at the local farmers' market, where her work generates additional income necessary to pay many of her bills. When her shift at her primary job changed suddenly, she was forced to seek alternative employment that allowed her to maintain sufficient control over her schedule. Her current job as a prep cook at the health food store provides a fixed schedule, and while she doesn't have schedule flexibility, she is able to have input into what her schedule looks like.

At the same time, her sister, Alice, has begun a new, high-paying, knowledge-intensive job at an insurance company. Alice now has schedule flexibility that allows her to start work at 7:00 AM so that she can leave at 4:30 PM and make a 5:30 PM event at the university where her husband is provost. Other days she begins her workday at 9:00 AM and works until 6:30 PM, allowing her to attend her 7:00 AM yoga class. For both of these women, schedule flexibility is key to managing work-life balance. While neither woman has children, Alice's stepson provides a good example of how these issues are intensified when children are present in the home. Recently separated from his wife and with primary custody of children ages two and five, the flexible schedule provided by the ability to conduct

*his work at a tech firm via technology is key to his successfully navigating
his responsibilities as a single parent.*

One external factor that might have bearing on the experiences of employees like Ramona and Alice is the outcome of a presidential election, as with the 2016 US presidential election. Rather than elect a woman who was a champion of women's and workers' rights, the Electoral College (in contrast to the popular vote) elected a president who appeared so hostile to women's and employees' rights that the day after his inauguration, the streets of most major cities and many small ones in the United States (and in many other countries) were filled with participants in the Women's March for Rights, alarmed at the potential policy shifts they expected from the new president. At stake was whether working conditions and employees' control would tighten or loosen. Despite campaign rhetoric championing the working class, Trump was a billionaire tycoon not known for supportive workplace practices and held a strong focus on the bottom line and the "art of the deal." The past has shown that the ideological stance of key figures in government signals to the business community what are acceptable or unacceptable business and workplace practices.[1] For instance, when President Reagan busted an important US trade union strike in 1981 (PATCO, the Professional Air Traffic Controllers Organization), it signaled to the business community that it was open season on unions and workplaces became much bolder in their antiunion strategies. So it is an empirical question, in the context of the 24/7 economy, with the prevalence of Amazon's and Starbucks's "just-in-time" staffing, what the political climate will do to workplaces. Yet, what much of the literature that interrogates work-life balance fails to query is what, if anything, happens at the state level? Further, what are the consequences if women move into positions of political power? That is what we ask in this chapter.

BACKGROUND

Globalization, Organizations, and Schedule Control

Schedule control refers to the ability to decide *when* one's job gets done. Because of the decision latitude involved, schedule control is also often viewed as schedule flexibility. Both terms are intended to capture the opportunity for employees to shape their work schedule to the needs that arise in their family or personal lives. The general consensus among scholars is that schedule control is important to work-life balance, or the global assessment that an employee has enough resources to manage work and family demands,[2] because the very essence of control is that employees are able to adjust and decide when they work, thus allowing for balance.

In the competitive global economy, organizations use "temporal flexibility" as a tool to minimize costs and increase efficiency.[3] "Temporal flexibility" means that organizations structure the workday as needed and no longer adhere to a traditional five-day-a-week, nine-to-five schedule.[4] This temporal flexibility contributes to business organizations' ability to innovate, identify diverse markets, and develop new products and services faster than can their competitors. The fast changes that occur on the larger global scale also influence the temporal structuring of work, particularly how employers schedule their employees' work activities. Most notable are departures from the previous normative Monday through Friday, nine-to-five workweek that, among other things, contribute to increased employment insecurity.[5] That insecurity derives from a number of factors that includes employers' disregard for the schedule needs of employees, which often results in either over- or underwork.[6] Both Ramona and Alice worry about the changing political climate because they know that political climate can embolden employers in their disregard. Given the global changes in the nature of organizations and work, scheduling has become increasingly important for managing work and family demands.

Scheduling challenges are, for instance, particularly great in the United States compared to Western Europe, where employment policies are far more supportive of workers and of supporting work and family. Gornick and Meyers[7] note in a cross-national comparison that industrialized, European countries with strong labor parties and proworker governments have far more policies and protections that address leave, time off, vacation, and work time than does the United States. Of course, most Western countries differ from the United States in size (European countries tend to be smaller) and composition (European countries, until recently, tend to be more homogenous). The United States, in contrast, is a large country with a great deal of *state-by-state* variation in institutional environments that are consequential for understanding the impact of public policy.

When organizations do allow their employees to have discretion over their schedules, employer attention turns from the hours that employees work and instead focuses on the results employees are able to produce. Instead of providing select employees with certain schedule-flexibility options, this workplace system attempts to shift the organizational culture such that flexibility is the norm. Employees are able to change their schedules without permission from their supervisors, labels such as "telecommuter" are removed, and higher-level executives buy into, and support, the change.[8] These innovative practices improve employee schedule control and, in turn, this increased schedule control is associated with positive outcomes, such as reduced work-family conflict, increased sleep, and positive health behaviors, for employees.[9]

What influences organizations to provide more schedule control to employees? We suggest that the broader institutional climate is an important part of the answer. The legislation in a particular state may influence how organizations respond to employee needs. Likewise, political scientists have found that women representatives in legislative bodies influence both the types of bills proposed and the legislation passed that support "women's issues" (e.g., autonomy and well-being of women).[10] It is possible that women's representation in state legislatures influences employee experiences of schedule control, given the evidence that schedule control is an important factor for achieving work-life balance. Sociologists who examine these questions have used gender structure theory to explain these influences.

Women's Substantive Representation and Policy

Gender structure theory provides an explanation for why women in power may influence various aspects of social life that differ from the influences of men in positions of power. According to this theory, gender is structured into all institutions, organizations, and practices.[11] The presumed differences between men and women (e.g., men are strong, assertive, and ambitious; women are nurturing, supportive, and primarily concerned with family) are mutually shared, internalized, and embedded in institutions from the most microlevel to the macrolevel. Risman argues that the most enduring of these institutions is the household division of labor premised on a breadwinning husband and home-making wife. These normative expectations persist despite women's increased participation in the workforce and government. Given that observation, gender structure theory would suggest that women in positions of power would be more likely to promote policies that support the health and well-being of the family.

When considering women in power, there is a question about whether the influence of women is simply descriptive (adding demographic diversity) or substantive (women's participation in politics has a distinct influence on policy).[12] Analyses of women in the US Congress and state-level legislatures support the substantive representation of women and show that by sponsoring particular bills, women are able to foreground—not just support—issues that they consider legislatively important. For example, Swers's[13] analysis of the US Congress found that women promoted policy focused specifically on "women's issues" that address gender inequality, education, and child protection. Further, examining bills in the lower state houses of 12 states in the United States, Thomas[14] found that women prioritize bills concerning family, women, and children more than men and that, as the proportion of women in the state legislature increased, so did the passage rates of those bills.

A reasonable question asks whether political figures simply act in ways that align with the interests of their political parties, districts, and other political supporters to get them reelected, a dynamic known as "constituency representation."[15] Legislators may seek votes from various constituencies such as their respective political party, in which case legislators would simply push their party's view on an issue. They may also align policies based on the region they represent. Often, these regional distinctions represent differences in the general political culture. For instance, states in a "traditional" region tend to raise less money per capita and have lower levels of political liberalism. "Moralist" regions, however, have higher levels of political innovation and liberalism.[16] While alignment with constituents is important to legislators maintaining their elected office, empirical evidence indicates that the effect of gender holds even after accounting for region[17] and political party.[18] That is, the gender composition of the legislature remains important even after researchers account for the region and political party a politician represents.

When we see an effect of gender on legislative action remaining even after accounting for other variables, this effect indicates there is something specific about women in legislative bodies. Gender and work-family scholars suggest that these differences occur because women have traditionally been responsible for the maintenance of families. Thinking about our current investigation, we posit that when more women have political power, the policies they pass are likely to shape organizations in ways that support employees so they can have the schedule flexibility and control needed to maintain work-life balance.

Political Party and Women's Political Power

While more women being elected to political office may influence working conditions in organizations, the political party representation in the state legislature may influence the degree to which the bills and policies women propose will actually affect employees. Swers's analysis of women in the US Congress compared the Democratic-controlled 103rd US Congress (1993–1994), often called the "Year of the Woman," to the Republican-controlled 104th US Congress (1995–1996), or "Contract with America," which was the first Congress since the 1950s to have Republican Party majorities in both chambers.

During the 103rd Congress, even Republican women voted for progressive women's policies, against their conservative political alignment, that the Democratic majority enabled. In contrast, the 104th Congress removed women from committee positions that enabled those women to sponsor bills and defunded resources necessary to sustain legislative service organizations. Similar findings occur at the state level as well, with evidence of higher commitment at the state level to women-friendly policies when Democrats control the legislature.[19]

CASE STUDY

Women in the State Legislature: Do They Matter?

Three questions suggested by the literature review above guide our analyses. First, is schedule control greater in states where female representation is greater? Second, does the impact of women's political power depend on the political party of the women in office? Finally, does the impact of women in the legislature on schedule control depend on whether the legislature as a whole leans more heavily Democratic or Republican? We suggest the answer to all three of these questions is yes. Specifically, we hypothesize (1) female representation in state legislatures has a positive relationship with schedule control of employees in those states, (2) the effect of female representation is stronger when those women are Democrats, and, finally, (3) the effect of female representation is stronger as the percentage of total Democrats increases.

To investigate the above questions, we analyze a multilevel data set compiled from the 2008 National Study of the Changing Workforce, the Rutgers's Center for American Women and Politics, and the Statistical Abstract of the United States. We used two questions to capture schedule control. First, *control in scheduling working hours* was measured by asking, "Overall, how much control would you say you have in scheduling your work hours?" Responses ranged from 1 (none) to 4 (complete). Second, *control over starting/quitting times* was measured by asking, "Are you allowed to choose your own starting and quitting times within some range of hours?" Respondents answered yes or no. Given that these outcome variables are not continuous, we analyzed each using ordered logit and logistic regression, respectively. When using these regression techniques, we estimate the likelihood of a participant choosing a particular response choice.[20] Although these analyses estimate probabilities, the direction of the

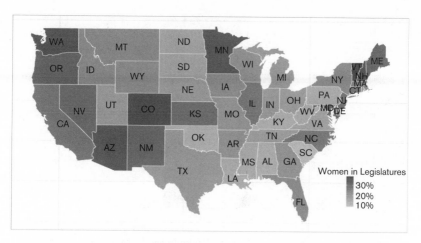

FIGURE 10.1. Geographic Distribution of the Percentage of Women in State Legislatures.

coefficients (i.e., positive or negative) can be interpreted in a manner similar to linear regression.

To measure women's representation in state legislatures, we calculated the percentage of women's state-level representation in both chambers of the legislature for each state and the District of Columbia (we exclude Hawaii and Alaska), regardless of party affiliation. To address the second question above, we also calculated the percentage of non-Republican women in the legislature (the majority of whom are Democrat; this percentage also includes women in the legislature who identify as independent, as progressive, or as having no party affiliation). To capture the overall political climate of the state, we calculated the percentage of the state legislature, both male and female, who identified as Republican versus non-Republican. Our multivariate analyses include several control variables, including age, race/ethnicity, marital status, education, and occupation, tenure and union membership of employees, as well as the presence of children in the household and household income.

The mean percentage of women in state legislatures is 23 percent. Figure 10.1 displays how this percentage varies by state. Darker shading on the map represents higher percentages of women in the state legislature. The figure suggests that the variation is not captured by simple regional differences because female representation does not appear to be densely concentrated in any particular region.

Some results involving our control variables are of interest. While married respondents reported less control over their start/quit times than those

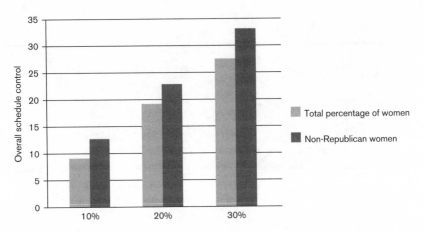

FIGURE 10.2.   Results of the Effect of Women in the State Legislature on Schedule Control.

who were single, parents have more control over start/quit times than respondents who do not have a child living in the home. Similar to Alice, employees in higher-skilled occupations with higher incomes and more education also have higher levels of schedule control compared to other employees.

Figures 10.2–10.5 summarize the key finding of our analyses, providing answers to the questions raised above. The percentage of women in the state legislature has positive effects on employees' abilities to schedule working hours (figure 10.2) and their control over starting/quitting times (figure 10.3). What these analyses demonstrate is that as the percentage of women in the state legislature increases (regardless of party affiliation), the overall ability of employees to control their work schedule increases and the likelihood that employees have control over their start and quit times also increases. When we consider increases in the percentage of non-Republican female legislators alone, the positive impact on both forms of schedule control is even stronger.

We further ask whether the political party in power matters for the effect of women's representation on employee schedule control. When the total percentage of non-Republican legislators increases, women's representation in the legislature has a stronger effect on increasing the likelihood that employees have some control over their start and quit times. This dynamic is more pronounced when the women themselves were non-Republican (compare the left and right panels of figure 10.4). In figure 10.5, we see a similar pattern in part for overall schedule control. Specifically,

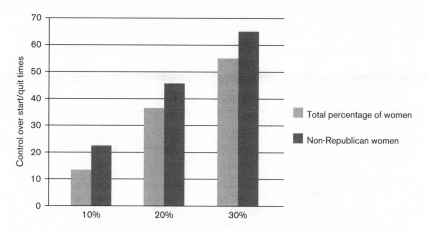

FIGURE 10.3. Results of the Effect of Women in the State Legislature on Control over Start/Quit Times.

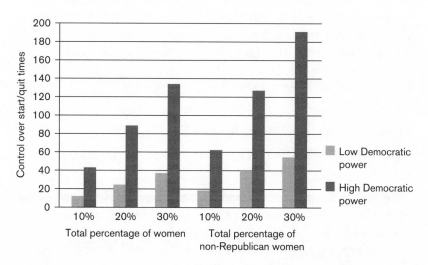

FIGURE 10.4. Results of the Interaction Effect of Women in the State Legislature on Control over Start/Quit Times.

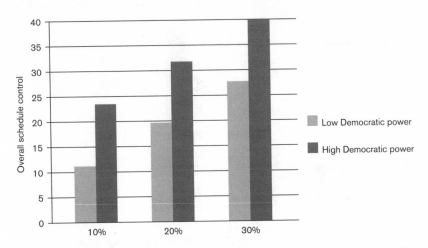

FIGURE 10.5.   Results of the Interaction Effect of Non-Republican Women in the State Legislature on Schedule Control.

when the overall percentage of non-Republicans is high, the effect of non-Republican women on overall schedule control is also stronger. The relationship between the total percentage of women in the state legislature and individual schedule control, however, is not influenced by the overall percentage of non-Republicans in the legislature (as we saw with control over start/quit times in figure 10.4).

UPDATING THE CONTEMPORARY SITUATION

Women Legislators, Work-Family, and Gender-Equitable Environments

We demonstrate that the gender composition of state legislatures does influence outcomes for individual employees. This evidence suggests that when women hold positions of political power, their influence extends beyond their role in sponsoring and passing legislation. The political leadership by women alters the larger institutional environment and reflects change that in turn results in a more favorable family-supportive climate and practice in organizations. Institutional theories say that organizations adopt policies for three reasons: legal mandates, mimicking other organizations, and conforming to social norms.[21] Legal structures and public policy have been discussed for other workplace issues such as discrimination[22] and unfair labor practices.[23] Feminist policy analysts have discussed the ways in which policy addresses a variety of women's issues that include body-related policy (marital rape, abortion, birth control) as well as employment-related policy (equal pay, sexual harassment, affirmative action, parental leave, and, most relevant to our study, working time policies).[24] Our findings are consistent with both perspectives.

Our findings support institutional perspectives that would expect that women in power both directly support practices that enhance work-life balance through legislative efforts and alter the larger environment by changing the normative structure to support organization-level policies that recognize new configurations of work (e.g., just-in-time staffing, lack of career ladders, 24/7 web-based technologies) and family (e.g., dual-earner couples, single-parent households, LGBTQ families) that affect both women and men. These normative understandings diffuse throughout the larger political and cultural context in a geographic state and are incorporated into organizational practices. Our results are also consistent with gender structure theory, which views gender as structured into institutions and which would predict differential policy outcomes from women's greater political representation and power.

FUTURE DIRECTIONS AND POLICIES

Stories like Ramona's, Alice's, and Alice's stepson's are illustrative of the lives of many employees in the contemporary workforce. Our research suggests that rather than focusing on individual schedules or even specific workplace policies, scholars should begin to consider the institutional forces that drive the creation of workplace policies and environments. Research that considers institutional forces shifts the focus away from individuals and organizations to *challenge* institutions and their broader influence on work and on life outcomes.

As Harriet Gross[25] urges, social and political factors determine what is relevant to discussion of work and family. The issues of work and family should not remain tucked away within the day-to-day strategies of individual families but should instead be part of shaping public policy. Issues such as decreased job stability and the lack of protections and supports for employees become a critical part of the work-family conversation, derived from examining the political and legal environment in which these issues are discussed.

A focus on institutional forces also highlights the important connections among work, family, and the community. Voydanoff's[26] research documents that physical and social disorder within neighborhoods and communities can have negative implications for work-family spillover and acts as an additional stressor as individuals attempt to balance work and family demands. Affordable housing, safe neighborhoods, and quality schools provide the stability needed to both work and protect one's family. When women, especially progressive women, occupy public office, these are the very issues for which they tend to advocate. Advancing women to positions of power can work to increase community supports such as child-care and afterschool programs as well as strengthen community ties to encourage neighborhood cohesion and support that can informally assist to balance work and family.

The concerns of scheduling are significant for all workers. Like Alice, those with higher education and incomes have experienced the biggest increases in working hours, primarily because of the rise of dual-earner couples as more women have entered the labor force.[27] These individuals are also the most likely to experience work-family conflict, time pressures, and other job strains. Although high-skilled jobs provide them with autonomy and flexibility, these jobs often come with heavy workloads that blur boundaries between work and family and limit workers' ability to fully take advantage of the flexibility afforded to them.[28]

Schedule control is also necessary for lower-level workers with less autonomy and flexibility, as formal workplace supports are even less likely to be present. For example, Netflix was initially lauded in 2015 for offering workers unlimited parental leave during the first year following a childbirth or adoption.[29] This benefit is, however, only available to Netflix's salaried, white-collar employees and is not offered to its lower-paid, distribution center, blue-collar employees. In terms of schedule control, low-income workers are also more likely to "bear the brunt" of irregular scheduling over higher-income workers.[30] Such a bifurcated system leads workers like Ramona to quit their primary job (for one that offers less money) in order to get the schedule control they need. For these employees, schedule predictability and adequate hours are critical to managing work and family.[31]

Our findings here may also support the notion that organizations strategically improve work conditions to stay ahead of undesired regulation and legislation. Unions have long known and used the threat of militancy[32] to gain employer concessions. Employers will raise wages or improve working conditions to forestall union organizing efforts and strike activity. When women obtain positions of formal political power, it may increasingly signal a more worker-friendly environment and thus organizations may choose to relax more egregious practices under these conditions, such as Walmart's recent decision to increase hourly wages to avoid potential government-mandated minimum wage increases. As institutional theory would predict, following Walmart's public decision to increase wages, major US retailers TJ Maxx and Target quickly followed suit.

One challenge our study highlights, though, is that the institutional supports for balancing work and family vary across states. Although well intended, a drawback of state-level actions is that they may perpetuate the lack of coherent family- and worker-supportive policies at the national level. In the absence of federal laws, protections for workers remain a patchwork of policies that are inconsistent for families and workers across state lines. It is clear that not only should working families seek to put more women in office but, once there, those women should push for federal change; their voices should be clear and strong.

NOTES

1. Rubin, Beth A. *Shifts in the Social Contract*. Thousand Oaks, CA: Sage.
2. Voydanoff, Patricia. 2014. *Work, Family, and Community: Exploring Interconnections*. New Jersey: Psychology Press.
3. Rubin, Beth A. 2007. "New Time Redux: Layering Time in the New Economy." In *Workplace Temporalities: Research in the Sociology of Work*, vol. 17, edited by Beth A. Rubin, 527–44. Oxford: JAI.
4. Rubin, Beth A. 1995. "Flexible Accumulation: The Decline of Contract and Social Transformation." In *Research in Stratification and Mobility*, 297–323. Oxford: JAI.
5. Brody, Charles J., and Beth A. Rubin. 2011. "Generational Differences in the Effects of Insecurity, Restructured Workplace Temporalities, and Technology on Organizational Loyalty." *Sociological Spectrum* 31 (2): 163–192.
6. Rubin, Beth A. 2014. "Employment Insecurity and the Frayed American Dream." *Sociology Compass* 8 (9): 1083–1099.
7. Gornick, Janet C., and Marcia K. Meyers. 2003. "Does Policy Matter? Linking Policies to Outcomes." In *Families That Work: Policies for Reconciling Parenthood and Employment*, 236–267. New York: Russell Sage Foundation.
8. Kelly, Erin L., Phyllis Moen, and Eric Tranby. 2011. "Changing Workplaces to Reduce Work-Family Conflict: Schedule Control in a White-Collar Organization." *American Sociological Review* 76 (2): 265–290.
9. Moen, Phyllis, Erin L. Kelly, Eric Tranby, and Qinlei Huang. 2011. "Changing Work, Changing Health: Can Real Work-Time Flexibility Promote Health Behaviors and Well-Being?" *Journal of Health and Social Behavior* 52 (4): 404–429.
10. Childs, Sarah, and Mona Lena Krook. 2009. "Analyzing Women's Substantive Representation: From Critical Mass to Critical Actors." *Government and Opposition* 44 (2): 124–145.
11. Risman, Barbara J. 2004. "Gender as a Social Structure: Theory Wrestling with Activism." *Gender & Society* 18 (4): 429–450.
12. Paxton, Pamela, Sheri Kunovich, and Melanie M. Hughes. 2007. "Gender in Politics." *Annual Review of Sociology* 33 (1): 263–284.
13. Swers, Michele L. 1998. "Are Women More Likely to Vote for Women's Issues Bills Than Their Male Colleagues?" *Legislative Studies Quarterly* 23 (3): 435–448.
14. Thomas, Sue. 1991. "The Impact of Women on State Legislative Policies." *Journal of Politics* 53 (4): 958–976.
15. Paxton et al. (2007).

16. Morgan, David R., and Sheilah S. Watson. 1991. "Political Culture, Political System Characteristics, and Public Policies among the American States." *Publius* 21 (2): 31–48.

17. Thomas (1991).

18. Little, Thomas H., Dana Dunn, and Rebecca E. Deen. 2001. "A View from the Top." *Women & Politics* 22 (4): 29–50.

19. Caiazza, Amy. 2004. "Does Women's Representation in Elective Office Lead to Women-Friendly Policy? Analysis of State-Level Data." *Women & Politics* 26 (1): 35–70.

20. Long, J. Scott. 1997. *Regression Models for Categorical and Limited Dependent Variables.* London: Sage.

21. Dimaggio, Paul J., and Walter W. Powell. 1983. "The Iron Cage Revisited: Institutional Isomorphism and Collective Rationality in Organizational Fields." *American Sociological Review* 48 (2): 147–160.

22. Stainback, Kevin, and Donald Tomaskovic-Devey. 2012. *Documenting Desegregation.* New York: Russell Sage Foundation.

23. Befort, Stephen F. 2001. "Labor and Employment Law at the Millennium: A Historical Review and Critical Assessment." *Boston College Law Review* 43: 351–460.

24. Gottfried, Heidi. 2013. *Gender, Work and Economy: Unpacking the Global Economy.* Cambridge: Polity.

25. Gross, Harriet. 2001. "Work, Family, and Globalization: Broadening the Scope of Policy Analysis." In *Working Families,* edited by Rosanna Hertz and Nancy L. Marshall, 187–203. Berkeley: University of California Press.

26. Voydanoff (2014).

27. Jacobs, Jerry, and Kathleen Gerson. 2001. "Overworked Individuals or Overworked Families? Explaining Trends in Work, Leisure, and Family Time." *Work and Occupations* 28 (1): 40–63.

28. Schieman, Scott, and Paul Glavin. 2015. "The Pressure-Status Nexus and Blurred Work-Family Boundaries." *Work and Occupations* 43 (1): 3–37.

29. Balding, Susan. 2015. "Netflix's Paid Parental Leave Policy Reflects a Sad Reality Facing Working Families." Economic Policy Institute, September 3. www.epi.org/blog/netflixs-paid-parental-leave-policy-reflects-a-sad-reality-facing-working-families/.

30. Danny Vinik. 2015. "Low-Wage Workers Deserve Predictable Work Schedules." *New Republic,* April 14. https://newrepublic.com/article/121528/lack-scheduling-flexibility-low-income-workers-big-problem.

31. Jacobs, Anna. W., and Irene Padavic. 2015. "Hours, Scheduling and Flexibility for Women in the US Low-Wage Labour Force." *Gender, Work & Organization* 22 (1): 67–86.

32. Rubin, Beth A. 1986. "Class Struggle American Style : Unions, Strikes and Wages." *American Sociological Review* 51 (5): 618–633.

11. Black, Women, or Black Women

An Intersectionality Approach to Health Inequalities

Jielu Lin and Susan W. Hinze

Paula Upshaw was a 36-year-old respiratory therapist from Laurel, Maryland. In 1991 she had a heart attack; as a health professional she was more knowledgeable than most about her symptoms—they were the so-called "classic" signs of a heart attack (terrible chest pain, numbness on her left side, sweating, and nausea). She says, "they never ever considered my heart . . . they were all sure it was my stomach." At her insistence (she was an assertive patient) she received three separate electrocardiograms. But, she reports, the emergency room physicians said her symptoms were normal (for stomach problems) and they sent her home to take antacids and ulcer medications. Her heart condition was not diagnosed until she made a third visit to the ER on a Friday evening and refused to go home. Even though she was eventually admitted to the hospital, she says no one was even thinking about her heart. The following day, a cardiologist on weekend duty was flipping through a stack of Saturday's electrocardiograms that included Paula Upshaw's. Paying no attention to gender, he asked, "Who's the 36-year-old with the massive heart attack?"[1]

The above case of Paula Upshaw opens the now classic article by John B. McKinlay on gender inequalities and heart disease.[2] This story illustrates the value of a gender-neutral patient—without knowing gender, the cardiologist examined the test and correctly diagnosed a massive heart attack. But patients are not gender-neutral—they come into the ER and doctor's offices with gender, and race, and ethnicity, and social class, and sexuality, and age all wrapped up in one body with a lifetime of experiences. Often implicitly, physicians' own biases shape their judgments about patients and eventually influence their medical decisions.[3] The good news is that the past few decades have brought about greater public awareness of how *sex* (generally viewed as a biological category, and increasingly as a continuum) and *gender* (generally viewed as a social status, a legal designation, and a personal identity) each shape diagnoses, treatment, and health outcomes.[4]

Keep in mind that although gender is often viewed as synonymous with women, health researchers have highlighted the importance of attending to how gender shapes men's health as well as women's health.[5] In fact, much of the research on gender and health attempts to answer the question of why men and women differ in health outcomes such as morbidity and mortality.[6] From these gender-based comparisons, we know that higher social and economic status does not necessarily translate into better health outcomes for men. In Western countries, women live longer than men—*even while they continue to lag behind men in occupational prestige, power in the home, earnings, and status in religious and educational institutions.* Why? This is a knotty question many have worked to untangle.

In the United States, women live an average of five years longer than men, and men die at higher rates of 14 of the top 15 causes of death (figures 11.1 and 11.2). Despite women's survival advantage, research shows that Western women get sicker than do men. Women live longer than men, but they have more chronic conditions,[7] and more functional limitations,[8] and they spend more years disabled[9] during later life. Gender-based patterns in health outcomes have been attributed to how men and women are "doing" or "performing" gender, that is, how culturally defined gender roles influence disease risk, illness roles, and health-related behaviors.[10] For example, higher mortality rates among men can be attributed to their higher rates of alcoholism, substance abuse, and death by homicide and accidents—in part due to demonstrations of power in line with hegemonic masculinity, including the denial of weakness and vulnerability.[11] On the other hand, for women, the stress associated with a lifetime of caregiving and the economic consequences of unpaid or underpaid labor has led to their diminished quality of life in later years.[12]

Let's return to Paula Upshaw for a moment. Notice that the description did not disclose her ethnoracial status. Why not? Does it matter for physician perceptions? The answer is very clear here: it matters enormously, but as a social construct, not as something biological or genetic. What if Paula Upshaw was a black or Hispanic woman? In an extensive review of social determinants of risk and outcomes for cardiovascular disease, the American Heart Association makes it clear that ethnoracial status and racism contribute to health inequalities.[13] They note that blacks are two to three times more likely to die of heart disease compared with whites. In an interesting twist, they cite a study by Schulman et al.[14] in which actors portray patients

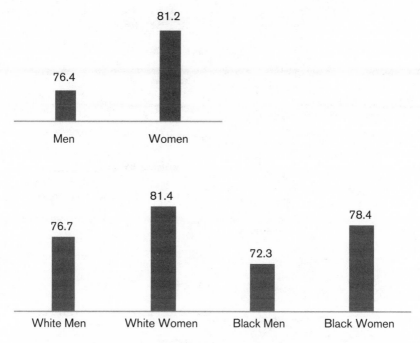

FIGURE 11.1.   Average Life Expectancy (In Years) at Birth: United States, 2013.
Source: Centers for Disease Control and Prevention, Deaths: Final Data for 2013.

with chest pain. The script is the same, and scenarios are videotaped. Results show no difference in the rate of physician-recommended catheterization for black men and white men. So, holding gender constant reveals no racial disparity for men. What happens if we cross gender and race? Shulman et al. found that physicians were less likely to recommend catheterization for black women than for white men with the same symptoms. Clearly, the intersection of race and gender is critical for physician decision making and for understanding the social determinants of population health more generally.

This takes us back to figure 11.2. Notice for nearly all causes of death, men are more likely to die than women, and blacks are more likely to die than whites. If being black generally means having a higher mortality rate, and being a woman generally means having a lower mortality rate, then do the effects of race and gender cancel each other out for black women? The answer is no. However, in health research, scholars have often attempted to disentangle the independent contributions of patients' race, gender, and social class to poor health outcomes and/or access to healthcare. Isolating

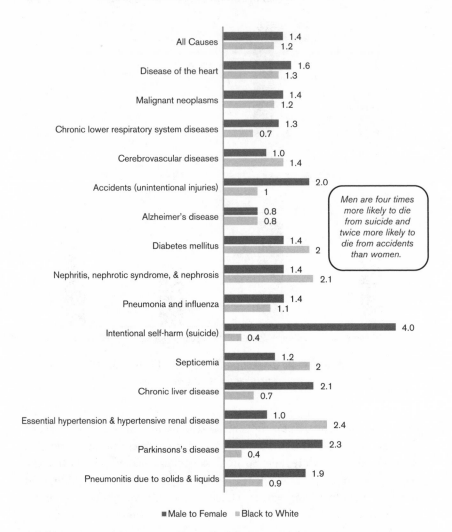

FIGURE 11.2. Death Rate Ratios by Gender and Race for Leading Causes of Death: United States, 2010. *Note:* = 1 means that men (blacks) and women (whites) are equally likely to die from that cause; > 1 means that men (blacks) are more likely to die from that cause than women (whites); < 1 means that men (blacks) are less likely to die from that cause than women (whites). *Source:* Centers for Disease Control and Prevention, Deaths: Final Data for 2013.

the effect of each social factor has become a commonly used analytic approach, even though these social positions cannot and should not be separated for a given individual.

In this chapter, we discuss a recent strand of quantitative research examining population health from the perspective of intersectionality, with an explicit focus on the overlapping, simultaneous production of health inequalities by race/ethnicity, gender, and socioeconomic status. In the first section, we provide an overview of the concept of intersectionality that includes the value of a multiplicative approach in research on health inequalities, the placement of marginalized groups at the center of research, and categorical approaches to health inequalities that better capture the complexities of power differentials between groups and variation of experiences within groups. In the second section, we showcase our own findings—we show how inequalities "get under the skin," resulting in worse health through behavioral pathways (e.g., smoking), relationship pathways (e.g., family and friend network size), psychological pathways (e.g., depressive symptoms), and physiological pathways (e.g., C-reactive protein). In the third section, we discuss our findings in the broader framework of gendered health inequalities. In the final section, we reflect on the recent shift toward a more gender-equal and -equitable approach to health research, and the degree to which an intersectionality approach takes us further toward fairness.

BACKGROUND

Intersectionality and Health Inequalities:
New Questions and New Frontiers

The concept of intersectionality is not entirely new. As Bowleg reminds us, freed slave Sojourner Truth's famous speech "Ain't I a Woman?" from 1851 challenges the exclusivity of being black and being a woman:

> That man over there says that women need to be helped into carriages, and lifted over ditches, and to have the best place everywhere. Nobody ever helps me into carriages, or over mud-puddles, or gives me any best place! And ain't I a woman?[15]

In the late 1980s and early 1990s, black feminist scholars began to challenge more systematically traditional feminist scholarship as reflecting prototypical white, middle-class, US women's experiences, and thus neglecting the lived experiences of women of color.[16] A perspective rooted in "intersectionality," a term coined by legal scholar and critical race theorist Kimberle Crenshaw, emerged with an intensified focus on the multifaceted nature of women's oppressions, and a shift toward developing theories and conceptual models that encompass those realities.[17] Besides being an essential component of the feminist theory discourse, the concept of intersectionality has broad-scale appeal across many social science disciplines, as evidenced by the proliferation of research utilizing intersectionality to attend to issues of political and economic marginalization,[18] disability,[19] health,[20] and aging.[21]

In particular, intersectionality resonates with the line of sociological inquiry of sociostructural inequality, which views race, gender, and class as fundamental, joint determinants of the opportunity structure and life chances.[22] This has led to the rise of a strand of literature applying an intersectionality approach to the studies of racial/ethnic, gender, and socioeconomic health inequalities. Much of this body of work has used qualitative methodologies,[23] but more recently, we have observed an expanding use of an intersectionality approach in large-scale, quantitative analyses of health,[24] generating several streams of novel thinking, analysis, and findings. While sociological and epidemiological studies of health and well-being have contributed much to our understanding of the structure of inequality, the challenges that intersectionality brings to this line of inquiry are threefold. First, should the effect of race, gender, and socioeconomic status be disaggregated in empirical studies of health disparities? Second, what are the potential gains of putting marginalized groups at the center of research? Third, what are the new ways of looking at race, gender, and class beyond categories?

Additive, Competing, or Multiplicative?   In the literature, it is hardly controversial that substantial disparities in health, functioning, well-being, and longevity exist across groups defined by race/ethnicity, gender, and socioeconomic status, highlighting the heterogeneity in population health.[25] Drilling down into these disparities, a wealth of research and analysis has been stimulated and guided by conceptual developments and methodological innovations.

For example, concepts like double jeopardy and multiple jeopardy attempt to explain inequalities as a consequence of disadvantages associated with race, gender, and class accumulating in an additive manner. Let's pretend the woman with the heart attack that opens our chapter, Paula, is a high-income, white man named Paul. In earlier studies, it would be assumed that his social class + his ethnoracial status + his gender would add up to a triple advantage. Yet we know from a rich body of literature on race, socioeconomic status, and gender that it doesn't work that way. Higher-class white men might have more access to resources, but gendered cultural norms and expectations serve as major stressors and psychological strains that disproportionately contribute to risky and unhealthy behaviors in men.

Another important line of inquiry has taken up the task of examining whether gender and racial disparities can be explained by differences in socioeconomic status.[26] Very frequently in this literature, researchers test for whether controlling for socioeconomic status can partial out the independent effects of race or gender. The logic of this approach views socioeconomic status as a competing explanation. It would be assumed that a black woman's health problems are caused by her low socioeconomic status, since black women tend to have fewer years of schooling and lower income as compared to others. As a result, if the race or gender effect disappears after socioeconomic status is accounted for, researchers are often inadvertently "locked in" to proclaim that race does not matter, a problem articulated by Bonilla-Silva and Baiocchi.[27]

An intersectionality approach is distinct from these prior approaches that have examined race/ethnicity, gender, and socioeconomic status together yet as separate dimensions of social stratification. While intersecting race, gender, and education, Hinze et al. report that being black and female has an effect on health beyond what is already accounted for by race and gender.[28] In other words, the health of black women can only be understood if we appreciate that their experiences are greater than the sum of racism and sexism. Similarly, Warner and Brown have found that black women, regardless of their socioeconomic status, have a unique health profile, which they call accelerated disablement, characterized by a more rapid accumulation of functional limitations.[29] Other studies include Sen et al.'s examination of long-term illness in India, showing how class works through gender in securing healthcare access,[30] and Veenstra's use of a multiplicative model to find that South Asian men and women have different experiences of health, with a race effect for women but not for men.[31] This collection of studies consistently suggests the need for a multiplicative, intersectional approach to race, gender, and social class.

Put Marginalized Groups as Center of Research   Although our example above is of a white man with economic privilege, intersectional scholars have long argued the importance of placing marginalized groups at the center of research and analysis. Historically excluded from the production of knowledge, their experiences and perspectives have been missing.[32] The center, or "mythical norm," has been "defined as white, thin, male, young, heterosexual, Christian, and financially secure."[33] Health concerns of those not conforming to the dominant cultural norms have been marginalized, devalued, and treated differently. For example, placing poor women at the center of analysis reveals factors that lead to the underutilization of health services, including limited financial resources that force a focus on food and shelter rather than healthcare.[34] In addition, lack of transportation and child care are barriers to healthcare for poor women. In the case of Paula Upshaw, if she had been African American and poor—let's call her Paulina in this scenario—she might not have even made it to the hospital for care. And if she had made it and been sent home with antacids, her lack of knowledge about the symptoms of a heart attack might have caused her to die at home—unlike the health professional in our vignette, who knew the symptoms and returned three times before she was appropriately diagnosed and treated.

Understanding structural and sociocultural contexts (including the language, systems of meaning, and ideas about community) has been central to health promotion among marginalized people and those living in marginalized communities. Beyond collecting data, health researchers can be advocates, partnering with those in underserved communities to implement community-based sustainable health promotion projects.[35] This type of research, often using anthropological and qualitative sociological approaches, holds promises for extending this line of inquiry in new empirical directions.

Inter- and Intracategorical Complexities To the extent that scholars embrace intersectionality as a research paradigm, there has been little consensus in how to address the issue of intersectionality methodologically (see Bowleg and McCall).[36] It is particularly challenging in the studies of population health, most of which rely on secondary survey data that have already been collected. In these data, race, gender, and social class are measured as demographic variables. They approximate, yet hardly represent precisely, one's social standing. In such a scenario, we do not have the ideal tool for capturing the relationships between multiple dimensions of inequality.

This, however, does not make quantitative analysis ill suited for studying intersectionality. In fact, it urges us to think beyond demographic variables and about more creative ways to analyze quantitative health data, in order to better understand the overlapping system of stratification.

In her influential discussion, McCall introduced three feminist, intersectional approaches—anticategorical, intracategorical, and intercategorical complexities, laying the foundations for many feminist analyses that followed.[37] In simple terms, intercategorical complexities compare power differentials between socially meaningful groups (e.g., men versus women, black versus white) and intracategorical complexities document the lived experience of individuals within each group. Surprisingly, we see relatively little quantitative health research applying these approaches. Instead, the vast majority of the analyses on health inequalities in large-scale population studies tend to be focused exclusively on average differences by race, by gender, or by class, devoting little attention to complexities within each group.

Inter- and intracategorical complexities in particular speak to the central weakness of comparing average differences by race, gender, or class. While informative, the differences reported in this type of analysis are not very closely tied to power differentials between categories. Moreover, such analysis implicitly assumes that individuals in the same category have the same experiences, by collapsing all individuals under one umbrella. Therefore, the reliance on between-group comparisons of average can to some extent contribute to the reification of fundamental group differences. At the same time, these lost distinctions may be very important for us to detect other dimensions of inequality beyond what have been captured by race, gender, and social class.

Complexities within status group are an inherent element of the subject matter of social inequality and can be properly addressed in quantitative health research. Such analysis does not necessarily contradict prior findings on group differences. Rather, it will help us understand whether these subgroup differences are fundamental or definitive and make meaningful conceptualizations and interpretations of within-group differences in health outcomes. In the following section, we describe our own research as an example of disentangling inter- and intracategorical complexities in large-scale quantitative studies of population health outcomes.

CASE STUDY

Now we turn our attention to some empirical health patterning in a nationally representative sample of white and black men and women aged from 57 to 85 years old from the National Social Life, Health, and Aging Project (NSHAP). We begin by examining race/ethnic, gender, and educational difference in self-rated physical health (5-point scale; 0 = Poor, 4 = Excellent), which is a robust indicator of one's overall functioning and strongly inversely correlated with mortality. Not surprisingly, we found that 14 percent of whites rated their health as "excellent." In contrast, only 7 percent of blacks did so. A greater percentage of blacks rated their health as "poor" compared with whites. Fourteen percent of respondents who completed high school or more rated their health as "excellent," whereas only 6 percent of those who did not complete high school did so. Fifteen percent of the less educated individuals, in comparison with only 6 percent of the more educated, rated their health as "poor."

However, we find no patterning when we cross-tabulate gender and self-rated physical health. Does this mean that gender is not associated with health and it is all about race and education? In fact, we have found a myriad of ways through which gender intersects with race and education to influence health. We do this using an intersectionality approach, specifically by examining inter- and intracategorical complexities across groups with different social standing.

Social Standing and Pathways to Health: Intercategorical Complexities

Figure 11.3 compares three groups: (1) black women with less than a high school education, (2) white men with greater than a high school education, and (3) everybody else in the sample. We label (1) the "low-power" group and (2) the "high-power" group to indicate a relational rather than distributional quality. We conceptualize four pathways through which social standing influences health: behavioral, relationship, psychological, and physiological. We show an example for each pathway.

Those in the low-power group are more likely to be smokers, with 29 percent reportedly smoking, compared with 13 percent of the high-power group and 18 percent of the medium-power group (behavioral pathway). Black women with less than a high school education have significantly fewer close connections with friends and family members/relatives, as compared to the other two groups (relationship pathway). In contrast, white men with greater than high school education have more network connections with family and friends (relationship pathway). While low-power individuals show the highest degree of depressive symptoms, one surprising finding is that people in the high-power group, though less depressed than the low-power group, have higher levels of depressive symptoms than the medium-power group (psychological pathway).

With respect to the physiological pathway, we look at differences in C-reactive protein (CRP) by social standing. Normally, there should be no CRP detectable in the blood. When there is an acute infection or injury, the immune system responds and CRP is produced. Chronically elevated levels of CRP is linked to stress-induced chronic inflammation and associated

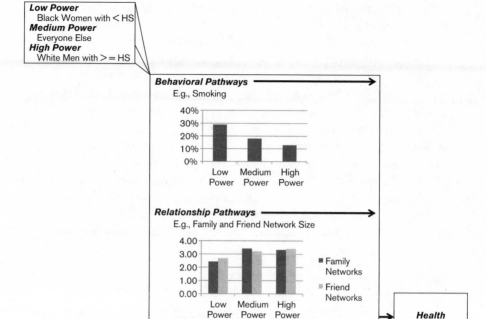

FIGURE 11.3.   Intersectionality, Social Standing, and Pathways to Health.

with a wide range of diseases, including heart disease, diabetes, and stroke in a number of population studies.[38] Therefore, examining differences in CRP levels by social standing as defined by race, gender, and education is useful for establishing a biological mechanism linking social inequalities and health outcomes. As shown in figure 11.3, chronic inflammation as indicated by CRP is highest in the low-power group and lowest in the high-power group, suggesting that social inequalities may lead to biological changes in human bodies.

These patterns together contribute to what we have seen in self-rated health. Gender matters in all of the pathways to health, when we look at the joint, multiplicative effect of race, gender, and education. Comparing blacks with whites or women with men would not capture the same relationships that we captured in our approach. In addition, the more highly educated white men are not simply the converse of lower-educated black women.

Inequalities Get under the Skin: Intra- and Intercategorical Complexities

We have shown that social standing, as jointly determined by one's race, gender, and education, influences health through various pathways. In the following analysis, we focus on the physiological pathway to health and look at patterns in CRP by social standing. Consistent with what we have found, many studies have shown elevated CRP levels among the socially disadvantaged—racial/ethnic minorities, women, and individuals with lower levels of socioeconomic status.[39]

Now we want to take a closer look at CRP levels within each status group. We discuss three measures—the average CRP levels of a group, which give a "pooled" assessment of all individuals in that group, the standard deviation of CRP for a group, which represents how much variability or dispersion there is in that group, and, finally, how CRP is distributed within a group. From figure 11.3 in the previous section, we know that there likely is an average difference between groups with different social standing (i.e., intercategorical complexities), but do all groups have the same, or at least similar, within-group distribution of CRP (as indicated by standard deviations and the shapes of histograms)? If not, how do these intracategorical complexities influence our conclusion regarding average differences between groups in CRP? What do these complexities, both between and within categories, tell us about inequalities based on race, gender, and education?

Figure 11.4 shows the distribution of CRP by social standing. To capture chronic inflammation, we eliminate any CRP levels of 10 mg/l and higher because such values would be indicative of acute infections or injury. We first discuss results from Panel A in figure 11.4, which includes individuals with less than a high school education. Both the average differences and within-group variability in CRP appear to be similar between white men and black men with less than high school education. Neither the average difference nor the standard deviation scores of CRP significantly differ between black and white men with less than a high school education.

Turning to black and white women with less than high school education, we see that black women have higher levels of CRP—a finding that is consistent with prior literature. Does this mean, however, that *all* black women with less than high school education experience the same degree of chronic inflammation? This requires us to tackle the intracategorical complexities. Although there is no difference in the amount of variability (as measured by standard deviations) between white and black women with less than high school education, the distribution of CRP levels differs across these two groups. CRP shows a right-skewed distribution for white women, a pattern that we also see in white and black men. For black women, however, CRP levels are more evenly distributed, exhibiting a more rectangular shape. This suggests that the elevated average CRP levels among black women with less than high school education are caused by two empirical phenomena combined together: (1) there are more black women with elevated CRP levels; *and* (2) there are fewer black women with normal CRP levels, when compared with white women with the same level of education.

Panel B in figure 11.4 shows the distribution of CRP for individuals with high school or greater than high school education. Similarly, we compare racial differences for men and women separately. Black men have the highest CRP levels with the greatest variability in CRP, as compared to white men with the same education level. The same pattern is also found for women. Black women with a high school or greater than high school education also have the highest average with the greatest variability in CRP, as compared to their white counterparts.

When we compare across all four graphs in panel B, figure 11.4, we found a considerable amount of overlap between groups with different social standing. So, the majority of the individuals in the study do *not* differ from one another in terms of chronic inflammation, regardless of their race, gender, and education. The reason that black women with more education have on average elevated CRP levels is because there is a small group of black women with high CRP levels, pulling the group average upward. Such a pattern, although more muted, is also observed for black men with high school or greater education. Even though we have dissected three

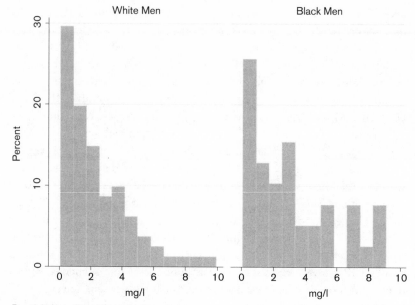

Panel A: Less than high school

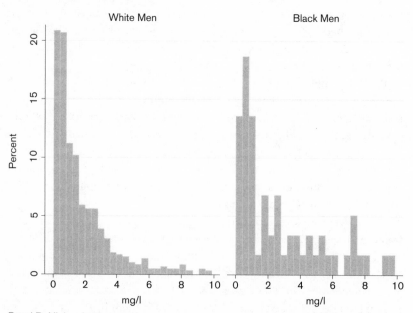

Panel B: High school or greater

FIGURE 11.4. Distribution of C-Reactive Protein by Social Standing.

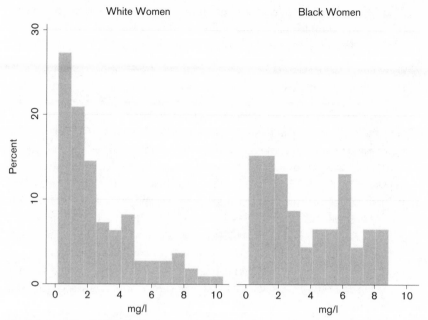

Panel A: Less than high school

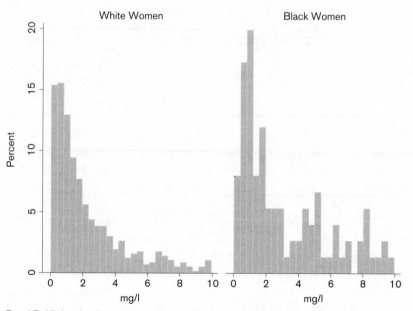

Panel B: High school or greater

FIGURE 11.4. *(continued)*

dimensions—race, gender, and education—the intracategorical complexities that we found indicate other dimensions of inequality that may be intersecting and need to be taken into consideration.

UPDATING THE CONTEMPORARY SITUATION

Let's return to the classic question that we posed at the beginning of the chapter: Why do men and women differ in health outcomes? This is a question that scholars have attempted to answer in many ways. As early as in 1985, Verbrugge outlined her central hypothesis, emphasizing differential exposure: "sex differences in health are principally the outcome of differential risks acquired from roles, stress, life styles, and preventive health practice."[40] In the decades that followed, a large body of literature, predominantly grounded in demographic and epidemiological analyses, has been devoted to explaining why differential exposure matters for women's health—men and women differ systematically in health outcomes because of women's disadvantaged economic status and elevated exposure to stressors associated with such status.[41]

Is it all about exposure? In the early 2000s, a feminist, intersectional perspective was brought into the field of health research, marking an important shift in this line of inquiry from differential exposure to the dynamics of social inequality. Weber and Parra-Medina made a clear distinction between distributional models and relational models, moving from the question of "who has more resources" (distributional) to "who has control over whom" (relational).[42] This perspective has refined scholarly thinking on health inequalities as resulting from the hierarchical ordering of influence or resources rather than from deprivation. In this sense, the issue is no longer "gender and health," but rather "gender inequality and health inequality," which requires scholars to recognize race, gender, and class as social constructs that define status and location in the opportunity structure. As a consequence, race, gender, and class are implicated together not only because the distribution of social resources strongly correlates with one's race and gender, but also because the disparities in resource distribution are reproduced through the individual's race and gender identity.[43]

While research applying an intersectionality approach to the studies of population health is not yet prolific, the collection of studies we discussed in this chapter has provided a more nuanced view of heath inequality, yielding relationships that are otherwise obscured when race/ethnicity and gender are examined in a separate fashion. The way we approach intersectionality—

addressing inter- and intracategorical complexities—bridges a feminist framework and traditional quantitative approaches to race-, gender-, and class-based health inequalities. Consistent with prior studies looking at *intercategorical complexities* in the context of health research, our findings suggest that being a black woman with less than a high school education has its uniqueness in determining one's health status, in terms of both pathways to health and overall physical well-being. The fact that more educated white men are not simply the converse of the low-power group complicates the easy interpretation of how power and privilege manifest. These findings together provide support for the value of a multiplicative approach and suggest the need to explore everyday, consequential experiences of men and women in order to reveal more fully the power of structured inequalities.

With respect to *intracategorical complexities*, we found a substantial amount of within-group heterogeneity in CRP among older white and black men and women, an empirical phenomenon that has been largely overlooked in prior research examining health disparities. These patterns do not just offer a diverse demographic content. Rather, they highlight that relying solely on between-group comparisons, and consequently assuming within-group homogeneity, may put researchers at risk of erroneously concluding that a specific health pattern holds true for all individuals in a given category. Identifying and describing patterns of within-group heterogeneity are, therefore, a necessary first step to understanding the complex, interlocking systems of inequality. Are the same social mechanisms generating intercategorical complexities (i.e., between-group differences) also responsible for intracategorical complexities (i.e., within-group heterogeneity)? If so, why? If not, what other dimensions of inequalities are intersecting with race, gender, and class and producing these complexities?

As does most quantitative research on gender and health inequalities, the exemplar studies that we discussed, as well as our own work, are not immune from feminist criticisms. Though innovative, this line of research still largely hinges on individual-level analysis, preventing us from fully understanding power relationships between women and men and between blacks and whites. An ideal intersectional study might look at how gendered racism influences health. Nevertheless, our work demonstrates how to better utilize existing data to reveal new aspects of health inequalities. Our simultaneous consideration of inter- and intracategorical complexities allows a more comprehensive and meaningful depiction of the intersections of race/ethnicity, gender, and education and their impact on health, based on standard health survey data.

FUTURE DIRECTIONS AND POLICIES

The theorization and a wider application of intersectionality can open up questions about dimensions of oppression and privilege that we have not captured.[44] For example, how do privilege and marginalization function together to impact health? Past research and resulting public policies for improving health have been predominantly biomedical, neglecting people's lives in context. Feminist approaches to health have emphasized placing women at the center of analyses, and in consequence have helped reshape global (e.g., WHO), national, and local policies to improve health.

Indeed, there is good news in the move toward gender equity in health research and policy. A science produced primarily by upper-middle-class men and reflecting a narrow set of political and cultural experiences has shifted to include women.[45] In part due to organizations like the National Women's Health Network, understandings of illnesses have broadened past "men's diseases" and "women's diseases"—resulting in an understanding that will help future Paula Upshaws: heart disease is not a "man's" disease.

On the other hand, institutional barriers to advancing scientific knowledge about women's health persist. For example, it has been decades since scientists have learned that heart disease affects women just as much as it does men, but it was not until very recently that a few pioneering women's health researchers started to advocate "making heart disease a women's disease."[46] While clinical studies now increasingly include women, we see interesting twists in the story: unless they are included in a couple of all-women trials initiated in the 1990s (Women's Health Study, Women's Health Initiative), women's enrollment in cardiovascular clinical trials has *not* increased since 1965.[47] More generally, the number of studies awarded funding by the National Institutes of Health (NIH) to study gender difference in health has decreased by 16 percent, despite a 20-percent increase in the funding rate across the board.[48]

Of late, as intersectional health scholars push us to move beyond discrete groups, more emphasis has been placed on expanding the focus to include ethnoracial status, social class, sexuality, and other social characteristics that shape experience.[49] Scholars championing an intersectional approach—one that places marginalized groups at the center—have historically incorporated political strategies into their work[50] but because intersectionality is in nascent stages of development, understanding how new knowledge can translate into improvements in practices and policies to improve health is an ongoing challenge.[51] As Bowleg eloquently notes, in 2001, the NIH produced "Policy and Guidelines on the Inclusion of Women and Minorities as Subjects of Clinical Research," but the title of the guideline implies a mutual exclusivity of these populations.

The need to assure fairness in clinical studies has long been recognized—"no one group—gender, racial ethnic, or socioeconomic group—[should] receive disproportionate benefits or bear disproportionate burdens of research."[52] As this chapter demonstrates, an intersectionality approach takes us further toward fairness by revealing the complicated relationship between health and the simultaneously socially constructed dimensions of race, class, gender, and age—providing direction for policy-oriented research. The United States may have much to learn from attention to global approaches to health inequalities. In the European Union, a pioneer in gender-equality policies, members are moving toward policies addressing interlocking strands of inequality.[53] In the end, the thoughtful incorporation of intersectionality into population-level interventions might result in more accurate diagnoses, better treatment, and a chance at longer and healthier lives for the Pauls, Paulas, *and* Paulinas of the world.

ACKNOWLEDGMENTS

We thank Casey Albitz for research assistance. This research was primarily conducted while the first author was at Case Western Reserve University. The opinions expressed in the article are the authors' own and do not reflect the official views of the National Institutes of Health, the Department of Health and Human Services, or the United States Government.

NOTES

1. Henig, Robin M. 1993. "Are Women's Hearts Different?" *New York Times Magazine*, October 3, 58–61.

2. McKinlay, John B. 1996. "Some Contributions from the Social System to Gender Inequalities in Heart Disease." *Journal of Health and Social Behavior* 27:1–26.

3. Blair, Irene V., John F. Steiner, Diane L. Fairclough, Rebecca Hanratty, David W. Price, Holen K. Hirsh, Leslie A. Wright et al. 2013. "Clinicians' Implicit Ethnic/Racial Bias and Perceptions of Care among Black And Latino Patients." *Annals of Family Medicine* 11:43–52; Hinze, Susan W., Noah J. Webster, Heidi T. Chirayath, and Joshua H. Tamayo-Sarver. 2009. "Hurt Running from Police? No Chance of (Pain) Relief: The Social Construction of Deserving Patients in Emergency Departments." *Research in the Sociology of Health Care* 27:235–261; Sabin, Janice A., Brian A. Nosek, Anthony G. Greenwald, and Frederick P. Rivara. 2009. "Physicians' Implicit and Explicit Attitudes about Race by MD Race, Ethnicity, and Gender." *Journal of Health Care for the Poor and Underserved* 20:896–913; Sarver, Joshua H., Susan W. Hinze, Rita K. Cydulka and David W. Baker. 2003. "Racial/Ethnic Disparities in Emergency Department Analgesic Prescription." *American Journal of Public Health* 93:2067–2073.

4. Bird, Chloe E., and Patricia P. Rieker. 2008. *Gender and Health: The Effects of Constrained Choices and Social Policies.* New York: Cambridge University Press; Davis, Angela Y. 1990. "Sick and Tired of Being Sick and Tired: The Politics of Black Women's Health." In *The Black Women's Health Book,* edited by Evelyn C. White, 18–26. Seattle: Seal; Krieger, Nancy. 2003. "Genders, Sexes, and Health: What Are the Connections—and Why Does It Matter?" *International Journal of Epidemiology* 32:652–657; Lorber, Judith. 2012. *Gender Inequality.* New York: Oxford University Press; Lucal, Besty. 2008. "Building Boxes and Policing Boundaries: (De)Constructing Intersexuality, Transgender and Bisexuality." *Sociological Compass* 2:519–536; note that sex and gender are not entirely separable. Many of the male-female differences are due to the "irreducibly entangled phenomenon" of "sex/gender" and are "inextricably interwoven factors"; Springer, Kristen W., Jeanne Mager Stellman, and Rebecca M. Jordan-Young. 2012. "Beyond a Catalogue of Differences: A Theoretical Frame and Good Practice Guidelines for Researching Sex/Gender in human Health." *Social Science & Medicine* 74:1817–1824.

5. Courtenay, Will H. 2000. "Constructions of Masculinity and Their Influence on Men's Well-Being: A Theory of Gender and Health." *Social Science & Medicine* 50:1385–1401; Griffith, Derek M. 2012. "An Intersectional Approach to Men's Health." *Journal of Men's Health* 9:106–112; Lorber, Judith, and Lisa Jean Moore. 2002. *Gender and the Social Construction of Illness.* Walnut Creek, CA: Altamira; Verbrugge, Lois M. 1985. "Gender and Health: An Update on Hypotheses and Evidence." *Journal of Health and Social Behavior* 26:156–182.

6. Case, Anne, and Christina Paxson. 2005. "Sex Differences in Morbidity and Mortality." *Demography* 42:189–214; Crimmins, Eileen M., Jung Ki Kim, and Aïda Solé-Auró. 2010. "Gender Differences in Health: Results from SHARE, ELSA and HRS." *European Journal of Public Health* 21:81–91.

7. Gorman, Bridget K., and Jen'nan Ghazal Read. 2006. "Gender Disparities in Adult Health: An Examination of Three Measures of Morbidity." *Journal of Health and Social Behavior* 47:95–110.

8. Murtagh, Kirsten Naumann, and Helen B. Hubert. 2004. "Gender Differences in Physical Disability among an Elderly Cohort." *American Journal of Public Health* 94:1406–1411; Read, Jen'nan Ghazal, and Bridget K. Gorman. 2006. "Gender Inequalities in US Adult Health: The Interplay of Race and Ethnicity." *Social Science & Medicine* 62:1045–1065.

9. Laditka, Sarah B., and James N. Laditka. 2002. "Recent Perspectives on Active Life Expectancy for Older Women." *Journal of Women & Aging* 14:163–184; Newman, Anne B., and Jennifer S. Brach. 2001. "Gender Gap in Longevity and Disability in Older Persons." *Epidemiologic Reviews* 23:343–355.

10. Lorber and Moore (2002); Rieker, Patricia P., Chloe E. Bird, and Martha E. Lang. 2010. "Understanding Gender and Health." *Handbook of Medical Sociology,* edited by Chole E. Bird, Peter Conrad, Allen M. Fremont, and Stefan Timmermans, 52–74. Nashville: Vanderbilt University Press.

11. Courtenay, Will H. 2000. "Constructions of Masculinity and Their Influence on Men's Well-Being: A Theory of Gender and Health." *Social Science & Medicine* 50:1385–1401.

12. Hinze, Susan W. 2016. "Gender and Health." In *Gender: Sources, Perspectives and Methodologies,* edited by Renée C. Hoogland. New York: Macmillan.

13. Havranek, Tomas, Roman Horvath, Zuzana Irsova, and Marek Rusnak. 2015. "Cross-Country Heterogeneity in Intertemporal Substitution." *Journal of International Economics* 96:100–118.

14. Schulman, Kevin A., Jesse A. Berlin, William Harless, Jon F. Kerner, Shyrl Sistrunk, Bernard J. Gersh, Ross Dube et al. 1999. "The Effect of Race and Sex on

Physicians' Recommendations for Cardiac Catheterization." *New England Journal of Medicine* 340:618–626.

15. Bowleg, Lisa. 2012. "The Problem with the Phrase Women and Minorities: Intersectionality—an Important Theoretical Framework for Public Health." *American Journal of Public Health* 102:1267–1273.

16. Collins, Patricia Hill. 1986. "Learning from the Outsider Within: The Sociological Significance of Black Feminist Thought." *Social Problems* 33:14–32; Crenshaw, Kimberle. 1991. "Mapping the Margins: Intersectionality, Identity Politics, and Violence against Women of Color." *Stanford Law Review* 43:1241–1299; hooks, bell. 1990. *Yearning: Race, Gender and Cultural Politics.* Boston: South End.

17. King, Deborah K. 1988. "Multiple Jeopardy, Multiple Consciousness: The Context of a Black Feminist Ideology." *Signs: Journal of Women in Culture and Society* 14:42–72.

18. Glenn, Evelyn Nakano. 1985. "Racial Ethnic Women's Labor: The Intersection of Race, Gender and Class Oppression." *Review of Radical Political Economics* 17:86–108.

19. Liasidou, Anastasia. 2013. "Intersectional Understandings of Disability and Implications for a Social Justice Reform Agenda in Education Policy and Practice." *Disability & Society* 28:299–312.

20. Schulz, Amy J., and Leith Mullings. 2006. *Gender, Race, Class, and Health: Intersectional Approaches.* San Francisco: Jossey-Bass; Weber, Lynn, and Deborah Parra-Medina. 2003. "Intersectionality and Women's Health: Charting a Path to Eliminating Health Disparities." *Advances in Gender Research* 7:181–230.

21. Calasanti, Toni. 2009. "Theorizing Feminist Gerontology, Sexuality, and Beyond: An Intersectional Approach." *Handbook of Theories of Aging* 2:471–486.

22. Choo, Hae Yeon, and Myra Marx Ferree. 2010. "Practicing Intersectionality in Sociological Research: A Critical Analysis of Inclusions, Interactions, and Institutions in the Study of Inequalities." *Sociological Theory* 28:129–149; DiPrete, Thomas A., and Gregory M. Eirich. 2006. "Cumulative Advantage as a Mechanism for Inequality: A Review of Theoretical and Empirical Developments." *Annual Review of Sociology* 32:271–297.

23. Schulz and Mullings (2006).

24. Hinze, Susan W., Jielu Lin, and Tanetta E. Andersson. 2012. "Can We Capture the Intersections? Older Black Women, Education, and Health." *Women's Health Issues* 22:91–98; Robinson, Margaret, and Lori E. Ross. 2013. "Gender and Sexual Minorities: Intersecting Inequalities and Health." *Ethnicity and Inequalities in Health and Social Care* 6:91–96; Sen, Gita, Aditi Iyer, and Chandan Mukherjee. 2009. "A Methodology to Analyse the Intersections of Social Inequalities in HEALTH." *Journal of Human Development and Capabilities* 10:397–415; Veenstra, Gerry. 2013. "Race, Gender, Class, Sexuality (RGCS) and Hypertension." *Social Science & Medicine* 89:16–24; Warner, David F., and Tyson H. Brown. 2011. "Understanding How Race/Ethnicity and Gender Define Age-Trajectories of Disability: An Intersectionality Approach." *Social Science & Medicine* 72:1236–1248.

25. Berkman, Lisa F., Ichiro Kawachi, and Maria Glymour, eds. 2014. *Social Epidemiology.* New York: Oxford University Press; Marmot, Michael G. 2004. *The Status Syndrome: How Social Standing Affects Our Health and Longevity.* New York: Holt.

26. House, James S., Ronald C. Kessler, and A. Regula Herzog. 1990. "Age, Socioeconomic Status, and Health." *Milbank Quarterly* 68:383–411; Matthews, Sharon, Orly Manor, and Chris Power. 1999. "Social Inequalities in Health: Are There Gender Differences?" *Social Science & Medicine* 48:49–60.

27. Bonilla-Silva, Eduardo, and Gianpaolo Baiocchi. 2007. "Anything but Racism: How Sociologists Limit the Significance of Racism." In *Handbooks of the Sociology of Racial and Ethnic Relations*, edited by Herman Vera and Joe R. Feagin, 79–100. New York: Springer.

28. Hinze, Lin, and Andersson (2012).

29. Warner and Brown (2011).

30. Sen, Iyer, and Mukherjee (2009).

31. Veenstra (2013).

32. Collins (1986); Ruzek, Sheryl Burt, Virginia L. Olesen, and Adele Clarke, eds. 1997. *Women's Health: Complexities and Differences*. Columbus: Ohio State University Press.

33. Lorde, Audre. 1984. *Sister Outsider: Essays and Speeches*. Trumansburg, NY: Crossing.

34. Marshall, Alicia A., and Janet K. McKeon. 1996. "Reaching the 'Unreachables': Educating and Motivating Women Living in Poverty." In *Communication and Disenfranchisement: Social Health Issues and Implications*, edited by Eileen Berlin Ray, 137–155. New York: Routledge.

35. Farmer, Paul. 1999. *Infections and Inequalities*. Berkeley: University of California Press; Ford, Leigh Arden, and Gust A. Yep. 2003. "Working along the Margins: Developing Community-Based Strategies for Communicating about Health with Marginalized Groups." In *Handbook of Health Communication*, edited by Teresa L. Thompson, 241–226. New York: Lawrence Erlbaum.

36. Bowleg (2012); McCall, Leslie. 2005. "The Complexity of Intersectionality." *Signs: Journal of Women in Culture and Society* 30:1771–1800.

37. McCall (2005).

38. Danesh, John, Jeremy G. Wheeler, Gideon M. Hirschfield, Shinichi Eda, Gudny Eiriksdottir, Ann Rumley, Gordon D.O. Lowe, Mark B. Pepys, and Vilmundur Gudnason. 2004. "C-Reactive Protein and Other Circulating Markers of Inflammation in the Prediction of Coronary Heart Disease." *New England Journal of Medicine* 350:1387–1397; Mendall, M.A., Praful Patel, Lydia Ballam, D. Strachan, and T.C. Northfield. 1996. "C Reactive Protein and Its Relation to Cardiovascular Risk Factors: A Population Based Cross Sectional Study." *BMJ* 312:1061–1065; Ridker, Paul M., Charles H. Hennekens, Julie E. Buring, and Nader Rifai. 2000. "C-Reactive Protein and Other Markers of Inflammation in the Prediction of Cardiovascular Disease in Women." *New England Journal of Medicine* 342:836–843.

39. Das, Aniruddha. 2013. "How Does Race Get 'Under the Skin'? Inflammation, Weathering, and Metabolic Problems in Late Life." *Social Science & Medicine* 77:75–83; Herd, Pamela, Amelia Karraker, and Elliot Friedman. 2012. "The Social Patterns of a Biological Risk Factor for Disease: Race, Gender, Socioeconomic Position, and C-Reactive Protein." *Journals of Gerontology Series B: Psychological Sciences and Social Sciences* 67:503–513; Schafer, Markus H., Kenneth F. Ferraro, and Sharon R. Williams. 2011. "Low Socioeconomic Status and Body Mass Index as Risk Factors for Inflammation in Older Adults: Conjoint Influence on C-Reactive Protein?" *Journals of Gerontology Series A: Biological Sciences and Medical Sciences* 66:667–673; Nazmi, Aydin, and Cesar G. Victora. 2007. "Socioeconomic and Racial/Ethnic Differentials of C-Reactive Protein Levels: A Systematic Review of Population-Based Studies." *BMC Public Health* 7:212–224.

40. Verbrugge (1985).

41. Read, Jen'nan Ghazal, and Bridget K. Gorman. 2010. "Gender and Health Inequality." *Annual Review of Sociology* 36:371–386.

42. Weber and Parra-Medina (2003).

43. Bauer, Greta R. 2014. "Incorporating Intersectionality Theory into

Population Health Research Methodology: Challenges and the Potential to Advance Health Equity." *Social Science & Medicine* 110:10–17; Hankivsky, Olena. 2012. "Women's Health, Men's Health, and Gender and Health: Implications of Intersectionality." *Social Science & Medicine* 74:1712–1720.

44. Bauer (2014).

45. Ruzek, Olesen, and Clarke (1997).

46. Bird, Chole. 2013. "Making Heart Disease a Women's Issue." *Ms. Magazine,* March 20.

47. Harris, David J., Pamela S. Douglas. 2000. "Enrollment of Women in Cardiovascular Clinical Trials Funded by the National Heart, Lung, and Blood Institute." *New England Journal of Medicine* 343:475–480.

48. Simon, Viviana R., Tajrina Hai, Sarah K. Williams, Erica Adams, Kristen Ricchetti, Sherry A. Marts. 2005. "National Institutes of Health: Intramural and Extramural Support for Research on Sex Differences, 2000–2003." *Scientific Report Series: Understanding the Biology of Sex Differences.* Washington, DC: Society for Women's Health Research.

49. Ruzek, Olesen, and Clarke (1997).

50. Luft, Rachel E., and Jane Ward. 2009. "Toward an Intersectionality Just out of Reach: Confronting Challenges to Intersectional Practice." *Perceiving Gender Locally, Globally, and Intersectionally* 13:9–37.

51. Hankivsky (2012).

52. Mastroianni, Anna C., Ruth Faden, and Daniel Federman, eds. 1994. *Women and Health Research: Ethical and Legal Issues of Including Women in Clinical Studies.* Washington DC: National Academies Press.

53. Hankivsky (2012).

12. Interactions between Gender and Immigration in Wage Inequality among STEM Workers, 1980–2010

Erin M. Stephens, Joshua D. Tuttle, and James C. Witte

Amita and her young children followed her husband from India to the United States when he was recruited by a biotechnology research institute. Amita is trained as a physician and finds work with a local hospital. Despite her considerable experience, she finds that she is not offered pay increases or career opportunities at the same pace as her male counterparts. Moreover, without the support she had in her home country, she struggles to find the time to build her career with the heavier burden of care work at home. Amita wonders if she will ever be rewarded for her work at the same level as immigrant men who practice medicine in the United States.

INTRODUCTION

In the twentieth century, the American workforce transformed as the proportion of women and immigrants in the workforce grew rapidly. Women grew from being approximately a third of the labor force in 1950 to over 60 percent in 2000.[1] The immigrant population swelled with the passing of the Immigration and Nationality Act of 1965, which ended nation-based quotas and policies of exclusion for Asian and Latin American countries and allowed naturalized immigrants to sponsor family members for immigration. Not only did this act facilitate the entry of a larger and more heterogeneous pool of immigrants, but women immigrants steadily became a larger proportion of the immigrant population. Between 1950 and 2010 the foreign-born population in the United States grew from 7.5 percent to 12.9 percent, while the share of women among the foreign-born grew from 48.7 percent to 51.0 percent.[2] Combining these two trends, along with overall population growth in the United States, the estimated number of foreign-born women in the country grew nearly fourfold, from 5.5 million to 20.4 million.

Despite the growth in labor force participation for both groups, compensation for work has been characterized by a different trend. While the gap between men's and women's pay closed from approximately 60 percent in 1955 to 74 percent in the mid-1990s,[3] there has been little change to the gap since then. However, the trend for wages between immigrant men and women tells a different story. Between 1950 and 2000, the gap between immigrant men and women closed from 67 percent to 83 percent. Between 2000 and 2010, the gap closed further, to 87 percent.[4] There is an abundance of research that explores the stagnation in the pay gap among the general population, but *what explains the variation in the pay gap among immigrants?*

This chapter explores trends in wage earnings for immigrant men and women from 1980 to 2010 with an interest in understanding the interaction between gender and immigrant characteristics as it relates to gender pay disparities. In the context of laws regarding gender equity and immigrant rights in the workplace, we review common explanations for the gender pay gaps for women and men more broadly and specific factors as they pertain to immigrants. Using US Census data from 1980 to 2010, we then present a case study on immigrants in science, technology, engineering, and mathematics (STEM) occupations to explore how certain factors help explain gender pay disparities between high-skill immigrant men and women over time. Our findings indicate that within this group, the gap closed significantly between 1980 and 1990, held constant from 1990 to 2000, and had a slight decline between 2000 and 2010. Further, we observe among STEM workers that immigrant men earn more than native-born men, and immigrant women also earn more than native-born women. Finally, among all STEM workers, the wages of native-born men were relatively flat between 1980 and 2010, such that earnings of immigrant women were nearly equal to those of native-born men in 2010.

BACKGROUND

The persistent gap in median and average earnings between men and women in the United States has been well documented by social scientists and successfully brought into public discourse by feminist activists and others. Researchers have done exhaustive analyses to explore whether the wage gap is due to gender discrimination or can be explained by other individual and labor market factors. Economists, in particular, have been interested in explaining the disparity, attributing much of the wage gap to gendered differences in the quantity and quality of human capital. They have often employed human capital models to study the gender wage gap, concluding that gender-based differences in occupational choices, college majors, work experience, abilities, and noncognitive skills explain much of the gap.[5] Further, they argue that the wage gap can be fully explained by accounting for gender differences in labor market tastes. For example, a study showed that though more women are in higher-status jobs, they are more likely to work in people-oriented jobs than in jobs that pay more, such as data- or "thing"-oriented occupations.[6]

However, sociologists and other social scientists have critiqued the strength of the human capital model for explaining gender wage disparities. Psychologist Hilary Lips argues that the conceptualization and operationalization of the "investments" and "outcomes" that are central to human capital theory are themselves not gender-neutral, such that understanding the gender gap requires a more nuanced theoretical framework.[7] Sociologists have argued that gender socialization plays a key factor in informing labor market participation and outcomes. Okamoto and England found that men and women exhibit distinct and different patterns of job preferences and employment patterns in accordance with cultural standards.[8] Sociological research has also shown that women tend to accumulate less labor market experience due to familial gender roles and have more intermittent work lives.[9] Budig and England argued that women experience a *motherhood wage penalty*, especially when they are married, such that women with children earn less than women without children.[10] The gendered dimensions of care work means that, compared to women without children, mothers are more likely to interrupt their career to have children (diminishing future earnings), seek parent-friendly jobs that may pay less, face employer discrimination for family obligations, and be distracted by needs of children.

The Immigrant Employment Context

An analysis of the wage gap between immigrant men and women requires an understanding of the additional barriers that face immigrant workers, as well as their gendered dimensions. While the Immigration and Nationality Act of 1965 facilitated the exponential growth of immigrants in the workforce, legislation passed in the 1980s and 1990s had different economic implications for various classes of immigrants. The Immigration Reform and Control Act (IRCA) in 1986 was the first piece of legislation aimed at undocumented migrants. It introduced penalties for employing undocumented immigrants, increased border control, and offered amnesty to undocumented migrants. The legislation resulted in increased wage penalties for undocumented workers,[11] greater discrimination for undocumented workers and Hispanics, and feminized migration from Mexico.[12] Further restrictions were added in the Illegal Immigration Reform and Immigrant Responsibility Act of 1996. Alternatively, the Immigration Act of 1990 eased restrictions on temporary skilled workers and raised the cap on employment-based visas, thus increasing the admissions of skilled immigrant workers.[13] These policies further articulated the difference between documented and undocumented, and low-skilled and high-skilled, workers, which in turn has had particular implications for women as explored below.

When it comes to labor participation and wage earnings among immigrants, there are additional barriers at play. Factors that can affect wage earnings among immigrants include

- *Country of Origin:* Research has shown that highly educated immigrants are less likely to hold highly skilled jobs, particularly those from Eastern European, Middle Eastern, and Latin American countries.[14] Immigrants from Canada, Oceania, and other European countries have been found to have earning advantages.[15]

- *Translation of Foreign Degree into the US Labor Market:* Though some immigrants arrive in the United States with advanced training and degrees, depending on the country of origin and type of qualification, these degrees may not transfer into the labor market, and additional certification or licensing may be required to practice in the United States. Immigrants from the same country may find that while technical degrees translate easily into the workforce, medical degrees do not. For example, physicians face particular challenges transferring their skills and training to the workforce. Alternatively, scientists and engineers are more easily able to enter equivalent jobs.[16] This can result in immigrants who are overskilled for their current occupations, such as the ubiquitous Uber and taxi drivers who practiced medicine in their home countries.

- *Place of College Education:* Related to the issue of degree translation, research shows that obtaining an undergraduate college degree in the United States, rather than another country, is associated with higher earnings, regardless of where graduate degrees are obtained.[17] This may be due to challenges related to acculturation and language, but also to employers' preference for and familiarity with "made in America" higher education.[18]

- *Acculturation:* While all immigrants may struggle to assimilate to a new country, the more dissimilar a country is to the United States, the more difficult it can be to be successful in the US labor market. For example, unspoken codes of conduct in the workplace regarding dress, relationships, language, time, and other ways of being can affect an immigrant's ability to obtain and be successful in certain types of jobs. Access to social networks, or the lack thereof, can affect one's ability to obtain jobs as well. Cultural and racial bias in the workplace may limit promotion opportunities and wages. Low or poor English skills serve as a barrier for many jobs, especially those that require strong communication skills, such as customer service and many professional jobs (e.g., teaching, sales, or marketing).

- *Visa and Citizenship Status:* Requirements related to nativity or visa/citizenship may control access to certain jobs, such as those in the public sector. Immigrants on student or working visas may struggle to find employers who are willing and able to cover visa expenses. Additionally, US citizenship status has been shown to moderate the relationship between sociodemographic characteristics and wages. Among Mexican immigrants, undocumented status has been associated with slower wage growth and lower returns to human capital.[19] And, most obviously, undocumented status or documents showing expired legal residence exclude immigrants from legal, formal employment.

Intersections of Gender and Immigration

There are also gendered dimensions to the immigration-employment context as described above. Social scientists have argued that immigrant women experience a cumulative disadvantage due to their gender and the context of their immigration in the labor market.[20] To begin with, the gender dynamics from the home country can also impact labor market participation in the United States. The labor force participation for first-generation women has been shown to be associated with the gender gaps in labor force participation in their home countries.[21] There are often generational shifts in women's workforce participation, with the first generation of women immigrants less likely to work than future generations. Further, men and women often have different immigration and assimilation paths that affect their labor participation and earning trajectories.[22] Refugee flows are more likely to initially be dominated by women and children and there is evidence that since 9/11 the US refugee resettlement programs, including employment services, have deteriorated.[23] Immigrant women have tended to concentrate in certain occupations in the US labor force.[24] Low-status occupations in domestic service and the garment industry have continued to be occupations with high concentrations of immigrant women, though over time the population for both has shifted from being primarily European migrants to Latin American and Asian migrants. Though foreign-born men are more likely to be self-employed, immigrant women also are likely to work in entrepreneurial small businesses.

The social consequences of gender impact highly skilled immigrant women as well. Emigration rates for skilled women have been shown to be higher than that of skilled men, particularly for migrants from Africa, Oceania, and Latin America.[25] Indeed, women are an increasing proportion of the highly educated immigrant population. Yet, a study of 2010 Census data showed that despite having higher rates of naturalization, schooling, and years in the United States than immigrant men, highly skilled immigrant women who worked in managerial, professional, and related occupations still earned less than their counterparts.[26] Moreover, this study showed that these women experienced a double earnings penalty on the basis of gender and nativity, with a greater proportion of the gap being explained by nativity.

Additionally, different labor participation outcomes can be observed between women who come to the United States for familial reasons and those who come to work. Women are more likely to be permanent migrants accompanying men and bring their children through family unification visas, prioritizing their husband's career over their own.[27] As dependents, immigrant women have less power than men performing the institutional interactions necessary to enter the job market (such as engaging with accreditation institutions). In one study of highly skilled Asian Indian women, who emigrated under family reunification clauses, the demands of care and house work made it more difficult to overcome barriers such as devalued credentials, gaining access to professional networks, occupational segregation, and glass ceilings.[28]

CASE STUDY: GENDER DISPARITY AMONG IMMIGRANT STEM WORKERS

Based on the existing literature, our empirical goal in this chapter is to further explore how factors that have been shown to contribute to gender wage inequity in the US population interact with immigrant-related characteristics to explain gender wage inequity among the US immigrant labor force. In order to consider the interactions between gender and immigration in wage earnings over time, our analysis specifically focuses on comparing men and women immigrants, rather than comparing them to native-born workers. This allows us to more precisely consider potential changes to the male and female earnings structures among immigrants over time. We engage a cumulative disadvantage perspective that considers the social consequences of gender among immigrant workers and considers the consequences of citizenship status, race, and the development status of home countries. Additionally, we have chosen to focus specifically on STEM workers in order to control for variation in occupational demands, skill level, and education. Due to the limitations of our data, we were not able to include legal status among noncitizen immigrants as a variable in the analysis.

The STEM workforce experienced major growth in the 20th century: increasing nearly eightfold between 1950 and 2000.[29] Though women make up approximately half of the overall US workforce, the STEM occupations have and continue to be disproportionately filled by men. In the 1970s, women made up 3 percent of engineers, 14 percent of life and physical scientists, 17 percent of social scientists, and 15 percent and math and computer occupations. While women have increasingly entered these fields—in 2011, women were 13 percent of engineers, 41 percent of life and physical scientists, 27 percent of computer occupations, 47 percent of math occupations, and 61 percent of social scientists—significant differences according to gender remain.[30] There has been substantial federal funding and energy put toward recruiting and retaining women in STEM careers, yet women remain only one-fourth of the total STEM labor force.

The persistent gender imbalance has been attributed to the lack of women role models, gender stereotypes, gender socialization of girls away from math and sciences, and fewer women pursuing STEM degrees. For example, though computer science and information technology is one of the nation's fastest growing fields, there has been a growing gap between women and men earning these degrees.[31] Indeed, since the 1990s, women have declined as a proportion of computer occupations.[32] Computer occupations are approximately 80 percent of STEM occupations, but only a fourth of positions held by women.[33] Gender stereotypes and bias contribute to the imbalance.

Women also face gendered challenges in the workplace. College-educated women make 20 percent more in STEM careers than in non-STEM careers, making it a lucrative career choice for women.[34] Nonetheless, in a comparison of women in STEM careers to other high-skill professional women, a study found that women in STEM occupations were significantly more likely to leave the field, though they often remain the labor force.[35] Women engineers, in particular, have been found to be less likely to persist in STEM careers, primarily due to lack of advancement and dissatisfaction with pay.[36] In addition, the wage gap between men and women with STEM college degrees jumped from men earning 22.5 percent more than women in 1993 to 44 percent in 2003. In a longitudinal cohort study of college graduates in STEM careers, women were found to experience earning penalties as their family obligations grew.[37]

While women in STEM careers are paid more than their non-STEM counterparts,[38] there remains a substantial gap between men and women in these careers. A Department of Commerce report in 2011 found that after controlling for a number of characteristics, men and women earned $36.34 and $31.11 per hour, respectively, in private sector STEM jobs. That amounted to an overall pay gap of 14 percent. The field of computer science and math, which has some of the highest average salaries, also has relatively large gender imbalances in employment and wage gaps, with women making 12 percent less than what men earned. When considering the implications for earnings over a career, in addition to factoring in potential earning penalties associated with motherhood, the persistent wage inequality is troubling.

Method

This chapter draws upon US Census data from the Integrated Public Use Microdata Series (IPUMS). We combine unweighted 5 percent state data samples from the 1980, 1990, and 2000 US Decennial Census and the 2010 five-year American Community Survey (ACS). Our analysis was limited to immigrants who were at least 25 years of age, who worked full-time in STEM occupations, and who had worked for the entire year prior to participating in each survey. To avoid undue influence of outliers, we also limited our analysis to immigrant STEM workers who earned more than $0 and less than $200,000 dollars, annually. Here we define STEM occupations according to the occupational categories included in the ACS. Seven STEM occupational groupings were identified: software developers, engineers, mathematicians and computer scientists, natural scientists, technicians, drafters and surveyors, and healthcare practitioners (see appendix 12.A for a detailed list of individual occupations in each group).

We analyzed the effect of gender on annual wage and salary income with a multiple regression model. A multiple regression model is a mathematical model that measures the relationship between a continuous dependent variable and a set continuous or discrete independent variables. The model assumes that the dependent variable shares a linear relationship with each independent variable. That is, a change in each independent variable ought to be related to a linear change in the dependent variable. In this case, annual wage and salary income served as the dependent variable, while gender served as the independent variable of interest. Other independent variables that are known to share a relationship with income (and the incomes of immigrants in particular) were included in the model, such as educational attainment, marital status, parenthood, English proficiency, age, race, occupation, self-employment, and the level of economic development that characterized an immigrant's country of birth. These control variables allowed us to more clearly measure the relationship between gender and annual wage and salary income while accounting for the effect of other social and economic characteristics.

To accurately model change over time, it was necessary to control for economic and demographic variations across years of data. We accomplished this with the inclusion of dummy variables for each year of data. Dummy variables are also known as indicator variables in the sense that they indicate the presence or absence of a categorical trait that is thought to have some kind of effect on a dependent variable. Thus, a dummy variable was included for individuals who responded to the ACS in 1990, 2000, and 2010. A dummy variable for 1980 was excluded as a reference category, which allowed us to observe how the effect of responding to the ACS in 1990, 2000, and 2010 affected wage and salary income relative to the effect of responding to the ACS in 1980. We also included several interaction terms that measured the effect of gender on wage and salary income per year. Again, the effect of gender in 1980 was omitted as a reference effect, which allowed us to compare the impact of gender on wage and salary income in subsequent years of data. Sample sizes for each year and descriptive statistics for all variables can be found in appendix 12.B.

Foreign-born workers have progressively become a larger proportion of the STEM workforce over time. As depicted in figure 12.1, the share of immigrants in the STEM workforce is much greater than the share of immigrants in the general workforce and in the general population. More specifically, the share of immigrants in the STEM workforce grew from approximately 9 percent in 1980 to approximately 19 percent in 2010, while the share of immigrants in the total population grew from approximately 6 percent to 13 percent. In each case the population more than doubled, but the starting point for immigrants in the STEM workforce was much higher than in the general population.

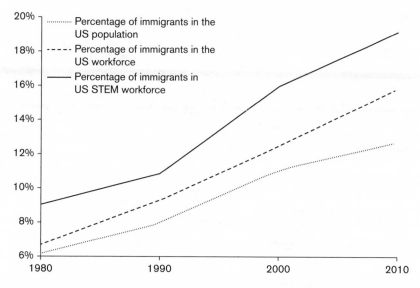

FIGURE 12.1. Trends in the US Immigrant Population over Time.

Trends in median wage and salary income by gender and nativity are presented in figure 12.2. In comparison to females, male STEM workers were characterized by higher median incomes across all years of data. However, male and female immigrant STEM workers fared better than their native-born counterparts. Indeed, in 2010, immigrant males enjoyed a median income that was $7,664 larger than native-born males, while immigrant females enjoyed a median income that was $11,073 larger than native-born females. While it may be surprising to some, there are two potential explanations: specific occupation and level of education. Immigrant STEM workers are overrepresented among the specific occupational group with the highest median wage, such as software developers, while the native-born are disproportionately found in occupations with the lowest median wages, such as technicians, drafters, surveyors (see appendix 12.B). Second, the proportion of the immigrant-born STEM workers with a graduate degree is nearly double that of native-born STEM workers across all years of data. Among immigrant STEM workers, the pay gap between males and females was smallest in 1990, with immigrant men enjoying a median income that was $8,792 larger than immigrant females. Nevertheless, this gap grew in subsequent years. By 2000, the gender pay gap between male and female immigrant STEM workers approached $13,000. However, by 2010, the gap was reduced to $9,300.

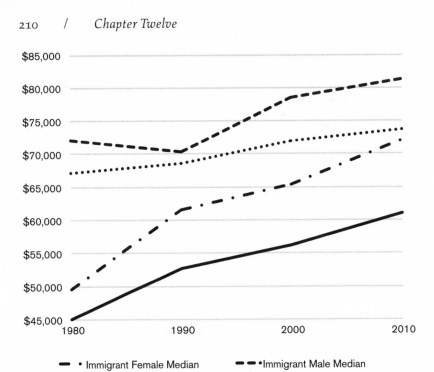

FIGURE 12.2. Trends in the Median Income of STEM Workers by Gender and Nativity.

The results of the linear regression model (see appendix 12.C) demonstrate that gender shares a significant relationship with annual wage and salary income. More specifically, when compared to male immigrant STEM workers, female immigrant STEM workers were characterized by an average wage penalty of $24,272 dollars. Moreover, female immigrant STEM workers who were married with children were characterized by an additional average wage penalty of $682, while male immigrant STEM workers who were married with children enjoyed an average wage advantage of $924.

However, the results of the linear regression model demonstrate that female immigrant STEM workers have enjoyed pay increases since the 1980s, with the largest pay increase occurring between the years 2000 and 2010. As a result, the gender pay gap among male and female immigrant STEM workers shrank significantly during those years. Nevertheless, the gender pay gap has persisted, which means that more must be done if the pay inequities that female immigrant STEM workers experience in the US labor market are to be addressed.

Gender pay gap aside, the results of the analyses indicate that female immigrant STEM workers who hail from developing regions enjoy a wage advantage over their counterparts from developed regions. Indeed, this wage advantage approached $9,000. The reason for this wage advantage is not yet clear, but it may be explained by the locations in which these female immigrants received their education. It may be that female immigrant STEM workers who originated in developing nations also sought out a college or graduate degree when they arrived in the United States, while their counterparts from developed nations were educated before emigrating. A college or graduate degree earned in the United States may be worth more than those earned abroad.[39]

FUTURE DIRECTIONS AND POLICIES

The results of this analysis indicate that wage and salary income among immigrant STEM workers continues to be stratified along the lines of gender. Indeed, the effect of gender proved to be the largest in comparison to the other social and economic factors considered in this case study, with female immigrants suffering from an estimated average wage penalty of $24,272 relative to male immigrants between 1980 and 2010. Of course, immigrant women are not alone in their disadvantaged situation. Over the years, the literature has consistently found that on average, female workers are remunerated at a lower rate than male workers, even when controlling for other factors that influence one's income.[40] Thus, the persistence of the gender pay gap among immigrant STEM workers must be viewed as a particular example of a larger social problem: wage discrimination on the basis of gender.

As this analysis and other analyses have demonstrated, wage discrimination is felt most acutely by mothers. That is, mothers experience a double wage penalty: first they are penalized because of their gender; then they are penalized once again because they are mothers. Here, the wage *penalty* associated with motherhood among immigrant STEM workers was an estimated at $682. On the other hand, fatherhood yielded an estimated wage *advantage* of $924. This is further evidence of wage discrimination on the basis of gender, and also supports the cumulative disadvantage perspective that is highlighted in studies of skilled immigration and gender in the United States.[41]

Indeed, the gender pay gap has been studied in a number of different economic contexts and across time. Here it was found that the gender pay gap has persisted for at least 30 years among immigrant STEM workers, despite the increases in wages among immigrant females—though it did narrow significantly between 1980 and 2010. Given the durability of this pay gap, it seems that labor policies are needed to ameliorate it, as employers have failed to address it voluntarily. An obvious policy recommendation is equal pay for equal work. That is, females must receive the same pay as males if they are involved in work of equal standing. Such a policy would accomplish two objectives. First, it would certainly increase the well-being of females who work in the United States. Second, it would make the United States a more appealing locale for immigrant women, particularly those who specialize in the STEM fields.

As the United States continues to prioritize STEM careers, another policy recommendation would be to address credentialing barriers for immigrants. Immigrants who are unable to translate their education and skills into the US labor market result in an abundance of brain waste that disadvantages immigrant families, particularly women. Creating more pathways for skill translation, especially for immigrants from developing countries, would allow the American economy to benefit from currently underused skills. Additionally, initiatives aimed at recruiting girls and women into STEM career pathways should engage immigrant and first-generation populations as well. Moreover, recruitment efforts for immigrant STEM workers should make recruiting talented women part of their recruitment strategy.

Finally, future social policies should also address the wage discrimination that mothers face in the US economy. As the only industrialized nation without paid maternity leave, such policies could include nonpunitive paid maternity leave that does not harm women's ability to receive raises and promotions. Workplaces should institutionalize child-care provisions for working mothers, which would allow women to focus on their careers and their families simultaneously while minimizing the wage penalty associated with motherhood. Also, social policies regarding child care for working mothers ought to consider culturally sensitive child-care issues, such as language accessibility and environments that allow for different cultural practices. This would allow all women to utilize child-care programs for the benefit of themselves and their families. This too could give US employers a competitive advantage in the highly competitive international labor market for STEM workers.

APPENDIX 12.A   STEM Occupation Groups and Specific STEM Occupations per Group by Nativity and Gender, Pooled across Years

Occupation, and Median Income in 2010	Weighted Total Per Occupational Group			
	Native Male	Native Female	Foreign Male	Foreign Female
Software Developers ($82,453)	1,660,893 (12.2%)	549,513 (7.1%)	494,072 (20.2%)	171,533 (12.7%)
Engineers ($81,322)	4,316,348 (31.8%)	376,986 (4.9%)	730,739 (29.9%)	83,594 (6.2%)
Aerospace engineers				
Metallurgical and materials engineers				
Petroleum, mining, and geological engineers				
Chemical engineers				
Civil engineers				
Electrical engineers				
Industrial engineers				
Mechanical engineers				
Other engineers				
Mathematicians and Computer Scientists ($66,066)	2,361,846 (17.4%)	1,099,535 (14.3%)	395,170 (16.1%)	145,150 (10.8%)
Computer systems analysts and computer scientists				
Operations and systems researchers and analysts				
Actuaries				
Statisticians				

(continued)

APPENDIX 12.A (Continued)

Occupation, and Median Income in 2010	Native Male	Native Female	Foreign Male	Foreign Female
		Weighted Total Per Occupational Group		
Mathematicians and mathematical scientists				
Natural Scientists ($64,863)	854,457 (6.3%)	319,984 (4.1%)	201,108 (8.2%)	118,571 (8.8%)
Physicists and Astronomers				
Chemists				
Atmospheric and space scientists				
Geologists				
Agricultural and food scientists				
Biological scientists				
Foresters and conservation scientists				
Medical scientists				
Other natural scientists				
Healthcare Practitioners ($65,962)	1,612,677 (11.9%)	4,455,449 (58.2%)	340,840 (13.9%)	718,913 (53.6%)
Physicians				
Dentists				
Veterinarians				
Optometrists				
Podiatrists				
Registered Nurses				
Pharmacists				

Other healthcare practitioners				
Social Scientists ($65,962)	374,405 (2.7%)	320,221 (4.1%)	43,059 (1.7%)	33,188 (2.4%)
Economists				
Psychologists				
Sociologists				
Other social scientists				
Technicians, Drafters, Surveyors ($50,621)	2,355,171 (17.4%)	532,557 6.9%)	235,117 (9.6%)	76,122 (5.6%)
Electrical engineering technicians				
Mechanical engineering technicians				
Other engineering technicians				
Drafters				
Surveyors, cartographers, and mapping technicians				
Biological technicians				
Chemical technicians				
Other science technicians				
Total	13,535,797 (99.7%)	7,654,244 (99.9%)	2,440,105 (99.6%)	1,341,264 (100.1%)

NOTE: Column percentages do not total 100% due to rounding.

APPENDIX 12.B Unweighted Descriptive Statistics for All Variables Included in the Regression of Wage and Salary Income

	1980 N=17,019		1990 N=27,484		2000 N=51,497		2010 N=78,959	
	Mean	SD	Mean	SD	Mean	SD	Mean	SD
Continuous Variables								
Wage and Salary Income	70568.39	34930.94	73072.54	33207.00	78012.76	36278.56	83232.85	36038.48
Age	40.07	10.22	40.58	10.20	40.29	10.08	42.18	10.40
# of Children in Home	01.18	01.22	01.08	01.14	00.96	01.08	01.01	01.06
	Percent		Percent		Percent		Percent	
Dichotomous Variables								
Female	28.3		34.3		35.3		37.3	
Naturalized Citizens	56.9		60.1		54.2		58.2	
Developing Regions	57.8		69.2		75.8		80.7	
English Speaking	80.2		79.5		79.0		80.3	
Self-Employed	05.0		04.1		03.1		03.1	
Hispanic	11.0		11.5		09.4		10.1	
Married	77.4		73.5		72.8		74.8	
Race								
Black	05.3		07.5		07.2		08.1	
White	55.3		43.2		36.9		29.7	
Asian	11.0		14.5		16.6		15.6	
Other Races	28.4		34.8		42.1		46.6	

Education				
High School	10.0	05.8	03.6	03.7
Some College	17.8	19.0	13.6	11.5
Bachelor's Degree	21.8	35.0	38.1	38.6
Graduate Degree	50.4	40.2	44.7	46.2
Occupations				
Software Developers	04.3	09.0	20.7	21.1
Healthcare Practitioners	34.3	29.8	26.7	28.3
Engineers	32.3	28.7	19.9	17.2
Mathematicians and Computer Scientists	05.2	10.0	14.8	17.2
Natural Scientists	07.0	06.6	09.2	08.5
Social Scientists	02.7	02.5	01.6	01.9
Technicians, Drafters, Surveyors	14.2	13.4	07.1	05.8

APPENDIX 12.C Predictors of Constant Wage and Salary Income, 1980–2010

	Unstandardized Ordinary Least Squares Regression Coefficient	Standard Error of the Estimate
Females	−24341.59**	603.99
Males	Reference category	—
Naturalized Citizens	3849.75**	166.06
Noncitizens	Reference category	—
Developing Regions	−4452.11**	281.12
Developed Regions	Reference category	—
English Speaking	8390.59**	193.77
Non-English Speaking	Reference category	—
Self-Employed	1392.64*	414.43
Employee	Reference category	—
Hispanic	−5770.75**	285.70
Non-Hispanic	Reference category	—
Black	−9725.01**	367.66
White	Reference category	—
Asian	1554.30**	289.68
Other Races	47.55	245.11
Married	2813.52**	214.97
Nonmarried	Reference category	—
Number of Own Children in Home	760.40**	234.34
High School or Less	−11469.32**	405.56
Some College	−9366.73**	246.10
Bachelor's Degree	Reference category	—
Graduate Degree	11532.86**	177.28
Age	3144.58**	57.29
Age-Square	−28.50	0.63
Software Developers	1459.56**	256.03
Healthcare Practitioners	Reference category	—
Engineers	−4105.17**	245.46
Mathematicians and Computer Scientists	−4975.71**	266.34
Natural Scientists	−18963.90**	313.94
Social Scientists	−5467.99**	550.67
Technicians, Drafters, and Surveyors	−21833.20**	327.88
1980	Reference category	--

1990	2253.04**	369.48
2000	5651.78**	330.77
2010	7585.22**	330.77
Interaction Terms		
Female*1990	6079.67**	666.88
Female*2000	6135.00**	612.32
Female*2010	8553.71**	612.32
Female*Developing Regions	8811.20**	371.06
Female*Married*Children	-687.47*	255.45
Male*Married*Children	934.99**	254.07
Constant	-7432.61	1263.85
Adjusted R-Square	.237	—

NOTE: N = 174,959; * = p < .01; ** = p < .001.

NOTES

1. O'Neill, June. 2003. "The Gender Gap in Wages, circa 2000." *American Economic Review* 93 (2): 309–314.

2. Based on calculations from the 1950 1% Decennial Census and the 2010 American Community Survey using Steven Ruggles, Katie Genadek, Ronald Goeken, Josiah Grover, and Matthew Sobek. 2015. *Integrated Public Use Microdata Series: Version 6.0.* Machine-Readable Database. Minneapolis: University of Minnesota.

3. Ruggles et al. (2015).

4. Authors' estimations based upon data from the Integrated Public Use Microdata Series American Community Survey, 1950–2010.

5. Blau, Francine D., and Lawrence M. Khan. 2000. "Gender Differences in Pay." *Journal of Economic Perspectives* 14 (4): 75–99; Grove, Wayne A., Andrew Hussey, and Michael Jetter. 2010. "The Gender Pay Gap beyond Human Capital: Heterogeneity in Noncognitive Skills and in Labor Market Tastes." *Journal of Human Resources* 46 (4): 827–874.

6. Lippa, Richard A., Kathleen Preston, and John Penner. 2014. "Women's Representation in 60 Occupations from 1972 to 2010: More Women in Higher-Status Jobs, Few Women in Things-Oriented Jobs." *PLoS One* 9 (5): e95960.

7. Lips, Hilary. 2013. "The Gender Pay Gap: Challenging the Rationalizations: Perceived Equity, Discrimination, and the Limits of Human Capital Models." *Sex Roles* 68 (3/4): 169–185.

8. Okamoto, Dina G., and Paula England. 1999. "Is There a Supply Side to Occupational Gender Segregation?" *Sociological Perspectives* 42:557–582.

9. Blau and Khan (2000).

10. Budig, Michelle J., and Paula England. 2001. "The Wage Penalty for Motherhood." *American Sociological Review* 66:205–225.

11. Hall, Matthew, Emily Greenman, and George Farkas. 2010. "Legal Status and Wage Disparities for Mexican Immigrants." *Social Forces* 89 (2): 491–513.

12. Donato, Katherine M., Chizuko Wakabayashi, Shirin Hakimzadeh, and Amada Armenta. 2008. "Shifts in the Employment Conditions of Mexican Migrant Men and Women." *Work and Occupation* 35 (4): 462–495.

13. Lowell, B. Lindsay. 2010. "A Long View of America's Immigration Policy and the Supply of Foreign-Born STEM Workers in the United States." *American Behavioral Scientist* 53 (7): 1029–1044.

14. Mattoo, Aaditya, Illeana Cristina Neagu, and Caglar Ozden. 2008. "Brain Waste? Educated Immigrants in the US Labor Market." *Journal of Development Economics* 87:255–269.

15. Tong, Yuying. 2010. "Place of Education, Gender Disparity, and Assimilation of Immigrant Scientists and Engineers Earnings." *Social Science Research* 39:610–626.

16. Tong (2010).

17. Tong (2010).

18. Bergson-Shilcock, Amanda, and James Witte. 2015. *Steps to Success: Integrating Immigrant Professionals in the U.S.* New York: World Education Services.

19. Hall, Greenman, and Farkas (2010).

20. Pedraza, Silvia. 1991. "Women and Migration: The Social Consequences of Gender." *Annual Review of Sociology* 17:303–325.

21. Antecol, Heather. 2000. "An Examination of Cross-Country Differences in the Gender Gap in Labor Force Participation Rates." *Labour Economics* 7:409–426.

22. Pedraza (1991).

23. Kerwin, Donald. 2012. "The Faltering US Refugee Protection System: Legal and Policy Responses to Refugees, Asylum-Seekers, and Others in Need of Protection." *Refugee Survey Quarterly* 34 (4): 1–33.

24. Pedraza (1991).

25. Lopez, Mary J. 2012. "Skilled Immigrant Women in the US and the Double Earnings Penalty." *Feminist Economics* 18 (1): 99–134.

26. Lopez (2012).

27. Goyette, Kimberly, and Yu Xie. 1999 "The Intersection of Immigration and Gender: Labor Force Outcomes of Immigrant Women Scientists." *Social Science Quarterly* 80 (2): 395–408.

28. Purkayastha, Bandana. 2005. "Skilled Migration and Cumulative Disadvantage: The Case of Highly Qualified Asian Indian Immigrant Women in the US." *Geoforum* 36:181–196.

29. Lowell (2010).

30. Landivar, Liana Christin. 2013. "Disparities in STEM Employment by Gender, Race and Hispanic Origin." US Department of Commerce. Washington, DC: US Census Bureau. www.census.gov/prod/2013pubs/acs-24.pdf.

31. Change the Equation. 2013. "Vital Signs: What Is the STEM Where You Live and Work?" http://vitalsigns.changetheequation.org/.

32. Landivar (2013).

33. Landivar (2013).

34. Beede, David, Tiffany Julian, David Langdon, Beethika Khan, and Mark Doma. 2011. "Women in STEM: A Gender Gap to Innovation, Executive Summary." US Department of Commerce, Economics, and Statistics Administration, Washington, DC. www.esa.doc.gov/sites/default/files/womeninstemagaptoinnovation8311.pdf.

35. Glass, Jennifer L., and Sharon Sassler. 2013. "What's So Special about STEM? A Comparison of Women's Retention in STEM and Professional Occupations." *Social Forces* 92 (2): 723–756.

36. Fouad, Nadya, Romila Singh, Mary E. Fitzpatrick, and Jane P. Liu. 2011. *Stemming the Tide: Why Women Leave Engineering.* University of Wisconsin-Milwaukee. www.studyofwork.com/files/2011/03/NSF_Women-Full-Report-0314.

pdf; Hunt, Jennifer. 2010. "Why Do Women Leave Science and Engineering?" NBER Working Paper No. 15853, National Bureau of Economic Research.

37. Xu, Yonghong. 2015. "Focusing on Women in STEM: A Longitudinal Examination of Gender-Based Earning Gap of College Graduates." *Journal of Higher Education* 86 (4): 489–523.

38. Beede et al. (2011).

39. Bergson-Shilcock and Witte (2015) in their study of immigrant professionals found that economic success in terms of salary, use of one's higher education, and employment in a professional or managerial position was significantly more likely among those with at least some higher education in the United States.

40. Okamoto and England (1999); Blau and Kahn (2000); Lips (2013).

41. Purkayastha (2005).

13. Queer Eye on the Gay Rodeo

D'Lane R. Compton

Cowboys Are Frequently Secretly (Fond of Each Other) . . . Say,
what do you think all them saddles and boots was about?

—WILLIE NELSON, "Cowboys Are
Frequently Secretly (Fond of Each Other)"

*I do not remember how or when I first heard about gay rodeos, but I do
remember how excited I felt. Yet this excitement was coupled with some
hesitation. I felt the need to disguise my excitement among my queer
friends. I presented the gay rodeo's allure as rooted in simple curiosity, a
chance to further my academic study of queer life. However, I was personally interested in finding others like me—other queers who appreciated
country as a lifestyle or one might even say as an ethnicity—rather than
simply as a place. Country meant good things to me; I dreamt of owning
land and livestock and I loved country music and dancing.*

*One of the most difficult aspects of coming out for me was how drasti-
cally the setting for my social life changed. My previous "straight" life
involved what one could call "country" entertainment. It took place in
dusty arenas, around animals, and in bars that played country music.
Upon coming out, my social life moved to house parties or venues that
played dance and pop music and I rarely took road trips to small towns for
markets, fairs, or rodeos. Rather, I was more likely to make trips to a big
city for nightlife, shopping, and art. While I know this sounds like a sim-
plistic juxtaposition of bad stereotypes, it really felt that way to me at the
time. The sociologist in me often reflected on why this occurred. I now
suspect one influential factor was the lack of mainstream knowledge
regarding the true diversity of queer life at the time, which was almost two
decades ago.*

*On the level of appearances, it seemed simple. Queer people were unwel-
come in country places—places associated with rednecks, Republicans, and
ignorance. Thus, we did not go there. After all, the mass media had taught
us that country was a place where we would die not only from isolation,
but also from even more horrible cruel, painful, violent, and undignified*

deaths like Brandon Teena's or Matthew Shepard's. Yet, at times I was uncomfortable in ostensibly safe, queer spaces due to my country background. Ironically, it often felt like my rural conservative friends and acquaintances were less disapproving of my sexual orientation than my liberal queer friends were of my country tastes. So one can understand why I was so excited to hear about a gay rodeo. I anticipated a queer country wonderland extravaganza that encompassed all of the "good" that country culture had to offer and none of the bad. I did not have to worry about coming out or being too gay and cowboy hats were not associated with fears of homophobic harassment.

INTRODUCTION

I have given numerous sociological presentations on topics of sexual orientation over the past 10 years and the majority of my postpresentations conversations have not been directly about the presentation itself, but rather my experience living and working in Texas. The questions have typically centered on my experience of being an openly queer person doing queer work in Texas. To then state that I was well funded, supported, and even encouraged to be who I am and do the work I do in Texas and, even more, that I like living in Texas and have a preference for the country and country lifestyle seems to further incite interest. The social psychologist in me realized that what was occurring was a clash of stereotypes. "Texas" and "country" denote rural, conservative, red state, intolerant, and resistant to change, while the images associated with LGBT people include liberal, blue state, urban, and progressive. Queer stereotypes do not mix with the stereotype of rural or country; rather, queer stereotypes encompass places and lifestyles that are the opposite of rural and country stereotypes. In few instances does this perhaps become more exaggerated than at the gay rodeo.

This chapter addresses whether gay rodeo is a transgressive performance from the vantage point of someone who is both queer and country. Indeed, one of the reasons I draw on queer theory is the social constructionism and its assumptions that give a queer lens to heteronormative[1] settings—in this case the rodeo.[2] I also draw on queer theory because of its focus on gender as performance and performance politics.[3] This framework of social constructionism and situated knowledges is employed to develop my own narrative of what being both queer and country means for interpreting gay rodeos. I then provide a brief discussion of prior research relevant to this topic, as well as a brief overview of the history of gay rodeo. An analysis of my participant observations of gay rodeo and insights from formal interviews follow this historical and textual grounding.

BACKGROUND

On an academic level, I am always fascinated with identities and stereotypes—how they come about, how they are employed, when they are salient, and, above all, when they clash and how those clashes are overcome. Once again, I attribute this to my social location of being queer and spending most of my life in rural spaces. This combination of personal and academic interests leads me to question how sexual minorities deal with and create queer spaces in what I call "unexpected places"—where stereotypes of sexual orientation clash with those of place or lifestyles. Fortunately, there has been a recent increase in scholarly attention on this topic. This work examines Log Cabin Republicans, gays and lesbians in the military, gay and lesbian Christians, and LGBT experiences in the South, the Midwest, and rural places, in addition to other queer subcultures.[4] A significant portion of this work is also explored through documentary films, such as *Queens and Cowboys, Small Town Gay Bar, Southern Comfort,* and a whole series of minidocumentaries on LOGO—a LGBT television network.[5]

City, Place, and LGBT Life

Academic research also challenges reigning assumptions regarding queer identities and place. In "Get Thee to a Big City," Kath Weston explains how past queer thought uncritically suggests that if a person is struggling to come out in rural America, then they should go to San Francisco or at least to a "big city."[6] Weston's work questions taken-for-granted associations of meaning between categories of queer identities and place. For example, she notes how much earlier work focuses on "gay" as meaning white, male, and college-educated. Thus, it overlooks the experiences of queers of different genders, races, and classes. She also notes how many queer narratives link more free and open sexualities and sexual practices to the city, posing an opposition between the city and the country. Yet it is unclear to Weston whether this opposition actually exists.[7] Scott Herring's work on queer anti-urbanism further asserts the urban and the city as the largely exclusive focus of studies of queer culture in America although there is much more beyond the "city limits."[8] Moreover, he documents how this assumption of metronormativity is pervasive throughout LGBT art, culture, and politics.[9]

We know that rural queers exist. While there is no way to count exactly how many gay, lesbian, bisexual, or transgender people live in America, demographers extrapolate through the censuses and nationally representative social science and health surveys that there are approximately nine million people that identify as LGBT living in the United States.[10] The 2000 US Census data shows that 99 percent of US counties have same-sex partners living in them, with 15 percent of the same-sex partners (approximately 180,000) residing in nonmetropolitan areas.[11] Although these same-sex partners are located throughout the United States, they are not distributed equally. Rather, there is considerable variation in their rates of prevalence across these areas; some cities have larger presences of gay and lesbian partners in comparison to other cities, just as some rural towns and counties have larger presences in comparison to other rural towns and counties.[12]

US Census data from 2000 also shows that lesbian households are more likely to be found in rural areas in comparison to their gay male counterparts and that they have higher prevalence rates in almost 90 percent of the nonmetropolitan counties.[13] Among nonmetropolitan counties, the most influential variables for explaining geographic distributions of same-sex households are whether the counties are retirement counties, whether they are rural, and whether they are farming-dependent. These findings indicate a higher concentration of gay male and lesbian households in isolated nonmetropolitan communities, rather than in communities in closer proximity to cities. Work drawing on the 2010 Census suggests more gay men are moving out of metropolitan areas although the above trend of lesbian couples being more likely to live in rural spaces still holds.[14] Qualitative work further supports that LGBT individuals do not just live in gay enclaves and cities.[15] Some suggest that a combination of increasing social tolerance, assimilation, increasing rates of parenthood, rising costs of city living, the wage gap, and the Internet is contributing to this shift.[16] Additionally, Michael Rosenfeld theorizes that the extension of the independent life stage experienced by young adults has reduced parental control over mate selection, adding to the complications of understanding how and where LGBT individuals may move and settle.[17] There is evidence to suggest that single LGBT individuals may move to "known as" gay cities and enclaves to find community and partners, and may be more likely to leave or interact less in "gay spaces" once partnered.[18]

This empirical work may be counterintuitive to the average person—queer or otherwise. One might suppose that few queers would choose to live in a place like Texas, but Texas housed the third largest queer population in the country in 2000 and the fourth in 2004, dropping behind Florida by less than 2100 couples.[19] Furthermore, legislation concerning issues of sexual orientation does not have a significant impact on where gay male and lesbian couples reside, whether they have children, or how they organize their households.[20] It appears that gay men and lesbians who reside in rural areas or "red states" may understand, use, or avoid the law differently than their urban or "blue state" counterparts.[21] In any case, these individuals exist regardless of stereotypes and expectations—LGBT individuals do live and thrive in rural places and red states.

Gay Rodeos

Regarding gay rodeos specifically, there is little academic literature on the subject. One informative piece by Patricia Nell Warren responds to the *Brokeback Mountain* backlash.[22] Warren's article "Real Cowboys, Real Rodeos" details a more accurate version of cowboy and rodeo life from the romanticized and nostalgic Americana portrayals. She asserts that few occupations are more conducive to a secret same-sex relationship and draws on a "real-life Jack Twist" to exemplify her point. She further analyzes the birth of rodeo and various types of rodeos from ranch rodeos to the larger professional rodeos and gay rodeos. She emphasizes the heterosexism within rodeo and how openly gay contestants are only found in gay rodeo although many may compete in the mainstream rodeo before coming out. For Warren, gay rodeo is just as "real" as any rodeo because in the end it pits human against animal and seeks to answer: "which of the two will win?"[23]

Other work employing various frameworks to analyze gay rodeos, their events, and their functions is found in graduate theses and dissertations. Three common themes emerge from this work. First, gay rodeos serve primarily as entertainment and social gathering places for gay men.[24] Second, gay rodeos are masculine venues, although there is less consistency in what this means for the rodeos and the participants. Third, gay rodeos involve paradoxes. On the one hand, they appear to challenge traditional gender and sexual norms via the introduction of gay culture and the eradication of gender barriers in events. On the other, they uphold these traditional norms through the idealization of heteronormative masculinity.[25]

HISTORICALLY GROUNDING GAY RODEO

According to the International Gay Rodeo Association, the first gay rodeo was held in 1976 in Reno, Nevada. It began as a fundraiser for the Muscular Dystrophy Association (MDA). First conceptualized in 1975, the idea of an amateur gay rodeo was expected to be fun, raise money, and erase gay stereotypes. However, it was difficult and expensive to find a location and animals for a gay event.[26] It was not until the following year that Ragsdale, the event's founder, was able to secure a location and animals. Approximately 125 people took part in the event and it was considered "great fun and a minor success."[27]

In 1977, the gay rodeo and fundraiser were introduced as the National Reno Gay Rodeo. It included the "Mr., Ms., and Miss National Reno Gay Rodeo" contests and titles to further benefit the Muscular Dystrophy Association (MDA). This event raised only $214.00 for the MDA. Nevertheless, the rodeo became a new outlet for the gay community with additional events and activities that complemented the rodeo like theme parties such as country/western parties, dance events (including square dancing, clogging, line-dancing, and two-stepping), and 24-hour casinos. Three years later, 10,000 people attended the 1980 Reno Gay Rodeo and $40,000 was raised for MDA. Gay rodeo had been transformed from a "minor success" to a major new entertainment venue for gays and lesbians.

Throughout the 1980s numerous rodeo events and rodeo associations formed across the United States. (The "Urban Cowboy" phenomenon was taking hold within both the gay community and mainstream America.) In 1985 the International Gay Rodeo Association (IGRA) was founded and by 1991 the association had spread across the United States and split into three regions. The mission of IGRA was to support other regional or state rodeo associations and their communities. In addition to providing resources to produce quality events and supporting amateur sportsmanship, the IGRA promotes a LGBTQ country/western lifestyle.

Currently, the IGRA includes over 25 member organizations that represent nearly 30 states, the District of Columbia, and four Canadian provinces.[28] The IGRA maintains year-round events, fundraisers, and a Hall of Fame, and has national sponsors that have included Miller Light, Bud Light, Jack Daniels, Logo, American Airlines, and Whole Foods.[29] In short, gay rodeo became an institution in the LGBT community. I have attended a number of gay rodeo events in my lifetime; for the purpose of this work I focus on three events that took place in Texas and Louisiana.

CASE STUDY

Growing up in rural Texas, I have attended rodeos my entire life. They range in size, location, and whether they are amateur or professional. A small town or high school rodeo is quite different from a national-level, professional event. Small town rodeos are more bare bones with less glitz

and glamour, while a professional event generally caters to audience entertainment and involves a great show (such as musical entertainment by professional recording artists and fireworks or pyrotechnics) in addition to the
rodeo events. However, most audiences have an expectation of what should
be happening—stereotypical or otherwise: it will take place in an arena, the
contests rarely change, and there will be cowboys, boots, and hats. As such,
I went to my first gay rodeo expecting a rodeo—albeit one with more
"glam" and, perhaps, rainbows. I expected it to be very much like any other
amateur rodeo, but with an out and proud audience.

Rodeoing

Upon arrival, I found a smaller version of a mainstream rodeo. It was more
like an exhibition or high school rodeo, but with far less foot traffic, especially in regard to spectators. Most people appeared to be participating in
the rodeo, working the event, or attending to support a friend or loved one.
All seemed to have some direct connection to the rodeo. Although attendance was sparse, there was a diverse mix of ages, sexes, races, and sexual
orientations (largely thanks to many heterosexual vendors). This regional-
level rodeo felt somewhat family-oriented and lighthearted over all.

On the surface, the rodeo did not appear all that queer and was quite
heteronormative. It began with the national anthem and a prayer, which is
typical for mainstream rodeos. Most participants and onlookers could have
passed as heterosexual at any rodeo. However, there were a few touches of
flair—the occasional rainbow flag accessory (such as a rainbow flag hat pin,
patch, or belt buckle) and men sporting sleeveless shirts, tank tops, or no
shirts at all. Such attire (or lack thereof) is seldom seen at mainstream
rodeos. In addition, a rainbow flag hung alongside state and national flags
and queer specialty tables were mixed in with vendors who attend all types
of rodeos. The gay rodeo had many of the same events or contests as a
mainstream rodeo. Notably, however, it also included a few events never
seen in mainstream rodeo—such as the wild drag race (a three-person
event that involves one male, one female, and one person in drag—either
male or female—who must work together to maneuver a steer across part
of the arena, and then must mount the drag contestant on the steer and
cross back over the finish line with the drag contestant on top).

The rodeo seemed most queer when I ran into or interacted with drag
queens, who represented rodeo royalty in heavily starched shirts and jeans
with pageant sashes that stated their rodeo affiliations and, of course, big
hair and sparkly makeup and bedazzled accessories. Drag was also employed
as a replacement to the rodeo clowns in mainstream rodeo. This drag was

not the camp drag commonly expected at a queer event. Rather it was a male participant in a sequined bra and underwear combo over his jeans and a brightly colored wig. This was "clownish" drag, rather than campy drag, that could be employed by any male and their role was to do the job of mainstream rodeo clowns but with a colorful and bedazzled twist.

I attended my first gay rodeo as a volunteer, where I sat at a table for a political organization. We were seated behind the bleachers with other organizations and commercial vendors. Our table was next to a table giving away the "Gay and Lesbian Yellow Pages" and across from other tables that sold or promoted various merchandise from the conventional (such as cowboy hats and leather belts) to the more risqué (such as a "private club" for gay men or candles in various masculine scents, which included leather and tobacco). For a majority of the vendors, this was also their first time at a gay rodeo.

Overall, I was pleased to have experienced my first gay rodeo. It did seem that a community was present and that it was a tolerant place—open and accepting—no matter one's sexual orientation. Furthermore, queer country interests were shared in an open and accepting environment. As I explain below, the event also felt empty and inconsequential. While it may have entertained attendees for a day, as a new comer I was especially left with the impression that I only played "rodeo" for the day.

While my first gay rodeo met my initial expectations, my next rodeo experience suggested that, as with mainstream rodeos, gay rodeos were also varied in their levels of participation, competition, and attendance—factors that often were based on their location and promotion. Indeed, promotion and attendance greatly affected the atmosphere of the rodeo. When attendance was low, the event seemed more diverse regarding age, sex, race, and even sexual orientation. As attendance increased, the rodeo became a less heterosexual and a more white, male event. For example, the first rodeo I attended felt more family-oriented because there were numerous children playing in and around the venue. These were children of gay parents and some heterosexual vendors. However, there were very few children at the second event I attended, which felt more like a gay cowboy social event.

The Scene

There was a social merriment quality to the gay rodeo that can also be found at professional rodeos. However, it was more exaggerated and closely mirrored what I deem a cowboy-themed circuit party. It was almost as if an entirely different event was taking place in spaces that flanked the arena. There was a cruising culture or vibe in these adjacent spaces. In fact, many individuals did not make it into arena seating; rather, they milled around in the spaces that border the arena and high foot traffic areas (near the entrance, expo areas, and concession stands) with drinks in hand. In these spaces, the rodeo was a mere prop and contributed to the party setting and theme. The vast majority of these individuals were voyeurs and "dudes" dressed in cowboy clothes. They appeared to be more concerned with the social goings-on of the other "party"-goers than they were with the actual rodeo events. Further, individuals at this party were overwhelmingly white and male. As a female-bodied person, I felt invisible in these areas. I was constantly bumped into and it was very hard to get served drinks—even just a mere coke. The vendors just seemed to not see me. At first I felt very stealth, but after an hour became quite annoyed.

The gay rodeo merged gay male and leather cultures with cowboy style. The spectators were dressed to impress with their boots, jeans, hats, and chaps (many of which appeared to be new). However, this attire had visible queer accents. Shirts were much tighter or revealed more or in a few cases were nonexistent. Some articles of clothing indicated gay pride with rainbow colors or made sexual innuendos. Some individuals sported various forms of leather. Most commonly, leather vests and black biker-style chaps were combined with jeans and cowboy boots so that a country/western style was created. A select few did not dress for the theme at all; rather, they dressed in what one would have assumed to be their usual "going-out" attire. The only thing that differentiated this scene from an actual themed circuit party was the lack of a full-service bar and of a dance floor with music and the time of day.

The diversity in rodeo events and those that attend, coupled with the lack of academic literature on the subject, led me to review other materials that address gay rodeos, including documentaries, periodicals, online communities, and association websites, in order to provide a more complete understanding of gay rodeo. In addition, I spoke with approximately 30 individuals (academics and lay persons) who have attended or participated in gay rodeos concerning their experiences and opinions; 15 were formal interviews. A central theme that arose from these sources is that gay rodeo is an event that remains open to numerous interpretations.

UPDATING THE CONTEMPORARY SITUATION: IS GAY RODEO A TRANSGRESSIVE PERFORMANCE?

The gay rodeo deconstructs the core features and assumed identities of traditional rodeos. There is often an association of the rodeo with the rural country and the heterosexuality of strictly gender binary males and females, with the main performance being the bull riding. While it is stereotypical to assume that mainstream rodeo does not recognize the rural gay males who ride (e.g., those performers who hide or do not advertise their sexual identity), the gay rodeo is an example of how an excluded population is able to dismantle social constructs—or social fictions—by deconstructing the event's association with hegemonic systems of discourses and symbols as they appear in mainstream rodeos.

Resisting identity categories is not simply a destructive process, but can also be creative and dynamic because it can open new spaces for assertion of difference.[30] When nonheterosexual individuals rodeo, they create a new space that is challenging and disruptive to the system; an action becomes a form of performance politics whether intended or not. While it may be assumed that the gay rodeo will be drastically different from a traditional rodeo, what is actually different is that the focus is less on bull riding and other traditional events, and more on other side events that are not typical at mainstream rodeos.

The essential detail here is the word "gay" in gay rodeo, which deconstructs our typical idea of traditional rodeo and its surrounding expectations. We rarely recognize how often categories of language govern our beliefs and assumptions of what is "real," "natural," or "legitimate." Language governs our sense of difference and what should be based upon categories and identities as activated by that language.[31] Take, for example, the word "cowboy" and how one would interpret that in a gay rodeo. Heteronormative America associates cowboys with heterosexuality and this would make a "gay cowboy" seem "unnatural" and less "real." However, there is the possibility of deconstructing these social fictions and of creating counterdiscourses and practices. In this way, the gay rodeo challenges dominant assumptions and opens new spaces for difference and transformation. Below I examine some of the ways gay rodeos do and do not serve as transgressive performances.

The Rural/Urban Divide

While advocates of queer politics do an excellent job of dismantling binary or dualistic thinking in regard to sex and gender, they are less successful in applying it to other areas of social life. The rural/urban divide is precisely one of those binaries that are only recently beginning to receive greater attention or serious consideration by academics—think bona-fide lumberjacks and tradesmen vs. lumbersexuals. Social discourses and social fictions surrounding the rural/urban divide help explain why the notion of gay rodeos creates a sensational effect. The social psychologist in me understands that this sensational effect is due to the clash of expectations stemming from stereotypes. Just as a divide between culture and nature is used to deem many marginalized peoples as closer to nature and, hence, lesser—such as women (in opposition to men) and people of color (in opposition to whites)—so too does the notion of country appear as closer to nature and less rational, more traditional, and having less sophistication in comparison to urban areas.[32] Indeed, while the cowboy image is an exaggeration of the image of heteronormative masculinity, it also is an image of a male who is rugged, closer to nature, and more robust because of it. However, with American modernization and development across its transcontinental boundaries, the closing of the frontier makes the "cowboy" and "country" historical icons steadily on the decline. In contrast to an urban population, the country represents the past whether through a farmer or a rancher. The image is a throwback to a nostalgic time, but this image connects itself to an unrefined and unpolished past, unlike its urban counterpart.[33]

In contrast to rugged, robust cowboys who live in rural spaces, urban males are more likely to be associated with overrefinement and delicate while queer males are additionally associated with the effeminate. Urban also implies a distance from nature, and it can be argued that queer is viewed as reflecting a "crime against nature."[34] Thus, in many ways the notions of both cowboys and country counterpose stereotypes of both urban and queer males. The stereotype of queer women as dykes or masculine women would appear to bring them closer to the rugged, robust images of country and cowboy and therefore seem to open more doors—perhaps this would also help to account for the breakdown of gender barriers (such as men and women not having sex-specific events—both can barrel race or ride broncs) in gay rodeo as compared to mainstream rodeo. However, this association "against nature" may preclude queer women from being truly "country." Underlying all of these binary images is a notion of lifestyles that should not mix. By mixing these stereotypes the "gay rodeo" is exciting, intriguing, and, potentially, transgressive.

Imitation and Spoof

There is nothing inherently transgressive in any given performance.[35] While the gay rodeo may resemble a mainstream rodeo, it definitely feels different. In many ways, it feels like an imitation. This is not to say that it feels inauthentic. But there are fewer smells (food and animal), less activity, and much less attention centering on the actual events inside the arena. Most of the action appears to be taking place around the vendors, around the concessions, and perhaps even in the bathrooms. Loud conversations and joking occur among event-goers in these areas. The actual spectators in the arena are rather quiet in comparison. Some appear to just be patiently waiting, rather than actively engaging or having interest. Cheering is very sporadic and there are many empty seats and sparse spaces around the audience seating where the events take place. However, the crowd does become more lively for the more "queer" events—goat dressing, steer decorating, and any events involving participants in queer drag.

These events, however, make the rodeo seem more like a spoof. When animals are dressed up or rodeo clowns look more like "frat boys" in bad drag the rodeo definitely becomes more play, more jest, and less "business." Further, it feels more misogynistic. Within the arena, femininity is not visibly displayed, taken seriously, or possibly even allowed.

Paradoxically, to me as an audience member, the gay rodeo often feels as if it is trying too hard to imitate a "real" (heteronormative) mainstream rodeo. The event coordinators and participants are quite serious about the event as a whole. They walk around with purpose and actively seek to fulfill their roles—to rodeo. They also encourage others to play their parts and do rodeo work. Event coordinators recognize the lack of focused attention on the arena and the rodeo participants. They work to refocus the event-goers and get more cheers via announcing various events, riders with teasers, and related statistics and trivia. Announcing over speakers as they walk past groups of people, they try to entice people to the arena by noting "favorite," "toughest," and "most competitive" events or pointing out that a rider is new, back from a long break, or extremely good or attractive. The tone of activity fluctuates from serious to lighthearted, which stems from one's involvement or investment in performing a "real" rodeo. The more investment one has in taking part in a real rodeo, the more serious they appear and the more active they become in getting others to do the same. This leads to a polarization between the serious rodeo workers and an audience with less investment or interest.

The more serious moments go beyond imitating a mainstream rodeo and contribute to a more over-the-top feeling of playing rodeo. Announcers try to draw an audience to the arena in a way that reminds me of when the assistant principal tries to corral students back into a building after a fire drill. It is at these times that the rodeo fails most in its imitation of a mainstream rodeo but has the most potential to be transgressive.

Spoofing Gay Rodeo, Cowboys, and Gender Play

The gay rodeo is also a spoof—spoofing cowboys and masculinity. To begin with, it spoofs mainstream rodeos by the mere notion that it has an association with anything "gay." Mainstream rodeos have a heteronormative premise—not a gay one. A gay rodeo entails many "campy" attributes that draw on gay male culture, such as drag queens in the rodeo royalty and a running dance mix of iconic gay music playing in both the background and the foreground as events take place. Thus the rodeo competition itself becomes like a mainstream rodeo with added queer flair. The shops are oriented toward a gay male crowd where flavored vodkas sell alongside Bud Lite (an official sponsor), while hats and leather vests and underwear sell along with masculine scented candles and sex toys. In many ways, the gay rodeo manages to uphold the gender binary and value masculinity, but the campy accessories assert its gay existence.[36]

The notion of cowboys and rodeo is already heavily gendered toward hypermasculinity in US society. At the gay rodeo this becomes more exaggerated. For example, there is very little space for cowgirls, although men are able to demonstrate greater flexibility of femininity—most extremely as drag queens with over-the-top glam and humor. Women typically perform in a more butch and masculine cowboy way. At the gay rodeo, one is or plays cowboy, there are no roles for cowgirls. In turn, cowboys and cowboy culture become hypersexualized and women and cowgirls become unseen and arguably irrelevant.

The hypermasculinity of traditional mainstream rodeo further complicates why gay rodeos are not consistently subversive. Distinguishing between the effeminacy and hypermasculinity within gay male culture and rodeo culture becomes problematic. There may be a subtle line between spoofing masculinity and mirroring hypermasculinity, one that is entangled and intersects with notions of gender, sexuality, and self-identity, and with each subculture—gay male culture and rodeo culture.

FUTURE DIRECTIONS

Gay rodeo wants to be taken as seriously as mainstream rodeo. However, it also must hold the attention of the individuals that sustain it, namely, a LGBT community. This LGBT focus ironically may require gay rodeo to do less of the traditional activities and to incorporate more camp. This analysis would encourage future research to consider whether gay rodeos are queer spaces for queer practices. Queer culture means more than collections of queer people, and whether gay rodeos are or even desire to be a part of that is a question that deserves more attention. For example, initially gay rodeos appear to be an inclusive space and community. Some gender barriers are broken down in that men and women can participate in all events, including those that historically and for mainstream rodeo have been sex-segregated.

Yet, there is little space for lesbian culture or heteronormative femininity. In fact, women seem quite invisible, contributing to the complexities and paradoxes of gay rodeo.

Ultimately, gay rodeo is a venue that is open to possibility for play. However, overwhelmingly it is only open for demonstrations of masculinity and men's gender play. Butler highlights the artificial nature of gender construction and the deconstruction of social fictions through performance politics. This type of politics uses the performance of contradictory or stigmatized gender practices to denaturalize gender roles and to resist normalizing tendencies. To illustrate such performative resistance in *Gender Trouble*, Butler points to "drag" as a subversive performance. She writes:

> I would suggest . . . that drag fully subverts the distinction between inner and outer psychic space and effectively mocks the expressive model of gender and the notion of a true gender identity.[37]

And in later writing, Butler more carefully qualifies the argument by discussing how drag can be used in a progressive manner to deconstruct gender roles or in a regressive way to idealize them.[38] In application to gay rodeo, performances, not only of participants but also of its audience members, generate its hypermasculinity, particularly with their cowboy drag. While mainstream rodeo is subject to much of the same pressure to perform, perhaps mainstream rodeo actions and expectations have been ritualized over a longer period of time and saturated into an expectation set that has seeped into the lay society. In this way, neither rodeo is more or less real than the other. In fact, gay rodeo is just as "real" as any rodeo because in the end it pits human against animal and seeks to answer: "which of the two will win?"[39] Moreover, rodeo—both gay and mainstream—can be more than one thing and can hold many different meanings for any single individual.

In talking with those active in the gay rodeo as participants or royalty, it was often described as a family, not just something to do—by most definitions a community. For most they were also looking for an accepting culture and to merge their nostalgia for cowboy culture with their status as sexual minorities. It was also a place for testing their strength—which initially sounded physical, but was also psychological. For audience-goers it was just something fun to do, and mostly a different or new experience. Some small town LGBT communities have successfully formed bridges across boundaries of gender, age, race, and ethnicity that may help LGBT individuals to think about how to create larger versions of these networks. Urban LGBT communities might want to think about the ways in which the dominant queer narrative (coming out, leaving home, moving to the city) might itself be a model of assimilation and normativity, and if that is the desired goal.

NOTES

1. Heteronormative is "the assumption that everyone is heterosexual unless there are signs indicating otherwise." Wade, Lisa, and Myra M. Ferree. 2014. *Gender: Ideas, Interactions, Institutions.* W.W. Norton.

2. Rodeos are typically considered to be a public exhibition of cowboy skills, such as bull and bronco riding, calf roping, and barrel racing.

3. Mann, Susan A. 2012. *Doing Feminist Theory: From Modernity to Postmodernity.* New York: Oxford University Press.

4. Abelson, Miriam. 2014. "Men in Context Transmasculinities and Transgender Experiences in Three US Regions." PhD diss., Department of Sociology, University of Oregon, Eugene; Barton, Bernadette. 2012. *Pray the Gay Away: The Extraordinary Lives of Bible Belt Gays.* New York: New York University Press; Dews, Carlos L., and Carolyn Lest Law. 2001. *Out in the South.* Philadelphia: Temple Press; Gray, Mary. L. 2009. *Out in the Country: Youth, Media, and Queer Visibility in Rural America.* New York: New York University Press; Hennen, Peter. 2008. *Faeries, Bears, and Leathermen: Men in Community Queering the Masculine.* Chicago: University of Chicago Press; Howard, John. 1997. *Carryin' On: In the Lesbian and Gay South.* New York: New York University Press; Hubbs, Nadine. 2014. *Rednecks, Queers, & Country Music.* Berkeley and Los Angeles: University of California Press; Kazyak, Emily. 2012. "Midwest or Lesbian? Gender, Rurality, and Sexuality." *Gender and Society* 26:6; Woodell, Brandi, Emily Kazyak, and D'Lane R. Compton. 2015. "Reconciling LGB and Christian Identities in the Rural South." *Social Sciences Special Issue: LGBTQ Lives in Context: The Role of Place* 4 (3): 859–878.

5. *Queens and Cowboys: A Straight Year on the Gay Rodeo.* Dir. Matt Livadary. Gravitas Ventures; *Small Town Gay Bar.* 2006. Dir. Malcolm Ingram. View Askew Productions; *Southern Comfort.* 2001. Dir. Kate Davis. Q-Ball Productions.

6. Weston, Kath. 1995. "*Get Thee to a Big City: Sexual Imagery and the Great Gay Migration.*" GLQ: A Journal of Lesbian and Gay Studies 2 (3): 253–277.

7. Weston (1995).

8. Herring, Scott. 2010. *Another Country: Queer Anti-Urbanism.* New York: New York University Press.

9. Herring (2010).

10. Gates, Gary. J. 2011. *How Many People are Lesbian, Gay, Bisexual and Transgender?* Los Angeles: Williams Institute Report. http://williamsinstitute.law.ucla.edu/wp-content/uploads/Gates-How-Many-People-LGBT-Apr-2011.pdf.

11. Baumle, Amanda K., D'Lane Compton, and Dudley Poston, 2009. *Same-Sex Couples: The Demography of Sexual Orientation.* Albany: State University of New York Press; Gates, Gary J., and Jason Ost. 2004. *The Gay and Lesbian Atlas.* Washington, DC: Urban Institute Press; The 2000 US Census counted almost 1.2 million same-sex unmarried partners in the country; 301 thousand were male-male households, and 293 thousand were female-female households (Baumle, Compton, and Poston 2009).

12. Baumle, Compton, and Poston (2009); while there are many issues with the US Census data, it is the best, and only, data available to geographically examine distributions and patterns of gay and lesbian households in the United States.

Additionally, prior analyses have found the data to be valid and useful Baumle et al. 2009; Gates and Ost 2004; Williams Institute. 2011. United States—Census Snapshot 2010. http://williamsinstitute.law.ucla.edu/category/research/census-lbgt-demographics-studies/. Black, Dan, Gary Gates, and Lowell Taylor. 2000. "Demographics of the Gay and Lesbian Population in the United States: Evidence from Available Systematic Data Sources." *Demography* 37 (2): 139–154.

13. Baumle et al. (2009).

14. Compton, D'Lane R., Dudley Poston, Qian Xiong, and Emily Knox. 2015. "The Residential Segregation of Gay and Lesbian Households from Heterosexual Households in 100 MSAs of the United States, circa 2010." Paper presented at American Sociological Association Annual Meeting Conference, Chicago, IL.

15. Ghaziani, Amin. 2014. *There Goes the Gayborhood?* Princeton: Princeton University Press; Gray (2009).

16. Compton, D'Lane R. 2015. "LG(BT) and Counting." *Sociological Compass* 9 (7): 597–608; Ghaziani (2014); Gray (2009).

17. Rosenfeld, Michael. 2009. *The Age of Independence: Interracial Unions, Same-Sex Unions, and the American Family.* Cambridge, MA: Harvard University Press.

18. Baumle et al. (2009); Compton, D'Lane R., and Amanda K. Baumle. 2012. "Beyond the Castro: Examining Gay and Lesbian Enclaves in the San Francisco Bay Area." *Journal of Homosexuality* 59 (10): 1327–1356.

19. Gates and Ost (2004); Williams Institute (2011).

20. Baumle et al. (2009).

21. Baumle et al. (2009); Baumle, Amanda K., and D'Lane Compton. 2015. *Legalizing LGBT Families: How the Law Shapes Parenthood.* New York: New York University Press.

22. Warren, Patricia Nell. 2006. "Real Cowboys, Real Rodeos." *Gay and Lesbian Review.* July/August, 19–23.

23. Warren (2006).

24. Gauthier, Paula. 2000. "Steers and Queers." MFA thesis, Department of Visual Arts, the University of California, San Diego; Heibel, Todd D. 2005. "An Arena for Belonging? A Spatial Hingepoint Perspective of Citizenship at the Gay Rodeo." PhD diss., Department of Geography, Pennsylvania State University; McClain, Craig W. 2005. "Gay Rodeo: Carnival, Gender, and Resistance." MA thesis Department of American Studies, University of New Mexico, Albuquerque.

25. Gauthier (2000); Heibel (2005); McClain (2005).

26. International Gay Rodeo Association (IGRA). 2008. www.igra.com.

27. IGRA (2008).

28. Heibel (2005); IGRA (2008).

29. Armour, Lawrence A. 2003. "Bridle Accessories." *Fortune,* October 13, 60–64; IGRA (2008); McGovern, Celeste. 1994. "Homo on the Range." *Alberta Report,* July 18, 29.

30. Mann (2012); Ward, Jane. 2012. "Postmdernism, Poststructuralism, Queer, and Transgender Theories." In *Doing Feminist Theory: From Modernity to Postmodernity,* edited by Susan A. Mann, 211–255. New York: Oxford University Press.

31. Mann (2012); Ward (2012).

32. Mann (2012).

33. Warren (2006).

34. Sodomy laws and laws associated with nontraditional marital sex have been classified under these terms (see Louisiana as one example).

35. Butler, Judith. 1990. *Gender Trouble*. New York: Routledge; Butler, Judith. 1993. *Bodies That Matter*. New York: Routledge.

36. Newton, Esther. 1972. *Mother Camp: Female Impersonators in America*. Chicago: University of Chicago Press.

37. Butler (1990).

38. Butler (1993).

39. Warren (2006).

Review Questions

Part II: Gender Politics and Policies

1. Rubin and colleagues note that women's representation in the political system yields substantial benefits for all workers through the construction of more favorable family-supportive working environments. The chapters on political and economic leadership (Burke & Hartmann and Garcia & Lopez) suggest that quota systems may be most effective at achieving gender and racial parity on corporate boards and in the political system. Why would quota systems be more effective in creating gender and racial parity than would traditional hiring and electoral systems? How does gender at the interactional and/or individual level influence the hiring and electoral process to impede gender equity?

2. Lin and Hinze's findings highlight the importance of using an intersectional approach to studying health. Building on their findings, interview at least two women and two men who identify with differing racial/ethnic groups about their experiences with the healthcare system. Ask them to describe their experiences with doctors and others in the healthcare profession across their life course, from their childhood through adolescence and young adulthood and into adulthood. What have you learned about how gender and race simultaneously influence experiences with the healthcare system? Did your interviews reveal anything about how socioeconomic status may impact health? Do the results of your interviews seem consistent with or divergent from the general findings of Lin and Hinze?

3. Stephens, Tuttle, and Witte suggest that the gender wage gap is smaller among immigrant STEM workers than among native-born STEM workers in part due to immigrant women's choices of occupations. Thinking about the influence of gender at the individual, interactional, and institutional levels, why might we see differences in the occupational choices of US-born women and immigrant women who work in STEM? That is, what

individual, interactional, and institutional forces differentially shape the occupational choices of US-born women and immigrant women who work in STEM?

4. Compton's research documents how the gay rodeo serves as a site for community-building among individuals with similar gendered interests. Attend a local event that is aimed at building community or solidarity among attendees. Describe the extent to which the event draws upon shared norms and beliefs around gender (as well as other characteristics like race/ethnicity, social class, and nativity) to try to facilitate connections between individuals. Does the event combine two (or more) stereotypically divergent cultures or identities? How does it do so? Are you among the "target audience" for this event? How do you know? If not, how, if at all, does the event address or incorporate "outsiders"?

PART III

Conclusion

14. Unstalling the Revolution: Policies toward Gender Equality

Sarah Winslow, Shannon N. Davis, and David J. Maume

The pieces in this volume have demonstrated a number of things. First, gender is embedded in interactions and institutions in ways that have implications for individual lives. Second, gender intersects with a number of other dimensions—race, ethnicity, nationality, class, sexual orientation, religion—to shape the lives of men and women. Third, a myriad of policy options could or do exist to "unstall" the gender revolution. After a brief review of the first two points, we focus our attention in this chapter on the last point, elaborating on policy recommendations for addressing continued gender inequality. Just as we've focused on how gender operates at several levels, we argue that policies designed to address it must as well. Moreover, just as we are all not just men and women but men and women of particular races, ethnicities, sexual orientations, etc., we recognize that effective policy must address the intersection of gender and other dimensions of inequality.

GENDER AT THE INDIVIDUAL, INTERACTIONAL, AND INSTITUTIONAL LEVELS

All of the pieces in this volume highlight the multilevel nature of gender, as well as the complex connections within and between these levels. The chapter by Kathleen Gerson (chapter 2) exemplifies this perspective by pointing out how rising insecurity in the economy and increasing demands in both paid labor and family life have augmented conflicts between work and family. At the institutional level, the workplace and the family—both highly gendered institutions—compete for time and energy of individuals. At the interactional level, men and women must negotiate divisions of labor within workplaces and families, as well as between the two, amid gendered cultural expectations of appropriate roles and behaviors. And at the individual level, men and women are forced to make often-difficult choices between employment and family.

Schnable (chapter 5) considers a different historically gendered institution, religion, but similarly emphasizes how this gendered institutional context shapes interactions and individual selves and, ultimately, permeates other institutions. The True Love Waits movement, she argues, deploys the patriarchal assumptions embedded in religion to encourage sexual purity for individual women and, indeed, to make this purity a part of their identities. Reflecting this relationship between the institutional and individual levels, she argues that young women's bodies become "the battleground upon which patriarchy and progress war for control of sexuality." Further, young women's purity is pledged to and protected by their fathers so that it can be promised to their future husbands and thus is deeply embedded in interactions between men and women. This logic, Schnable argues, is not just limited to the institution of religion but pervades current approaches to sex education in the United States, which emphasize abstinence over a more comprehensive approach to healthy sexual behavior.

As Gerson and Schnable document, gender as an institution intersects with other social institutions, such as the family and religion. However, gender also pervades organizational life through the same institutional mechanisms. Garcia and Lopez (chapter 9) highlight the institutional logics, policies, and procedures that have prohibited Latinas from gaining ground in holding corporate leadership positions in the United States. Institutional practices that hire based on social networks and homophily constitute key mechanisms through which access to leadership opportunities is denied to nonwhite, nonmale individuals. The reciprocal relationship between the institutional practices and interactional experiences that yield familiarity with and access to others with the same social and cultural backgrounds, argue Garcia and Lopez, should be the target of policy intervention. Disrupting the practices that define familiarity as a sufficient qualification for employment has the potential for changing not only institutional and organizational culture and interactional expectations but also individual identities as Latinas and other groups previously shut out of the corporate boardroom will come to see themselves as potential leaders and advocate for themselves as such.

INTERSECTIONALITY

Several of the pieces in this volume focus our attention specifically on the ways in which gender intersects with other dimensions of inequality.

Intersectionality as a theoretical framework has the potential to underscore both differences and similarities in individuals' experiences across dimensions and levels of inequality. Using an intersectional lens can also uncover conditions for facilitating greater equality when investigating the intersection of dimensions of inequality.

Lin and Hinze (chapter 11) detail the progression of considerations of difference in health research, from the historical exclusion of attention to gender and women to an approach that assumed that privileges (and disadvantages) accrued in an additive manner to the current focus on intersectional analyses which assume that the experiences of any given group are greater than the sum of race, class, gender, and any other dimension of inequality. Focusing on inter- and intracategorical complexities, they generate two important overall findings that emphasize the importance of intersectional analyses. First, in comparing black women with less than a high school education to highly educated white men, they find that the former are not simply the converse of the latter, suggesting "the need to explore every day, consequential experiences of men and women, in order to reveal more fully the power of structured inequalities." Second, they find a substantial amount of within-group heterogeneity, offering caution in relying on between-group comparisons and assuming that specific patterns—in their case, for health and health behaviors—are common among all members of a given group.

While also highlighting the way that gendered interactions shape individual experiences in the workplace, Wingfield (chapter 4) pays special attention to the intersection of race and gender in shaping this process. Although a large body of research documents the myriad ways in which women face barriers to full inclusion when entering male-dominated occupations, Wingfield argues that applying an intersectional lens allows us to see the ways in which gender, race, and class combine to inform the ways that men interact with women in the workplace, thereby shaping the experiences of women in these fields. Specifically, she finds that, as a result of their own experiences with racial discrimination, black professional men were more cognizant of the disadvantages faced by their female colleagues than were their white male counterparts and simultaneously attempted to utilize their male privilege to produce more equitable conditions. While emphasizing the interactional biases and processes that underlie women's marginalization, Wingfield's analysis also sheds light on the policies and conditions necessary for realizing equality in the workplace, such as placing greater weight on work done to support underrepresented groups (e.g., mentoring) in performance appraisals and reemphasizing affirmative action rather than broad-based calls for diversity. In so doing, her intersectional analysis emphasizes the ways in which policy efforts must extend beyond the individual and interactional to the institutional level.

Focusing on immigrant STEM workers, Stephens, Tuttle, and Witte (chapter 12) further illuminate the mechanisms underlying—and potentially alleviating—gender inequality. The gender gap in wages is lower among immigrant STEM workers than among native-born STEM workers. While emphasizing the primacy of gender as a social institution and dimension of inequality in shaping worker experiences by documenting the continuation of the gender wage gap, Stephens, Tuttle, and Witte also call our attention to the variations in how the social institution of gender operates culturally. If the gender wage gap is narrower among immigrant STEM workers than among native-born STEM workers due to differing occupational choices and educational attainment across native-born and immigrant women, as Stephens and colleagues argue, then using an intersectional lens has uncovered two key mechanisms through which gender as a social institution operates to create inequality—and two key mechanisms through which greater equality could be achieved.

POLICIES AND INTERVENTIONS TO UNSTALL THE REVOLUTION

A major contribution of this volume has been not just to explore elements and examples of gender inequality, but to utilize empirical research to suggest policies and interventions that might ameliorate it. Just as gender operates at multiple levels, the pieces in this volume suggest that policy must do so as well. In what follows, we highlight policies and interventions at the community, organizational, and governmental levels. While we have grouped the policies into these overarching categories, we remain mindful of their multiple points of overlap and recognize that a complete gender revolution requires simultaneous change at all levels. At the same time, as our contributors have recognized the intersection of gender and other forms of inequality, we also attend to the ways in which effective policy must be guided by an intersectional lens.

Community Level

Several of our pieces suggest policies and practices that originate at the community level. Compton (chapter 13) highlights the way in which gay rodeos challenge stereotypes juxtaposing "gay" and "country," creating an inclusive space for those whose identities challenge traditional boundaries of place and sexuality. At the same time, gay rodeos remain grounded in traditional hypermasculinity. Compton's piece suggests that community-level initiatives to broaden gay rodeo's incorporation of lesbian culture and heteronormative femininity would make gay rodeo more gender-inclusive and potentially challenge the ways in which a particular form of masculinity is institutionalized in both gay and mainstream rodeo culture.

While higher education is a broad social institution, Smith's chapter (chapter 3) argues that colleges that serve local communities will themselves be strengthened if they embody as their mission the goal of being a core resource provider at the community level. Individualized strategies of uncovering the needs of local communities and developing mechanisms for training that meet those needs will situate (community) colleges as potential locations for a sense of community to emerge. Shared values regarding education and employment, contextualized within local communities' and families' experiences and histories, can frame higher education as a public good while simultaneously undermining economic inequality at the local level.

Gerson's work (chapter 2) points to the necessary role of communities in carework, while also enlarging the definition of community to encompass broad cultural norms about work and care. Specifically, Gerson calls for abandoning the "ideal worker" and "intensive parenting" norms that simultaneously require incompatible single-minded devotion to work, on the one hand, and family, on the other.[1] In their place, she advocates a "flexible worker" norm that values contributions over time and allows workers—both men and women—time with their families without sacrificing career success and a "flexible parenting" norm that recognizes and values the necessary involvement of a large circle of caregivers.

Organizational Level

The contributors in this volume highlight the critical role of organizational policies in ameliorating gender (and other) inequality. Gerson (chapter 2) contends that the normative and community-level changes discussed above are necessary but not sufficient conditions for transformation in the gendered work-family nexus. They must be accompanied by a restructuring of jobs and careers to allow employees—men and women alike—to combine paid labor and caregiving in the way that's best for their individual and family needs. Wingfield (chapter 4) similarly recommends a number of workplace policy provisions, in her case building on the lessons learned from black men's efforts to support female colleagues in male-dominated occupations. Recognizing and valuing service work done to support underrepresented groups and placing greater emphasis on systematic and explicit affirmative action policies would incorporate the ways in which race, gender, and class intersect for workers, change both the structure and the culture of workplaces, and ultimately lead toward a more gender-equitable employment environment.

Lin and Hinze's work (chapter 11) is similar to that of Wingfield in that it is centrally focused on intersectionality, although in this case applying it to healthcare and health research. Their policy recommendations flow from this research. Their work serves as a caution to healthcare providers to take gender, race, class, and other dimensions of difference—and, importantly, the power dynamics associated with these categories and their combinations—seriously in evaluating and treating patients. Moreover, health research, which began with a sole focus on men, gradually moved to incorporate women (although such work remains limited), and has increasingly incorporated additional dimensions of inequality, must incorporate an intersectional lens rather than treating women and minorities as discrete and mutually exclusive categories. Finally, they suggest that scholars and researchers will need to translate their more nuanced findings into improved healthcare policies and practices.

In many cases, organizations and institutions have influences on one another. Schnable's chapter (chapter 5) demonstrates how religion, perhaps one of the most deeply and historically gendered institutions, influences education. Specifically, she argues that the evangelical purity movement's focus on abstinence pervades approaches to sex education, despite no empirical evidence suggesting that abstinence-only sex education reduces premarital sex, teen pregnancy, or the transmission of sexually transmitted infections. Schnable advocates shifting to an approach that doesn't deny the religious backgrounds that young men and women bring to sex education but instead presents a "holistic focus on the overall emotional, sexual, and intimate wellness of young adults that considers abstinence to be one choice among many." The two institutions remain linked, but the focus becomes a comprehensive approach to sex education that is less controlling of women's sexuality and thus more likely to contribute to "unstalling" the gender revolution.

Hattery and Smith (chapter 7) direct our attention to the nexus of two other organizations—universities and the NCAA, the governing and regulatory body for college athletics. Outlining the gendered implications of conference realignment, they advocate for a range of policy modifications guided by a single principle—"funding should be driven by need not want." Specific recommendations include reasonable travel accommodations with limited time away from campus, adequate food, safe equipment, and financial resources to minimize out-of-pocket costs of attendance for all athletes, male or female. Such provisions would require the cooperation of individual universities and athletics departments and would ultimately necessitate changes in a highly masculinized athletic arena that prioritizes the interests and desires of male athletes.

The implementation of quotas within organizations is a key mechanism through which diversity in organizational leadership can be achieved, especially if it is voluntarily enacted. Despite the negative connotation around quotas, Garcia and Lopez (chapter 9) and Burke and Hartmann (chapter 8) both provide evidence that women and other minorities do gain economic and political power when formal policies are in place that require individuals from diverse gender, racial, and ethnic backgrounds to hold positions of power within corporations and political institutions. And given the positive impact of having diverse leadership on corporate, political, and social outcomes that these and other chapters (see chapter 10, Rubin et al.) have documented, this particular policy is one that, if implemented, has the potential for reverberating impact in creating spaces for greater gender (and racial/ethnic) equality in the United States.

Governmental Level

Attention tends to focus on federal policy as the main source of intervention when working to undermine inequality. There is good reason for this; federal policy has national-level ramifications that are tied to funding mechanisms for communities, organizations, and state and local municipalities. Federal policy can impact lives directly, such as by criminalizing discrimination against individuals during applications for marriage as well as employment. But federal policy can also impact lives indirectly by shaping the opportunity landscape for individuals in their local communities.

Economic power is potentially both the most important component of gender equality and the one that requires policy intervention for the creation of opportunities and sustainability over time. Policies that support women's control of economic resources, including greater labor force participation and entrepreneurship, are extensions of federal nondiscrimination policies that can directly reduce gender inequality.

Federal employment policies have the potential to directly facilitate greater gender equality. Specifically, Rubin et al. (chapter 10) and Stephens, Tuttle, and Witte (chapter 12) argue that policies that support worker flexibility and contemporary family life, to include paid maternity/parental leave for workers at all jobs, can reduce job-related stress among workers and create stronger economic opportunities for women and families overall. Policies that allow for flexible work schedules for nonprofessional workers will have as much an impact on facilitating gender equality as telework and

other new economy-flexibility options were expected to have for professional workers.[2] Federal policy has already focused on closing the gender
pay gap; it is important step toward gender equality, but so too is providing
paid leave for the short time after the birth or adoption of a child. Not only
will both parents have the opportunity to bond with their children, but
caregiving responsibilities will be more equally divided by parents, something that has significant ramifications for both parents' work and family
lives after the arrival of children in two-parent homes.[3] Paid maternity
leave is also one key mechanism that can reduce the gender wage gap, making it a crucial policy lever in the fight against gender inequality that needs
to be deployed.

Helmuth and Bailey (chapter 6) take a different approach to studying
federal policy, by examining military employment and benefits and their
relationship to residential segregation. Arguing that military employment
and veteran's benefits represent a tremendous social safety net, they assert
that women's increased military participation, particularly in light of the
recent opening of all military occupations to women, potentially represents
a significant transfer of public resources (historically disproportionately
received by men) to women. Helmuth and Bailey's work also suggests the
need for revisions to housing policy, including a focus on policies promoting integration, such as rental vouchers for low-income households, inclusionary zoning, and incentives for developers to build affordable family
housing. Each of these efforts will produce a more equitable division of
governmental and public resources and opportunity along the lines of gender, race, and class.

CONCLUDING THOUGHTS

As Marcia and Mark, the teenagers from our introductory chapter, transition into young adulthood, the world around them will continue to change.
Technological advances will continue to shift how they communicate with
others, how and where work is performed, and how and where knowledge
is stored. One constant is that their lives will still be influenced by gender
as a social institution at the individual, interactional, and institutional levels. The policy interventions our contributors present are suggestions for
how we can work toward greater gender equality in the United States and
beyond in order to unstall the gender revolution. Because gender is a social
institution, it has staying power that will outlast any individual actors. But
the details of how it organizes our social lives have and can continue to shift
such that differences do not necessarily equate with inequality. Marcia and

Mark can earn equal pay for equal work, can both be expected to be committed to their chosen work and to their families (in whatever form their families may take), and can both have the opportunity to be productive members of their respective communities. Policies that afford equal opportunities for all to live up to their potential will continue to facilitate the construction of gendered selves that reflect the diversity that exists in our population. Indeed, providing equal opportunities and choices to individuals regardless of gender, race, ethnicity, sexuality, nativity, or other dimensions of inequality may yield greater diversity in how gender (and other dimensions) is enacted at the individual level. And while the resulting shifts in how gender is embodied, and as a result enacted in everyday life, could feel a little like vertigo,[4] we argue that it is up to all of us to work to overcome this vertigo in order for the Marcias and Marks, the Julias and Julios, and Tomekas and Taquans of the world to have a chance to make the most significant contributions they possibly can for humankind.

NOTES

1. Blair-Loy, Mary. 2003. *Competing Devotions: Career and Family among Women Executives*. Cambridge, MA: Harvard University Press.

2. Blair-Loy (2003).

3. Bianchi, Suzanne M., and Melissa A. Milkie. 2010. "Work and Family Research in the First Decade of the 21st Century." *Journal of Marriage and Family* 72 (3): 705–725.

4. Risman, Barbara. 1998. *Gender Vertigo: American Families in Transition*. New Haven: Yale University Press.

Review Questions

Part III: Conclusion

Visit the website of the Institute for Women's Policy Research and find the latest (2015 as of the publication of this volume) report on the "status of women in the states." Describe the criteria by which they grade the status of women in each of the 50 states. How do these criteria relate to the chapter readings in the book? What are the five best and the five worst states for women in the United States? Comment on the pattern you see when you look at the best and worst states for women in the United States. How do the findings presented in this report relate to (1) gender at the individual, interactional, and institutional levels and (2) the intersection of gender and other dimensions of inequality? What policy initiatives might be necessary to make the five worst states look more like the five best states? Are these community, organizational, and/or governmental policies?

References

2020 Women on Boards. 2014. "Steady Gains Made by Women on Fortune 1000 Company Boards." www.2020wob.com/about/press/release/2020-women-boards-releases-2014-gender-diversity-index.

Abelson, Miriam. 2014. "Men in Context Transmasculinities and Transgender Experiences in Three US Regions." PhD diss., Department of Sociology, University of Oregon, Eugene.

Accreditation Board for Engineering and Technology. 2015. "Engineering vs. Engineering Technology." Baltimore: Accreditation Board for Engineering and Technology. www.abet.org/accreditation/new-to-accreditation/engineering-vs-engineering-technology/.

Acker, Joan. 1990. "Hierarchies, Jobs, Bodies: A Theory of Gendered Organizations." *Gender & Society* 4:139–158.

———. 2006. "Inequality Regimes: Gender, Class, and Race in Organizations." *Gender & Society* 20:441–464.

Acosta, Vivian, and Linda Carpenter. 2015. *Women in Intercollegiate Sport: A Longitudinal National Study, Thirty-Seven Year Update, 1977–2014.* www.acostacarpenter.org/.

Aguilar, Luis A., "Speech by SEC Commissioner: Board Diversity: Why It Matters and How to Improve It." New York, November 4, 2010. www.sec.gov/news/speech/2010/spch110410laa.htm.

Alexander, Bryant Keith. 2014. "Call for Papers—Special Issue 'Hands Up! Don't Shoot!': Policing Race in America." *Cultural Studies ↔ Critical Methodologies* 14 (6): 626–626.

Amesen, Eric, ed. 2007. *Encyclopedia of U.S. Labor and Working-class History.* Vol. 1. New York: Routledge.

Antecol, Heather. 2000. "An Examination of Cross-Country Differences in the Gender Gap in Labor Force Participation Rates." *Labour Economics* 7:409–426.

Armour, Lawrence A. 2003. "Bridle Accessories." *Fortune,* October 13, 2003, 60–64.

Asch, Beth J., Christopher Buck, Jacob Alex Klerman, Meredith Kleykamp, and David S. Loughran. 2009. *Military Enlistment of Hispanic Youth: Obstacles and Opportunities.* Santa Monica, CA: RAND Corporation.

Asch, Beth J., M. Rebecca Kilburn, and Jacob Alex Klerman. 1999. *Attracting College-Bound Youth into the Military: Toward the Development of New Recruiting Policy Options.* Santa Monica, CA: RAND Corporation.

Attwell, Paul, Scott Heil, and Laurel L. Reisel. 2011. "Competing Explanations of Undergraduate Noncompletion." *American Educational Research Journal* 48 (3): 536–559.

Balding, Susan. 2015. "Netflix's Paid Parental Leave Policy Reflects a Sad Reality Facing Working Families." Economic Policy Institute. September 3. www.epi.org/blog/netflixs-paid-parental-leave-policy-reflects-a-sad-reality-facing-working-families/.

Bartkowski, John P. 2001. *Remaking the Godly Marriage: Gender Negotiation in Evangelical Families.* New Brunswick, NJ: Rutgers University Press.

Bartkowski, John P., and Xiaohe Xu. 2000. "Distant Patriarchs or Expressive Dads? The Discourse and Practice of Fathering in Conservative Protestant Families." *Sociological Quarterly* 41 (3): 465–485.

Barton, Bernadette. 2012. *Pray the Gay Away: The Extraordinary Lives of Bible Belt Gays.* New York: New York University Press.

Bauer, Greta R. 2014. "Incorporating Intersectionality Theory into Population Health Research Methodology: Challenges and the Potential to Advance Health Equity." *Social Science & Medicine* 110:10–17.

Baumgardner, Jennifer. 2011. *F'em! Goo Goo, Gaga, and Some Thoughts on Balls.* Berkeley: Seal.

Baumle, Amanda K., and D'Lane Compton. 2015. *Legalizing LGBT Families: How the Law Shapes Parenthood.* New York: New York University Press.

Baumle, Amanda K., D'Lane Compton, and Dudley Poston, 2009. *Same-Sex Couples: The Demography of Sexual Orientation.* Albany: State University of New York Press.

Beamon, Karen, and Patricia Bell. 2002. "Going Pro: The Differential Effects of High Aspirations for a Professional Sports Career on African-American Student-Athletes and White Student-Athletes." *Race and Society* 5:179–192.

Beck, Ulrich. 1992. *Risk Society: Toward a New Modernity.* Thousand Oaks, CA: Sage.

Becker, Julia C., and Janet K. Swim. 2011. "Seeing the Unseen: Attention to Daily Encounters with Sexism as Way to Reduce Sexist Beliefs." *Psychology of Women Quarterly* 35 (2): 227–242.

Beede, David, Tiffany Julian, David Langdon, Beethika Khan, and Mark Doma. 2011. "Women in STEM: A Gender Gap to Innovation, Executive Summary." US Department of Commerce, Economics and Statistics Administration, Washington, DC. www.esa.doc.gov/sites/default/files/womeninstemagapto innovation8311.pdf.

Befort, Stephen F. 2001. "Labor and Employment Law at the Millennium: A Historical Review and Critical Assessment." *Boston College Law Review* 43:351–460.

Belkin, Lisa. 2003. "The Opt-Out Revolution." *New York Times Magazine,* October 26.

Bell, Ella, and Stella Nkomo. 2001. *Our Separate Ways*. Cambridge, MA: Harvard Business Review.

Bellafaire, Judith Lawrence. 2006. "Public Service Role Models: The First Women of the Defense Advisory Committee on Women in the Service." *Armed Forces and Society* 32 (3): 424–436.

Bem, Sandra L. 1993. *The Lenses of Gender: Transforming the Debate on Sexual Inequality*. New Haven: Yale University Press.

Benard, Stephen, and Shelley Correll. 2010. "Normative Discrimination and the Motherhood Penalty." *Gender & Society* 24:616–646.

Bergson-Shilcock, Amanda, and James Witte. 2015. *Steps to Success: Integrating Immigrant Professionals in the U.S.* New York: World Education Services.

Berkman, Lisa F., Ichiro Kawachi, and Maria Glymour, eds. 2014. *Social Epidemiology*. New York: Oxford University Press.

Berkowitz, Steve, and Andrew Kreighbaum 2015. "College Athletes Cashing In with Millions in New Benefits." *USA Today*. http://usat.ly/1hmqsBj.

Bernard, H.R. 2011. *Research Methods in Anthropology: Qualitative and Quantitative Approaches*. 5th ed. Walnut Creek, CA: Altamira.

Berrey, Ellen. 2015. *The Enigma of Diversity*. Chicago: University of Chicago Press.

Bersamin, Melina M., Samantha Walker, Elizabeth D. Waiters, Deborah A. Fisher, and Joel W. Grube. 2005. "Promising to Wait: Virginity Pledges and Adolescent Sexual Behavior." *Journal of Adolescent Health* 36 (5): 428–436.

Bertrand, Marianne, Sandra E. Black, Sissel Jensen, and Adriana Lleras-Muney. 2014. *Breaking the Glass Ceiling? The Effect of Board Quotas on Female Labor Market Outcomes in Norway*. Cambridge, MA: National Bureau of Economic Research. www.nber.org/papers/w20256.

Betts, Julian R., and Laurel L. McFarland. 1995. "Safe Port in a Storm: The Impact of Labor Market Conditions on Community College Enrollments." *Journal of Human Resources* 30:741–765.

Bianchi, Suzanne M., and Melissa A. Milkie. 2010. "Work and Family Research in the First Decade of the 21st Century." *Journal of Marriage and Family* 72 (3): 705–725.

Bianchi, Suzanne M., Melissa A. Milkie, Liana C. Sayer, and John P. Robinson. 2000. "Is Anyone Doing the Housework? Trends in the Gender Division of Household Labor." *Social Forces* 79:191–228.

Bianchi, Suzanne A., John P. Robinson, and Melissa A. Milkie. 2007. *Changing Rhythms of American Family Life*. New York: Russell Sage Foundation.

Binder, Ulrike, and Guido Zeppenfeld. 2015. "Germany Introduces Rules on Female Quota for Supervisory Boards." www.mondaq.com/x/381586/Employee+Benefits+Compensation/Germany+Introduces+Rules+on+Female+Quota+for+Supervisory+Boards.

Bird, Chole. 2013. "Making Heart Disease a Women's Issue." *Ms. Magazine*, March 20.

Bird, Chloe E., and Patricia P. Rieker. 2008. *Gender and Health: The Effects of Constrained Choices and Social Policies*. New York: Cambridge University Press.

Black, Dan, Gary Gates, and Lowell Taylor. 2000. "Demographics of the Gay and Lesbian Population in the United States: Evidence from Available Systematic Data Sources." *Demography* 37 (2): 139–154.

Blair, Irene V., John F. Steiner, Diane L. Fairclough, Rebecca Hanratty, David W. Price, Holen K. Hirsh, Leslie A. Wright et al. 2013. "Clinicians' Implicit Ethnic/Racial Bias and Perceptions of Care among Black And Latino Patients." *Annals of Family Medicine* 11:43–52.

Blair-Loy, Mary. 2003. *Competing Devotions: Career and Family among Women Executives.* Cambridge, MA: Harvard University Press.

Blau, Francine D., and Lawrence M. Khan. 2000. "Gender Differences in Pay." *Journal of Economic Perspectives* 14 (4): 75–99.

Bloch, Jon P. 2000. "The New and Improved Clint Eastwood: Change and Persistence in Promise Keepers Self-Help Literature." *Sociology of Religion* 61 (1): 11–31.

Bonilla-Silva, Eduardo, and Gianpaolo Baiocchi. 2007. "Anything but Racism: How Sociologists Limit the Significance of Racism." In *Handbooks of the Sociology of Racial and Ethnic Relations,* edited by Herman Vera and Joe R. Feagin, 79–100. New York: Springer.

Bowleg, Lisa. 2012. "The Problem with the Phrase Women and Minorities: Intersectionality—an Important Theoretical Framework for Public Health." *American Journal of Public Health* 102:1267–1273.

Brady, Diane. 2014. "The Crumbling Case against Women on U.S. Boards." *Bloomberg Business.* www.bloomberg.com/bw/articles/2014–04–17/the-crumbling-case-against-adding-more-women-to-u-dot-s-dot-corporate-boards.

Branch, Taylor. 2011. "Shame of College Sports." *Atlantic.* http://theatln .tc/1MD1D1H.

Breazeale, Kathlyn A. 2010. "There Goes the Bride: A Snapshot of the Ideal Christian Wife." In *Women and Christianity,* edited by Cheryl A. Kirk-Duggan and Karen Jo Torjesen, 3–25. Santa Barbara: ABC-CLIO.

Breitenberg, Mark. 1993. "Anxious Masculinity: Sexual Jealousy in Early Modern England." *Feminist Studies* 19 (2): 377–398.

Britton, Dana. 2003. *At Work in the Iron Cage.* New York: New York University Press.

Brody, Charles J., and Beth A. Rubin. 2011. "Generational Differences in the Effects of Insecurity, Restructured Workplace Temporalities, and Technology on Organizational Loyalty." *Sociological Spectrum* 31 (2): 163–192.

Brooke-Marciniak, Beth A., and Debra Perry. 2014. *Every Other One: More Women on Corporate Boards: An Update of a Policy Statement. Committee for Economic Development's Policy and Impact Committee.* Washington, DC: Committee for Economic Development. www.ced.org/reports/single /every-other-one-more-women-on-corporate-boards.

Brubaker, Pamela K. 2010. "Gender and Society: Competing Visions of Women's Agency, Equality, and Well-Being." In *Women and Christianity,* edited by Cheryl A. Kirk-Duggan and Karen Jo Torjesen, 93–114. Santa Barbara: ABC-CLIO.

Brückner, Hannah, and Peter Bearman. 2005. "After the Promise: The STD Consequences of Adolescent Virginity Pledges." *Journal of Adolescent Health* 36 (4): 271–278.

Budig, Michelle, and Paula England. 2001. "The Wage Penalty for Motherhood." *American Sociological Review* 66:204–225.

Burk, Martha. 2014. *Your Voice, Your Vote: The Savvy Woman's Guide to Power, Politics, and the Change We Need.* Austin, TX: A.U.

Butler, Judith. 1988. "Performative Acts and Gender Constitution: An Essay in Phenomenology and Feminist Theory." *Theatre Journal* 40 (4): 519–538.

———. 1990. *Gender Trouble.* New York: Routledge.

———. 1993. *Bodies That Matter.* New York: Routledge.

Byers, Walter. 1995. *Unsportsmanlike Conduct: Exploiting College Athletes.* Ann Arbor: University of Michigan Press.

Caiazza, Amy. 2004. "Does Women's Representation in Elective Office Lead to Women-Friendly Policy? Analysis of State-Level Data." *Women & Politics* 26 (1): 35–70.

Calasanti, Toni. 2009. "Theorizing Feminist Gerontology, Sexuality, and Beyond: An Intersectional Approach." *Handbook of Theories of Aging* 2:471–486.

Campbell, Alec. 2004. "The Invisible Welfare State: Establishing the Phenomena of Twentieth Century Veteran's Benefits." *Journal of Political and Military Sociology* 32 (2): 249–267.

Carnevale, Anthony, Nicole Smith, and Michelle Melton. 2011. "STEM: Science, Technology, Engineering, Mathematics." Washington, DC: Georgetown University Center on Education and the Workforce. https://cew.georgetown.edu/wp-content/uploads/2014/11/stem-complete.pdf.

Carnevale, Anthony P., Nicole Smith, and Jeff Strohl. 2013. "Recovery: Job Growth and Education Requirements through 2020." Georgetown Public Policy Institute, Center on Education and the Workforce. http://cew.georgetown.edu/recovery2020.

Carpenter, Laura M. 2005. *Virginity Lost: An Intimate Portrait of First Sexual Experiences.* New York: New York University Press.

Case, Anne, and Christina Paxson. 2005. "Sex Differences in Morbidity and Mortality." *Demography* 42:189–214.

Cashin, Sheryll. 2005. *Failures of Integration: How Race and Class Are Undermining the American Dream.* New York: PublicAffairs.

Catalyst. 2015a. *2014 Catalyst Census: Women Board Directors.* New York: Catalyst. February 6, 2015. www.catalyst.org/knowledge/2014-catalyst-census-women-board-directors.

———. 2015b. *New Global 2014 Catalyst Census: Women Board Directors.* www.catalyst.org/media/new-global-2014-catalyst-census-women-board-directors.

———. 2015c. *Still Too Few Women on Boards.* New York: Catalyst.

Change the Equation. 2013. "Vital Signs: What Is the STEM Where You Live and Work?" http://vitalsigns.changetheequation.org/.

Childs, Sarah, and Mona Lena Krook. 2009. "Analyzing Women's Substantive Representation: From Critical Mass to Critical Actors." *Government and Opposition* 44 (2): 124–145.

Choitz, Vickie, and Heath Prince. 2008. *Flexible Learning Options for Adult Students*. Washington, DC: US Department of Labor. www.jff.org/sites /default/files/publications/FlexibleLearning.pdf.

Choo, Hae Yeon, and Myra Marx Ferree. 2010. "Practicing Intersectionality in Sociological Research: A Critical Analysis of Inclusions, Interactions, and Institutions in the Study of Inequalities." *Sociological Theory* 28:129–149.

Chou, Rosalind. 2013. *Asian American Sexual Politics*. New York: Routledge.

Cianni, Mary, and Beverly Romberger. 1997. "Life in the Corporation: A Multi-Method Study of the Experiences of Male and Female Asian, Black, Hispanic and White Employees." *Gender, Work, and Organizations* 4 (2): 116–129.

Colby, Sandra L., and Jennifer M. Ortman. 2015. "Projections of the Size and Composition of the U.S. Population: 2014 to 2060: Population Estimates and Projections." *Current Population Reports*. US Census Bureau. March 2015.

Collins, Jane L., and Victoria Mayer. 2010. *Both Hands Tied: Welfare Reform and the Race to the Bottom in the Low-Wage Labor Market*. Chicago: University of Chicago Press.

Collins, Patricia Hill. 1986. "Learning from the Outsider Within: The Sociological Significance of Black Feminist Thought." *Social Problems* 33:14–32.

———. 1990. *Black Feminist Thought: Knowledge Consciousness, and the Politics of Empowerment*. New York: Routledge.

———. 2000. *Black Feminist Thought: Knowledge Consciousness, and the Politics of Empowerment*. 2nd ed. New York: Routledge.

Collins, Sharon. 2011. "Diversity in the Post Affirmative Action Labor Market: A Proxy for Racial Progress?" *Critical Sociology* 37 (5): 521–540.

Compton, D'Lane R. 2015. "LG(BT) and Counting." *Sociological Compass* 9 (7): 597–608.

Compton, D'Lane R., and Amanda K. Baumle. 2012. "Beyond The Castro: Examining Gay and Lesbian Enclaves in the San Francisco Bay Area." *Journal of Homosexuality* 59 (10): 1327–1356.

Compton, D'Lane R., Dudley Poston, Qian Xiong, and Emily Knox. 2015. "The Residential Segregation of Gay and Lesbian Households from Heterosexual Households in 100 MSAs of the United States, circa 2010." Paper presented at American Sociological Association Annual Meeting Conference, Chicago, IL.

Connell, R.W. 2005. *Masculinities*. 2nd ed. Berkeley: University of California Press.

Cook, Alison, and Christy Glass. 2014. "Above the Glass Ceiling: When Are Women and Racial/Ethnic Minorities Promoted to CEO?" *Strategic Management Journal* 35:1080–1089.

Cooky, Cheryl, Michael A. Messner, and Michela Musto. 2015. "It's Dude Time!: A Quarter Century of Excluding Women's Sports in Televised News and Highlight Shows." *Communication and Sport* 3:1–27.

Cooney, Richard T., Mady Wechsler Segal, David R. Segal, and William W. Falk. 2003. "Racial Differences in the Impact of Military Service on the

Socioeconomic Status of Women Veterans." *Armed Forces and Society* 30 (1): 53–86.

Cooper, David, Mary Gable, and Algernon Austin. 2012. *The Public-Sector Jobs Crisis: Women and African Americans Hit Hardest by Job Losses in State and Local Governments.* Washington, DC: Economic Policy Institute. www.epi.org/publication/bp339-public-sector-jobs-crisis/.

Cooper, Marianne. 2014. *Cut Adrift: Families in Insecure Times.* Berkeley and Los Angeles: University of California Press.

Coser, Lewis A. 1974. *Greedy Institutions: Patterns of Undivided Commitment.* New York: Free.

Costello, Cindy. 2012. "Increasing Opportunities for Low-Income Women and Student Parents in Science, Technology, Engineering and Math at Community College." Washington, DC: Institute for Women's Policy Research. www.iwpr.org/publications/pubs/increasing-opportunities-for-low-income-women-and-student-parents-in-science-technology-engineering-and-math-at-community-colleges.

Cotter, David A., Joan M. Hermsen, and Reeve Vanneman. 2011. "End of the Gender Revolution? Gender Role Attitudes from 1977 to 2008." *American Journal of Sociology* 117:259–289.

———. 2014. *Back on Track? The Stall and Rebound in Support for Women's New Roles in Work and Politics.* Council on Contemporary Families Gender Rebound Symposium. https://contemporaryfamilies.org/gender-revolution-rebound-brief-back-on-track/.

Courtenay, Will H. 2000. "Constructions of Masculinity and Their Influence on Men's Well-Being: A Theory of Gender and Health." *Social Science & Medicine* 50:1385–1401.

Covert, Bryce. 2014. "Sweden May Establish Quotas If Companies Don't Hire More Female Board Members." *Think Progress*, February 13. http://thinkprogress.org/economy/2014/02/13/3287791/sweden boards quota/.

Craig, Jessica, and Holly Foster. 2013. "Desistance in the Transition to Adulthood: The Roles of Marriage, Military, and Gender." *Deviant Behavior* 34 (3): 208–223.

Crenshaw, Kimberle. 1991. "Mapping the Margins: Intersectionality, Identity Politics, and Violence against Women of Color." *Stanford Law Review* 43:1241–1299.

Crimmins, Eileen M., Jung Ki Kim, and Aïda Solé-Auró. 2010. "Gender Differences in Health: Results from SHARE, ELSA and HRS." *European Journal of Public Health* 21:81–91.

Danesh, John, Jeremy G. Wheeler, Gideon M. Hirschfield, Shinichi Eda, Gudny Eiriksdottir, Ann Rumley, Gordon D. O. Lowe, Mark B. Pepys, and Vilmundur Gudnason. 2004. "C-Reactive Protein and Other Circulating Markers of Inflammation in the Prediction of Coronary Heart Disease." *New England Journal of Medicine* 350:1387–1397.

D'Angelo, Mary Rose. 2003. "'Knowing How to Preside over His Own Household': Imperial Masculinity and Christian Asceticism in the Pastorals, Hermas, and Luke-Acts." In *New Testament Masculinities,* edited by

Stephen D. Moore and Janice Capel Anderson, 265–295. Atlanta: Society of Biblical Literature.

Das, Aniruddha. 2013. "How Does Race Get 'Under the Skin'? Inflammation, Weathering, and Metabolic Problems in Late Life." *Social Science & Medicine* 77:75–83.

Davies, E. Mervyn. 2011. *Women on Boards.* February. United Kingdom Government. www.gov.uk/government/uploads/system/uploads/attachment_ data/file/31480/11-745-women-on-boards.pdf.

————. 2014. *Women on Boards: Davies Review Annual Report 2014.* United Kingdom Government. March. www.gov.uk/government/publications /women on boards 2014 third annual review.

Davis, Angela Y. 1990. "Sick and Tired of Being Sick and Tired: The Politics of Black Women's Health." In *The Black Women's Health Book,* edited by Evelyn C. White, 18–26. Seattle: Seal.

Davis, Kate. 2001. *Southern Comfort.* Q-Ball Productions.

Davis, Shannon N., and Theodore N. Greenstein. 2009. "Gender Ideology: Components, Predictors, and Consequences." *Annual Review of Sociology* 35:87–105.

del Río, Coral, and Olga Alonso-Villar. 2015. "The Evolution of Occupational Segregation in the United States, 1940–2010: Gains and Losses of Gender– Race/Ethnicity Groups." *Demography* 52:967–988.

Dennie, Christian. 2011. "Conference Realignment: From Backyard Brawls to Cash Cows." *Mississippi Sports Law Review* 1:249–279.

Department of Veterans Affairs. 2014. *FY 13 Summary of Expenditures by State, Expenditures in $ 000s.* www.va.gov/vetdata/expenditures.asp.

DePaulo, Bella. 2006. *Singled Out: How Singles are Stereotyped, Stigmatized, and Ignored, and Still Live Happily Ever After.* New York: St. Martin's.

Dews, Carlos L., and Carolyn Lest Law. 2001. *Out in the South.* Philadelphia: Temple Press.

Dezso, Cristian L., and David Gaddis Ross. 2012. "Does Female Representation in Top Management Improve Firm Performance? A Panel Data Investigation." *Strategic Management Journal* 33:1072–1089. http://onlinelibrary.wiley .com.proxygw.wrlc.org/doi/10.1002/smj.1955/pdf>.

Dickerson, Niki T. 2002. "Is Racial Exclusion Gendered? The Role of Residential Segregation in the Employment Status of Black Women and Men in the US." *Feminist Economics* 8 (2): 199–208.

Dimaggio, Paul J., and Walter W. Powell. 1983. "The Iron Cage Revisited: Institutional Isomorphism and Collective Rationality in Organizational Fields." *American Sociological Review* 48 (2): 147–160.

DiPrete, Thomas A., and Claudia Buchmann. 2013. *The Rise of Women: The Growing Gender Gap in Education and What It Means for American Schools.* New York: Russell Sage Foundation.

DiPrete, Thomas A., and Gregory M. Eirich. 2006. "Cumulative Advantage as a Mechanism for Inequality: A Review of Theoretical and Empirical Developments." *Annual Review of Sociology* 32:271–297.

DiTomaso, Nancy, Corinne Post, and Rochelle Parks-Yancy. 2007. "Workforce Diversity and Inequality: Power, Status, and Numbers." *Annual Review of Sociology* 33:473–501.

Dobbin, Frank, Alexandra Kalev, and Erin Kelly. 2007. "Diversity Management in Corporate America." *Contexts* 6 (4): 21–27.

Donato, Katherine M., Chizuko Wakabayashi, Shirin Hakimzadeh, and Amada Armenta. 2008. "Shifts in the Employment Conditions of Mexican Migrant Men and Women." *Work and Occupation* 35 (4): 462–495.

Dow, Dawn Marie. 2016. "The Deadly Challenges of Raising African American Boys Navigating the Controlling Image of the 'Thug.'" *Gender & Society* 30 (2): 161–188.

Ducat, Stephen J. 2004. *The Wimp Factor: Gender Gaps, Holy Wars, and the Politics of Anxious Masculinity.* Boston: Beacon.

Edwards, Harry. 1979. "The Olympic Project for Human Rights: An Assessment Ten Years Later." *Black Scholar* 10:2–8.

Eikhof, Doris Ruth. 2012. "A Double-Edged Sword: Twenty-First Century Workplace Trends and Gender Equality." *Gender in Management: An International Journal* 27 (1): 7–22.

Embrick, David. 2011. "The Diversity Ideology in the Business World: A New Oppression for a New Age." *Critical Sociology,* 1–16.

England, K. 1991. "Gender Relations and the Spatial Structure of the City." *Geoforum* 22 (2).

England, Paula. 2010. "The Gender Revolution: Uneven and Stalled." *Gender & Society* 24:149–166.

England, Paula, and Su Li. 2006. "Desegregation Stalled: The Changing Gender Composition of College Majors, 1971–2002." *Gender & Society* 20:657–677.

Ephesians 5:22–33. New King James Version.

Epstein, Cynthia Fuchs. 2007. "Great Divides: The Cultural, Cognitive, and Social Bases of the Global Subordination of Women." *American Sociological Review* 72:1–22.

Erikson, Erik. 1963. *Childhood and Society.* New York: Norton.

European Commission. 2012. *Women on Boards: Commission Proposes 40% Objective—European Commission.* http://ec.europa.eu/justice/newsroom /gender-equality/news/121114_en.htm#Press.

Fahs, Breanne. 2010. "Daddy's Little Girls: On the Perils of Chastity Clubs, Purity Balls, and Ritualized Abstinence." *Frontiers: A Journal of Women's Studies* 31 (3): 116–142.

Faludi, Susan. 1991. *Backlash: The Undeclared War against American Women.* New York: Anchor.

Farmer, Paul. 1999. *Infections and Inequalities.* Berkley: University of California Press.

Fenner, Lorry M. 1998. "Either You Need These Women or You Do Not: Informing the Debate on Military Service and Citizenship." *Gender Issues* 16 (3): 5–32.

Ferree, Myra Marx, and David A. Merrill. 2000. "Hot Movements, Cold Cognition: Thinking about Social Movements in Gendered Frames." *Contemporary Sociology* 29 (3): 454–462.

Ford, Leigh Arden, and Gust A. Yep. 2003. "Working along the Margins: Developing Community-Based Strategies for Communicating about Health with Marginalized Groups." In *Handbook of Health Communication*, edited by Teresa L. Thompson, 241–261. New York: Lawrence Erlbaum.

Forde, Pat. 2015. "NCAA Interviewed Ohio State's JaQuan Lyle about Louisville Recruitment." *Yahoo Sports,* October 7. http://yhoo.it/1LDmr8V.

Fouad, Nadya, Romila Singh, Mary E. Fitzpatrick, and Jane P. Liu. 2011. *Stemming the Tide: Why Women Leave Engineering.* University of Wisconsin-Milwaukee. www.studyofwork.com/files/2011/03/NSF_Women-Full-Report-0314.pdf.

Frankenberg, Ruth. 1993. *White Women, Race Matters.* Minneapolis: University of Minnesota Press.

Friedman, Lawrence M. 1966. "Public Housing and the Poor: An Overview." *California Law Review* 54 (2): 642–669.

Gardner, Christine J. 2011. *Making Chastity Sexy: The Rhetoric of Evangelical Abstinence Campaigns.* Berkeley: University of California Press.

Gates, Gary J. 2011. *How Many People Are Lesbian, Gay, Bisexual and Transgender?* Los Angeles: Williams Institute Report. http://williamsinstitute.law.ucla.edu/wp-content/uploads/Gates-How-Many-People-LGBT-Apr-2011.pdf.

Gates, Gary J., and Jason Ost. 2004. *The Gay and Lesbian Atlas.* Washington, DC: Urban Institute Press.

Gaul, Gilbert. 2015. *Billion Dollar Ball: A Journey through the Big-Money Culture of College Football.* New York: Viking.

Gauthier, Paula. 2000. "Steers and Queers." MFA thesis, Department of Visual Arts, University of California, San Diego.

Gerson, Kathleen. 2011. *The Unfinished Revolution: Coming of Age in a New Era of Gender, Work, and Family.* New York: Oxford University Press.

———. 2016. "Different Ways of Not Having It All: Work, Care, and Shifting Gender Arrangements in the New Economy." In *Beyond the Cubicle: Insecurity Culture and the Flexible Self,* edited by Allison Pugh. New York: Oxford University Press.

Ghaziani, Amin. 2014. *There Goes the Gayborhood?* Princeton: Princeton University Press.

Giddens, Anthony. 1984. *The Constitution of Society: Outline of the Theory of Structuration.* Berkeley: University of California Press.

Giscombe, Katherine, and Mary Mattis. 2002. "Leveling the Playing Field for Women of Color in Corporate Management: Is the Business Case Enough." *Journal of Business Ethics* 37:103–119.

Giunta, Tara, and Michelle Cline. 2014. *Breaking the Glass Ceiling: Women in the Boardroom: A Study of Major Global Exchange.* Washington, DC: Paul Hastings Law Firm. www.paulhastings.com/docs/default-source/PDFs/gender_parity_report_exchanges.pdf.

Glass, Jennifer L., and Sharon Sassler. 2013. "What's So Special about STEM? A Comparison of Women's Retention in STEM and Professional Occupations." *Social Forces* 92 (2): 723–756.

Glenn, Evelyn Nakano. 1985. "Racial Ethnic Women's Labor: The Intersection of Race, Gender and Class Oppression." *Review of Radical Political Economics* 17:86–108.

———. 2004. *Unequal Freedom: How Race and Gender Shaped American Citizenship and Labor.* Cambridge, MA: Harvard University Press.

Glynn, Sarah Jane. 2014. *Breadwinning Mothers, Then and Now.* Washington, DC: Center for American Progress.

Goldman Sachs. 2011. *Global Economics, Commodities & Strategy Research: BRICS Monthly Issue 11/06.*

Goldrick-Rab, Sara, and Kia Sorensen. 2011. *Unmarried Parents in College: Pathways to Success.* Fast Focus. Institute for Research on Poverty University of Wisconsin-Madison. www.irp.wisc.edu/publications/fastfocus/pdfs /FF9–2011.pdf.

Goodley, Simon. 2015. "Cable Hints at Mandatory EU Quotas for Female Executives." *Guardian*, February 3.

Gorman, Bridget K., and Jen'nan Ghazal Read. 2006. "Gender Disparities in Adult Health: An Examination of Three Measures of Morbidity." *Journal of Health and Social Behavior* 47:95–110.

Gornick, Janet C., and Marcia K. Meyers. 2003. "Does Policy Matter? Linking Policies to Outcomes." In *Families That Work: Policies for Reconciling Parenthood and Employment*, 236–267. New York: Russell Sage Foundation.

Gottfried, Heidi. 2013. *Gender, Work and Economy: Unpacking the Global Economy.* Cambridge: Polity.

Goyette, Kimberly, and Yu Xie. 1999 "The Intersection of Immigration and Gender: Labor Force Outcomes of Immigrant Women Scientists." *Social Science Quarterly* 80 (2): 395–408.

Grant Thornton LLP. 2015. "U.S. Businesses Show Little Progress in Advancing Women during Past Decade." *MarketWatch*, March 5. www.marketwatch .com/story/us-businesses-show-little-progress-in-advancing-women- during-past-decade-2015–03–05.

Gray, Mary. L. 2009. *Out in the Country: Youth, Media, and Queer Visibility in Rural America.* New York: New York University Press.

Greene, Linda. 2012. "Head Football Coaches: Ending the Discourse of Privilege." *Wake Forest Journal of Law & Policy* 2 (1): 115–142.

Greene, Solomon, and Erika C. Poethig. 2015. *Creating Place of Opportunity: HUD's New Data and Community Driven Approach.* Washington, DC: Urban Institute.

Griffith, Derek M. 2012. "An Intersectional Approach to Men's Health." *Journal of Men's Health* 9:106–112.

Gross, Harriet. 2001. "Work, Family, and Globalization: Broadening the Scope of Policy Analysis." In *Working Families,* edited by Rosanna Hertz and Nancy L. Marshall, 187–203. Berkeley: University of California Press.

Grove, Wayne A., Andrew Hussey, and Michael Jetter. 2010. "The Gender Pay Gap beyond Human Capital: Heterogeneity in Noncognitive Skills and in Labor Market Tastes." *Journal of Human Resources* 46 (4): 827–874.

Groysberg, Boris, and Katherine Connelly. 2013. "Great Leaders Who Make the Mix Work." *Harvard Business Review* September 2013:2–10.

Gulati, Mitu, and Devon Carbado. 2013. *Acting White.* New York: Oxford University Press.

Guttmacher Institute. 2015. "State Policies in Brief: Sex and HIV Education." www.guttmacher.org/statecenter/spibs/spib_SE.pdf.

Hacker, Jacob S. 2008. *The Great Risk Shift: The New Economic Insecurity and the Decline of the American Dream.* New York: Oxford University Press.

Hafner-Burton, Emilie M. 2008. "Sticks and Stones: Naming and Shaming the Human Rights Enforcement Problem." *International Organization* 62 (4): 689–716.

Hall, Matthew, Emily Greenman, and George Farkas. 2010. "Legal Status and Wage Disparities for Mexican Immigrants." *Social Forces* 89 (2): 491–513.

Hankivsky, Olena. 2012. "Women's Health, Men's Health, and Gender and Health: Implications of Intersectionality." *Social Science & Medicine* 74:1712–1720.

Harris, David J., and Pamela S. Douglas. 2000. "Enrollment of Women in Cardiovascular Clinical Trials Funded by the National Heart, Lung, and Blood Institute." *New England Journal of Medicine* 343:475–480.

Hartmann, Chester, and Gregory Squires. 2010. *The Integration Debate: Competing Futures for American Cities.* New York: Routledge.

Hattery, Angela J. 2012. "They Play Like Girls: Gender and Race (In)Equity in NCAA Sports." *Wake Forest Journal of Law & Policy* 2:247–265. http://bit.ly/1IODKNc.

Haurwitz, Ralph, and John Maher. 2011. "UT Sets New Standard with $300 Million ESPN Deal: Few If Any Other Schools Could Match Such a TV Network Arrangement, Officials Say." *American-Statesman.* http://atxne.ws/1PmhyS7.

Havranek, Tomas, Roman Horvath, Zuzana Irsova, and Marek Rusnak. 2015. "Cross-Country Heterogeneity in Intertemporal Substitution." *Journal of International Economics* 96:100–118.

Hayden, Dolores. 2005. "What Would a Nonsexist City Be Like? Speculations on Housing, Urban Design, and Human Work." In *Gender and Planning: A Reader,* edited by Susan S. Fainstein and Lisa J. Servon, 47–66. New Brunswick, NJ: Rutgers University Press.

Hays, Sharon. 1996. *The Cultural Contradictions of Motherhood.* New Haven: Yale University Press.

Heath, Melanie. 2003. "Soft-Boiled Masculinity: Renegotiating Gender and Racial Ideologies in the Promise Keepers Movement." *Gender & Society* 17 (3): 423–444.

Heibel, Todd D. 2005. "An Arena for Belonging? A Spatial Hingepoint Perspective of Citizenship at the Gay Rodeo." PhD diss., Department of Geography, Pennsylvania State University.

Henig, Robin M. 1993. "Are Women's Hearts Different?" *New York Times Magazine*, October 3, 58–61.

Hennen, Peter. 2008. *Faeries, Bears, and Leathermen: Men in Community Queering the Masculine*. Chicago: University of Chicago Press.

Herd, Pamela, Amelia Karraker, and Elliot Friedman. 2012."The Social Patterns of a Biological Risk Factor for Disease: Race, Gender, Socioeconomic Position, and C-Reactive Protein." *Journals of Gerontology Series B: Psychological Sciences and Social Sciences* 67:503–513.

Herring, Cedric. 2009. "Does Diversity Pay? Race, Gender, and the Business Case for Diversity." *American Sociological Review* 74:208–224.

Herring, Scott. 2010. *Another Country: Queer Anti-Urbanism*. New York: New York University Press.

Higginbotham, Elizabeth, and Lynne Weber. 1997. "Perceptions of Workplace Discrimination among Black and White Professional-Managerial Women." In *Latinas and African American Women at Work*, edited by Irene Browne. New York: Russell Sage Publications.

Hill, Catherine, Christianne Corbett, and Andresse St. Rose. 2010. *Why So Few? Women in Science, Technology, Engineering, and Mathematics*. Washington, DC: American Association of University Women. www.aauw.org/files/2013/02/Why-So-Few-Women-in-Science-Technology-Engineering-and-Mathematics.pdf.

Hill, Shirley, and Joey Sprague. 1999. "Parenting in Black and White Families: The Interaction of Gender with Race and Class." *Gender & Society* 13:480–502.

Hillard, Tom. 2011. *Mobility Makers*. New York: Center for an Urban Future. https://nycfuture.org/pdf/Mobility_Makers.pdf.

Hinze, Susan W. 2016. "Gender and Health." In *Gender: Sources, Perspectives and Methodologies*, edited by Renée C. Hoogland. New York: Macmillan.

Hinze, Susan W., Jielu Lin, and Tanetta E. Andersson. 2012. "Can We Capture the Intersections? Older Black Women, Education, and Health." *Women's Health Issues* 22:91–98.

Hinze, Susan W., Noah J. Webster, Heidi T. Chirayath, and Joshua H. Tamayo-Sarver. 2009. "Hurt Running from Police? No Chance of (Pain) Relief: The Social Construction of Deserving Patients in Emergency Departments." *Research in the Sociology of Health Care* 27:235–261.

Hispanic Association on Corporate Responsibility. 2013. *Corporate Governance Study*.

Hochschild, Arlie R., with Anne Machung. 1989. *The Second Shift: Working Parents and the Revolution at Home*. New York: Metropolitan.

Hoffer, Adam, and Jared Pincin. 2014. "The Effects of Conference Realignment on NCAA Athletic Departments." http://ssrn.com/abstract = 2578333.

Hooks, B. 1990. *Yearning: Race, Gender and Cultural Politics*. Boston: South End.

Hosick, Michael. 2014. "Student-Athletes Earn Diplomas at Record Rate." *NCAA*. http://on.ncaa.com/1PF38YA.

House, James S., Ronald C. Kessler, and A. Regula Herzog. 1990. "Age, Socioeconomic Status, and Health." *Milbank Quarterly* 68:383–411.

House of Representatives of the Ninety-Ninth General Assembly of the State of Illinois. 2015. Resolution HR0439. Illinois. www.ilga.gov/legislation /billstatus.asp?DocNum'0439&GAID'13&GA'99&DocTypeID'HR&LegID' 91204&SessionID'88.

Howard, Clayton. 2013. "Building a Family-Friendly Metropolis: Sexuality, the State, and Postwar Housing Policy." *Journal of Urban History* 39 (5): 933–955.

Howard, John. 1997. *Carryin' On: In the Lesbian and Gay South*. New York: New York University Press.

Howard, Madeline. 2013. "Subsidized Housing Policy: Defining the Family." *Berkeley Journal of Gender, Law, and Justice* 22 (1).

Hubbs, Nadine. 2014. *Rednecks, Queers, & Country Music*. Berkeley and Los Angeles: University of California Press.

Hunt, Jennifer. 2010. "Why Do Women Leave Science and Engineering?" NBER Working Paper No. 15853, National Bureau of Economic Research.

Ingram, Malcolm. 2006. *Small Town Gay Bar*. View Askew Productions.

Institute of Women's Policy Research. 2015. "The Status of Women in the States: 2015 Employment and Earnings." Washington, DC: Institute of Women's Policy Research. http://statusofwomendata.org/app/uploads /2015/02/EE-CHAPTER-FINAL.pdf.

International Gay Rodeo Association (IGRA). 2008. www.igra.com.

Investopedia. 2016. www.investopedia.com/terms/s/sec-form-def-14a.asp.

Jackson, Kenneth T. 1985. "Federal Subsidy and the Suburban Dream: How Washington Changed the American Housing Market." In *Crabgrass Frontier: The Suburbanization of the United States*, 190–218. New York: Oxford University Press.

Jackson, Mareshah. 2013. *Fact Sheet: The State of Latinas in the United States*. Center for American Progress. www.americanprogress.org/issues/race /report/2013/11/07/79167/fact-sheet-the-state-of-latinas-in-the-united-states/.

Jacobs, A.W., and I. Padavic. 2015. "Hours, Scheduling and Flexibility for Women in the US Low-Wage Labour Force." *Gender, Work & Organization* 22 (1): 67–86.

Jacobs, Jerry, and Kathleen Gerson. 2001. "Overworked Individuals or Overworked Families? Explaining Trends in Work, Leisure, and Family Time." *Work and Occupations* 28 (1): 40–63.

———. 2004. *The Time Divide: Work, Family, and Gender Inequality*. Cambridge, MA: Harvard University Press.

———. 2016. "Unpacking Americans' Views on the Employment of Mothers and Fathers: Lessons from a National Vignette Survey." *Gender & Society* 30 (3): 413–441. http://gas.sagepub.com/content/early/2015/08/05/089124 3215597445.full.pdf?ijkey = HyVJlcqtcMnTnWg&keytype = finite.

Janowitz, Morris. 1960. *The Professional Soldier: A Social and Political Portrait*. Glencoe, IL: Free.

Johnson, Nate. 2015. "The Unemployment-Enrollment Link." Washington, DC: Inside Higher Education. www.insidehighered.com/views/2015/08/27/unemployment-rate-community-college enrollments-and-tough-choices-essay.

Johnson, Waldo E., Lauren M. Rich, and Lance C. Keene. 2016. "Father–Son Communication." *Journal of Men's Studies* 24 (2): 151–165.

Jones, Katherine. 2013. "Children of Christ and Sexual Beings: Sexuality and Gender in an Evangelical Abstinence Organization." *International Journal of Religion and Spirituality in Society* 3 (2): 1–14.

Joy, Lois, Nancy M. Carter, Harvey M. Wagner, and Sriram Narayanan. 2007. *The Bottom Line: Corporate Performance and Women's Representation on Boards.* Chubb Corporation. New York: Catalyst. www.catalyst.org/system/files/The_Bottom_Line_Corporate_Performance_and_Womens_Representation_on_Boards.pdf.

Kain, J.F. 1968. "Housing Segregation, Negro Employment and Metropolitan Decentralization." *Quarterly Journal of Economics* 82:175–197.

Kalev, Alexandra, Frank Dobbin, and Erin Kelly. 2006. "Best Practices or Best Guesses? Assessing the Efficacy of Corporate Affirmative Action and Diversity Policies." *American Sociological Review* 71 (4): 589–617.

Kalleberg, Arne L. 2011. *Good Jobs, Bad Jobs: The Rise of Polarized and Precarious Employment Systems in the United States, 1970s to 2000s.* New York: Russell Sage Foundation.

Kamonjoh, Edward. 2014. *Gender Diversity on Boards: A Review of Global Trends.* Institutional Shareholder Services.

———. 2015. *Boardroom Refreshment: A Review of Trends at U.S. Firms.* Institutional Shareholder Services.

Kane, Mary Jo. 2013. "The Better Sportswomen Get, the More the Media Ignore Them." *Communication & Sport* 1 (3): 231–236.

Kanter, Rosabeth Moss. 1977. *Men and Women of the Corporation.* New York: Basic.

Kantrowitz, Mark. 2011. "Reasons Why Students Do Not File the FAFSA." Student Aid Policy Analysis. http://finaid.org/educators/20110118nofafsareasons.pdf.

Katz, Jonathan Ned. 1995. *The Invention of Heterosexuality.* New York: Penguin.

Katznelson, Ira. 2006. *When Affirmative Action Was White: The Untold History of Racial Inequality in Twentieth Century America.* New York: Norton.

Kazyak, Emily. 2012. "Midwest or Lesbian? Gender, Rurality, and Sexuality." *Gender & Society* 26 (6).

Kelly, Erin L., Phyllis Moen, and Eric Tranby. 2011. "Changing Workplaces to Reduce Work-Family Conflict: Schedule Control in a White-Collar Organization." *American Sociological Review* 76 (2): 265–290.

Ken, Ivy. 2008. "Beyond the Intersection: A New Culinary Metaphor for Race-Class-Gender Studies." *Sociological Theory* 26 (2): 152–172.

———. 2010. *Digesting Race, Class, and Gender: Sugar as a Metaphor.* New York: Palgrave MacMillan.

Kerwin, Donald. 2012. "The Faltering US Refugee Protection System: Legal and Policy Responses to Refugees, Asylum-Seekers, and Others in Need of Protection." *Refugee Survey Quarterly* 34 (4): 1–33.

Kim, Nami. 2011. "'Lord, I Am a Father!': The Transnational Evangelical Men's Movement and the Advent of 'Benevolent' Patriarchy." *Asian Journal of Women's Studies* 17 (1): 100–131.

Kim, Soohan, Alexandra Kalev, and Frank Dobbin. 2012. "Progressive Corporations at Work: The Case of Diversity Programs." *NYU Review of Law and Social Change* 36:171–213.

Kimmel, Michael. 1994. "Masculinity as Homophobia: Fear, Shame, and Silence in the Construction of Gender Identity." In *Theorizing Masculinities*, edited by Harry Brod and Michael Kaufman, 119–141. Thousand Oaks, CA: Sage.

———. 1996. *Manhood in America: A Cultural History.* New York: Free.

———. 2010. *Misframing Men: The Politics of Contemporary Masculinities.* New Brunswick, NJ: Rutgers University Press.

King, Clayton. 2014. *The True Love Project: How the Gospel Defines Your Purity, Student Book.* Nashville: B & H.

King, Clayton, and Sharie King. 2014. *True Love Project: How the Gospel Defines Your Purity.* Nashville: B & H.

King, D. 1988. "Multiple Jeopardy, Multiple Consciousness: The Context of a Black Feminist Ideology." *Signs: Journal of Women in Culture and Society* 14:42–72.

King, Sharie, and Clayton King. 2014. *True Love Project: 40 Days of Purity for Girls.* Nashville: B & H.

Kirk, David S., and Robert J. Sampson. 2013. "Juvenile Arrest and Collateral Educational Damage in the Transition to Adulthood." *Sociology of Education* 86:36–62.

Klinenberg, Eric. 2012. *Going Solo: The Extraordinary Rise and Surprising Appeal of Living Alone.* New York: Penguin.

Kmec, Julie. 2011. "Are Motherhood Wage Penalties and Fatherhood Bonuses Warranted?" *Social Science Research* 40:444–459.

Korbel, Pam Watson, and Donna Evans. 2012. *Women on Boards = Peak Performance in Organizations: A White Paper on the High Value That Women Directors Bring to Corporations and Non-Profit Organizations.* February 2. Denver: Women's Leadership Foundation. http://cloud.chambermaster.com/userfiles/UserFiles/chambers/427/File/womenonboardswhitepaperver4p-wkde.pdf.

Kramer, Vicki, and Toni Wolfman. 2011. "Major Approaches to Making Change." Thirty Percent Coalition. New York: 30 Percent Coalition. www.30percentcoalition.org/files/Major%20Approaches%20to%20Making%20Change.pdf.

Krieger, Nancy. 2003. "Genders, Sexes, and Health: What Are the Connections—and Why Does It Matter?" *International Journal of Epidemiology* 32:652–657.

Laditka, Sarah B., and James N. Laditka. 2002. "Recent Perspectives on Active Life Expectancy for Older Women." *Journal of Women & Aging* 14:163–184.

Landivar, Liana Christin. 2013. "Disparities in STEM Employment by Gender, Race and Hispanic Origin." US Department of Commerce. Washington, DC: US Census Bureau. www.census.gov/prod/2013pubs/acs-24.pdf.

Lang, Molly Monacan, and Barbara J. Risman. 2010. "A 'Stalled' Revolution or a Still Unfolding One?" In *Families as They Really Are*, edited by Barbara J. Risman, 408–412. New York: Norton.

Lareau, Annette. 2011. *Unequal Childhoods: Class, Race, and Family Life*. 2nd ed. with an Update a Decade Later. Berkeley: University of California Press.

Lee, Linda-Eling, Ric Marshall, Damion Rallis, and Matt Moscardi. 2015. *Women on Boards: Global Trends in Gender Diversity on Corporate Boards*. MSCI ESG Research. www.msci.com/documents/10199/04b6f646-d638–4878–9c61–4eb91748a82b.

Lester, Jamie 2010. "Women in Male-Dominated Career and Technical Education Programs at Community Colleges: Barriers to Participation and Success." *Journal of Women and Minorities in Science and Engineering* 16 (1): 51–66.

Liasidou, Anastasia. 2013. "Intersectional Understandings of Disability and Implications for a Social Justice Reform Agenda in Education Policy and Practice." *Disability & Society* 28:299–312.

Lienesch, Michael P. 1990. "Anxious Patriarchs: Authority and the Meaning of Masculinity in Christian Conservative Social Thought." *Journal of American Culture* 13 (4): 37–55.

Lippa, Richard A., Kathleen Preston, and John Penner. 2014. "Women's Representation in 60 Occupations from 1972 to 2010: More Women in Higher-Status Jobs, Few Women in Things-Oriented Jobs." *PLoS One* 9 (5): e95960.

Lips, Hilary. 2013. "The Gender Pay Gap: Challenging the Rationalizations: Perceived Equity, Discrimination, and the Limits of Human Capital Models." *Sex Roles* 68 (3/4): 169–185.

Little, Thomas H., Dana Dunn, and Rebecca E. Deen. 2001. "A View From the Top." *Women & Politics* 22 (4): 29–50.

Livadary, Matt. 2014. *Queens and Cowboys: A Straight Year on the Gay Rodeo*. Gravitas Ventures.

Long, J. Scott. 1997. *Regression Models for Categorical and Limited Dependent Variables*. London: Sage.

Lopez, Mary J. 2012. "Skilled Immigrant Women in the US and the Double Earnings Penalty." *Feminist Economics* 18 (1): 99–134.

Lorber, Judith. 1995. *Paradoxes of Gender*. New Haven: Yale University Press.

———. 2012. *Gender Inequality*. New York: Oxford University Press.

Lorber, Judith, and Lisa Jean Moore. 2002. *Gender and the Social Construction of Illness*. Walnut Creek, CA: Altamira.

Lorde, Audre. 1984. *Sister Outsider: Essays and Speeches*. Trumansburg, NY: Crossing.

Lowell, B. Lindsay. 2010. "A Long View of America's Immigration Policy and the Supply of Foreign-Born STEM Workers in the United States." *American Behavioral Scientist* 53 (7): 1029–1044.

Lucal, Besty. 2008. "Building Boxes and Policing Boundaries: (De)Constructing Intersexuality, Transgender and Bisexuality." *Sociological Compass* 2:519–536.

Luft, Rachel E., and Jane Ward. 2009. "Toward an Intersectionality Just out of Reach: Confronting Challenges to Intersectional Practice." *Perceiving Gender Locally, Globally, and Intersectionally* 13:9–37.

Lundquist, Jennifer Hickes. 2008. "Ethnic and Gender Satisfaction in the Military: The Effect of a Meritocratic Institution." *American Sociological Review* 73:477–496.

Mandel, Stewart. 2015. "Biggest Winners, Losers Five Years after Realignment Hell Broke Loose." http://foxs.pt/20bBEEZ.

Mann, Susan A. 2012. *Doing Feminist Theory: From Modernity to Postmodernity.* New York: Oxford University Press.

Marmot, Michael G. 2004. *The Status Syndrome: How Social Standing Affects Our Health and Longevity.* New York: Holt.

Marshall, Alicia A., and Janet K. McKeon. 1996. "Reaching the 'Unreachables': Educating and Motivating Women Living in Poverty." In *Communication and Disenfranchisement: Social Health Issues and Implications,* edited by Eileen Berlin Ray, 137–155. New York: Routledge.

Martin, Patricia Yancey. 2004. "Gender as Social Institution." *Social Forces* 82:1249–1273.

Massey, Douglass S., and Nancy A. Denton. 1993. *American Apartheid: Segregation and the Making of the Underclass.* Cambridge, MA: Harvard University Press.

Mastroianni, Anna C., Ruth Faden, and Daniel Federman, eds. 1994. *Women and Health Research: Ethical and Legal Issues of Including Women in Clinical Studies.* Washington, DC: National Academies Press.

Matthews, Sharon, Orly Manor, and Chris Power. 1999. "Social Inequalities in Health: Are There Gender Differences?" *Social Science & Medicine* 48:49–60.

Mattoo, Aaditya, Illeana Cristina Neagu, and Caglar Ozden. 2008. "Brain Waste? Educated Immigrants in the US Labor Market." *Journal of Development Economics* 87:255–269.

Maume, David J., and Leah Ruppanner. 2015. "State Liberalism, Female Supervisors, and the Gender Wage Gap." *Social Science Research* 50:126–138.

McCall, Leslie. 2000a. "Gender and the New Inequality: Explaining the College/Non-College Wage Gap." *American Sociological Review* 65 (2): 234–255.

———. 2000b. "Explaining Levels of Within-Group Wage Inequality in US Labor Markets." *Demography* 37 (4): 415–430.

———. 2005. "The Complexity of Intersectionality." *Signs: Journal of Women in Culture and Society* 30:1771–1800.

McClain, Craig W. 2005. "Gay Rodeo: Carnival, Gender, and Resistance." MA thesis, Department of American Studies, University of New Mexico, Albuquerque.

McFadden, Joan R. 1993. "Housing Policy in the United States: A Contemporary Analysis." *Housing and Society* 19 (2).

McGovern, Celeste. 1994. "Homo on the Range." *Alberta Report*, July 18, 1994, 29.

McKinlay, John B. 1996. "Some Contributions from the Social System to Gender Inequalities in Heart Disease." *Journal of Health and Social Behavior* 27:1–26.

McKinney, Lyle, and Heather Novak. 2012. "The Relationship between FAFSA Filing and Persistence among First-Year Community College Students." *Community College Review* 41 (1): 63–85.

Meernik, James, Rosa Aloisi, Marsha Sowell, and Angela Nichols. 2012. "The Impact of Human Rights Organizations on Naming and Shaming Campaigns." *Journal of Conflict Resolution* 56 (2): 233–256.

Mendall, M.A., Praful Patel, Lydia Ballam, D. Strachan, and T.C. Northfield. 1996. "C Reactive Protein and Its Relation to Cardiovascular Risk Factors: A Population Based Cross Sectional Study." *BMJ* 312:1061–1065.

Merton, Robert. 1988. "The Matthew Effect in Science, II." *ISIS* 79:606–623.

Messner, Michael A. 1997. *Politics of Masculinities: Men in Movements.* Lanham, MD: Altamira.

Miller, Kevin, Barbara Gault, and Abby Thorman. 2011. "Improving Child Care Access to Promote Postsecondary Success among Low-Income Parents." Washington, DC: Institute for Women's Policy Research. www.iwpr.org /publications/pubs/improving-child-care-access-to-promote-postsecond-ary-success-among-low-income-parents.

Mills, Scott. 2014. *True Love Waits: The Complicated Struggle for Sexual Purity.* DVD. LifeWay Films.

Moen, Phyllis, Erin L. Kelly, Eric Tranby, and Qinlei Huang. 2011. "Changing Work, Changing Health: Can Real Work-Time Flexibility Promote Health Behaviors and Well-Being?" *Journal of Health and Social Behavior* 52 (4): 404–429.

Moen, Phyllis, and Patricia Roehling. 2004. *The Career Mystique: Cracks in the American Dream.* Lanham, MD: Rowman & Littlefield.

Moore, Maya. 2014. "(In)visibility." http://bit.ly/1EUxXto.

Morgan, David R., and Sheilah S. Watson. 1991. "Political Culture, Political System Characteristics, and Public Policies among the American States." *Publius* 21 (2): 31–48.

Murtagh, Kirsten Naumann, and Helen B. Hubert. 2004. "Gender Differences in Physical Disability among an Elderly Cohort." *American Journal of Public Health* 94:1406–1411.

National Science Board. 2016. "Science and Engineering Indicators 2016." Arlington, VA: National Science Foundation. www.nsf.gov/statistics/2016 /nsb20161/#/report.

National Women's Law Center. 2014. "Underpaid and Overloaded: Women in Low-Wage Jobs." Washington, DC: National Women's Law Center. https:// nwlc.org/wp-content/uploads/2015/08/executivesummary_nwlc_lowwa-gereport2014.pdf.

Nazmi, Aydin, and Cesar G. Victora. 2007. "Socioeconomic and Racial/Ethnic Differentials of C-Reactive Protein Levels: A Systematic Review of Population-Based Studies." *BMC Public Health* 7:212–224.

Newman, Anne B., and Jennifer S. Brach. 2001. "Gender Gap in Longevity and Disability in Older Persons." *Epidemiologic Reviews* 23:343–355.

Newton, Esther. 1972. *Mother Camp: Female Impersonators in America.* Chicago: University of Chicago Press.

Newton-Smalls, Jay. 2013. "Women Are the Only Adults Left in Washington." *Time,* October 16. http://swampland.time.com/2013/10/16/women-are-the-only-adults-left-in-washington/.

New York City Comptroller. "Comptroller Stringer, NYC Pension Funds Launch National Campaign to Give Shareowners a True Voice in How Corporate Boards Are Elected." November 2014. http://comptroller.nyc.gov/boardroom-accountability/.

Nielsen. 2013. *Latinas Are a Driving Force Behind Hispanic Purchasing Power in the U.S.* Nielsen: New York. www.nielsen.com/us/en/insights/news/2013/latinas-are-a-driving-force-behind-hispanic-purchasing-power-in-.html.

———. 2014. *A Fresh View of Hispanic Consumers.* www.nielsen.com/us/en/insights/news/2014/a-fresh-view-of-hispanic-consumers.html.

Office of Public and Intergovernmental Affairs. 2013a. "VA and the Post 9/11 GI Bill." US Department of Veterans Affairs. www.va.gov/opa/issues/post_911_gibill.asp.

———. 2013b. "One Million Now Benefit from Post-9/11 GI Bill." November 8. http://va.gov/opa/pressrel/pressrelease.cfm?id = 2490.

Office of the Deputy Assistant Secretary of Defense (Military Community and Family Policy). 2013. *2012 Demographics. Profile of the Military Community.* Washington, DC: Department of Defense.

Okamoto, Dina G., and Paula England. 1999. "Is There a Supply Side to Occupational Gender Segregation?" *Sociological Perspectives* 42:557–582.

Olson, Jack. 1968. "The Black Athlete—a Shameful Story." *Sports Illustrated,* July 1. http://sportsillustrated.cnn.com/vault/article/magazine/MAG1081325/.

O'Neill, June. 2003. "The Gender Gap in Wages, circa 2000." *American Economic Review* 93 (2): 309–314.

Orsagh, Matt. 2014. "Women on Corporate Boards: Global Trends for Promoting Diversity." CFA Institute Market Integrity Insights. September 24. http://blogs.cfainstitute.org/marketintegrity/2014/09/24/women-on-corporate-boards-global-trends-for-promoting-diversity/.

Ozyegin, Gul. 2009. "Virginal Facades: Sexual Freedom and Guilt among Young Turkish Women." *European Journal of Women's Studies* 16 (2): 103–123.

Paap, Kris. 2006. *Working Construction.* Ithaca, NY: ILR.

Padavic, Irene, and Barbara F. Reskin. 2002. *Women and Men at Work.* 2nd ed. Thousand Oaks, CA: Sage.

Pager, Devah. 2007. *Marked: Race, Crime, and Finding Work in an Era of Mass Incarceration.* Chicago: University of Chicago Press.

Paik, Anthony, Kenneth J. Sanchagrin, and Karen Heimer. 2016. "Broken Promises: Abstinence Pledging and Sexual and Reproductive Health." *Journal of Marriage and Family* 78 (2): 546–561.

Pascoe, C.J. 2007. *Dude, You're a Fag: Masculinity and Sexuality in High School.* Berkeley: University of California Press.

Patten, Eileen, and Kim Parker. 2012. *A Gender Reversal on Career Aspirations: Young Women Now Top Young Men in Valuing a High-Paying Career.* April 25. Washington, DC: Pew Research Center.

Paxton, Pamela, and Melanie M. Hughes. 2017. *Women, Politics, and Power: A Global Perspective.* 3rd ed. Thousand Oaks, CA: Sage.

Paxton, Pamela, Sheri Kunovich, and Melanie M. Hughes. 2007. "Gender in Politics." *Annual Review of Sociology* 33 (1): 263–284.

Pedraza, Silvia. 1991. "Women and Migration: The Social Consequences of Gender." *Annual Review of Sociology* 17:303–325.

Pedulla, David, and Sarah Thebaud. 2015. "Can We Finish the Revolution? Gender, Work-Family Ideals, and Institutional Constraint." *American Sociological Review* 80 (1): 116–139.

Pew Research Center. 2008. *Hispanic Women in the United States, 2007.* www.pewhispanic.org/2008/05/08/hispanic-women-in-the-united-states-2007/.

Pierce, Jennifer. 1995. *Gender Trials.* Berkeley: University of California Press.

Polanyi, Karl. 1944 (reissued in 1957). *The Great Transformation: The Political and Economic Origins of Our Time.* Boston: Beacon.

Proverbs 31:10–31. New King James Version.

Pruss, Alexander. 2013. *One Body: An Essay in Christian Sexual Ethics.* Notre Dame: University of Notre Dame Press.

Pugh, Allison J. 2014. *The Tumbleweed Society: Working and Caring in an Age of Insecurity.* Oxford: Oxford University Press.

Purkayastha, Bandana. 2005. "Skilled Migration and Cumulative Disadvantage: The Case of Highly Qualified Asian Indian Immigrant Women in the US." *Geoforum* 36:181–196.

Putnam, Robert D. 2000. *Bowling Alone: The Collapse and Revival of American Community.* New York: Simon & Schuster.

Read, Jen'nan Ghazal, and Bridget K. Gorman. 2006. "Gender Inequalities in US Adult Health: The Interplay of Race and Ethnicity." *Social Science & Medicine* 62:1045–1065.

———. 2010. "Gender and Health Inequality." *Annual Review of Sociology* 36:371–386.

Reid, Megan. 2010. "Gender and Race in the History of Housing Policy and Research: From Industrialization to Hurricane Katrina." *Sociology Compass* 4:180–192.

Reskin, Barbara. 1998. *The Realities of Affirmative Action in Employment.* Washington, DC: American Sociological Association.

Rich, Adrienne. 1980. "Compulsory Heterosexuality and Lesbian Existence." *Signs* 5:631–660.

Ridker, Paul M., Charles H. Hennekens, Julie E. Buring, and Nader Rifai. 2000. "C-Reactive Protein and Other Markers of Inflammation in the Prediction of Cardiovascular Disease in Women." *New England Journal of Medicine* 342:836–843.

Ridpath, David. 2015. "Who Actually Funds Intercollegiate Athletic Programs?" *Forbes*. http://onforb.es/1VvIDSp.

Rieker, Patricia P., Chloe E. Bird, and Martha E. Lang. 2010. "Understanding Gender and Health." In *Handbook of Medical Sociology*, edited by Chole E. Bird, Peter Conrad, Allen M. Fremont, and Stefan Timmermans, 52–74. Nashville: Vanderbilt University Press.

Risman, Barbara J. 1998. *Gender Vertigo: American Families in Transition*. New Haven: Yale University Press.

———. 2004. "Gender as a Social Structure: Theory Wrestling with Activism." *Gender & Society* 18 (4): 429–450.

Robinson, Andrew. 2011. "Conference Expansion Affects More Than Football." *Daily Collegian*. http://bit.ly/1VUTnZS.

Robinson, Christine M., and Sue E. Spivey. 2007. "The Politics of Masculinity and the Ex-Gay Movement." *Gender & Society* 21 (5): 650–675.

Robinson, Margaret, and Lori E. Ross. 2013. "Gender and Sexual Minorities: Intersecting Inequalities and Health." *Ethnicity and Inequalities in Health and Social Care* 6:91–96.

Roman, Caterina Gouvis, and Jeremy Travis. 2006. "Where Will I Sleep Tomorrow? Housing, Homelessness, and the Returning Prisoner." *Housing Policy Debate* 17 (2): 389–418.

Rosenbaum, Janet Elise. 2009. "Patient Teenagers? A Comparison of the Sexual Behavior of Virginity Pledgers and Matched Nonpledgers." *Pediatrics* 123 (1): e110–e120.

Rosenbaum, Janet E., and Byron Weathersbee. 2013. "True Love Waits: Do Southern Baptists? Premarital Sexual Behavior among Newly Married Southern Baptist Sunday School Students." *Journal of Religion and Health* 52 (1): 263–275.

Rosenberg, Matthew, and Dave Phillips. 2015. "All Combat Roles Now Open to Women, Defense Secretary Says." *New York Times*, December 3.

Rosenfeld, Michael. 2009. *The Age of Independence: Interracial Unions, Same-Sex Unions, and the American Family*. Cambridge, MA: Harvard University Press.

Rosin, Hanna. 2012. *The End of Men and the Rise of Women*. New York: Riverbed.

Rubin, B.A. 1986. "Class Struggle American Style: Unions, Strikes and Wages." *American Sociological Review* 51 (5): 618–633.

———. 1995. "Flexible Accumulation: The Decline of Contract and Social Transformation." In *Research in Stratification and Mobility*, 297–323. Oxford: JAI.

———. 1996. *Shifts in the Social Contract*. Thousand Oaks, CA: Sage.

———. 2007. "New Time Redux: Layering Time in the New Economy." In *Workplace Temporalities: Research in the Sociology of Work*, vol. 17, edited by Beth A. Rubin, 527–544. Oxford: JAI.

———. 2014. "Employment Insecurity and the Frayed American Dream." *Sociology Compass* 8 (9): 1083–1099.

Rubin, Gayle. 1975. "The Traffic in Women: Notes on the 'Political Economy' of Sex." In *Toward an Anthropology of Women,* edited by Rayna Reiter, 157–210. New York: Monthly Review Press.

Ruether, Rosemary Radford. 1993. *Sexism and God-Talk: Toward a Feminist Theology.* Boston: Beacon.

Ruggles, Steven, Katie Genadek, Ronald Goeken, Josiah Grover, and Matthew Sobek. 2015. *Integrated Public Use Microdata Series: Version 6.0.* Machine-Readable Database. Minneapolis: University of Minnesota.

Russell Reynolds Associates. 2014. *Diversity in Leadership: Minority and Female Representation on Fortune 250 Boards and Executive Teams.* Washington, DC: Russell Reynolds Associates.

Ruzek, Sheryl Burt, Virginia L. Olesen, and Adele Clarke, eds. *Women's Health: Complexities and Differences.* Columbus: Ohio State University Press, 1997.

Sabin, Janice A., Brian A. Nosek, Anthony G. Greenwald, and Frederick P. Rivara. 2009. "Physicians' Implicit and Explicit Attitudes about Race by MD Race, Ethnicity, and Gender." *Journal of Health Care for the Poor and Underserved* 20:896–913.

Sarver, Joshua H., Susan W. Hinze, Rita K. Cydulka and David W. Baker. 2003. "Racial/Ethnic Disparities in Emergency Department Analgesic Prescription." *American Journal of Public Health* 93:2067–2073.

Satariano, Adam. 2014 "Apple Facing Criticism about Diversity Changes Bylaws." *Bloomberg Business,* January 6. www.bloomberg.com/news/articles /2014-01-06/apple-facing-criticism-about-diversity-changes-bylaws.

Schafer, Markus H., Kenneth F. Ferraro, and Sharon R. Williams. 2011. "Low Socioeconomic Status and Body Mass Index as Risk Factors for Inflammation in Older Adults: Conjoint Influence on C-Reactive Protein?" *Journals of Gerontology Series A: Biological Sciences and Medical Sciences* 66: 667–673.

Schieman, Scott, and Paul Glavin. 2015. "The Pressure-Status Nexus and Blurred Work-Family Boundaries." *Work and Occupations* 43 (1): 3–37.

Schrader, Steve. 2015. "Former Pacer Jalen Rose on College Recruiting: It's Like a Bachelor Party." *Detroit Free Press,* October 21. http://indy.st/1PX5C8O.

Schulman, Kevin A., Jesse A. Berlin, William Harless, Jon F. Kerner, Shyrl Sistrunk, Bernard J. Gersh, Ross Dube et al. 1999. "The Effect of Race and Sex on Physicians' Recommendations for Cardiac Catheterization." *New England Journal of Medicine* 340:618–626.

Schulz, Amy J., and Leith Mullings. 2006. *Gender, Race, Class, and Health: Intersectional Approaches.* San Francisco: Jossey-Bass.

Segal, David R. 1989. *Recruiting for Uncle Sam: Citizenship and Military Manpower Policy.* Lawrence: University Press of Kansas.

Seidler, Victor J. 2006. *Transforming Masculinities: Men, Cultures, Bodies, Power, Sex and Love.* London: Routledge.

Sen, Gita, Aditi Iyer, and Chandan Mukherjee. 2009. "A Methodology to Analyse the Intersections of Social Inequalities in HEALTH." *Journal of Human Development and Capabilities* 10:397–415.

Shapiro, Doug, Afet Dundar, Phoebe Khasiala, Xin Yuan Wakhungu, Angel Nathan, and Youngsik Hwang. 2015. *Completing College: A National View of Student Attainment Rates—Fall 2009 Cohort (Signature Report No. 10).* Herndon, VA: National Student Clearinghouse Research Center. https://nscresearchcenter.org/wp-content/uploads/SignatureReport10.pdf.

Sherrill, Andrew. 2015. *Corporate Boards: Strategies to Address Representation of Women Include Federal Disclosure Requirements.* Washington, DC: United States Government Accountability Office. www.gao.gov/assets/680/674008 .pdf.

Silva, Jennifer. 2103. *Coming Up Short: Working Class Adulthood in an Age of Uncertainty.* New York: Oxford University Press.

Simon, V.R., T. Hai, S.K. Williams, E. Adams, K. Ricchetti, S.A. Marts. 2005. "National Institutes of Health: Intramural and Extramural Support for Research on Sex Differences, 2000–2003." In *Scientific Report Series: Understanding the Biology of Sex Differences.* Washington, DC: Society for Women's Health Research.

Slaughter, Anne-Marie. 2012. "Why Women Still Can't Have It All." *Atlantic,* July.

Smale, Alison, and Claire Cain Miller. 2015. "Germany Sets Gender Quota in Boardrooms." *New York Times,* March 6.

Smith, Earl. 2014. *Race, Sport and the American Dream.* 3rd ed. Durham, North Carolina: Carolina Academic Press.

Smith, Earl, and Angela J. Hattery. 2015. "Conference Realignment and the Demise of the Academic Mission." In *Introduction to Intercollegiate Athletics,* edited by Eddie Comeaux, 219–230. Baltimore: Johns Hopkins University Press. http://bit.ly/144Noza.

Smith, Earl, Angela J. Hattery, and E. Staurowsky. 2008. "They Play Like Girls: Gender Equity in NCAA Sports." *Journal for the Study of Sports and Athletes in Education* 1:249–272.

Smith, Erick. 2011. "Syracuse Coach Jim Boeheim Not Happy about Move to ACC." *USA Today.* http://usat.ly/pfvTid.

Snyder, R. Clare. 2003. "The Citizen-Soldier Tradition and Gender Integration in the U.S. Military." *Armed Forces & Society* 29 (2): 185–204.

Soares, Rachel, and Liz Mulligan-Ferry. 2013. *2013 Catalyst Census: Fortune 500 Women Board Directors.* Catalyst. New York: Catalyst. www.catalyst .org/knowledge/2013-catalyst-census-fortune-500-women-board-directors.

Spain, Daphne. 2005. "What Happened to Gender Relations on the Way from Chicago to Los Angeles?" In *Gender and Planning: A Reader,* edited by Susan S. Fainstein and Lisa J. Servon, 15–30. New Brunswick, NJ: Rutgers University Press.

Sprague, Joey, and Kelley Massoni. 2005. "Student Evaluations and Gendered Expectations: What We Can't Count Can Hurt Us." *Sex Roles* 53:779–793.

Springer, Kristen W., Jeanne Mager Stellman, and Rebecca M. Jordan-Young. 2012. "Beyond a Catalogue of Differences: A Theoretical Frame and Good Practice Guidelines for Researching Sex/Gender in Human Health." *Social Science & Medicine* 74:1817–1824.

Staggenborg, Suzanne. 2011. *Social Movements.* New York: Oxford University Press.

Stainback, Kevin, and Donald Tomaskovic-Devey. 2009. "Intersections of Power and Privilege: Long-Term Trends in Managerial Representation." *American Sociological Review* 74:800–820.

———. 2012. *Documenting Desegregation.* New York: Russell Sage Foundation.

Starobin, Soko S., and Laanan, Frankie Santos. 2010. "Broadening Female Participation in Science, Technology, Engineering, and Mathematics: Experiences at Community Colleges." *New Directions for Community Colleges* 16 (1): 67–84.

Stein, Arlene. 2005. "Make Room for Daddy: Anxious Masculinity and Emergent Homophobias in Neopatriarchal Politics." *Gender & Society* 19 (5): 601–620.

Streitfeld, David. 2012. "Lawsuit against Kleiner Perkins Is Shaking Silicon Valley." *New York Times,* June 2.

St. Rose, Andresse, and Catherine Hill. 2013. *Women in Community Colleges: Access to Success.* Washington, DC: Women in Community Colleges, Access to Success. www.aauw.org/files/2013/05/women-in-community-colleges .pdf.

Sullivan, Laura, Tatjana Meschede, Lars Dietrich, Thomas Shapiro, Amy Traub, Catherine Ruetschlin, and Tamara Draut. 2015. *The Racial Wealth Gap: Why Policy Matters.* New York: Demos and the Institute for Assets and Social Policy, Brandeis University.

Swers, Michele L. 1998. "Are Women More Likely to Vote for Women's Issues Bills Than Their Male Colleagues?" *Legislative Studies Quarterly* 23 (3): 435–448.

Taylor, Verta. 1999. "Gender and Social Movements: Gender Processes in Women's Self-Help Movements." *Gender & Society* 13 (1): 8–33.

Teachman, Jay, and Lucky Tedrow. 2014. "Delinquent Behavior, the Transition to Adulthood, and the Likelihood of Military Enlistment." *Social Science Research* 45:46–55.

Thirty Percent Coalition. "CalSTRS and the Thirty Percent Coalition Expand Campaign for More Women on Corporate Boards." California State Teacher's Retirement System. October 22, 2014. www.30percentcoalition .org/news.

Thomas, Melvin, and Richard Moye. 2015. "Race, Class, and Gender and the Impact of Racial Segregation on Black-White Income Inequality." *Sociology of Race and Ethnicity* 1 (4): 490–502.

Thomas, Sue. 1991. "The Impact of Women on State Legislative Policies." *Journal of Politics* 53 (4): 958–976.

Tomaskovic-Devey, Donald, and Kevin Stainback. 2007. "Discrimination and Desegregation: Equal Opportunity Progress in U.S. Private Sector Workplaces since the Civil Rights Act." *Annals of the American Academy of Political and Social Science* 609:49–84.

Tong, Yuying. 2010. "Place of Education, Gender Disparity, and Assimilation of Immigrant Scientists and Engineers Earnings." *Social Science Research* 39:610–626.

Trillium Asset Management. "Trillium Files Four Board Diversity Shareholder Proposals for 2015." December 2014. www.trilliuminvest.com/14405/.

United States Census Bureau. 2014. *Facts-for-Features: Hispanic Heritage Month 2015.* www.census.gov/newsroom/facts-for-features/2015/cb15-ff18.html.

United States Census Bureau, Population Division. 2015. *Annual Estimates of the Resident Population by Sex, Age, Race, and Hispanic Origin for the United States and States: April 1,2010 to July 1,2014.* http://factfinder.census.gov/faces/tableservices/jsf/pages/productview.xhtml?src = bkmk.

United States Department of Labor. 2012. *The Latino Labor Force at a Glance.* www.dol.gov/_sec/media/reports/HispanicLaborForce/HispanicLaborForce.pdf.

United States Government Accountability Office. 2011. *DOD Education Benefits: Increased Oversight of Tuition Assistance Program Is Needed.* Washington, DC: United States Government Accountability Office.

United States Hispanic Chamber of Commerce. 2010. *America's Business Trailblazers—the Impact of Hispanic Business Women.* http://ushcc.com/americas-business-trailblazers-the-impact-of-latina-entrepreneurs/.

US Bureau of Labor Statistics. 2015. "Labor Force Characteristics by Race and Ethnicity, 2014." *BLS Reports: Report 1057,* November 2015.

US Riot Commission. 1968. *Report of the National Advisory Commission on Civil Disorders.* New York: Bantam.

Valenti, Jessica. 2010. *The Purity Myth: How America's Obsession with Virginity Is Hurting Young Women.* Berkeley: Seal.

Veenstra, Gerry. 2013. "Race, Gender, Class, Sexuality (RGCS) and Hypertension." *Social Science & Medicine* 89:16–24.

Verbrugge, Lois M. 1985. "Gender and Health: An Update on Hypotheses and Evidence." *Journal of Health and Social Behavior* 26:156–182.

Vinik, Danny. 2015. "Low-Wage Workers Deserve Predictable Work Schedules." *New Republic,* April 14. https://newrepublic.com/article/121528/lack-scheduling-flexibility-low-income-workers-big-problem.

Voydanoff, Patricia. 2014. *Work, Family, and Community: Exploring Interconnections.* New Jersey: Psychology.

Wade, Lisa, and Myra M. Ferree. 2014. *Gender: Ideas, Interactions, Institutions.* New York: Norton.

Wang, Wendy. 2014. *Record Share of Wives Are More Educated Than Their Husbands.* February. Washington, DC: Pew Research Center.

Wang, Wendy, Kim Parker, and Paul Taylor. 2013. *Breadwinner Moms.* May 29. Washington, DC: Pew Research Center.

Ward, Jane. 2012. "Postmdernism, Poststructuralism, Queer, and Transgender Theories." In *Doing Feminist Theory: From Modernity to Postmodernity*, edited by Susan A. Mann, 211–255. New York: Oxford University Press.

Warner, David F., and Tyson H. Brown. 2011. "Understanding How Race/ Ethnicity and Gender Define Age-Trajectories of Disability: An Intersectionality Approach." *Social Science & Medicine* 72:1236–1248.

Warren, Patricia Nell. 2006. "Real Cowboys, Real Rodeos." *Gay and Lesbian Review*, July/August, 19–23.

Weber, Lynn, and Deborah Parra-Medina. 2003. "Intersectionality and Women's Health: Charting a Path to Eliminating Health Disparities." *Advances in Gender Research* 7:181–230.

West, Candace, and Sarah Fenstermaker. 1995. "Doing Difference." *Gender & Society* 9:8–37.

West, Candace, and Don H. Zimmerman. 1987. "Doing Gender." *Gender & Society* 1:125–151.

Western, Bruce, Anthony A. Braga, Jaclyn Davis, and Catherine Sirois. 2015. "Stress and Hardship after Prison." *American Journal of Sociology* 120 (5): 1512–1547.

Weston, Kath. 1995. "Get Thee to a Big City: Sexual Imagery and the Great Gay Migration." *GLQ: A Journal of Lesbian and Gay Studies* 2 (3): 253–277.

Wheeler, Lydia, and Tim Devaney. 2016. "Overnight Regulation: GAO Faults Corporate Boards on Diversity." *Hill*, January 4. http://thehill.com/regulation /overnights/264700-overnight-regulation.

Whitaker, Tracy R., and Cudore L. Snell. 2016. "Parenting While Powerless: Consequences of 'The Talk.'" *Journal of Human Behavior in the Social Environment* 26:303–309.

Wilcox, William Bradford. 2004. *Soft Patriarchs, New Men: How Christianity Shapes Fathers and Husbands*. Chicago: University of Chicago Press.

———. 2010. *When Marriage Disappears: The Retreat from Marriage in Middle America*. Charlottesville, VA: National Marriage Project.

Williams, Christine L., Kristine Kilanski, and Chandra Muller. 2014. "Corporate Diversity Programs and Gender Inequality in the Oil and Gas Industry." *Work and Occupations* 41 (4): 440–476.

Williams, Jean Calterone. 2011. "Battling a 'Sex-Saturated' Society: The Abstinence Movement and the Politics of Sex Education." *Sexualities* 14 (4): 416–443.

Williams, Joan. 2000. *Unbending Gender: Why Family and Work Conflict and What to Do about It*. New York: Oxford University Press.

Williams, Katherine, and Charles O'Reilly. 1998. "Demography and Diversity: A Review of 40 Years of Research." In *Research in Organizational Behavior*, edited by Barry M. Staw and Robert I. Sutton, 77–140. Greenwich, CT: JAI.

Williams Institute. 2011. United States—Census Snapshot 2010. http:// williamsinstitute.law.ucla.edu/category/research/census-lbgt-demographics-studies/.

Wilson, George, Vincent J. Roscigno, and Matt Huffman. 2015. "Racial Income Inequality and Public Sector Privatization." *Social Problems* 62:163–185. doi: 10.1093/socpro/spv001.

Wilson, William Julius. 1975. *The Truly Disadvantaged*. Chicago: University of Chicago Press.

———. 2009. *More Than Just Race: Being Black and Poor in the Inner City*. New York: Norton.

Wingfield, Adia Harvey. 2013. *No More Invisible Man: Race and Gender in Men's Work*. Philadelphia: Temple University Press.

———. 2016. "Advocating Affirmative Action in the Days of Diversity: How the Business Case Enables Attention to Race and Gender." In *Underneath the Thin Veneer: Critical Diversity, Multiculturalism, and Inclusion in the Workplace*, edited by David G. Embrick, Sharon Collins, and Michelle Dodson. Netherlands: Brill.

Winslow, Sarah. 2010. "Gender Inequality and Time Allocations among Academic Faculty." *Gender & Society* 24 (6): 769–793.

Wolverton. Brad. 2015. "Disparities in New Aid for Athletes Could Alter Recruiting Dynamics." *Chronicle of Higher Education*. http://bit.ly/1LhOFCM.

Woodell, Brandi, Emily Kazyak, and D'Lane R. Compton. 2015. "Reconciling LGB and Christian Identities in the Rural South." In *LGBTQ Lives in Context: The Role of Place*, special issue, *Social Sciences* 4 (3): 859–878.

Xu, Yonghong. 2015. "Focusing on Women in STEM: A Longitudinal Examination of Gender-Based Earning Gap of College Graduates." *Journal of Higher Education* 86 (4): 489–523.

Yip, Andrew K.T. 1997. "Gay Male Christian Couples and Sexual Exclusivity." *Sociology* 31 (2): 289–306.

Yoder, Janice, and Patricia Aniakudo. "Outsider within the Firehouse: Subordination and Difference in the Social Interactions of African American Women Firefighters." *Gender & Society* 11 (3): 324–341.

Zehner, Jackie. 2014. "The Road Not Taken: What If I Had Never Left Goldman Sachs?" *Linked In Pulse*, November 20. https://www.linkedin.com/pulse/road taken what i never left jacki zehner?trk = prof post.

Zimbalist, Andrew. 2013. "Inequality in Intercollegiate Athletics: Origins, Trends and Policies." *Journal of Intercollegiate Sport* 6:5–24.

Zimmerman, Jonathan. 2015. *Too Hot to Handle: A Global History of Sex Education*. Princeton: Princeton University Press.

Zwigenhaft, Richard L., and G. William Domhoff. 2006. *Diversity in the Power Elite: How It Happened, Why It Matters*. Lanham, MD: Rowman & Littlefield.

———. 2011. *The New CEOs: Women, African American, Latino, and Asian American Leaders of Fortune 500 Companies*. Lanham, MD: Rowman & Littlefield.

———. 2015. "Diversity in the Corner Office from 2005–2014: Yes but Mostly No." Unpublished manuscript.

Contributors

AMY KATE BAILEY is Assistant Professor of Sociology at University of Illinois-Chicago. Her research examines race and inequality with two key areas of focus. The first examines the military, especially the interplay between individual and collective outcomes. The second focuses on historical patterns of racial violence in the American South. Her work has been published in journals including the *American Journal of Sociology*, the *American Sociological Review*, *Population Research and Policy Review*, and *Historical Methods*.

CHARLES J. BRODY is currently Vice President of Academic Affairs at Misericordia University and Professor Emeritus of Sociology at University of North Carolina, Charlotte, where he was previously Associate Dean for Academic Affairs in the College of Liberal Arts and Sciences. His publications have dealt with a variety of issues in sociological methodology and a range of substantive topics, including interruptions, evaluating drug and alcohol treatment, gun ownership, and public opinion about nuclear energy. His most recent research has focused on management behaviors and a variety of workplace factors that influence employee outcomes such as organizational commitment, job satisfaction, perceptions of discrimination, and psychological well-being. Currently, he attempts to implement lessons learned from this research in his role as a university administrator.

MARTHA BURK is a political psychologist and women's issues expert who is cofounder of the Center for Advancement of Public Policy, a research and policy analysis organization in Washington, DC. She serves as the money editor for *Ms.* magazine, and she is a syndicated newspaper columnist and frequent front-page blogger for *Huffington Post*. In January 2012, she launched her national public radio show, *Equal Time with Martha Burk*. Her latest book *Your Voice, Your Vote: The Savvy Woman's Guide to Power, Politics, and the Change We Need* (2015) is a *Ms.* magazine book selection. Her work has been published in major US newspapers and she has appeared on all major television networks in the United States.

Burk is a frequent speaker on women's issues, civil society, and women's leadership. She is an active contributor to the Journalism and Women symposium, and is a contributing speaker to SheSource, a project of the Women's Media Center. Burk holds a PhD in psychology from the University of Texas, Arlington. Her background includes experience as a university research director, management professor, and advisor to both nongovernment organizations (NGOs) and political campaigns and organizations. Dr. Burk has served on the Commission for Responsive Democracy, the Advisory Committee of Americans for Workplace Fairness, the Sex Equity Caucus of the National Association for the Education of Young Children, and the board of directors of the National Committee on Pay Equity. She serves as an advisory board member to several other national organizations, including the US Committee for UNIFEM, as well as Women for World Peace, a project of the Twenty First Century Foundation, and the PAX World Fund.

D'LANE R. COMPTON is Associate Professor of Sociology at the University of New Orleans. Her two major research interests are social psychology and the demography of sexual orientation. Her research uses both approaches to examine sexual, gender, and family inequalities. Specifically, she questions how categorization or labeling processes yield different outcomes in treatment and resources. Additionally, she is interested in methodological issues related to these substantive concerns, in particular how different kinds of measurements can lead to different kinds of inferences. Compton is the coauthor of *Same-Sex Partner: The Social Demography of Sexual Orientation* (State University of New York Press, 2009) and *Legalizing LGBT Families: How the Law Shapes Parenthood* (New York University Press, 2016).

SHANNON N. DAVIS is Associate Professor of Sociology at George Mason University. Her research focuses on the reproduction of gender inequality in institutions, in particular within families and higher education as well as the construction and maintenance of beliefs about gender (gender ideologies). Other recent research has investigated the predictive power of theories on divorce, the division of household labor, and perceptions of fairness of the division of household labor using cross-national samples. In addition to numerous publications in scholarly journals such as *Journal of Family Issues, Marriage & Family Review, Community, Work, & Family, Sex Roles,* and *Research in Social Stratification and Mobility,* she is coauthor (with Theodore Greenstein) of *Methods of Family Research* (3rd ed., Sage).

TONYA K. FREVERT is an NSF-funded Postdoctoral Fellow in the College of Computing and Informatics at University of North Carolina, Charlotte. She holds a PhD in Organizational Science and an MA in Sociology from UNC Charlotte and an MA in Psychology from Northern Arizona University. Through an intersectional lens, Frevert studies the effects of categorical differences on worker outcomes, diversity and inclusion in STEM education, active learning pedagogies, and organizational change. She has published in *Sociology Compass.*

LISETTE M. GARCIA is Senior Director at the Hispanic Association on Corporate Responsibility (HACR) in Washington, DC. She takes the lead in facilitating HACR's investigative projects and developing new programs and research studies aimed at strengthening HACR's reputation as the key source for information on Hispanic inclusion in corporate America. Her research examines Hispanic inclusion and diversity at Fortune 500 companies and her primary focus is on helping companies understand how to leverage the growing diverse segments of the US population to meet their business needs. Her scholarly work has been published in the annals of the *American Academy of Political and Social Science, Research in Race and Ethnic Relations,* and *Research in Higher Education.* She is also a proud recipient of the NCID Exemplary Diversity Scholar Citation for her contributions in diversity-related research, practice, and teaching.

JIANHUA GE is Assistant Professor of Management at Renmin University of China. His research and teaching interests focus on organizational theory and economic sociology, with an emphasis on the institutional and political dynamics in and around organizations. His work has appeared in both business and sociology journals such as *Journal of World Business* and *Research in Social Stratification and Mobility.* His current research centers on the institutional embeddedness of interorganizational networks, the impact of multiple institutional logics on corporate behaviors, and the role of political uncertainty in shaping temporary employment in China.

KATHLEEN GERSON is Professor of Sociology and Collegiate Professor of Arts and Science at New York University, where she studies work-family connections and their links to the structuring of gender inequality. The author of numerous books and articles, her most recent book, *The Unfinished Revolution: Coming of Age in a New Era of Gender, Work, and Family* (Oxford University Press, 2011), is an award-winning study of how new generations have responded to the rapidly unfolding gender revolution of the last several decades. Now at work on a book about examining new forms of work and care in the new economy," her other books include *Hard Choices: How Women Decide about Work, Career, and Motherhood, No Man's Land: Men's Changing Commitments to Family and Work,* and *The Time Divide: Work, Family, and Gender Inequality* (with Jerry A. Jacobs). She has held visiting positions at the Stanford Center for Advanced Study in the Behavioral Sciences, the Russell Sage Foundation, and the Bremen Center for Status Passages in the Life Course. She is the recipient of the American Sociological Association's Jessie Bernard Award for distinguished contributions to the study of women and gender, the Rosabeth Kanter Award for excellence in work-family research, and the Eastern Sociological Society's Distinguished Merit Award for lifetime contributions.

HEIDI HARTMANN, a MacArthur fellow, is a leading economist and women's movement intellectual whose work has been translated into more than a dozen languages. In 1987, she founded the Institute for Women's Policy Research, the leading American think tank informing women's policy issues. Dr. Hartmann is sought after by the media to comment on the most pressing issues impacting the status of women, including the gender wag gap, paid family leave, Social Security, and the glass ceiling for women in leadership. She has appeared as an expert on NBC *Nightly News* with Brian Williams, has been featured on NPR's *Morning Edition*, and is frequently quoted in notable press outlets, including the *New York Times*, the *Washington Post*, and the *Wall Street Journal*. Dr. Hartmann is the recipient of honorary degrees from Swarthmore College and Claremont Graduate University, the Wilbur Cross Medal for distinguished alumni of the graduate school of Yale University, and the 2012 Women of Vision Award from the National Organization for Women. Most recently she was named the 2014 Charlotte Perkins Gillman Fellow of the American Academy of Political and Social Sciences. She is an economist with a BA from Swarthmore College and MPhil and PhD degrees from Yale University, all in economics, and is the President of the Institute for Women's Policy Research. She is also a Research Professor at George Washington University.

ANGELA J. HATTERY is Professor and Director of the Women & Gender Studies Program at George Mason University. Her research focuses on social stratification, gender, family, and race. She is the author of numerous articles, book chapters, and books, including *African American Families: Myths and Realities* (2012, 2015), *The Social Dynamics of Family Violence* (2012, 2016), *Prisoner Reentry and Social Capital* (2010), *Interracial Intimacies* (2009), *Interracial Relationships* (2009, 2012); *Intimate Partner Violence* (2008), *African American Families* (2007), *Women, Work, and Family* (2001), and *Gender, Power & Violence* (2016). She teaches classes on gender and sexuality, intersections of race, class, and gender, gender-based violence, and feminist methods. In addition to her academic work she administers the Women & Gender Studies Program and directs the graduate programs (MAIS and certificate) in Women and Gender Studies.

ALLISON SUPPAN HELMUTH is a graduate student in sociology at University of Illinois, Chicago, and a former analyst and Mariam K. Chamberlain Fellow at the Institute for Women's Policy Research. She previously studied gender and development at the University of the West Indies and used her Fulbright award to learn about urban backyard chicken farming in Kingston, Jamaica. She completed a master's degree in sociology at George Washington University and her recent research examines the relationships between race, class, gender, and space in Washington, DC.

SUSAN W. HINZE is Associate Professor of Sociology and Women's and Gender Studies at Case Western Reserve University. Her research and teaching interests are in medical sociology, gender, social inequality, and the work/family or work/life nexus. She has employed quantitative and qualitative methodologies to study sexual harassment and gendered experiences in medical training, family life, and the career paths and patterns of physicians, and racial/ethnic disparities in physician decision making and medical care. She has published work on health and human rights, and the intersections of gender, race, and class on health outcomes for older women. Her newest project is on the emergence of workplace coaching services, an increasingly mainstream enterprise used by individuals and organizations to navigate complex and rapidly changing work environments. Her work appears in *Women's Health Issues, The Handbook of Sociology and Human Rights, Research in the Sociology of Health Care, Health: An Interdisciplinary Journal for the Social Study of Health, Illness, and Medicine, Research in the Sociology of Work, American Journal of Public Health, Work and Occupations, The Annals of Internal Medicine, Academic Emergency Medicine, The Sociological Quarterly,* and *Social Forces.*

JIELU LIN is a Postdoctoral Fellow at National Institutes of Health. Her areas of specialization include health inequalities, life course, and quantitative methodologies. She is interested in disentangling the sociostructural mechanisms that give rise to late-life health inequalities, with a focus on the racial/ethnic, gender, and socioeconomic patterning in health and functioning over the life course. She has written on the patterns of intraindividual variability in health trajectories as new dimensions of inequalities. Her current project integrates genetics and social relationships to examine the link between social dynamics and life course processes. In another line of inquiry, she develops and evaluates methodologies to aptly test life course theories of health inequalities. Her work has appeared in *Journal of Gerontology: Social Sciences, Research on Aging, Women's Health Issues,* and edited volumes.

ERIC LOPEZ is Research Manager at the Hispanic Association on Corporate Responsibility (HACR). His primary responsibilities entail analyzing and collecting data from US-based companies in order to better understand where improvements need to occur to help advance the inclusion of Hispanics in corporate America. Through his current work, Lopez supports HACR's broader research efforts to ensure corporate responsibility among Fortune 500 companies in the areas of employment, procurement, philanthropy, and governance. He is also the recipient of a Fulbright research grant, which was awarded to him in 2008 to study the discrimination and integration of the Roma in Hungary.

DAVID J. MAUME is Professor of Sociology at the University of Cincinnati. His teaching and research interests are in gender inequality in work and family life, and the connections between the two. His recent studies include examinations of how work demands affect family life (e.g., gender differences in providing urgent child care, taking vacation time, getting enough sleep, etc.), and how family life affects work and careers (e.g., gender differences in placing restrictions on work efforts, and how gender stereotypes affect job assignments, pay, and mobility). Currently, he is analyzing how the gender of the immediate supervisor affects subordinate work outcomes, the effect of the welfare state (here and abroad) on the sex gap in pay and work-family conflict, gender differences in mobility in the new economy, and gender differences in the effects of sport participation on aggression, deviance, and sexual behavior in adolescents. In 2014 he received the Jocher-Beard Award for distinguished scholarly contributions to an understanding of gender and society from the Southern

Sociological Society. In addition to numerous publications in scholarly journals, he is coeditor (with Barbara Arrighi) of the four-part edited volume *Child Poverty in America Today* (2007, Praeger).

BETH A. RUBIN received her PhD at Indiana University, Bloomington, and is a Professor of Sociology, Organizational Science, Public Policy and Adjunct Professor of Management at University of North Carolina, Charlotte. She has served as Program Officer at the National Science Foundation and President of the Southern Sociological Society and is a member the Sociological Research Association. She recently stepped down from directing the interdisciplinary Public Policy PhD program. Rubin's research focuses on workplace, organizational, and economic transformation with a focus on various outcomes such as organizational commitment, work-family balance, generational differences, management citizenship behaviors, homelessness, and a variety of inequalities. She has published three books and numerous papers in top journals such as *American Sociological Review and Social Forces* and specialist journals such as *Work and Occupations, Industrial Labor Relations Review,* and *American Behavioral Scientist,* among others.

SIERRA A. SCHNABLE is a doctoral fellow in the Department of Sociology and Criminology & Law at the University of Florida and is also pursuing a Graduate Certificate in Women's Studies at UF. Her research and teaching interests center on how sexuality shapes other dimensions of daily life, such as parenthood and religious participation. Currently, she is studying the lived experiences of lesbian couples as they navigate conception, pregnancy, and birth, with special attention to how these experiences are understood and conveyed visually. Her other projects examine participation in LGBTQ-affirming religious traditions, the pregnancy and birth experiences of incarcerated women, and the politics of lesbian kinship structures.

CHRYSTAL A. S. SMITH, PhD, is Assistant Professor in Residence of Anthropology at the University of Connecticut. Her research interests include using anthropological and sociological theories and methodologies to broaden the understanding about the challenges that women and minorities encounter pursuing STEM degrees and working in STEM higher education. She is particularly interested in applications of her findings that lead to (1) improving the design and implementation of interventions that support the retention and degree attainment of women and minority students in STEM higher education, and (2) changing program culture so that women and minority STEM faculty are more likely to be recruited, retained, and advance in their careers. She is the Co-PI and Qualitative Lead of the National Science Foundation (NSF) grant The Effects of Social Capital and Cultural Models on the Retention and Degree Attainment of Women and Minority Engineering Undergraduates (#1432297; 8/1/2014–7/31/2018).

EARL SMITH is a professor of sociology, Rubin Distinguished and American Ethnic Studies at Wake Forest University. Professor Smith holds a PhD from the University of Connecticut. He is the author of 11 books (authored and coauthored), scores of research articles, and many book chapters. Most recently he and Dr. Angela J. Hattery have published *African American Families* (2nd edition, 2015), *The Social Dynamics of Family Violence* (2nd edition, 2016), and *Gender, Power & Violence* (2016). Several of his articles and books are sports-related, including *Sociology of Sport and Social Theory* (2010) and *Race, Sport and the American Dream* (3rd edition, 2014).

SABRINA SPEIGHTS is a doctoral student at the University of North Carolina, Charlotte. Her research examines the work-life interface, with a focus on leisure and gender inequality. She is currently interested the role of scheduling and attendance policies in the context of managing work and life.

ERIN M. STEPHENS is a doctoral student in sociology at George Mason University. Her primary research uses qualitative research methods and social media analysis to explore emotional labor, trauma, and intersectionality in the Black Lives Matter movement. Other projects include analyzing the self-articulation of black women and girls amid "post"-racial ideology and considering the impact of gender and immigration status on immigrants' experiences in the American labor market. Her work appears in the second volume of *Women War and Violence: Topography, Resistance and Hope* (edited by Mariam M. Kurtz and Leser R. Kurtz). Stephens earned her MPH at the Gillings School of Public Health at the University of North Carolina, Chapel Hill.

JOSHUA D. TUTTLE is a doctoral candidate of sociology at George Mason University. His research focuses on the role that religious institutions play in social and economic change, the relationship between religious institutions and socioeconomic inequality, and the role that immigration plays in economic development. Other recent research has examined the relationship between religious participation and patterns of marital infidelity and divorce in the United States, the perception of fairness in the division of household labor across a number European nations, and the rise of the Washington, DC, metropolitan area as an immigrant gateway in the contemporary United States. He has also published research in the *Journal of Divorce and Remarriage.*

ADIA HARVEY WINGFIELD is Professor of Sociology at Washington University in St. Louis. She specializes in research that examines the ways intersections of race, gender, and class affect social processes at work. In particular, she is an expert on the workplace experiences of minority workers in predominantly white professional settings, and specifically on black male professionals in occupations where they are in the minority. Dr. Wingfield has lectured internationally on her research in this area, and her work has been published in numerous peer-reviewed journals, including *Social Problems, Gender & Society,* and *American Behavioral Scientist.* She is also a contributing writer for the *Atlantic.* Professor Wingfield is the author of several books, most recently *No More Invisible Man: Race and Gender in Men's Work* (Temple University Press), and has won multiple awards from sections of the American Sociological Association.

SARAH WINSLOW is Associate Professor of Sociology at Clemson University. Her research focuses on gendered dynamics and processes in a number of contexts, with special attention to the intersections of employment and family life. Her work has been published in *Gender & Society, Journal of Marriage and Family, Social Currents, Journal of Family Issues, Community, Work, and Family,* and the *Annals of the American Academy of Political and Social Science.* She has written extensively on husbands' and wives' relative earnings and gender inequality and work-family issues among academic faculty. Her current research on gender inequality in academic careers focuses on trends in faculty time allocations and the implications of time allocation mismatches for job satisfaction, turnover, and attrition as well as the impact of institutional culture and policies on the attraction, retention, and advancement of women faculty. She is also working on a project (with Rebecca Joyce Kissane) examining how gender operates and is institutionalized in fantasy sports, with special attention to the primacy of men and masculinity and women's marginalization in this potentially gender-neutral context.

JAMES C. WITTE is professor of sociology, Director of the Center for Social Science Research (CSSR), and Director of the Institute for Immigration Research (IIR) at George Mason University. As part of his work with the IIR, he secured funding to survey immigrant professionals in six major US cities. Now with additional funding from the Corporation for National and Community Service, this project is being expanded to include the Washington, DC, metropolitan area. Along with leading the IIR, he is coordinating two major research projects in Pakistan with the University of Karachi and the National University of Sciences and Technology in Islamabad. With support from the National Science Foundation he is also co–principal investigator on a project to analyze the peer review publication process at journals published by the American Sociological Association.

Index